A Crime Unlike Any Other

What the Facts Say About
Dr. Bruce Edwards Ivins and
The Anthrax Attacks of 2001

by

Edward G. Lake
www.anthraxinvestigation.com

i

A Crime Unlike Any Other - What the Facts Say About Dr. Bruce Edwards Ivins and the Anthrax Attacks of 2001.

First American Paperback Edition

Library of Congress Control Number: 2012919171

ISBN: 978-0-9766163-4-4

Author: Edward G. Lake
Edited by: Edward G. Lake
Cover by: Edward G. Lake
Published by: Edward G. Lake, Racine, WI

Table of Contents

List of Exhibits

Introduction

For nearly 30 years, from August 27, 1978 until July 29, 2008, a "mad scientist" worked for the United States Government. For the last 28 of those years, his job involved working with lethal pathogens in one of the U.S. Army's primary medical laboratories - The United States Army Medical Research Institute for Infectious Diseases, a.k.a. USAMRIID (pronounced "you-SAM-rid"), located at Ft. Detrick in Frederick, Maryland, not far from Washington, D.C.

Dr. Bruce Edwards Ivins wasn't any comic book "mad scientist," however. While he considered *himself* to be paranoid and schizophrenic, his actions indicate he was also - at minimum - a borderline *functioning sociopath*. That means, even though he had severe mental problems, he was able to function fairly well in the world of "normal" people. He was fully capable of holding down a complex and well paying job, raising a family, paying his bills and getting along with his neighbors and co-workers.

But, unknown to most of his neighbors and co-workers, this seemingly helpful, industrious, amiable scientist and microbiologist was secretly devising complex plans for revenge over perceived slights. He was committing burglaries, harassing women, damaging private property, making veiled threats, developing plans for murder, collecting bomb-making ingredients, spying on co-workers and driving long distances to perform bizarre activities - some benign, some criminal - so that those acts could not be traced back to him.

The facts say that two of those long drives took place during September and October of 2001, after he allegedly prepared at least 7 letters containing powders consisting of deadly anthrax spores. He drove roughly 200 miles each way from Fredrick, Maryland, to Princeton, New Jersey, to mail the letters. While the facts tend to indicate that he merely planned to frighten journalists, politicians, and

1

290 million other Americans into seeing his way of thinking, his reckless, sociopathic actions resulted in the deaths of 5 people, injury to at least 17 others, billions of dollars in damage, and helped start a war with Iraq.

This book uses hundreds of news media reports, many thousands of pages of official documents, interviews with key people, and a careful analysis of countless facts and scientific reports, to "fill in the blanks" in order to tell the true story of how and why Dr. Ivins did what he did, and also to describe how, in spite of countless false leads and incessant pressures to look elsewhere, the FBI eventually managed to identify Dr. Ivins as the person who sent the anthrax letters of 2001.

This book will also show how some people in the media, numerous conspiracy theorists, and others with their own agendas, endlessly misled the public about what was happening in the case, and how they continue to do so to this day.

Chapter 1

Ivins the Burglar

Dr. Bruce Edwards Ivins committed his first burglary in 1976 or '77, while he was at the University of North Carolina (UNC) at Chapel Hill. It wasn't a "college prank." Dr. Ivins was 30 or 31 years old at the time, an awkward, lean and wiry science nerd who wore dark rimmed glasses and possessed a massive but fragile ego, and he already had a doctorate in microbiology from the University of Cincinnati. He'd been married for over a year to Diane Betch, a tall, sturdy registered nurse, a fellow lover of music and sports who was 8 years younger than Ivins.

Unknown to his wife, Ivins had a secret, nearly uncontrollable obsession with the Kappa Kappa Gamma sorority, an obsession he claimed began after a KKG member turned him down when he asked her for a date while at the University of Cincinnati in 1966.

The burglary began with surveillance of the KKG sorority house at UNC, watching patterns, looking for which lights were always on even when the building was empty. Then, one night he entered the house through a first floor bathroom window which he'd found to be conveniently located behind a shrub, thus preventing anyone from seeing him as he climbed inside. There were several lights on inside the house, but he knew from his surveillance that they were always left on. Using a small pen light to help him see in unlighted rooms, he crept upstairs and looked for any drawer or cabinet which was locked and thus might contain secret sorority documents or materials.

In an unlocked closet, he found some blindfolds made from torn bed sheets. He assumed the blindfolds were used for the KKG initiation. Ivins also had a fascination with blindfolding, particularly the blindfolding of women, but left the blindfolds untouched.

On the opposite side of the same hallway, he found a closet which was locked. He used a coat hanger or some similar object to open it. Inside he found the KKG "Cipher" and some documents regarding KKG rituals. The Cipher was a document encased in glass, and it referred to a book of rituals for which he also hunted, but could not find.

Possibly the most unusual thing about his first burglary was the amount of time spent in the sorority house. A typical burglar would be in and out in a minimum amount of time, but Ivins lingered and poked around for nearly an hour before finally leaving. He left the same way he had entered, via the bathroom window. He took with him the KKG cipher and the ritual materials.[1]

Ivins must have realized that his actions and obsessions were not "normal," since appointment records for that time period show that for the first time in his life he had arranged for two sessions with a psychiatrist. But, unfortunately, no session records were ever found, so we don't know what he told the psychiatrist.[2]

Nancy Haigwood

What we do know is that Ivins didn't just suddenly decide one day to start committing burglaries because of a rejection he'd received from a KKG member ten years earlier. While at UNC, Ivins had met another KKG member who wasn't returning his overtures for a relationship. Her name was Nancy Haigwood, and Ivins became pathologically obsessed with her for the next 27 years.

Haigwood told FBI investigators many years after the anthrax attacks that she could still recall Ivins being "fixated" on Kappa Kappa Gamma sorority secrecy. She remembered how Ivins pressed her to reveal secret handshakes and initiation rites. She told him "that it was none of his business or to just go away." [3]

Haigwood had joined the KKG sorority as an undergraduate at UNC. When Ivins arrived at UNC, she was a graduate student in her mid-20s, and she held an advisory role there. She and Ivins shared neither office space nor advisors nor research interests. Nonetheless, Ivins later told Amerithrax investigators that he would read materials she left lying around on her desk, and in doing so, he learned of her KKG connection. Soon, by Ivins' own description, he became obsessed with Nancy Haigwood. "Because she was a member of KKG," he later told investigators, he paid close attention to all aspects of her life, and he would periodically ride by her house without making contact with her. Nearly thirty years later, Ivins could still remember details about Haigwood, such as the make and model of the car she drove at the time.[4]

Haigwood, the daughter of a Marine Corps officer, remembered in FBI interviews that she and Ivins and his wife may have gone out together for a sandwich at some point in time. And, she and about ten others from UNC joined in to help the Ivins move into a new house. But, there was never any romantic connection - at least from Haigwood's point of view. Nevertheless, Ivins somehow became obsessed with her.

One day, Ivins noticed that Haigwood was wearing a Kappa Kappa Gamma T-shirt, and he began pressing her for details. He wanted to know: Was she still involved with the sorority? What were its rituals, its practices? Haigwood told Ivins that she was no longer in the sorority, nor did she have any interest in discussing the subject, but Ivins persisted. According to Haigwood, "Most people, if you tell them to back off or change the subject, they would never come back to that. Bruce came back to it at least once a month -- maybe more frequently. He was always doing it in a very kind of *friendly* way." [5]

Ivins would later tell one of his psychiatrists that he admired Haigwood for her self-confidence, and he saw Haigwood as the ideal mother he never had - and possibly as his future wife. At one point, Ivins wrote a note to Haigwood lamenting that she wasn't returning his overtures of friendship.

A KKG member had spurned him when he was a freshman in college, and many years later he was again being spurned by a KKG member. Evidently as a result of his paranoia, he began to take action to learn more about the Kappa Kappa Gamma sorority, perhaps to learn why they were rejecting him. The codes in their Book of Rituals might hold the key. Codes were another subject that fascinated Ivins.

And there was another strange factor: Ivins' family on his father's side came from an area once called Monmouth, NJ, and before that they came from Monmouthshire, Wales. Kappa Kappa Gamma is one of the oldest sororities in America and was founded at Monmouth College in Monmouth, Illinois, in 1870. Bruce Ivins evidently saw some kind of mysterious connection between the "Monmouths" in the KKG sorority history and the "Monmouths" in his own family history.

After completing his post-doctoral work at UNC, Ivins and his wife moved to Maryland where Ivins went to work for the Uniformed Services University of Health Sciences (USUHS) in Bethesda, starting on August 27, 1978.[6] USUHS prepares scientists and health care practitioners for careers in government service, particularly in military hospitals and laboratories. It was also excellent preparation for his later work at USAMRIID.

Getting Psychiatric Help

In high school and college, Ivins found an interest in poisons, and if others verbally or physically intimidated him, he would tell them of pills he had in his possession which he could drop in their drinking water if they pushed him too far. He depicted himself as "evil" and a "clandestine-type" who knew chemistry and pharmacology better than anyone else, and could put those talents to use any time he wanted to.[7]

Possibly because he started thinking about using poisons to get back at Haigwood for rejecting him, Ivins began seeing another psychiatrist on September 12, 1978. Dr. Naomi Heller continued to assess him on an out-patient basis until the fall of 1979.[8]

The Expert Behavioral Analysis Panel which later reviewed all of Ivins' mental health records found that Dr. Ivins met the criteria for a diagnosis of "Borderline Personality Disorder." He also met the criteria for a diagnosis of "Paranoid Personality Disorder" in that he demonstrated a distrust and suspicion of others, often interpreting their motives as malevolent.

The pattern for paranoia was evident all the way back to his late adolescence. The EBAP report stated:

> He showed evidence of suspecting that others were exploiting, harming or deceiving him, without adequate basis. He frequently questioned his friends' loyalty and reacted as

6

if he could not count on them. He had difficulty confiding in others, fearing the information would be used maliciously against him. He read hidden, demeaning, or threatening meanings into benign remarks and, rather than forgiving insults, injuries or slights, persistently bore grudges. He perceived inquires into his work as attacks on his character and reputation and was quick to react angrily and to counterattack.[9]

Diagnoses of Borderline Personality Disorder and Paranoid Personality Disorder, however, fell short of providing a *complete* picture of Dr. Ivins' personality-disordered pathology. Also evident were characteristics supporting a diagnosis of "Personality Disorder Not Otherwise Specified, with Narcissistic and Antisocial Features".[10]

So, Bruce Ivins had a variety of mental disorders, and all seemed to originate in his formative years. In sessions with psychiatrists (and in FBI interviews), Ivins blamed a lot of his mental problems on his mother, whom he considered to be paranoid and schizophrenic, although there is no record that she ever sought treatment for any kind of mental problem. Mary Johnson Knight Ivins was a transplanted, petite, dark-haired Southern Belle from Brandon, Florida, with a degree in Home Economics. She and Randall Ivins met when he was vacationing in Florida.[9] Randall, a Princeton graduate, was co-owner of a drug store in Lebanon, Ohio. They were married in 1933 and produced three sons. Bruce, the youngest son, was born on April 22, 1946, when his bother Thomas, was eleven. Charles (known as "C.W.") was seven. There were family stories about how Bruce was an unwanted pregnancy, and Bruce's aunt once told him how his mother had tried various methods to cause a miscarriage, including bouncing down stairs on her rear-end. Ivins felt he'd not only been an unwanted pregnancy, he'd become an unwanted child.

People who knew the Ivins family described Mary as a strict disciplinarian, even tyrannical. There was also endless gossip about how Mary treated her husband. The EBAP report says:

Family and friends recalled that Mary Ivins could be extremely aggressive. ... According to one acquaintance [in Lebanon, Ohio], on one occasion Mrs. Ivins urgently contacted her husband's physician. "I think I killed Randall," she reported. When the doctor came to the house, Randall Ivins answered the door "covered in blood," having been beaten "with a broomstick."

Others from Lebanon recalled that Mrs. Ivins struck her husband on the head with a "frying pan," stuck a fork in her husband's hand, ran her husband "out of the house with a broom," and "got into fistfights" with him, leaving him with "a black eye" at least once if not on several occasions.[11]

Bruce Ivins described his mother as being "very controlling" and his father as very "subservient." He told FBI interviewers that he didn't have a good relationship with his father, either, and his father didn't care much about his wife or children. Ivins' father would occasionally even publicly ridicule and humiliate his son Bruce.

As a result, Bruce Ivins grew up feeling rejected by his parents and powerless to do anything about it. The way his father was dominated by his mother gave Bruce the sense that women were more powerful. He felt that, had his parents wanted another child at all, they would have wanted a girl. Psychiatrists felt that the resulting damage in his attachments to his parents and to his own self-worth may have created the foundation for the obsessions that controlled his future relationships with women.

Ivins would have explained most or all of his personal history to Dr. Heller. We know he told her that he was totally obsessed with the KKG sorority. It was one reason he'd sought out her help. He had begun devising plans to *poison* Nancy Haigwood.[12]

Burglary #2

While his sessions with Dr. Heller evidently convinced Ivins to drop his plans to murder Haigwood, it appears it was while being treated by Dr. Heller that Ivins committed his second burglary, one which seems to have required driving a very long distance to reach the scene of the crime. The exact dates are unclear. Haigwood and Ivins recalled the incident has having taken place in the spring of 1979. The FBI's summary report of the Amerithrax investigation, however, suggests that the date may have been sometime in 1977 or 1978, because in the spring of 1979 Ivins was living in Maryland, 300 miles from UNC.

Whatever the date, Ivins broke into Nancy Haigwood's locker at UNC and stole her lab research notebooks. The notebooks contained all the data Haigwood needed for her doctoral dissertation. They contained notes on all the experiments she had done for several years, along with photos and hypotheses she'd developed. And there were no duplicate copies anywhere. She had kept them in a locked room on the seventh floor of a laboratory building at UNC, and one day they were just gone. For Haigwood, it was a shattering loss of virtually irreplaceable materials.

The police were summoned after searches by Haigwood and her fellow scientists failed to turn up the notebooks.

Haigwood quickly suspected that Ivins may have done it, but when she called him to question him about it, he denied it.

Years later, Ivins admitted to the FBI that he'd taken the notebooks, and then he'd thought better of his actions, and he had returned to UNC to drop the notebook into a mail box near Haigwood's lab. Then he sent her an anonymous note via the mails describing where the notebook could be found. Eventually, the notebooks were returned to her. [13]

Psychiatrists point to this as Ivins' first use of the mails and mailboxes in his criminal activities.

He may also have broken a window on Haigwood's car around this time, his first admitted act of vandalism.

Ivins left a strong impression on Dr. Naomi Heller. More than 20 years later, when she heard about the anthrax letter attacks and their possible connection to Fort Detrick, her first thought was of Bruce Ivins. She "worried" that "the mailer was Ivins," she later told the FBI. She went so far as to try to compare the writing on the envelopes shown in the media with the handwriting she had from him on file. Finding no samples of his printing, however, she could not draw any conclusions. [14]

The Knoxville Incident

The exact time of the incident at the University of Tennessee at Knoxville is also not entirely clear. Some FBI documents state that it appears to have happened sometime in 1983 or 1984, but the EBAP report seems to be the most detailed and authoritative, the result of having access to Ivins' psychiatric records. The EBAP report says it happened in 1980, when Ivins was 34 years old and had been married for 5 years. At that time, he was completing his work at the USUHS and was looking for his next job.

Ivins had applied for a fellowship at the University of Tennessee and made the 8 hour drive (475 miles each way) to Knoxville to interview for the fellowship. He took his guitar along, so he may have had other reasons for the long drive.

While at the university, probably after the interview, he paid a visit to the KKG sorority house. He may have been planning another of his burglaries, but to his surprise, he found four sorority members having a meeting in the building. After starting a conversation with the four women about the sorority's secrets and rituals, he then started playing his guitar while singing the secret KKG ritual songs that no one but KKG members should have known. Because he displayed such extensive knowledge about the sorority's secrets, the young women became upset and called campus security. Ivins was escorted off the property.[15]

Ivins knew the incident left a record, and it worried him. He'd been there to interview for a fellowship, and he'd been escorted out of the KKG building by campus security which checked and noted his credentials.

His obsession with the KKG sorority could destroy his career and his entire life if he didn't get it under control.

Chapter 2

Ivins at USAMRIID

Ivins claimed that the anthrax outbreak in Sverdlovsk, Russia, in April of 1979 prompted him to become interested in anthrax.

The Sverdlovsk outbreak was the result of a human error when a maintenance worker failed to replace a filter on a vent. The mistake caused anthrax spores to be dispersed into the air from a bio-weapons factory, killing at least 64 townspeople and caused more than one thousand others to be hospitalized.[1]

It was also the Sverdlovsk incident which caused officials at USAMRIID to decide it was time to test America's only anthrax vaccine to see if it actually worked. And that opened up a new position in the research facility. A committee identified two possible people to fill the position. The first choice had already taken a job elsewhere, so Dr. Bruce Ivins was offered the job.

On December 1, 1980, Ivins resigned his position at USUHS and went to work for USAMRIID at Ft. Detrick, Maryland. Because his mental health records were "off limits" to investigators, his security clearance was approved on December 29.[2]

A Family Man

When Bruce and Diane Ivins moved to Frederick, Maryland, shortly after Ivins began working at USAMRIID, they moved into a gabled, 2-story home that was directly across the street from one of the gates of Ft. Detrick. From the front door of his new home, Ivins could bicycle the half mile to work in a matter of few minutes.

11

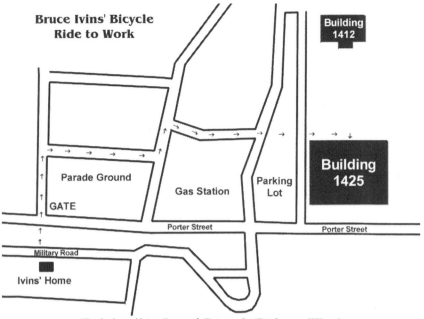

Exhibit #1 - Ivins' Bicycle Ride to Work

As Ivins and Diane settled into what promised to be a long career for Bruce at USAMRIID, it also seemed time to start a family. Bruce was incapable of having children, so, in the fall of 1984 they adopted 1-year-old twins, Andy and Amanda. Since that meant that Diane would become a stay-at-home mom, instead of finding another job as a registered nurse, she decided to bring in a little extra income by opening up a small day care center in her home, taking care of her own two children along with a few others whose working parents lived or worked nearby.[3]

Ivins worked primarily in Building 1425, in the maze of laboratories that occupied the back half of the large, two story building.

It was a guarded building that required a keycard to enter. Once past the guard at the door, Ivins could access his office in room 19 of the Staff Area, but he would have to use his keycard again to get into the Bacteriology Division, and again to get into the change room of Suite B3. After changing and leaving the keycard in is locker, he had to type his personal code into a keypad to get into the airlock designed to keep unwanted bacteria from entering or exiting the Biosafety Level-3 suite of laboratories. The airlock and negative

12

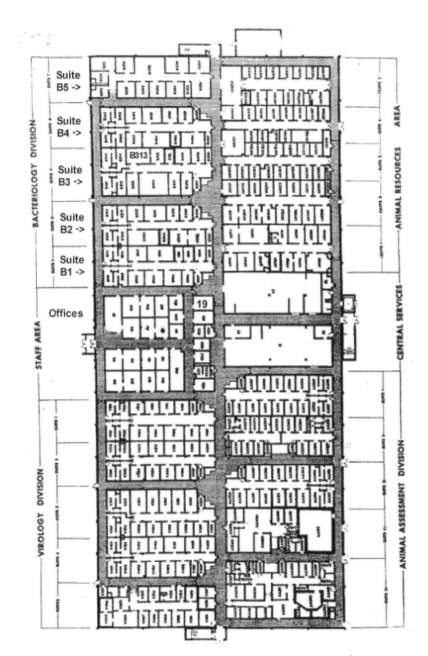

Exhibit #2 - Building 1425 Floor Plan [4]

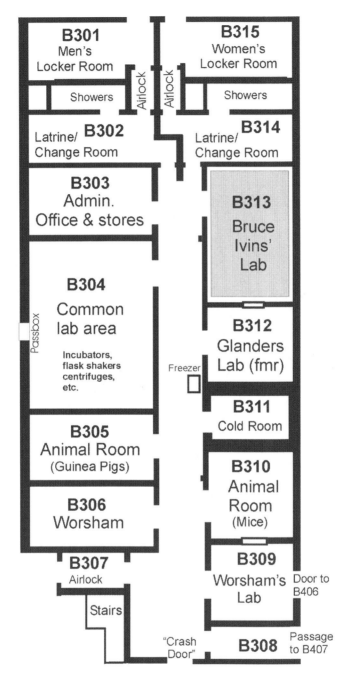

Exhibit #3 - Bacteriology Suite 3 [5]

air pressure kept airborne bacteria in the suite from escaping into the change room and hallway, and it helped keep outside bacteria from entering the labs and contaminating experiments. Employees were required to thoroughly shower before leaving the suite. Ivins' lab was located in room B313.

All aerosol tests on animals were done in Building 1412, a few hundred feet away, and Ivins also had a lab in that building for awhile, but most of his work time was spent in 1425.

Burglary #3

The change in jobs didn't affect Ivins' obsessions. It was in the early 1980's that he committed his third burglary. This time the target was the University of West Virginia's KKG sorority house at Morgantown. It was a night-time burglary, and he had to drive the 200 miles (3.5 hours each way) overnight to get there and back home again without being missed. Once again, he entered via a ground floor window. Spending about a half hour inside, he searched for any closet or cabinet that might be locked, and he finally found a locked cabinet. He broke it open and discovered the KKG book of rituals inside.[6] It was the "Holy Grail" he'd been looking for. He took it with him when he left.

It was his final KKG burglary, but Ivins was still committing other criminal acts related to his obsession with Nancy Haigwood.

Vandalism & Harassment

In the summer of 1982, Nancy Haigwood and her fiancé Gary Scandella moved into a townhouse in the Washington D.C. suburb of Montgomery Village. She'd gone to work for a private company nearby.

On November 29, 1982, Scandella found the initials KKG spray painted on the back window of his car. The initials were painted very carefully so that no damage was done to the paint on the car. And the same letters had been spray painted on their fence and on the sidewalk. Scandella reported the vandalism to the police, and Haigwood confronted Ivins about it when she encountered him one day. According to a newspaper report from decades later:

"He denied it, but there was no question it was he," she said. "He was really good at snooping, even in the 1980s."

After that confrontation, Ivins continued to send Haigwood e-mails that made her uncomfortable.

"He knew quite a lot about me without me telling him," she said. "He knew my sons' names and their years in school." [7]

In April 1982, Ivins wrote Haigwood a friendly letter expressing interest in her career and suggesting an opportunity for collaboration between her employer and USAMRIID. Although Haigwood apparently answered cordially and professionally (a 1983 letter she wrote alludes to this response), Ivins nonetheless followed up with a letter to her supervisor in which he claimed she had not replied. As was so typical of Ivins when rejected, he turned to acts of vengeance directed toward destroying Haigwood's professional career. This failure by Haigwood to respond, Ivins told her supervisor, had jeopardized the potential for a financially beneficial arrangement between the Army and Haigwood's employer. [8]

That particular letter seems to have done little harm to Haigwood's career, but, Ivins' revenge tactics didn't stop there.

The Hazing Letter

A year later, in May of 1983, Ivins prepared and sent a letter to the editors of the *Frederick News-Post* defending hazing by Kappa Kappa Gamma members, and he signed Nancy Haigwood's name to the letter. The letter was published by the *News-Post*, generating numerous angry responses from readers. [9]

After a colleague mentioned having read her letter in the *News-Post*, Haigwood found a copy of the paper and was stunned to see what had been done in her name. She immediately suspected Bruce Ivins. She confronted him about it on the telephone. Ivins, of course, denied being involved.

The letter said (in part):

As a member of Kappa Kappa Gamma, one of the nation's oldest and most prestigious college sororities, I am continually dismayed by attempts of the media and other outsiders to disparage the Greek System. I am *espe-cially* incensed at vitriolic attacks on our practices of "haz-ing," which non-Greeks fail to realize serve numerous valuable functions that I would like to briefly enumerate.[10]

Among the "valuable functions" Ivins listed was this claim in which active members are referred to as "actives":

> Charges that actives are to blame for accidental injuries which sometimes occur during pledge hazing are totally without foundation. No active ever forces any pledge or initiate to do anything in a sorority or fraternity - an individual is free to depledge at any time.

After Nancy Haigwood's protest that she hadn't written the letter that was being attributed to her, the *News-Post* sent her a letter of apology, but it did not publish a retraction.

And that wasn't the end of it. Apparently intent on further embarrassing Haigwood, or it may have been part of his original plan all along, Ivins soon went a step further: Within three weeks he re-contacted Eileen Stevens, the mother of a college student who had died in a 1978 hazing incident. He had first written Eileen Stevens in 1982, after she had become known as an outspoken critic of hazing and had been interviewed by Tom Brokaw on the *Today Show*. (Bro-kaw, it is worth adding, noted in that interview that his co-host Jane Pauley was a KKG alumna.)

On May 29, 1983, Bruce Ivins provided Eileen Stevens with a clipping of the fraudulently signed letter he'd sent to the *News-Post*. Stevens then gave the letter to the author of several books on hazing, Hank Nuwer, who then referred to Haigwood by name in a book he was writing, *Broken Pledges; The Deadly Rite of Hazing*. The book also quoted a KKG official as saying that Haigwood "does not speak for the organization and never has" and that "it is a 'most isolated' occur-rence to have a sorority woman come out in favor of hazing, which is 'strictly prohibited' by the national [KKG organization]."

The statements Ivins had fabricated in Haigwood's name have continued to be referenced and attributed to her in scholarly works, such as the 2004 thesis, *Definitions of Hazing: Differences Among Selected Student Organizations*. In fact, the letter triggered a libelous cascade of publications that led to a personal repudiation of Nancy Haigwood by the sorority's leadership and continuing damage to her reputation.[11]

The entire chain of events not only caused great embarrassment for Nancy Haigwood, but also demonstrated Dr. Ivins' deviousness and willingness to use others, as well as the United States Postal Service, to accomplish his stealthy retribution.

The *Frederick News-Post*, for example, did not know that the letter it received about hazing did not come from the person whose signature was attached; the mother of the student who died in a hazing accident had no idea that the published letter to the editor she later received in the mail from Ivins came from anyone but the woman who allegedly signed it; nor did the author of a book on hazing who received a copy of that letter from that mother suspect a fraud. All these parties were not only links in Dr. Ivins' smear campaign against Haigwood, they were unknowing links, in a chain consistently forged by Ivins via the Postal Service.

KKG Fights Back

During the course of the Amerithrax investigation, Ivins told investigators and others that he would drive three hours or more at night to visit various KKG sorority chapter houses. Once he arrived, he would look at the house for approximately ten minutes and then turn around to drive home again, often another drive of three hours or more. Ivins also told investigators he had developed a list "dozens and dozens and dozens" of KKG Sorority chapters throughout the eastern United States. He started the list by using a directory of colleges and universities maintained at the USUHS. Later, he went to the Library of Congress and reviewed telephone books from around the country to find the addresses of the KKG chapters and offices.[12] According to Ivins in a January 2008 on-the-record interview with DOJ prosecutors, he planned to mail copies of these secret materials to those who responded to ads he placed in *Rolling Stone* and *Mother Jones* magazines. In order to be sure he was not sending them to an actual KKG house, Dr. Ivins used his chapter address list from the Library of Congress as a cross-reference.[13]

Ivins at USAMRIID

There is no doubt that, in May of 1984, Ivins put an ad in *Mother Jones* magazine that said:

> **Attention "non-Greeks!" Receive a**
> **free copy of the secrets and initia-**
> **tion ritual of Kappa Kappa Gamma**
> **college sorority from an ex-mem-**
> **ber by sending SASE to: Carla**
> **Sander, P.O. Box 3536, Gaithers-**
> **burg, MD 20878.**[14]

"Carla Sander" appears to be a feminized, distorted version of Carl Scandella, Nancy Haigwood's fiancé at the time. In late 1984 or early 1985, Ivins put a similar ad in *Rolling Stone* magazine.

However, even though Ivins was working for USAMRIID at the time, and although he used a phony name in the magazine ads, he still left behind enough information (particularly at Knoxville) for people to tentatively figure out who was doing these things to harass and embarrass the Kappa Kappa Gamma sorority and its members.

KKG attorneys studied the matter. The copies of the Ritual Book that Ivins had given away for free on the campus of the University of Maryland were of particular concern. Although Ivins was technically violating copyrights, the Book of Rituals had not been formally copyrighted by sending copies to the Library of Congress along with the proper forms. Furthermore, prosecuting Ivins would be an expensive and difficult proposition, because only a few copies were involved, and they were given away for free. It would be difficult to prove damages. Thus, any lawsuit would be problematic. A Cease and Desist order might be more appropriate. But, that would require knowing for certain who was distributing the books.

A letter dated March 14, 1985 from a KKG attorney included some thoughts on how KKG could remedy the harassment situation if there was no actual legal remedy available to them. It said, "Since the identity of the passer out of the ritual in Maryland shows that it was probably Dr. Bruce Ivans [sic], perhaps a little more information can be discovered about who he is and then a confrontation with him for whatever good it would do." The letter also implied that no one was absolutely certain they could prove in court it was Ivins who had distributed the free copies.

Another letter dated September 10, 1985, also from KKG's attorney, addressed the "repeated problem" they had encountered with "unauthorized copying and disclosures of the content of the Kappa initiation manual." The attorney described the expense and delays that would be involved in fighting on the grounds of copyright violations, but if the "putative infringer" could be positively identified, there was the possibility of bringing harassment charges, although it would likely be only a misdemeanor. But, such an action could have a very strong deterrent effect.[15]

And, for a scientist in a responsible position at USAMRIID, it would definitely have a deterrent effect.

It can't be stated for certain that Ivins was contacted and deterred, but for the next *fourteen or fifteen years* he seems to have ceased all pathological actions regarding KKG or anyone else.

During that period of time, he became one of America's leading experts on creating and purifying deadly anthrax spores to use in the development of new anthrax vaccines.

Chapter 3

Ivins the Anthrax Expert

There's nothing that scares people more than something they do not understand. Anthrax, however, is pretty scary even if you do understand it. It's not like other bacteria which will live happily inside a host for months or years, anthrax quickly kills its victim - often in just a few days - because that is how its survival mechanism has developed. The *Bacillus anthracis* bacterium *lives to kill*. It *needs* to kill in order to survive. That's *very* scary.

Technically, anthrax is a disease. A disease cannot be placed into an envelope. Spores of *Bacillus anthracis* - the tiny bacterial organism that *causes* the anthrax disease - are what were in the envelopes mailed in 2001.

In many ways, anthrax spores are the stuff of science fiction. The lethal dose is delivered in a package too small to be seen by the human eye - tiny particles that are one hundredth the diameter of a human hair. A single gram of dry powder can contain between two and three *trillion* spores. A spore can survive for a century or more just a few centimeters underground - among the roots of grass. Then, when pulled up with the roots and ingested by a grazing animal, the anthrax spore "wakes up" within *minutes*.

In the warm and nutrient rich environment of an animal's body, like a deadly "seed" the spore begins to vegetate and turn into a living, rod-shaped organism. And it begins to grow. Each bacterium grows in length as it absorbs nutrients from its host. When it is roughly twice its original length, it divides in half, creating two identical rod-like bacteria. Under a microscope, you can literally *watch* them

21

grow exponentially! Under ideal conditions, they reproduce about once every 20 minutes. The two bacteria divide to create 4 bacteria, then 8, 16, 32, 64, 128, 256, 512, 1024 etc. All the rapidly growing bacteria contentedly take in nutrients from their suffering victim while at the same time secreting lethal toxins until the victim dies. If it had enough food and ideal living conditions, a single *Bacillus anthracis* bacterium could produce enough progeny to bury the Empire State Building in less than a week. But it kills its victim so rapidly that it can't possibly continue to reproduce at such a rate. The critically ill animal vomits and bleeds until it finally collapses and dies.

When the rapidly reproducing *Bacillus anthracis* bacteria are exposed to outside air through vomit or excretions from the dying animal, or from the carcass being picked apart by vultures - each living germ detects that conditions have changed so that it can no longer reproduce and survive. It begins a 15-hour transformation. It makes a copy of its chromosome - the string of DNA that carries all of its genes - and it starts to build a hard shell around that chromosome, much like the shell of a nut. It produces a spore.

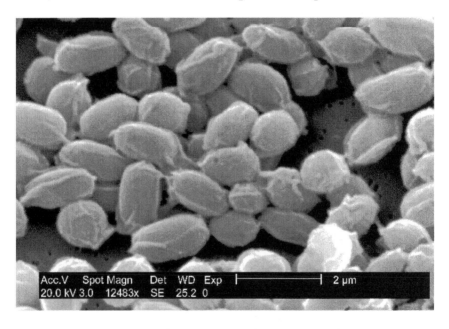

Exhibit #4 - A collection of spores[1]
(Photo courtesy of the CDC)

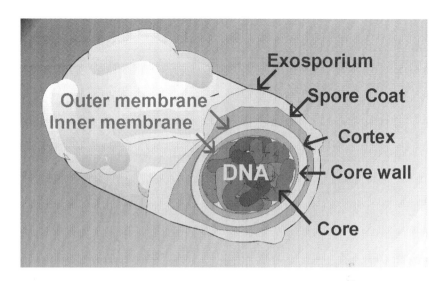

Exhibit #5 - The anatomy of an anthrax spore

But to create the single spore the "mother germ" must also die. It becomes a slimy husk which is dissolved away by natural enzymes until only the dry spore is left - or more properly, one of *billions* of spores, since that's how many bacteria would be going through the same process when killing a typical animal.

And if the spore managed to be transported underground by the dripping body fluids or by rainfall, it will settle somewhere among the roots of the grasses where it is safe from the lethal ultra-violet rays in sunlight, until - perhaps a month later, or maybe after another hundred years or so - it is ingested by another animal so it can start the killing process all over again

Anthrax Disease Types

As a disease, anthrax comes in three basic forms which are determined by how the bacteria or spores entered the body.

Inhalation anthrax is the most deadly form and can result when airborne spores are inhaled. It was once known as "woolsorter's disease", since it was common in factories during the Industrial Revolution where people handled wool and animal hides in factory environments which were inadequately ventilated. Anthrax spores floated in the air individually or as part of tiny dust particles. When inhaled, the tiny individual spores will pass through the lungs and lodge in the lymph nodes where they begin to germinate. An evaluation done in the 1920s indicated that people exposed to airborne spores could inhale as many as a hundred per hour without suffering any ill-effects. As a result, prior to the anthrax attacks of 2001, it was generally believed that it took at least 5,000 to 8,000 spores to overcome the human immune system and cause the inhalation version of the disease.

Cutaneous anthrax is the most common form of the disease. It generally results from spores entering the body through open cuts, sores, abrasions or even scratched acne pimples. Once lodged in something as small as a shaving cut, the spores begin to germinate and form a black lesion. (The name "anthrax" comes from the Greek and means "black" or "coal.") In theory, a single spore would be sufficient to cause cutaneous anthrax - but this form of the disease is rarely fatal if properly treated.

Gastrointestinal anthrax results from eating meat or other food contaminated with spores or living bacteria. The bacteria begin their work in the stomach or intestines. It is frequently fatal and occurs mainly in Third World countries.

Anthrax Strains

Anthrax has hundreds of different strains, the best known being Stern, Vollum and Ames.

The Stern strain is non-lethal and is used primarily for making vaccines. It was discovered in the 1930's and is missing the plasmid or DNA molecule that prevents it from forming a capsule. Thus, it's relatively harmless, although not completely so.

The Vollum strain was isolated in Oxford, England, in 1930, and it seems to be the strain of choice for making bioweapons. It's the strain used by most countries, including the U.S., England and Iraq, for such work.

The Ames strain which was obtained by USAMRIID in 1981 is primarily used in developing medicines. It grows very fast and can be killed by most antibiotics. Its critical attribute seems to be that it is more likely than other strains of anthrax to cause disease in animals immunized with the standard U.S. animal anthrax vaccine. So, there was also a veterinary need to find a vaccine which would effectively protect animals against Ames anthrax.

Ivins' Work with Anthrax

Anthrax has been used as a biological weapon since ancient times, when infected dead animals were catapulted over city walls to create havoc among the defenders inside.

President Nixon ended all American development and production of biological weapons in November, 1969, and since that time, work with anthrax in government labs has been defensive in nature. Such work involves the development of vaccines and antibiotics which can be used in the event of some other government or entity uses biological weapons against America.

The Sverdlovsk incident in April of 1979 demonstrated that the Soviet Union could not be trusted to adhere to signed treaties banning the building and stockpiling of biological weapons. Non-treaty countries - Iraq being a prime example - were known to have biological and chemical weapons development programs. During the Iran-Iraq War which lasted from September 1980 to August 1988, Iraq used chemical weapons against Iranian and Iraqi Kurds. And, during the First Gulf War, from August of 1990 to February of 1991, the risk that Saddam Hussein would use biological or chemical weapons upon American troops was a constant fear.

The only FDA-approved anthrax vaccine used in America (called AVA for "Anthrax Vaccine Adsorbed") was far from ideal. It provided immunity, but it required five shots to become truly effective: the initial vaccination, another after a month, then after 6, 12 and 18 months, plus annual booster shots. It was also a crude vaccine with unpurified bacterial proteins which could cause side effects ranging from swollen muscles to headaches. Plus, there were concerns about how effective it would be after long-term storage of two or three years. In 2001, only one company made the vaccine, Bio-Port Corp., a privately owned company in Michigan, and that company's only manufacturing facility in Lansing was barely functional.

A Crime Unlike Any Other

In November of 1994 and again in March of 2000, Ivins was listed as a co-inventor on patent documents for a new vaccine called rPA, for "recombinant Protective Antigen." It was a purer vaccine that was hoped to require fewer shots and cause fewer side effects.[2] But the new vaccine was far from being perfected or fully tested, and even farther from becoming FDA approved.

And there were other problems as well. The facilities at USAMRIID were worn and antiquated, not changed much from the 1950's when Ft. Detrick was the center of America's bioweapons research programs. Researchers were paid less than at civilian labs nearby, and grant money to purchase equipment and hire new researchers was difficult to come by. It was even a constant struggle to find enough money to buy the mice, guinea pigs, rabbits and monkeys used as test animals.[3]

Except for very rare instances when spores were killed with radiation and then dried into fine powders to test different kinds of airborne pathogen sensing equipment, personnel at USAMRIID only used "wet anthrax," which typically consists of spores suspended in distilled water. Because viable, dry spores float easily in the air and are too difficult to handle, too difficult to contain, and posed too great a danger for researchers, the spores Bruce Ivins and his staff created were almost always stored suspended in distilled water.

Ivins' key task was to produce purified anthrax spores for use in aerosol tests where a fine mist of spores and distilled water was sprayed into the mouths of the test animals. Ivins and his staff could routinely produce a trillion spores per week,[4] but there were also problems with consistency. For reasons having to do with purity and clumping of spores, one batch of spores might have slightly different effects upon animals than another batch. The spores also needed to be pure and relatively clump-free or the nozzles creating the mists to be inhaled by the animals would clog and produce irregular results.

The "art" of spore creation involved tricks to make certain that the spores were pure and free from debris, and that they didn't stick together and clog the equipment. Ivins learned those tricks and felt he was among the few who knew them.

RMR-1029

In 1997, to avoid consistency problems during a new series of animal tests, Ivins received funding and permission to contract with the U.S. Army laboratories at Dugway Proving Grounds in Utah to produce a large stock of purified anthrax spores that would last through years of tests.

Using seed bacteria from the original 1981 sample of the Ames strain stored in USAMRIID's freezers, Dugway performed 13 large production runs of anthrax spores while Ivins and his staff produced an additional 22 smaller production runs.[5] After rejecting some clumpy material from Dugway which didn't meet Ivins' strict requirements, the results consisted of over 164 liters of spore production, about 85% of it from Dugway. When purified, the end product was about 30 trillion spores suspended in distilled water and a few drops of antifungal chemical -- just enough to fill a single one-liter flask.

On October 22, 1997, Ivins placed the flask in the B311 cold room two doors down from his lab and recorded it into the USAMRIID inventory on Reference Material Receipt number 1029. Thereafter, it would be generally called material "RMR-1029," although Ivins usually referred to it as "the Dugway spores."

Ten years later, the FBI would begin referring to flask RMR-1029 as "the murder weapon."

Chapter 4

Return of the Mad Scientist

In the year 1993, after living what seems to have been a relatively "normal" life for about nine years, Bruce Ivins appears to have begun once again feeling the unrelenting, destructive urges symptomatic of his mental problems.

Even though he had a responsible position in a government laboratory, which would cause most people to be discreet in their public comments, Bruce Ivins felt the urge to express his far-from-normal feelings in letters to the editors of various periodicals using his own name. One such letter is worthy of note.

On September 29, 1993, The *Frederick News-Post* printed a letter to the editor written by Bruce Ivins in which he appeared to defend pedophilia, declaring it to be a matter of "sexual orientation." He complained that the North American Man-Boy Love Association (NAMBLA) had been denied the use of the campus facilities at the University of the District of Columbia to hold a conference. And he asked the readers of the *News-Post* if "individuals whose sexual orientation is children should be protected from discrimination in employment, housing, adoption rights and others areas."

The *News-Post* printed 10 responses from readers expressing anger, outrage and disgust. Ivins responded by backtracking, writing another letter in which he claimed that he'd been misunderstood, and agreeing that, "In our nation's season of 'tolerance' it is wise to remember that it is not morally wrong to be intolerant of pedophilia, and it is not a sin to discriminate against people who seek to legalize the sexual abuse of our children."[1]

28

Return of the Mad Scientist

Ivins' obsessions seem to indicate that he probably wasn't thinking of young boys or children in his wife's day care center. He was attracted to a pretty 18 year old girl who was the younger sister of his wife's best friend. The girl had evidently just gone off to college, but Ivins may have been fantasizing about her for a long time. The following summer, the girl, Mara Linscott, would be hired by Ivins as a lab assistant, and she would continue working summers for him until she became a full-time assistant after graduation.

Ivins' return to his vengeful ways were also partly attributed to problems at work. In May of 1999, reporter Gary Matsumoto had published an article in *Vanity Fair Magazine* that was critical of the AVA anthrax vaccine which Ivins and others had developed prior to the Gulf War of 1991. Unlike most other vaccines used in the United States and because of the rare chance of anyone in the general public getting the disease, the anthrax vaccine had not gone through large scale clinical trials. So, some considered the vaccine given to American military personnel to be "experimental." Although Matsumoto's claims would later be dismissed as invalid by nearly everyone, in 1999, 2000 and 2001, Matsumoto appeared to be blaming what had become known as "Gulf War Syndrome" on preservatives in the vaccine. He was also doing research for a book he was writing on the subject. Bruce Ivins was directly in the line of fire, because Matsumoto was submitting numerous Freedom Of Information Act (FOIA) requests to USAMRIID and Ft. Detrick for information to use in his book (which was eventually published in 2004 with the title *Vaccine A*). Ivins was largely responsible for responding to the FOIA requests, and it infuriated him.

In one email to a former colleague who had sent him a copy of Matsumoto's *Vanity Fair* article, Ivins responded by commenting, "I wonder when the National Enquirer will come out with its headlines on 'Guinea Pig Soldiers Get Killer Vaccine.'" [2]

While this was going on, 53-year-old Bruce Ivins had become fixated and dependant upon his two attractive female co-workers, Mara Linscott and a researcher named Patricia (or Pat) Fellows, who had started working for Ivins in 1988, when she was 27. [3] Mara worked as an assistant researcher while planning to continue with her education and efforts to obtain an MD degree.

Mara assisted Pat, and both of them assisted Ivins in his work. The three of them wrote scientific papers together.

While going about their daily tasks at USAMRIID, the three appear to have also discussed a variety of subjects unrelated to their work, everything from the progress and standings of their favorite baseball teams to personal issues. Mara had a great love for New York City and the New York Yankee baseball team in particular, a love that Ivins definitely did not share. He disliked New York City intensely, claiming it was the result of the way he'd been treated there years ago by waitresses and hotel clerks while he was attending a seminar.[4]

Judging from Ivins' emails, however, his own personal issues seem to have been his favorite subject of conversation. Being able to talk about his mental concerns with his two female subordinates invariably drew him closer to them - particularly to Mara. Although everything in his home life may have appeared happy and normal to outsiders, it was definitely not very satisfying for Ivins. He would sometimes come in to work alone in the evenings just to avoid being at home. If he didn't have any specific work to do, he claimed he'd just lie down in the men's locker room and think.

But trouble was brewing. Mara had made no secret of the fact that her work at USAMRIID was just temporary. She fully intended to return to the University of Buffalo to get her MD degree, then to a hospital residency and then, hopefully, a private practice of some kind. Ivins knew of her plans, but it still nagged at him that he could lose her at any time. For him, it was like being "spurned" in college all over again.

That time came in the summer of 1999 when Mara left USAMRIID to attend medical school. Ivins appears to have been absolutely shattered. He began sending Mara lengthy, very personal emails describing all the issues he could no longer discuss with her at work. Over time, he would send her *hundreds* of such emails.

And Pat was also talking about leaving USAMRIID. If she left, it would be another severe blow for Ivins.

Return of the Mad Scientist

Ivins felt betrayed, abandoned and unwanted. And, this was just a short time after the Gary Matsumoto article appeared in *Vanity Fair*, and at the time when Ivins was angered by Matsumoto's endless FOIA requests. As a result, Ivins appears to have begun suffering sociopathic episodes once again.

Ivins knew his thoughts were not healthy and dangerous to his career, and it worried him. He didn't understand what was happening. On October 27, 1999, Ivins sent this email to Mara:

> It's getting to be lately that I've felt there's nobody in the world I can confide in. You're gone now, and one of the reasons I was so sorry to see you go was a very selfish one - I could talk to you openly and honestly, and that was in itself a great lifter of my spirits. Losing [Pat] as someone I can spill my guts to is crushing - it would mean that I am truly alone completely alone. I know that you and [Pat] are such great friends - when you two are together, I've frequently felt like I totally don't belong. . . . I have come to learn, much to my surprise and disappointment, that [Pat] has been saying some very negative things behind my back. Apparently I am being made to appear mentally ill or just plain mean. It's hard to understand, especially since I've never spoken about her in other than glowing terms. It seems that whatever I say or do can get twisted, exaggerated or misconstrued by her, and now the bond of trust that I thought I had with her is gone. . . . Also, I know that the two of you are great friends, but please don't tell her that I told you about this. The whole thing is very disheartening.[5]

And, on November 1, 1999, he wrote this email to both Pat and Mara:

> There is something we should probably talk about. . . . It deals with some perceived interpersonal problems and some special "sensitivities" of mine. I'm including both of you on my emails. I can give you the information in one of three forms - you decide which one you would rather have, and email back: (1) A brief synopsis, probably no more than a paragraph, talking about the problem. (2) A longer explanation, going somewhat into the family historical

31

A Crime Unlike Any Other

background of the problem, but not getting into the
historical specifics. (3) The full exposition, including some
VERY dark family material, and possibly a few pages long.
(This would be the sort of stuff that would be talked about
in a clinical psych class.) If you choose this, I would need
you to agree to keep it to yourselves. There's nothing in it
about any unsolved crimes or something bad about to
happen to something [sic], but it's not the sort of thing I
would like spread around to others . . .[6]

The key words in that email may be "something bad about to
happen to something." The facts seem to indicate that Ivins had
begun planning some kind of crime, a crime intended to change
public attitudes toward the work he and others at USAMRIID were
doing on anthrax vaccines.

There's no way to know for certain what he was planning in
November of 1999, but in December something happened which
may have caused Ivins to do some additional thinking about his own
professional problems and what he could do to change things.

The LAX Bomb Plot

In August of 1999, an Algerian Muslim named Ahmed
Ressam began plotting to blow up Los Angeles International Airport
(a.k.a. LAX) that coming New Years' Eve. He would later be known
as "The Millennium Bomber," since that date would be commonly
(but incorrectly) viewed as the last day of the old century and the start
of a new millennium.

Ressam's plan was to place one or two large suitcases filled
with explosives and a timer onto a luggage cart and leave it in a
passenger waiting area where it would kill as many people as possible.

But first he had to get himself and the explosives into the
U.S. He planned to cross from Victoria, British Columbia, with the
explosives hidden in the spare tire wheel-well of a rented car.[7]

On December 14, 1999, Ressam managed to get as far as the
immigration station at Port Angeles, Washington. A customs officer,
Diana Dean, thought Ressam looked "hinky" and decided to have a
secondary search performed on his car. Opening the cover over the
space where the spare tire was supposed to be, the Customs

32

inspectors found over 130 pounds of chemicals used to create explosives, plus timers and detonators.

As one of the Customs inspectors began to escort him from the car, Ressam broke free and fled. Inspectors chased him for five to six blocks, and after he unsuccessfully tried to force his way into a car stopped at a light at an intersection, inspectors tackled him in the street and took him into custody.

The actions of the "millenium bomber" may have spurred Ivins into wondering about when the next attack by Muslim terrorists might come, and if it might be a bioweapons attack involving anthrax. If there ever was such an attack, it would certainly change the attitudes everyone currently had toward developing a new anthrax vaccine. *It would change everything.*

In January of 2000, Ivins purchased ammonium nitrate,[8] very likely for the purpose of constructing a "fertilizer bomb" similar to the one Timothy McVeigh used to blow up the Alfred P. Murrah Federal Building in Oklahoma City in April of 1995, killing 168 people, including 19 children, and injuring over 800 others.

Ivins wasn't a cold-blooded murderer, however, so his bomb would be much smaller, and his plan was very likely much more complex. The bomb he evidently planned to build would have to be something he could carry or transport in his car. It would just be the "attention getter," the first part of a two part plan. Perhaps he'd leave a critical wire unconnected so it wouldn't explode, or he'd arrange for the bomb to be found and disarmed before it was set to explode. The bomb's primary purpose would be to show America that common explosive devices were the least of their worries. Near the bomb, he planned to leave an envelope filled with anthrax powder and a warning people would assume was from Muslim terrorists stating that a biological attack was imminent. The anthrax letter would create a massive panic across America that would demand adequate protection from anthrax be made available to everyone.

And, Ivins would be at the center of whatever happened as a result of the threat. All the funding he and USAMRIID needed to fully develop and test the rPA vaccine would be happily provided. All the additional help he needed would be at his fingertips. Pat would certainly forget about leaving USAMRIID. Mara might even be convinced to return to work for him again. And, with the proper approach, Nancy Haigwood might even consider joining him in his work. If not, she would definitely be impressed by his new fame and importance.

Ivins was so convinced that his plan would turn him into a national hero that he felt compelled to make certain that no one else could steal any of his glory. If the time ever came when people began talking about how lucky they were that the anthrax letter had alerted them to the dangers of a bioweapons attack while they still had time to prepare for such an attack, Ivins might want to step forward and explain that it wasn't a matter of luck, it was his foresight and planning that did it.

In order to do that, he'd have to have some way to prove he was behind the bomb plot and the anthrax letter that resulted in America being fully prepared for the real anthrax attack when it came. And Nancy Haigwood would be the one most impressed.

The Coded Message

Ivins' had a long interest in secret codes, and his personal library contained a copy of a book Haigwood had recommended to him two decades ago, the 1980 Pulitzer Prize winning book *Gödel, Escher, Bach: An Eternal Golden Braid* by Douglas R. Hofstadter. Described by the author as "a metaphorical fugue on minds and machines in the spirit of Lewis Carroll", *Gödel, Escher, Bach* (also known as *GEB*) is a detailed and subtle exposition of concepts fundamental to mathematics, symmetry, and intelligence.

But, for Ivins and his obsessions with codes like those in the KKG book of rituals, *GEB* also contained a method of coding a hidden message within another message. Here is what *GEB* says in the chapter titled "The Location of Meaning" and in a section titled *Levels of Understanding of a Message* which describes how a phonograph record is a type of message within a message that would have to be "decoded" by an alien species which had never seen a phonograph record before:

> Nowadays, the idea of decoding is extremely widespread; it
> is a significant part of the activity of astronomers, linguists,
> archaeologists, military specialists and so on. It is often

suggested that we may be floating in a sea of radio messages from other civilizations, messages which we do not yet know how to decipher. And much serious thought has been given to the techniques of deciphering such a message. One of the main problems -- perhaps the deepest problem -- is the question, 'How will we recognize the fact that there is a message at all? How do we identify a frame?' The sending of a record seems to be a simple solution -- its gross physical structure is very attention-drawing, and it is at least plausible to us that it would trigger, in any sufficiently great intelligence, the idea of looking for information hidden in it.

Hofstadter also explained that deciphering a hidden message consists of three message layers:

The first layer is the frame message, which conveys that there is a message from the sender. Once the frame message is recognized, the attention is switched to the outer message, which is a set of triggers, patterns, and structures, telling the recipient how to decode the inner message, which is the third layer and the actual message to be conveyed.

The phonograph record idea would be great for sending a message to aliens on another planet, but Ivins' problem was to hide a message within another message in a way that humans would not immediately see as a message within a message.

Page 404 of *GEB* contained an illustration of a coding method that Ivins must have found to be of particular interest. The *GEB* example of a hidden message is contained within a list of six great mathematicians. The first letter of the first name is darkened, the second letter in the second name is darkened, the third letter of the third name is darkened, etc. The darkened characters draw the viewer's attention and suggest that something unusual and *deliberately* unnatural is occurring, particularly since the highlighted letters appear as a perfect, eye-catching diagonal string down the list.

However, the highlighted letters spell out "Dboups" which appears to be totally meaningless.

D e   M o r g a n
A b e l
B o o l e
B r o u w e r
S i e r p i ń s k i
W e i e r s t r a s s

Exhibit #6 - Coded Message from "GEB" page 404

But, Hofstadter provided a clue for his readers: "Subtract 1 from the diagonal, to find Bach in Leipzig."

Subtracting 1 means to use the prior letter in the alphabet, changing D to C, b to a, o to n, etc.

The result is "Cantor," which is the hidden message and what Johann Sebastian Bach was in Leipzig, a "cantor," a term for the leader of a church choir.

Needless to say, that is a *very* complex coding process. But, that's what Ivins wanted. If it was too simple, too many people might figure out that there was a hidden message in the anthrax letter, and everyone would be wondering why Muslim terrorists would do such a thing.

Ivins must have spent weeks putting together the carefully devised coded hidden message that would become part of the threat note left behind by the "Muslim terrorists" when they supposedly planted the ammonium nitrate fertilizer bomb that miraculously failed to explode. [9]

Here is the text of the letter Ivins gradually constructed:

THIS IS NEXT
TAKE PENACILIN NOW
DEATH TO AMERICA
DEATH TO ISRAEL
ALLAH IS GREAT

Except for the misspelling of penicillin, it seems straight forward enough. The bomb may have failed to explode, but an anthrax attack was coming next. And it would come from Muslim terrorists, just as the last three lines so clearly indicated.

Some might notice that the letter consists entirely of 3 word sentences, but that might not mean anything. Nearly everyone would probably notice that certain characters - specifically A's and T's - are traced over in the letter. But, why? Ivins knew why, but how many others would be able to figure it out?

If someone experienced with decoding messages was looking for a hidden message, the 3 word sentences might tell them that the number 3 is of importance. But, it would also take a solid knowledge of DNA to figure out what the 3 indicated.

The A's and T's spell out a series of 3-letter "codons," which are parts of DNA coding. In his personal library, Ivins had the November-December 1992 issue of *American Scientist Journal* which featured an article titled *The Linguistics of DNA* by David Searls. Among other things, the article described codons and DNA coding.

DNA coding uses A's, T's, G's and C's as abbreviations for adenine, thymine, guanine and cytosine. And, scientists with knowledge of DNA would know that adenine (A) forms a base pair with thymine (T), as does guanine (G) with cytosine (C). Thus, combinations of A's and T's have special meaning to someone with knowledge of DNA coding.

The person with knowledge of DNA coding might then notice that there are nine highlighted letters or three sets of three. The highlighted letters TTT AAT TAT are 3-letter combinations which have a specific meaning as codons:

```
TTT = Phenylalanine
      (single-letter designator F)
AAT = Asparagine
      (single-letter designator N)
TAT = Tyrosine
      (single-letter designator Y)
```

It must have been a sheer delight to Ivins when he found he could put together the 3 three-letter codons so they decoded into something that related to *both* of the female colleagues with whom he'd been fixated for years. Spelling out PAT also resulted in FNY as the single-letter designators, which ridiculed Mara's love of New York City. It's amazing that he didn't use that code elsewhere or tell people about it. (He did talk about similar codes, however.)

The misspelled word "PENACILIN" was particularly ingenious. It would attract the eye, and the "A" that didn't belong in the word was *highlighted*, making it doubly eye-catching. It was the type of "attention getter" that *GEB* described as being extremely important when hiding a message within a message.

However, as clever as the message with a message was, at some point, Ivins evidently realized that his overall plan was totally insane. The KKG burglaries had almost resulted in him getting arrested for harassment. He was now in a very different area. He was thinking about committing an act of *terrorism*.

Time to Re-Think

Was the hidden coded message in the letter too obvious? Would everyone seeing such a printed message immediately begin wondering why certain printed characters were larger and darker than others? Would everyone realize it must be a code of some kind? If the entire country was trying to figure out what the highlighted A's and T's meant, someone was bound to put the pieces together and figure out that it was a code derived from the book *Gödel, Escher, Bach*, that each sentence consisted of 3 words, and some geneticist could come forward and declare that the coding almost certainly referred to three letter codons: TTT AAT TAT. And that in turn translated to PAT or FNY.

And, he'd once given a copy of *Gödel, Escher, Bach* to Patricia Fellows in hopes that she might find it as fascinating as Nancy Haigwood had. If so, Pat might be among the first to put all the pieces together. If not her, then it could be Nancy Haigwood.

In the form of a typed or computer printed message, it might be too easy to decode, particularly by investigators. Ivins may also have tried writing a version using his left hand. But, that wouldn't have been much better if he deliberately traced over those nine A's and T's, plus it posed the additional risk that handwriting experts might be able to match his handwriting to the letters if he was somehow compelled to produce handwriting samples using his left hand. And there was a more serious problem: Planting an ammonium nitrate bomb in some public place was not as simple as breaking into a Kappa Kappa Gamma sorority house that he knew was empty and unguarded. If he were caught in the process of planting the bomb, the consequences would be a lot more severe than being caught inside a sorority house without a good explanation. No amount of explaining would ever convince people that he didn't actually intend to harm anyone with the bomb.

The whole thing was *totally insane*. And it was all Mara's fault. She'd left him to go out on her own. And now he was making plans that could put him in jail for life, or worse - the death penalty. But, he felt he was going to succumb to the impulse if things got too bad. And they could easily get worse than they already were.

So, to his credit, in early 2000 Bruce Ivins once again sought out the help of a psychiatrist.

Chapter 5

Ivins Plans a Murder

In late January 2000, it was again clear to Bruce Ivins that he needed professional psychiatric help. He telephoned Dr. Naomi Heller, who had treated him in 1978 and 1979, but she had retired and was no longer seeing patients. Dr. Heller referred Ivins to Dr. David S. Irwin, a forensic psychiatrist in Gaithersburg, Maryland.[1]

Records show that Ivins visited Dr. Irwin five times, starting on February 1, 2000. In one of the sessions, Ivins told Dr. Irwin that he'd purchased ammonium nitrate to build a bomb, but there's no public record that Ivins explained what he intended to do with the bomb.[2] There's also no record that Ivins told Dr. Irwin of any plans he had to seek vengeance upon Mara Linscott for leaving him. It appears that Ivins was a somewhat different person when talking with men than when talking with women - including health care professionals. Nevertheless, Dr. Irwin later described Ivins as being like "an overstretched rubber band," the "scariest" patient he had ever treated. He also made the diagnosis that later showed up in public records assessing Ivins as "homicidal, sociopathic with clear intentions."

After Ivins' fifth visit, due to reasons related to health care insurance coverage and driving distance, Dr. Irwin referred Ivins to another psychiatrist, Dr. Allan Levy who ran Comprehensive Counseling Associates (CCA) in Frederick, MD, only about a mile and a half from Ivins' home.

For the next eight years, Dr. Levy and his staff (including Dr. Levy's psychologist wife, Dr. Wendy Levy) provided Dr. Ivins with individual psychotherapy, group psychotherapy, and medication management.

Very soon after his first visit, Dr. Levy prescribed Celexa, an anti-depressant, to help Bruce Ivins deal with his mental problems. A month later, Dr. Levy doubled the prescription.[3]

But the pills didn't stop Ivins' obsessions. The effects of the pills only gave Ivins something else to discuss in emails sent to Pat and Mara. On June 27, 2000, Ivins described aspects of a visit he'd paid to Mara at her home a week earlier (At this time, Mara Linscott was evidently living in Ithaca, NY, about 300 miles, a 5½ hour drive, each way for Ivins):

> I apologized to [Pat] for my behavior and paranoia - that's exactly what it was, and I have no excuse for it, only regrets and apologies - last fall. Even with the Celexa and the counseling, the depression episodes still come and go. That's unpleasant enough. What is REALLY scary is the paranoia - you saw a brief flash of it last Tuesday night when, for no reason, I acted as I did. . . . Remember when I told you about the "metallic" taste in my mouth that I got periodically? It's when I get these "paranoid" episodes. Of course I regret them thoroughly when they are over, but when I'm going through them, it's as if I am a passenger on a ride. The metallic taste was there on Tuesday night. I don't want to become mean-spirited, hateful, angry, withdrawn and paranoid, and that's why I reach out to talk to you (a lot) and [Pat] (somewhat). . . . I think the problems started in 1997, and by the time you left, things were very bad. Your leaving then, even though we all knew it would happen, and even though we would keep in touch, was dreadfully painful. Then came the fall problems, [Pat]'s looking for a job, and finally my going to get professional help.[4]

We don't know what caused the "brief flash" of "paranoia" that Ivins wrote he exhibited during that Tuesday evening, which was evidently the evening of Tuesday, June 20, 2000. Nor do we know exactly what Ivins did. But, his obsessions with Pat and particularly Mara were deepening dramatically. At work, he had managed to steal Pat's computer password, and he was reading what she and Mara

A Crime Unlike Any Other

would say about him in emails they exchanged. What he read inflamed his paranoia.

Another Woman to Talk With

In late June, 2000, Dr. Levy turned Ivins' weekly therapy sessions over to CCA employee Judith McLean, a licensed clinical professional counselor. The fact that Ivins was again discussing his various problems with a woman instead of a man may have caused him to talk of different things.

McLean described Ivins as precise and unfailingly polite, but sometimes very cold and without emotion.[5]

Meanwhile, problems were getting worse for Ivins at work. On July 18, 2000, The *Washington Post* published an article titled *Anthrax Shots' Effect Challenged (Army Disputes Expert Who Reviewed Vaccine Tests)*. The article discussed a report Ivins had written, dated September 23, 1991, in which Ivins noted that although all ten of the vaccinated monkeys in a test had survived, "they appeared to be sick over the course of two weeks post-challenge." The *Washington Post* article drew the conclusion that vaccinated soldiers would have the same symptoms: "Soldiers who are exposed to anthrax may become quite sick and be incapacitated for up to two weeks, even if they have received the full set of anthrax vaccinations." The *Post* article went on to say:

> But if it turns out that even fully inoculated soldiers would be unable to fight after exposure to anthrax, the implications for U.S. military operations are enormous, said Chris Seiple, a former Marine officer who serves on a panel studying chemical and biological warfare issues at the Center for Strategic and International Studies.

Pressures at work seemed to increase Ivins' thoughts about seeking revenge upon women who had deserted him in his times of need.

It was the same day the *Washington Post* article was published - July 18, 2000 - that Ivins began opening up to his new counselor. He began telling Judith McLean about a "young woman" with whom McLean assumed Ivins was thinking of becoming involved. Ivins said her name was Mara. To McLean, Ivins appeared to be infatuated with Mara.[6] Ivins talked about driving to upstate New York to watch her play soccer. Although Ivins never mentioned his wife and their two adopted children, McLean suggested to Ivins that it was probably inappropriate for a man of his age to be so attracted to a woman so much younger than he.

Then, according to McLean, things "got bizarre." In a very cold and methodical way, Ivins described how he planned to *poison* Mara if she lost a critical soccer game they had talked about. He told McLean that he had already mixed the poison, and he "knew how to do things without people finding out."

Judith McLean was so alarmed by the deliberate way Ivins had laid out a specific homicidal plan that she prepared a statement for Ivins to sign declaring that he wouldn't do anything until after he'd consulted with her further. She explained to Ivins that she was duty-bound to report any homicidal threats to the police, and she asked if Ivins would be willing to consult with a psychiatrist about what he had told her. Ivins was willing, and, as soon as the session was over, McLean attempted to contact the head of the clinic, Dr. Levy, who happened to be out of town and traveling, making him unavailable for consultation. So, she consulted with Dr. Orrin Palmer, who was in charge of CCA while Dr. Levy was out of town.

Dr. Palmer called Ivins at home and confirmed what had been said, but he was uncertain if prescribing any new medications would help the situation.

In an effort to understand more about Bruce Ivins and his mental condition, McLean examined Ivins' past psychiatric records which included the diagnosis of sociopathy from Dr. Irwin. She called Dr. Irwin, and Dr. Irwin in turn called Ivins, further confirming what Ivins had told McLean. Dr. Irwin was uncertain if prescribing a different drug would remedy the situation.

McLean also contacted the CCA's malpractice insurance carrier, seeking legal advice. She was told that she didn't have enough information about the identity of the person Ivins planned to murder to warn anyone, and thus did not have any legal duty to do anything. Nevertheless, McLean contacted the Frederick Police Department. They merely told her the same thing: Without the full name of the person Ivins planned to murder or more information about where she was located, there wasn't anything the police could do.

On July 23, 2000, Ivins emailed Mara Linscott to report:

It's been a real stressful week, from all standpoints. Home, work, and it's not going well with the counselor I'm going to. (She said she thinks I went up to see you to have an affair.) I'm going to have to ask to get put with another counselor or into a group therapy session .... sometimes I think that it's all just too much.

When Ivins returned for the following week's counseling session, McLean was stunned to be told that, in spite of the pledge Ivins had signed, and in spite of all the talks with psychiatrists, Ivins had gone to watch the young woman play her soccer game.

Years later, McLean explained her final counseling session with Ivins this way to a *Washington Post* reporter:

That day, she said, he told her about the poison he had made but said he had not used it because the woman's team had won. She recalled that he also said he had grudges against several people from his past who he said deserved to be punished and that he knew how to find out where anyone lived.

He told her these things with "flat affect [and] total indifference," she said. "He obviously thought about this a lot. He made the poison, took it along. It was not a crime of impulse. It was planned with cunning." [7]

Once the planned murder of Mara Linscott was no longer a major issue preying on Ivins' mind, he seemed to relax a bit and return to his "normal self." In an August 23, 2000 email to Mara, he wrote that "suicidal thoughts were part of my life for the past few years until I got put on the medication." [8]

After Judith McLean refused to work with Ivins any further, Dr. Levy appears to have followed a suggestion from his patient and arranged for Ivins to go into group therapy. Group therapy seems to have gotten him past that particular mental crisis.

Ivins Plans a Murder

Seven months later, Ivins even mentioned the incident and the reaction from Judith McLean in an email to Mara dated March 4, 2001:

> The woman I saw before I went into group wanted to get me put in jail. [9]

Group therapy may have been a way of temporarily keeping Ivins from *discussing* plots for murder, but it didn't stop him from continuing to plot and plan to do things that were extremely dangerous and even insane.

Chapter 6

Motive & Means

In mid-2000, Dr. Ivins was sending e-mails to Mara expressing his increasing concern and eventual frustration that the Bioport Corporation, which had been producing the only approved anthrax vaccine available in the United States, was finding itself unable to produce quantities of anthrax vaccine that met the required potency standard, even though Ivins and other USAMRIID researchers were spending an increasingly large percentage of their time trying to help that company fix the problem. The problem continued into 2001.

The Office for the Assistant Secretary of Defense for Public Affairs stated in a news release on June 11, 2001, that the Anthrax Vaccine Immunization Program was being slowed due to a shortage of that vaccine. Vaccination would continue for special mission units and research purposes only. "This slowdown provides for a small reserve of FDA-released vaccine in the event of an emergency. Actions are being taken to ensure that personnel deployed to high-threat areas have sufficient antibiotics on hand for post-exposure treatment in case of an attack."

Pressure to improve the potency to meet the standards increased throughout the summer of 2001. Ivins was sending Mara emails telling her that USAMRIID was down to its last approved lot of the vaccine. That meant that, if Bioport could not get approval to resume production or somehow make existing lots of the vaccine meet the potency standard, the supply of anthrax vaccine would soon be completely depleted.

This would become a *major* problem, not only because the vaccine was needed for soldiers in the field, but also because it was needed for the researchers themselves. Without proper and up-to-date vaccinations, Dr. Ivins would not be allowed to enter BioSafety Level-3 laboratories to work with anthrax. It would become a "Catch-22" situation. He wouldn't be able to help develop a new vaccine because he wasn't properly vaccinated, and he couldn't be properly vaccinated because he wouldn't be allowed to work with anthrax to help develop a new vaccine to use in vaccinations.

And criticisms of the vaccine increased.

The claims from Gary Matsumoto and others that the current vaccine had not been thoroughly tested and could be unsafe were still in circulation, and in June of 2001, Senate majority leader, Tom Daschle of South Dakota, sent a letter to the Department of Defense expressing his concerns about the safety of the vaccine.

Because of all the criticism and controversy, the Army's Medical Research Material Command at USAMRIID was considering getting out of the anthrax vaccine business entirely and leaving it for private pharmaceutical companies to develop. They even began considering putting Dr. Ivins to work on finding a vaccine for *Burkholderia mallei*, also known as Glanders, for which there was no existing vaccine of any kind.

During the summer of 2001, Dr. Ivins learned that upper management was thinking of moving him into this entirely new area of research. He learned they felt that "anthrax research had matured beyond its mission," and the remaining work was too menial in nature and a waste of Dr. Ivins considerable talents. They didn't need someone with his experience at his pay grade to do little else but grow and purify anthrax spores.

Glanders primarily affected horses and mules, but, because no one had been able to develop a vaccine for Glanders, and because it only takes a few bacteria to kill, and those bacteria can be relatively easily aerosolized, it was considered to have considerable potential for use as a bioweapon.

USAMRIID management turned room B312 - the lab right next door to Ivins' lab - over to the study of Glanders.

A Crime Unlike Any Other

Bruce Ivins was extremely upset by this plan to transfer him into a totally different area of research, and he went around USAMRIID complaining, "I am an anthrax researcher. This is what I do." [1]

And the criticism of the existing anthrax vaccine continued, primarily from Gary Matsumoto, but also from a scientist, Internet conspiracy theorist and practicing physician in Maine by the name of Dr. Meryl Nass, and "Washington D.C. super lawyer" Mark S. Zaid who was accusing the Pentagon of covering up the real cause of Gulf War Syndrome.

According to page 40 of the FBI's Summary report,

> Dr. Ivins's offense at these criticisms grew as Matsumoto was making FOIA requests for information regarding the vaccine program for use in the critical Vaccine A. For example, just before the letter attacks, in August and September 2001, Dr. Ivins sent e-mails to a co-worker and a supervisor, a sample of which included, "Tell Matsumoto to kiss my ass. We've got better things to do than shine his shoes and pee on command. He's gotten everything from me he will get."

That was the situation in the summer of 2001 when Dr. Ivins apparently began considering once again taking some kind of action to turn the situation around. The truck bomb attack on the World Trade Center in 1993 by Muslim extremists was something else that most Americans would never forget. After that incident, there had been a great deal of talk about how bioweapons were the "poor country's atomic bomb." And on TV talk shows in November 1997, Secretary of Defense William S. Cohen told the American public that a five pound bag of anthrax spores could kill half the population of Washington D.C.

And, there was also that failed plan to blow up LAX.

To Bruce Ivins, the situation must have seemed like insanity. Muslims were almost certainly plotting to attack America again, just as they had in 1993 and tried in 1999. If they did it with a bioweapon like anthrax, America would be virtually defenseless. Soldiers would need to be protected. First responders, doctors and nurses would also have to be immunized. Yet, there was barely enough vaccine available to immunize scientists working on creating better vaccines. There wouldn't be any at all for the general public. And, even if they solved all the problems with getting a vaccine that could meet all the FDA requirements, it could still take *years* to gear up for mass production.

There was no need for anyone to die. It was just necessary that the American public get their pants scared off. And, the best way to do that was to show them how *easily* they could be attacked by Muslim extremists.

Ivins still had the unsent letter with the hidden message he had constructed after the LAX bomb plot was exposed. He still had the ammonium nitrate needed for a bomb. And he also had the Ames strain which was believed by everyone to be a common strain used in laboratories all over the world. That was perfect for Ivins' plan, since he didn't have easy access to any Middle-East strains. The information Ivins had about the Ames strain was that it was a strain routinely distributed by the United States Department of Agriculture (USDA) to any scientist with a need to study anthrax. Ivins understood that USAMRIID used a slant of Ames obtained in 1981 from the USDA in Ames, Iowa, which meant the USDA had been distributing it for twenty years since then, and possibly for a lot longer before 1981.

Garbage Anthrax

The cruder the powder, the better it was for Ivins' purposes. He wanted it to look like it had been made in a garage or in an unsophisticated lab. Plus, crude powders would be less dangerous. He didn't want anyone to be seriously harmed by the letter.

The crudest powder imaginable could probably be called "garbage anthrax," and Ivins just happened to have a nearly endless supply of "garbage anthrax."

When Ivins and his co-workers needed to prepare doses of anthrax spores for test animals, the process involved creating a lot of test plates to verify how many spores were in a dose.

There's no direct way to count the spores, since the spores were extremely small and there were so many of them. So, estimates were calculated and achieved via "serial dilutions."

A Crime Unlike Any Other

The serial dilution process involves first shaking the flask to get the spores as evenly distributed as possible in the distilled water. Starting with a liter of spores and water like that in flask RMR-1029, they would remove 1/1000th of the contents or one milliliter. The milliliter sample should contain 30 billion spores, far too many to count and far too many to use as a dose for a single animal.

The next step was to dilute the milliliter sample by adding 99 milliliters of water. The 100 milliliter diluted sample is then shaken to evenly distribute the spores in the water, and a one milliliter is removed. The dilution process is repeated until the correct dose quantity of 5,000 spores per milliliter is reached.

Just prior to 9/11, Ivins and his assistants provided doses of 5,000 spores each for 91 guinea pigs. To verify that each dose did indeed contain approximately 5,000 spores, six plates where inoculated from each sample and the number of colonies counted. That means to test 91 guinea pigs, 546 plates were inoculated, allowed to grow overnight, and then checked to verify the dosage quantity. Ivins reported they were doing 180 plates per day.[2]

And, after checking the plates to verify the number of colonies was within allowable limits and the dose was proper, the plates *and the anthrax on them* simply got tossed in the garbage.

But it was *biohazardous* garbage, which cannot be handled the same way as old magazines or coffee grounds. The plates had to be placed in day-glow orange biosafety bags for sterilization in a large autoclave. An autoclave uses high-pressure steam at temperatures far above the boiling point for 15 or 20 minutes or more to kill any living material inside closed plates or any other contaminated materials.

Then, the safely sterilized bags have to be hauled to the incinerator next to Building 1412 for final disposal. And that's where it became a distasteful and time-consuming chore. So, Ivins and his subordinates appear to have routinely allowed the autoclave bags to accumulate in his lab *for weeks*, thus reducing the amount of time they had to spend on such disagreeable house-keeping matters.[3]

This is a virtually unheard of practice in most microbiology labs where biohazardous material must be disposed of at the end of every day or even within a few hours after use. When Ivins briefly had a second lab in Building 1412 at Ft. Detrick, other scientists in that building even opened some of the autoclave bags to check what was inside, and they found Petri dishes totally covered with growth.

In layman's terms, they were covered with "garbage anthrax." The spores had been grown under the crudest of conditions. They were grown in ordinary agar used for all such growths in every lab in the world, and, instead of being grown in incubators, they were grown at "room" temperature like what might be found in someone's garage.

The 546 plates used for the guinea pig tests shortly before 9/11 contained enough "garbage" spores for dozens of letters.[4]

Of course, it would take some expertise to get the spores out of the Petri dishes and to dry them without contaminating the person doing the work and everything else nearby, but a Muslim scientist would be assumed to have at least some minimal lab equipment. Certainly they would have some ability to wash the spores off of the plates. They'd either have a glove box or an open-front biosafety cabinet to allow safe handling of the wet and dry spores, and a centrifuge would be needed to get rid of some of the unconsumed agar and to concentrate the spores somewhat before drying. A Muslim terrorist just wouldn't go through all the purification steps Ivins routinely performed when creating spores for vaccine testing. Without that purification step, creating spore powders would be an incredibly simple process. Almost anyone with microbiology experience could do it if they were immunized or if they assumed that Allah would protect them.

Demoted?

Ivins' mental problems, his constantly cluttered lab, and his obsessions with his female co-workers appear to have had a noticable effect on his work. During the 1990s, Ivins had been credited as the lead author on four out of 12 published journal articles. After Linscott left, he contributed to 16 articles, but was not named as the first author on *any* of the articles. His greatest prominence as a scientific author came during the 1980s, before Linscott started working for him, when Ivins was the lead writer on seven articles.

According to fellow USAMRIID scientist John Ezzell, "He got his name on a lot of these publications because he was providing the spores." "That is one of the reasons he was on so many publications. So many of the studies were conducted with his spores." [5]

Because his work was not up to his previous standards, USAMRIID officials decided at some point in the second half of 2001 to install a new supervisor between Ivins and the man who was currently his immediate supervisor, Jeffery Adamovicz, Deputy Chief of USAMRIID's Bacteriology Division. Ivins new direct superior would be a woman who was younger than Ivins and who had less experience, Patricia Worsham. Worsham's primary lab was in room B309, four doors down from Ivins.

For Ivins and his massive ego, the appearance of a demotion combined with the prospect of being supervised by a woman with less experience must have seemed like a degrading slap in the face. So, in August of 2001, Ivins was both mentally ill *and* wildly upset.

Chapter 7

Before 9/11

It appears that Ivins may have decided to go ahead with his bomb-plus-anthrax plan on Monday, August 13, 2001, since he spent more than three hours that evening in his BSL-3 lab, something he seems to have rarely done before.

Ivins undoubtedly knew his movements were being logged every time he swiped his key card in the card reader or typed his ID number into a keypad. But, there wasn't anything he could do about that. It would be a lot more incriminating if he tried to find some way to defeat the in-out logs and was caught at it. Plus, Ivins had already established a long pattern of going into Building 1425 at night to work in his office or just to get away from his family.

Besides if everything went as he hoped, no one would ever look at the in-out logs at USAMRIID, because they'd be suspecting terrorists from the Middle-East.

To collect the spores Ivins needed for his plans, all he had to do was come in at night or on a weekend to wash and scrape the spores off the plates in the autoclave bags and into a beaker. He'd then cover the beaker and put it into the B311 cold room among hundreds of other containers. When the autoclave bags were tossed into the autoclave, no one would know that they were sterilizing empty plates. And no one touched any one else's materials, so there was little danger that the beaker would be noticed, much less questioned. There were containers in the cold room that had been left behind by scientists who had left USAMRIID years ago.

A Crime Unlike Any Other

Developing a Plan

The next problem to solve was the letter he planned to leave with the fertilizer bomb. He'd use the most common kind of paper and envelope he could find. He'd have an untraceable fertilizer bomb, an untraceable anthrax powder in an untraceable letter in an untraceable envelope. And, to write the letter he'd use a common brand of felt tip or ballpoint pen that anyone could buy anywhere. But, one problem remained: the handwriting.

There was no way around it. He would almost certainly have to write the letter by hand.

Then, at some point in time, possibly around August 27, 2001, Ivins seems to have gotten an idea for the perfect way to write the letter as if it was being done by someone just learning English. And, there would be no possible match to his own handwriting.

The First Anthrax Letter

In the late summer of 2001, Diane's day care center was evidently still a going operation, but the twins had grown into young adults, seniors in high-school preparing to enter college and leave home for lives of their own.

The facts indicate that a child who had been in Diane's day care center was just starting first grade. The first day of school was evidently Monday, August 20. His mother would drop him off on her way to work, and the child would wait with Diane until the school bus arrived. Then, in the afternoon, the school bus would drop the child off in front of the Ivins' house, and Diane would be there to take him inside where he'd wait until his mother got out of work and could pick him up. And, if Diane and the mother were friends, they would often sit around and talk for awhile, leaving the child to do his homework or play with toys.

And that would be the situation when Bruce came home from work. He'd find two women talking in the kitchen, possibly talking about their husbands, sharing secrets with each other that they couldn't share with their husbands. And, Ivins' paranoia would be inflamed even more than it already was.

In another room, the child would be sitting and doing his homework - copying things to practice his newly learned skill of writing in block letters.

Click!

It must have seemed like an absolutely *brilliant* solution to the handwriting dilemma! A 6-year-old child would write about the same way a handwriting expert might assume an adult Muslim terrorist from Afghanistan or Iraq or Yemen or some other Middle-Eastern country would write in English. It would be crude, unsophisticated, awkward, and best of all, the handwriting could never be traced back to Ivins.

It was the *perfect* solution -- for a sociopath. It even had the added enjoyment for Ivins of allowing him to play a trick on Diane and her friend that they would never know about. It would never occur to them -- and probably not to forensic handwriting experts, either -- that someone would use a child in such a way. That made it an even more perfect solution.[1]

Of course, there was a definite risk that the child might tell his parents about writing the letter. But, Ivins' skills and experience with manipulating people could easily get around that problem. Children were infinitely easier to manipulate than the adults Ivins worked with and attempted to manipulate nearly every day.

So, the facts indicate that one afternoon in late August of 2001, Ivins decided to persuade the first grader to make a copy of the coded letter that Ivins had printed out. The child just had to make sure that all the highlighted characters - the A's and T's - were also traced over in the copy.

Perhaps Ivins attracted the six-year-old child's attention by doing some funny juggling. Then he'd ask if the child wanted to learn how to juggle. Ivins would offer to give him a few lessons in exchange for some help writing a letter. For Ivins, there would be yet another added benefit of having the child use a pen from his school backpack, making it almost impossible to trace.

And, the child would be focused on the fun of learning to juggle. If he talked about his time with Mr. Ivins, he'd talk about the juggling lesson, not about the chore he did for Mr. Ivins.

Later, when Ivins examined the letter the child had written, he saw that the child had done far less than a perfect job.[2]

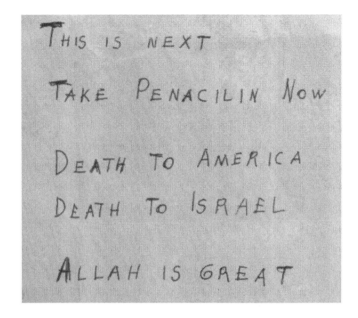

Exhibit #7 - The First Anthrax Letter

Ivins saw that some of the A's and T's were not as thoroughly darkened as others, and some additional characters seemed slightly traced over. However, the letter would be *perfect* because the coding in the letter was *not perfect*. If it ever became necessary, Ivins would still be able to explain things convincingly. But, the risk of having someone else figure out the code prematurely was *vastly reduced*. There wouldn't be much thought of hidden codes, because the thought would be that anyone deliberately putting a code into a letter would make certain that everything was clearly done.

So, in late August of 2001, Bruce Ivins had the handwritten letter he needed. But the risks of planting the bomb still remained. And, those risks still kept him from carrying out the bomb and anthrax plan he'd been thinking about for over a year and a half.

Other Coded Letters

The FBI investigation showed that Bruce Ivins had been sending other "coded" messages prior to this time. They weren't like the letter the child had written, but they were coded nevertheless.

And the recipients remembered the letters as having the same childlike block printing.

Using a false name and a post office far from Frederick, Ivins on one occasion mailed Linscott a soccer jersey in the name of Mia Hamm, a U.S. Olympic team star. On another occasion, Ivins used the name of New York Yankee's shortstop Derek Jeter to send Linscott some Yankees paraphernalia. Ivins mailed Linscott a jacket from Gettysburg, PA. He sent her a gift certificate and a birthday card from Gaithersburg, MD. But, most interesting of all, he mailed Mara Linscott *a box of detergent* when he was attending an Integrated Product Team meeting at Ft. Belvoir, VA. The return address on the package was "Laundry Boy." He later told investigators he did these things, in part, to test whether Linscott could "decode" the identity of the sender. She usually did.

The J-Lo Letter

In early September of 2001, Ivins *may* have mailed another box of detergent and some mysterious odds and ends to movie actress and singer Jennifer Lopez c/o the *Sun* magazine in Boca Raton, Florida. Some decoding was required for that letter, too. The large manila envelope contained a cigar tube with a cheap cigar inside, an empty can of chewing tobacco, an empty detergent box, and a tiny Star of David pendant buried in a mound of detergent around which a love letter had been carefully folded.

The unsigned letter contained some sexual innuendo, and the writer expressed how much he loved Lopez, asking her to marry him. The letter itself was on a business-size sheet of stationery decorated with pink and blue clouds around the edges.[3]

Jennifer Lopez's most recent movie was *The Cell*, which was about a beautiful psychotherapist who uses newly developed experimental technology to cause her mind to enter the mind of a comatose serial killer in an attempt to help stop another killing. Ivins had been looking for such a woman for decades - a beautiful, brilliant woman who could enter his mind and see what he saw and be fascinated by what fascinated Ivins. And he needed someone to stop him from doing the insane things he kept plotting.

A Crime Unlike Any Other

The J-Lo package was mailed around September 8 or 10, 2001. It was opened at the American Media Incorporated offices in Boca Raton on September 19, 2001.

But, while the J-Lo package was en route, Ivins' problems, his situation and the entire world suddenly changed on the morning that would become known forever as "9/11."

Chapter 8

9/11 and the First Mailing

According to his co-workers, Bruce Ivins was much more upset than most others at Ft. Detrick when the news about the first attacks of September 11, 2001, began to spread. Everyone with access to a TV or radio started watching and listening as the remaining events unfolded. Both Twin Towers of the World Trade Center in New York City had been struck by a hijacked aircraft, first one then the other. And while the whole world watched on TV, both buildings collapsed with horrific loss of life. Then it was learned that a third hijacked aircraft had crashed into the Pentagon, and the media was reporting that other hijacked aircraft could still be in the air somewhere.

After every aircraft in the skies over America had been ordered to land at the nearest airfield, it was learned that there was still an unaccounted for aircraft somewhere over the Eastern United States, and Ivins loudly argued that USAMRIID should be evacuated because the missing aircraft could be headed straight toward them. It appears his paranoia took over, for Ivins was yelling, "We got to get out of here!" [1]

A few days later, his fear turned to anger and he told a friend via email that he was "angry, very angry." He was "Angry at those who did this, who support them, who coddle them, and who excuse them." [2]

Ivins soon made some fateful decisions. He turned from a panicky potential victim of Islamic terrorism into a calculating planner of a major act of terrorism. From his point of view, there was a

59

chance that his act of "terrorism" could make him a national hero, even if it was only in his own eyes. People at USAMRIID were already talking about how a biological attack could come next, a second blow that could knock America to its knees.

USAMRIID's in-out logs show that on the evening of 9/11, Ivins spent nearly 2 hours in Building 1425, some of it in his lab, some in his office. It may have been during the time spent in his office that he dug out the address for the *National Enquirer* in Lantana, Florida. The Enquirer appears to have been popular reading material for Ivins and others at USAMRIID. Although it was someone else who actually bought the copies, many of the magazines reportedly ended up in a stack in Ivins' cluttered office.[3]

Ivins was developing a new plan for the coded letter and his stock of "garbage" anthrax. There was no longer any need for a bomb. The attacks that morning would become the first step in his plan, and all he needed was to implement the second step - a letter, or perhaps several letters - that would have to be sent through the mails.

The next evening, Wednesday the 12th, Ivins didn't enter building 1425 in the evening at all. It may have been on that evening that he decided he needed to send out five letters to get five times the impact. He'd send letters to the evening news anchors at the three top TV networks, Tom Brokaw at NBC, Dan Rather at CBS, Peter Jennings at ABC. Plus, he would send a letter to the *New York Post*, which would undoubtedly create one of its typically scary headlines when they received it. And lastly, he'd send a letter to the National Enquirer, since they would also produce scary headlines that would be seen at checkout lines in supermarkets all over America.

This new plan would have a hundred times - maybe a *thousand* times the impact of leaving an anthrax-filled letter left near an unexploded bomb.

He purchased two packs of pre-stamped envelopes at the local post office. They were untraceable and used all over the country, plus he bought them from a vending machine, which meant he never had to touch them. He handled them only by the white paper band that held the packs of five envelopes together. As soon as he was out of the post office, he put them into a Ziplock plastic bag to eliminate any further chance that he might accidentally leave fingerprints or other trace evidence on them.

On Thursday the 13th, Ivins was in Building 1425 for less than a half hour, evidently spending about ten minutes in Suite B5 where he had another lab in room B505 that wasn't a confinement area and didn't require keycard access. Then he spent a few minutes in his office before leaving the building at 9:56 p.m. Ivins may have spent that time looking through his records of KKG sorority locations, which he kept in his office.

News reports said that one of the hijacked planes had begun its flight at the airport in Newark, NJ. Ivins would try to mail the letters from near Newark. Like his other trips, he plotted his route on the Internet to determine how far he could expect to get in a trip that began after his family was asleep and would still get him back home to shave, change clothes and get to work on time the next morning.

And, since his obsession with the KKG sorority was never far from his mind, he evidently saw that his drive toward Newark could take him through or near Princeton. According his records of KKG sororities and office locations, KKG had some kind of office or meeting place he'd never visited right on the direct route to Newark.

Addressing the Envelopes

The addresses needed to be written on the five envelopes. Ivins evidently accomplished that by persuading the same first grader to do it, perhaps in return for another juggling lesson.

Ivins decided that the letters would more likely get immediate attention and get opened by the addressees if they appeared to have been written by a child. For most people, a letter from a child would arouse curiosity and even immediate attention. Only upon opening the letter would the addressee realize that the handwriting was *not* that of a child but of a barely literate Muslim terrorist whose handwriting simply appeared to be "childlike."

Along with his list of five addresses, Ivins had devised a return address that would be clever while at the same time eliminating some of his concerns about sending letters filled with anthrax through the mails. The return address he'd created combined more "codes" he could use if or when it became necessary to convince people he had written the letters. But the "codes" could never be decoded by anyone who didn't know what he knew.

He'd recently read about a 4th grade student at a school in Wisconsin who had been given corporal punishment - a spanking - which generated a public furor and a lawsuit. There had been a major article about it in the *American Family Association Journal,* to which he and Diane subscribed. They'd even made a donation to the AFA after they'd read about the case. The name of the school was The Greendale Baptist Academy.[4]

His travel calculations showed that the best place to mail the letters was Franklin Park, New Jersey. Franklin Park was about as close to Newark as he could reasonably get in an overnight round-trip night-time drive. Another reason for mailing the letters from Franklin Park was its proximity to Monmouth Junction, NJ. Having a place with the name "Monmouth" just a few miles from Franklin Park and just off the route to Newark must have seemed like fate to Ivins. Using the ZIP code for Monmouth Junction would be another secret "code" he could put in the return address that only he could decipher. The final result was:

4th GRADE
GREENDALE SCHOOL
FRANKLIN PARK NJ 08852 [5]

The address was a jumble of real places and had the additional benefit of eliminating any concern Ivins might have had that, if something went wrong in the post-9/11 confusion, the letters might be returned to sender. He didn't want to have letters filled with anthrax being returned to a real school. There wasn't any Greendale School anywhere near Franklin Park or Monmouth Junction.

Ivins probably helped the child avoid leaving fingerprints by putting a sheet of paper under his hand, but other things didn't go as Ivins planned. It appears that when asked to write the return address on the first envelope, the first grader wrote the only way he knew how to write, which was using characters so large that there was barely room left on the envelope for the actual destination address. And, the large writing of the return address would have left no doubt that a child was doing the writing, not an adult.

Having ruined one envelope, Ivins couldn't instruct the child on how to write smaller, since it would mean the child had done something wrong. It would turn the writing into something other than a favor. It would become a learning chore that the child would clearly remember and probably talk about with his parents later.

So, Ivins changed plans. No more return addresses. The next envelope addressed by the child looked okay:

Exhibit #8 - The Brokaw Envelope

The other four envelopes went equally well. As Ivins watched the child address the envelopes, he probably never noticed that during the past few weeks the child had learned the correct way to draw certain characters of the alphabet - particularly R's. In kindergarten, he'd been drawing the top of his R's as a small circle. In first grade, he'd been taught to properly draw it as an arc.

A Crime Unlike Any Other

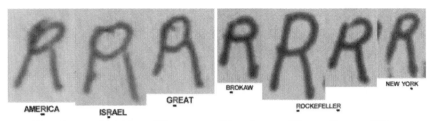

Brokaw Letter R's   Brokaw Envelope R's

Exhibit #9 - R's on the Brokaw Letter and Envelope

Then it appears that Ivins had a new thought. He borrowed the felt-tip pen from the child and, attempting to copy the child's hand-writing, he added the date "09-11-01" to the top of the letter to make another connection with the 9/11 hijackers.

Preparing the Anthrax

By the evening of the 14th, Ivins had made five copies of the letter. He just needed the spore powders and he'd be ready. He went into work at 9:21 p.m., entered Suite B3 at 9:45 and remained in the suite until just after midnight, about two hours and 15 minutes. Presumably, that time was spent washing the overgrown culture contents out of more plates and then centrifuging the wet material to squeeze out as much water as possible. The result would be a paste-like material which just needed to be dried.

On Saturday the 15th, Ivins worked another two and a quarter hours in his lab. And on Sunday the 16th he entered his lab at 7 p.m., left to go to his office at 8:16, then returned at 8:21 to spend another hour and a quarter in his lab. The drying of the spores didn't require that he be there to watch. It was on Sunday that the drying process most likely took place. It was a simple matter to spread the paste of spores and slime onto plates and let them air dry inside his biosafety cabinet, perhaps adding heat to aid the drying process.

At some point in time, perhaps while waiting for centrifuge runs to finish, he may have practiced folding a letter to contain the powder, stuffing the folded letter into the small post office envelope. As a scientist, he was familiar with the so-called pharmaceutical fold which had been used for centuries to wrap medicinal powders. It

64

involves folding the paper in thirds, first from the top and then from the bottom. And then the sides are folded toward the middle to keep the powder inside from falling out the ends.

If Ivins practiced the fold, he quickly learned there was a minor problem: an 8½ by 11 sheet of paper ends up slightly too large to fit neatly into the small envelope. So, Ivins trimmed down each letter to a smaller size. Trimming each letter in a slightly different way provided him with something else he may have wanted. He could save the irregular trimmed edges as additional proof that he sent the anthrax letters. And, since he'd be sending out copies, he'd have the original handwritten letter, too. The work was performed, of course, inside his biosafety cabinet using gloves to avoid leaving fingerprints or anything traceable.

Then, after he scraped the crusty dried powders into the letters one by one, he used a damp paper towel to seal the flaps. To make absolutely certain that no powder would leak from the envelopes, he taped the seams and corners shut. Lastly, he tucked the envelopes one by one into a Ziplock bag. When all five letters were ready, he sealed the bag, wiped down the exterior of the bag and the interior of the biosafety cabinet with bleach, and he was done. He probably finished late on the evening of the 16th. He then locked the Ziplock bag in a drawer of his desk and he went home.

Ivins and two lab assistants were scheduled to drive to the Covance research facility in Denver, Pennsylvania on Tuesday morning to deliver some vaccine samples. So, the mailing of the anthrax letters had to take place Monday night, which would mean they would be postmarked on Tuesday, exactly one week after 9/11.

On Monday morning, September 17, Ivins entered Building 1425 at 6:58 a.m. and worked until 11:14 a.m. Undoubtedly very anxious about what he was about to do, Ivins sent an email to Mara Linscott at about 10 a.m. that morning. The email indicated that he desperately needed someone to talk with. It said in part:

> I haven't been feeling so good lately because of all that's going on. I really can't talk to [my wife], and I don't say that much to [Patricia Fellows] or anyone else. The group I'm in is only moderately helpful. I'm glad some of us are going to Covance tomorrow with

some vaccine. It will be good to get away. I wish I had someone here that I could really open up to at times like this. [6]

But there was no one there to tell him he shouldn't do what he was planning on doing.

He took the rest of the day off as four hours of paid leave. He may have had his car checked to make sure everything was ready for the drive. It would be a disaster if he had car problems on the drive to New Jersey. Then, he had his regular Monday evening group therapy session, which ran from 5:30 to about 7 p.m.

Afterwards, it was only a five mile drive from CCA to Ft. Detrick and his office where he retrieved the plastic bag full of letters from his desk, slipped the bag inside his shirt and left, spending only 13 minutes inside Building 1425.

He most likely left the letters in his car when he went home. There would be no reason to take them inside.

The First Mailing

Sometime that night, between roughly 7:30 p.m. and about 11:30 p.m., Ivins left his house, got into his car and headed to New Jersey. The hours on the road gave him more time to think about what he was doing. But, he continued on - past Baltimore, past Wilmington, past Philadelphia, past Trenton.

It could have been around midnight when Ivins entered Princeton on Highway 206 and drove down Nassau Street looking for the address of the KKG office. It was a picturesque street lined by tall trees which, in mid-September, provided a green canopy of leafy branches that nearly turned the street into a tunnel.

The address of the KKG office at 20 Nassau Street was in an old, 4-story, red brick building with air-conditioners in nearly every window. The building stretched more than half the entire block, with small shops side by side at sidewalk level. The main door into 20 Nassau Street was in a recessed alcove between the Red Onion Restaurant and Tippy Toes, a shoe store selling only children's shoes. His father's alma mater, Princeton University, was across the street.

Ivins needed a closer look. At that time of night, he wouldn't have had a problem finding a place to park. If he'd looked through the twin glass doors of #20, he'd see that inside the interior consisted of business offices - doctors, psychologists, lawyers and the like. He knew the KKG office was on the 4th floor, so it was probably not something suitable for a future break-in. Perhaps he walked around the corner to see if there was a rear entrance or some place that would tell him more about what was behind the locked doors.

The time he spent checking out the KKG office location evidently drained him of his desire to continue on to Franklin Park. It was only another 10 miles, but, for all he knew, the mail from both towns could be collected and postmarked in the same place. So, he changed his plan.

He had passed a mailbox a block back on that same side of the street. He'd used it to mail the letters.

Making a U-Turn at the Chambers Street intersection, he drove back to the mailbox at 10 Nassau Street. He would have taken the Ziplock bag of envelopes to the mail box, and avoiding any chance of leaving fingerprints, he'd have simply opened the bag and dumped the envelopes into the box. There was a trash basket a few feet away, but, since his fingerprints were on the bag, he may have taken it with him and disposed of the bag on his way home.

He then drove back to Frederick - another three-plus hours on the road. The deed was done. Now, it was just a matter of waiting a few days until the letters caused total pandemonium.

Ivins was almost certainly still convinced that he was doing a heroic deed, warning America of the danger of a bioweapons attack via the mails. He'd taken every precaution he could think of to make sure that no one would be harmed by the letters - including giving medical advice. But, if someone was harmed, it would be for "the greater good" as defined in his favorite novel *Arrowsmith*.

Chapter 9

Between Mailings

Bruce Ivins arrived for work at 7:02 a.m. on the morning of Tuesday, September 18, 2001. He and two lab technicians then drove 100 miles to Denver, PA, a two and a half hour trip each way. If Ivins wasn't doing the driving, the trip may have given him a chance to catch a nap to help make up for the loss of sleep the night before. They were traveling to Covance to deliver a supply of anthrax vaccine for testing by one of the world's largest drug development service companies.[1]

They drove back to Frederick that evening, and Ivins was evidently feeling very satisfied with what he'd done. On the 19th, he sent Mara an email saying he'd exercised for the first time in months, and that he "felt good." [2]

The next day, the 20th, Ivins sent an email to someone at Battelle in Columbus, Ohio. Battelle also made anthrax spores for tests, but they were having problems making good spores. In the email, Ivins suggested that he pay a visit Battelle to "offer advice or suggestions with respect to spore production, purification, storage, etc." He explained how it had taken years for him to perfect the "art" and techniques "involved in getting spores which were stable, pure, unclumped, etc." He magnanimously explained how in a day or so he could save them months of experimenting and learning from trial and error.[3]

What he didn't say was that it would be perfect for him if, while at Battelle, he was summoned home because the nation had gone into a state of high alert as the result of anthrax letters being found in the mails. That would identify him as a top anthrax expert whose advice was needed to save America. It would probably even get his name into the newspapers.

On September 21, Ivins sent an email to Nancy Haigwood at the company where she worked in Seattle. When Haigwood read the email, she was both puzzled and stunned. Ivins not only knew where she worked, but he also inquired about her two sons and her plans for their education, which meant he was still researching and tracking her. He also made a comment about his own situation at USAM-RIID: "since we are the primary BW [Biowarfare] research center in this country, we are more than a bit on edge." When Haigwood didn't reply, Ivins called her to make sure she'd received his email.[4]

Although the call from Ivins was outwardly benign, Haigwood was greatly disturbed by this sudden burst of communication from Ivins who had repeatedly harassed her in the past and had even tried to destroy her career.

Years later, when the FBI asked Ivins about this call, he stated that he'd contacted her "after the anthrax attacks" in order to refresh their acquaintance. But, of course, on September 21, Bruce Ivins was the only person in the entire world who knew that there had been any kind of anthrax attack.[5]

On Saturday, September 22, Ivins filled out an application to join the American Red Cross as a volunteer. On the application he stated that he worked in "anthrax research," a term he'd never used before on any application. He'd always described himself as a "microbiologist" or as a "bacteriologist." [6]

During that week, he was undoubtedly anxiously waiting for the news of the anthrax letters to appear in the media.

But, *nothing happened.*

Frustrated

By the 25th, Ivins was becoming frustrated. Not only had his attack failed completely to create the panic he had expected, newspapers and TV were describing how politicians and others were trying to protect innocent Muslims living in America from harsh government actions intended to identify any additional terrorists who might be among them.

It was during this period of growing frustration that Patricia Worsham decided to implement her new supervisory power over Bruce Ivins. Although she was not yet officially Ivins' superior, she instructed him to clean up his lab, which was always notoriously dirty and cluttered.

Ivins did as ordered, but he was very upset about it. He went in to work on the evening of the 25th and spent one hour and 21 minutes in Suite B3. This time we know exactly what his was doing. Using his office computer, he wrote an email the next evening which explained what he had done in a manner that made it abundantly clear that he didn't like doing it. The email to his new boss read:

> Dear Queen of the Universe, Ruler of All that you Survey, Supreme and Grand Magisterial Potentate of Kindness and Favours to your Loyal Subjects (especially those who clear [redacted] ...)
>
> You asked me what I've done so far ....
>
> Tuesday evening - removed the light covers from the ceiling lights.
> Wednesday - cleaned the door jams where doors hit them (and trap dirt), took the pans out of the hoods (haven't cleaned them yet), picked up the junk from the floor of the [redacted] lab [redacted], cleaned the floor of [redacted]. BY the way, the sink in [redacted] is completely stopped up. Do you want to call a plumber? Maybe [redacted] should.[7]

He signed the email "Your ever humble servant, Bruce Badger." (Someone had once referred to USAMRIID employees as being like badgers in a tunnel system as they moved through the maze of hallways and labs doing their work.)

That same day, September 26, Ivins emailed Mara, telling her, "The News Media has been saying that some members of Congress and members of the ACLU oppose many of the Justice Department proposals for combating terrorism, saying that they are unconstitutional and infringe too much on civil liberties. Many people don't know it but the official ACLU position is to oppose all metal detectors in airports and schools and other public buildings. It's interesting that we may now be living in a time when our biggest threat to civil liberties and freedom doesn't come from the government but from enemies of the government. Osama Bin Laden has just decreed death to all Jews and all Americans, but I guess that doesn't mean a lot to the ACLU. Maybe I should move to Canada ....."

Significantly, Ivins used terms in that email that were similar to the terms used in his anthrax letters - "DEATH TO AMERICA" and "DEATH TO ISRAEL." But, once again, no one except Ivins knew at that time that the anthrax letters existed.[8]

There's no record of what happened between Worsham and Ivins as a result of his email. That may be because Ivins' simply shifted into "Good Bruce" mode to placate Worsham while he began developing a plan for a second batch of letters.

Making the Senate Powders

Although Ivins didn't work in his lab during the evening of the 27th, the following evening he once again began working long hours every evening in Suite B3, usually well over an hour, sometimes nearly three hours. He'd evidently decided that the letters for the second mailing wouldn't contain crude powders, they'd contain *highly refined* powders, something that would truly scare the hell out of everyone. And, he'd send the second batch of letters to politicians, not to media people.

Sophisticated anthrax powders took a lot longer to prepare. To create enough purified powder for just two letters would require about four times the amount of spores than had been in all five media letters. The crude powders in the media letters had been largely dried slime. Ivins would have to get rid of all that slime by adding water to dissolve it, shaking it to help the dissolving process, then centrifuging the results to separate the water and dissolved slime from the spores. One pass wouldn't be enough. He'd have to repeat the process again and again, exactly the way he'd been purifying spores for USAMRIID for the past twenty years. Only, he'd have to

71

do it alone and at night. So, he set to work, spending more hours in his lab at night than he'd spent in creating the media powders.

Friday, September 28 - 2 hours, 13 minutes
Saturday, September 29 - 1 hour, 20 minutes
Sunday, September 30 - 1 hour, 18 minutes
Wednesday, October 3 - 2 hours, 58 minutes
Thursday, October 4 - 2 hours, 33 minutes (in 2 sessions)
Friday, October 5 - 3 hours, 42 minutes (in 2 sessions)[9]

The Senate Letter & Envelopes

It was probably on the 1st or 2nd of October that Ivins again convinced the first-grader to write another letter and to address two more envelopes - one envelope addressed to Senator Tom Daschle of South Dakota, who was the Senate Majority Leader and the man who had questioned the safety of the vaccine Ivins had spent years helping to develop. The other envelope was addressed to Senator Patrick Leahy who was viewed as a civil libertarian and a leader in the efforts to protect the rights of innocent Muslims who might be caught up in the hunt for terrorists.

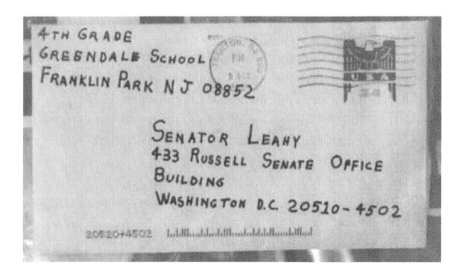

Exhibit #10 - The Leahy Envelope

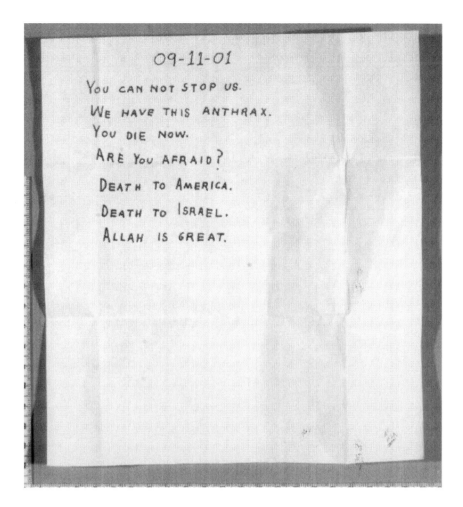

Exhibit #11 - The Leahy Letter

Since it was possible that the lack of a return address had caused the first set of letters to get tossed into the trash without ever being opened, Ivins would try to get the child to write smaller when writing the return addresses.

But, as it turned out, the child was already writing much smaller without being asked to do so. He had no problem fitting the return address into the corner, although he didn't specifically write it smaller. His writing was still just one size, but that size was smaller. Writing smaller was one of the first things they learned in first grade, where they had to write between the lines on lined paper, instead of on the blank drawing paper they used in kindergarten. In the space of just a few weeks, the child had also learned to write with greater confidence.

All the writing on the Senate letter and envelopes was roughly half the size of the writing on the media letter and envelopes.

There would be no coded message in the letter to the two Senators, so there would be no requirement that all sentences had to be three words long. There'd be a clear threat, but to make sure that the recipients realized they were dealing with a deadly pathogen, he'd state in the letter that the refined powder was anthrax. That should scare the hell out of them. It would certainly be a lot clearer than "Take penacilin now."

The child had also learned about punctuation, something else children were taught in the first weeks of first grade. Only the question mark seemed unfamiliar to the first grader. He constructed it as if he'd never seen one before, but it didn't really matter. All that mattered was that the child was more than willing to write the letters and address the envelopes in return for another lesson in juggling.

The results were totally satisfactory.

Ivins was evidently so pleased with himself that he sent Mara an email on the 3rd of October that seemingly hinted of an imminent biowarfare attack upon the United States and how Mara might play a role in it:

> I remember mentioning to you the possibility that after you get your degree you might be interested in being an 'on-call' physician for any suspected BW attacks in the country...I'm hoping such an attack doesn't happen, of course. On a more humorous note, if a BW 'crop duster' ever does buzz through your city, you can just look up in the sky, knowing your immune system is ready, and give him the finger.... [10]

It was probably on the evening of October 5 that Ivins took copies of the senate letter and the two envelopes to work. After he'd finished making the anthrax powders he divided the supply into two parts and wrapped the powders in the letters very much the way he'd done with the first letters.

He appears to have been undeterred by the latest news.

Bob Stevens

A 63-year-old photo editor for the *Sun* tabloid newspaper had become ill while he and his wife Maureen were on vacation visiting their daughter in North Carolina. The symptoms first hit Stevens at around 12:30 p.m. on Sunday, September 30, when he suddenly started shaking and shivering, and his face became flushed. He was sick and sweaty that night, but he felt well enough to drive home with his wife to Lantana, Florida, the next day.

That Monday night, he was ill again, and finally his wife took him to the hospital in nearby Atlantis. They arrived at around 2 a.m. in the morning of October 2, 2001.

The first recognition that Stevens might be infected with anthrax came when Dr. Larry Bush, an infectious disease specialist and chief of staff at JFK Medical Center in Atlantis, Florida, was called in to assist in the diagnosis of the ailing patient.

It took him about an hour to find that Stevens had somehow apparently contracted inhalation anthrax. As soon as Dr. Bush viewed the bacteria under a microscope he recognized it as *Bacillus anthracis*. But anthrax was *extremely* rare - particularly in humid Florida. The last case of inhalation anthrax in the entire United States had occurred twenty five years ago!

To be certain he wasn't about to make a fool of himself with a bad diagnosis, Dr. Bush checked his findings, did tests for similar bacteria. Those tests for similar bacteria proved negative. It was *definitely* anthrax. He then called in other experts - primarily for consultation, not for further testing.

The first question on his mind was: Was it a terrorist attack? The World Trade Center and the Pentagon had been hit by terrorists just a few weeks prior, and the media had been full of stories about how a biological attack might come next. Everyone was talking about anthrax. And suddenly there was a case in Florida.[11]

But it was just *one* case.

It was well known that some of the 9-11 hijackers had lived for awhile in that part of Florida. Even so, one case of anthrax still made no sense. Why would terrorists attack only some vacationing photo editor while he was in North Carolina? There were no other reported cases of anthrax - anywhere. Not in North Carolina, not in Florida, not anywhere.

The news broke in the media on Thursday, October 4. It was announced by Florida's Lieutenant Governor Frank Brogan who explained in detail that the disease could have been contracted naturally and that Stevens had just returned from a vacation in North Carolina where he had been spent a lot of time outdoors. Brogan also stated that there were no other known cases, and that Stevens' case was very likely to be fatal.

Ivins was still checking the Internet for some report about the anthrax letters he'd mailed in September. He saw an article about the Stevens case on the evening of the 4th, and he immediately sent an email to an acquaintance at the CDC:

> I just heard this evening (and read over internet news) that a case of pulmonary anthrax may have been identified in Florida. Is this true, or is this just hysteria? The only Florida strain of B. anthracis that I am familiar with is V770, which is the parent of V770-NP1-R, the strain used in production of the human anthrax vaccine. (I believe that V770 was originally isolated from a cow in Florida in the early 1950s.) The article said that this person was an "Outdoorsman," and had drunk water from a creek in North Carolina. If he really does have anthrax, could he have gotten it this way, or did he get it by tromping around some dusty field area. (Has North Carolina been dry this summer?)
>
> I know that in the wild in Africa, animals are supposed to be able to get it from water holes by stirring up spores and presumably ingesting and possibly inhaling them as an aerosol. Could this have happened? What if an animal had died upstream and the stream was contaminated? (Drinking from a stream or creek without boiling or purifying the water first is an invitation to intestinal disease or parasites, but have any other human anthrax cases been documented from people drinking contaminated water?)[12]

Ivins had sent an anthrax-laced letter to the *National Enquirer* in Lantana, Florida, and a photo editor who lived in Lantana had somehow contracted anthrax, apparently while on vacation in North Carolina. Ivins was undoubtedly rationalizing as he tried to think of some way that the Stevens case could just be a weird coincidence. To get inhalational anthrax a person needs to *inhale* spores into the lungs. The chances of a person contracting inhalation anthrax by drinking contaminated water out of a stream were next to nil. But it wasn't *totally* impossible.

Bob Steven died the next day, Friday October 5. Bruce Ivins spent a lot of time in his BSL-3 lab that evening. Perhaps he had convinced himself that the Stevens case was just a coincidence. Or he may have convinced himself that no one could possibly trace Stevens' case back to him, so it didn't make any difference to his plans. Stevens was dead. There was no way to bring him back to life. What was done was done. And, because the authorities were still suggesting that the Stevens case may possibly have been the result of natural causes, Ivins' had to continue with his plan for a second mailing. It was for "the greater good." The second mailing couldn't be ignored. The letter stated that the powder was anthrax, and after the Stevens case, that word alone would be enough to scare the hell out of the two senators.

Ivins didn't work on the evening of Saturday, the 6th of October, which was very likely when he drove again to New Jersey to mail the second set of anthrax letters. It appears he used the same mailbox he used for the first mailing.

Monday the 8th was Columbus Day. There wouldn't be any mail pickups. So, the second batch of letters would be postmarked on Tuesday the 9th of October.

Chapter 10

The Ames Strain

Public Health protocols require that the Centers for Disease Control (CDC) in Atlanta, GA, be notified of any confirmed case of inhalation anthrax. On October 3, 2001, the Florida Board of Health notified the CDC that they had a patient with a severe case of inhalation anthrax. Because the case had been diagnosed in an area where the 9/11 hijackers had stayed for awhile, and because of ongoing the concern that the 9/11 attacks might be followed by a bioweapons attack, the CDC notified the Federal Bureau of Investigation (FBI).

At about 1:30 p.m. on the afternoon of October 4, Dr. Paul Keim of Northern Arizona University (NAU) in Flagstaff was in his office when the phone rang. The six foot five, 46-year-old scientist picked up the phone. On the other end of the line was an FBI microbiologist, Douglas Beecher, who notified Keim that a plane had just left Atlanta on its way to Flagstaff carrying a cultured sample of bacteria taken from the fluid in the spine of Robert Stevens, the first victim of inhalation anthrax in America in nearly a quarter century. The FBI wanted Keim to analyze the DNA of bacteria in the sample to determine which strain of *Bacillus anthracis* Stevens had contracted.

According to Keim, his hands immediately began to tingle with anticipation and he broke into a sweat. He'd been expecting the call ever since he heard of the case in Florida. In the late 1990's, Keim and a colleague, Paul Jackson, had pioneered a DNA "fingerprinting technique" which could distinguish among the various anthrax strains. The FBI knew of Keim's reputation in analyzing anthrax, and they knew his lab at NAU had a database of about 2,000 anthrax samples from all over the world.[1]

About 4 hours after receiving that fateful phone call, Keim jumped into his 1990 Toyota 4Runner and headed for Flagstaff's Pulliam Airport, about a 15 minute drive from NAU. The sun was setting, and the sky was red gold as the small FBI jet landed. Keim walked out to it as it pulled to a stop near where he was waiting. The door swung down and a blonde woman stepped down the steps to the tarmac carrying a cardboard box in her hands.

For Keim, it was like a scene from a movie. It was "Casablanca"-like.

They went through the chain-of-custody processes, checking identification and filling out paperwork. Then the cardboard box was turned over to Dr. Keim who put it in the rear of his 4Runner, and he headed back to his lab.

When they opened the box at his lab, they found a single test tube inside - a "slant" - nestled in a bed of chipped ice. A slant is a standard form of culture used for long-term storage, particularly for evidence samples. To create a slant, a test tube is partially filled with liquid growth media, the test tube is then set down at about a 45 degree angle (slant) to provide more surface area on the top surface of the liquid media inside. The media is allowed to thicken. Then the media is inoculated with a sample of the bacteria. In this case, it was bacteria taken from Bob Stevens' spine. When it is certain that the bacteria are growing on the slanted surface of the media, producing a "culture," the culture is ready for transport.

Keim and a couple of his key researchers worked through the night, isolating, processing and magnifying the DNA from the slant. They used machines and computers similar to ones found in crime labs. In the early morning, they compared the results with their anthrax database. They found a match: Bob Stevens had been infected with "the Ames strain."

But, Keim and his colleagues didn't stop there. Among the 2,000 samples in their database, they had several samples of the Ames strain - and they had developed the capability of distinguishing one line of accession from another. For years, Keim and his team had been developing DNA analysis techniques that would not only enable them to distinguish one sample of Ames from another, but they were often able to tell which came first. A strain of anthrax found in Canada, for example, might have a line of accession that could be traced back to an ancient strain found in China.

In theory, it took a billion cell divisions to produce a mutation, and there might be many different mutations before one is generated that will produce a viable and enduring new version of a strain. But, *Bacillus anthracis* divided and produced a billion new cells in just over 10 hours. So, there were a lot more differences between batches of anthrax than most microbiologists and other scientists were thinking at the time. A sample of the Ames strain that Paul Keim's lab had obtained from Dugway Proving Grounds in Utah, for example, had 36 adenines in a row in its DNA, while another Ames sample obtained from USAMRIID had only 35 adenines in a row. And, the DNA of an Ames sample obtained from the Porton Down research facility in England was also slightly different from both the Dugway and USAMRIID samples.[2]

The version of the Ames strain that had infected Bob Stevens was a perfect match to the sub-strain used at USAMRIID, and it did not match the Ames sub-strains used by any other lab represented in the NAU database.

However, the sample NAU had obtained from USMAMRIID *would* very likely match the original supply at USAMRIID. Thus, NAU could - in theory - also have been the source of the anthrax that infected Stevens. And, if USAMRIID had sent other samples to other labs, those other labs might all have samples which contained no detectable DNA differences. And, of course, the same held true for whichever lab sent the original sample to USAMRIID.

Everything depended upon whether the sample was kept for reference or used in testing. Keim's lab at Northern Arizona University kept a sample for reference. USAMRIID, Dugway and Porton Down used their samples in testing. Thus, the bacteria in their stocks were the results of numerous re-growths as stocks dwindled and new stocks had to be created. Those labs had been re-grown their samples and then re-grown them again, creating many batches over the years, enough to produce detectable DNA differences in the current samples.

Paul Keim explained all this to the CDC and the FBI during a conference call on the morning of October 5, 2001. Bob Stevens had died that morning. The only known match to the strain that had killed Stevens was the version of the Ames strain stored at USAMRIID.

There could be hundreds of other labs with matching samples, but USAMRIID would be the right place to start looking.

The possibility that al Qaeda may have launched some kind of bioweapons attack that was only beginning to send victims to hospitals was also on everyone's mind. HazMat teams began checking every place the 9/11 hijackers had stayed and every place they may have visited to look for traces of anthrax. "We vacuumed everywhere they had been for residue," FBI officials stated. No traces of anthrax were found anywhere.[3]

Chapter 11

An Unexpected Mystery

On October 5, 2001, even though it was known that Bob Stevens had been exposed to the Ames strain of anthrax, no one really knew much about the Ames strain and how prevalent it might be in nature. The assumption was still that Stevens may have somehow been exposed to a natural source of the Ames strain of anthrax. Fifty investigators from the Florida Department of Health, the CDC and the FBI were trying to track Stevens' movements. They took samples around his home, wiping swabs in suspect areas - closets, halls, anywhere spores may have been tracked - and then tested the swabs for the presence of anthrax spores. They looked at furs and hides in any store he might have visited while on vacation. They found nothing.

They checked soil samples around his home and where he had vacationed in North Carolina. They determined that Stevens had driven with his wife to North Carolina on the 27th, staying that evening in Charlotte. The next day, the 28th, he went hiking with his daughter to Chimney Rock. On Saturday the 29th, he drove to Duke University and spent the day there. But his family said he was already showing signs of being ill on the 29th, so he must have been exposed before that time.

Investigators talked with everyone they could find who Stevens may have encountered during the two weeks before his death. And they kept checking local hospitals to see if anyone else might have come down with symptoms of the disease that may have been misdiagnosed. They found nothing - until they learned that 73 year old Ernesto Blanco, another employee at American Media Incorporated (AMI) in Boca Raton had recently been in the hospital for treatment of symptoms of pneumonia. His symptoms didn't appear to be a good match for anthrax, but medical investigators took swabs of his nostrils to see if there was any possibility that he'd been exposed.

The swabs tested positive. The tiny hairs within Ernesto Blanco's nostrils had trapped anthrax spores. Two people with nothing in common except that they worked for the same company had been exposed to aerosolized anthrax spores. The search immediately shifted to the AMI offices.

On the 7th of October, the AMI offices were shut down after what may have been a single spore was found on the keyboard of Stevens' computer. But, they had to swab the keyboard twice to find it. More spores, however, were found elsewhere in the building, particularly in the mailroom.[1]

By the 9th of October, the spores found in Blanco's nostrils were determined to also be the Ames strain, and no one any longer believed that Stevens had contracted anthrax from natural sources. It was becoming clear that the anthrax had arrived at the AMI building through the mails. The leading theory among AMI employees was that it had arrived in a package addressed to singer/movie star Jennifer Lopez c/o the *Sun*. The package had had been opened by a recently hired news assistant, Bobby Bender. Bob Stevens had looked at the letter and had sniffed at the detergent it contained. Perhaps the powder hadn't been only detergent. The problem was: the package and its contents were thrown away on the same day it arrived - probably September 19th.[2]

Then, on October 10, a third person at AMI tested positive for exposure to anthrax. Spores were found trapped in the hairs deep inside 36-year-old Stephanie Dailey's nostrils. Dailey had been on vacation during the time the J-Lo letter was opened and passed around, so she couldn't have been exposed to it. She worked in an office next to the first floor mail room, and one of her assigned tasks at AMI was to open mail addressed to *The National Enquirer*.

Dailey recalled opening a letter that contained a powder on September 24 or 25, the Monday or Tuesday after she returned from vacation. Since crank letters were frequently received at AMI, she'd simply thrown the letter, the envelope and the powder into the trash basket next to her desk and thought no more about it.

That third exposure at AMI ended all doubt. On the morning of Wednesday, October 10, 2001, Guy Lewis, the United States attorney for the Southern District of Florida informed the media, "It is now a criminal investigation." He also told the media that Bob Stevens had been infected with the Ames strain of anthrax, a strain primarily used in vaccine research.[3]

That announcement started *the media's* investigation of the source of the Ames strain. The first report seems to have been from CNN. The *Florida Sun-Sentinel* described what CNN reported:

> CNN reported Wednesday morning that the anthrax virus that killed a Lantana man and was found in his Boca Raton office appears to be manmade and apparently produced in an American lab about 50 years ago. [4]

The very idea that the anthrax was "manmade" and "manufactured" was totally preposterous, and there were no facts which said the Ames strain originated in the 1950's. It was guesses and nonsensical beliefs turned into hard news.

And, that was just the beginning.

The Media and Iowa State University

Reporters trying to determine the source of the Ames strain called USAMRIID and were told (possibly by Bruce Ivins) that the Ames strain was distributed to researchers by the United States Department of Agriculture (USDA) offices in Ames, Iowa.

In 1985, Dr. Gregory Knudson from USAMRIID had co-authored a scientific article which showed the source of the Ames strain as: Cow; Iowa, 1980. [5]

In 1996, Dr. Bruce Ivins was a co-author and the prime contact on a scientific paper titled, *Efficacy of a standard human anthrax vaccine against Bacillus anthracis aerosol spore challenge in rhesus monkeys.* The article stated:

> The virulent Ames strain of B. anthracis was obtained from the U.S. Department of Agriculture, Ames, Iowa.[6]

An Unexpected Mystery

On October 22, 1997, when filling out the "Reference Material Receipt Record" to keep track of the usage of the spores stored in flask RMR-1029, where the form asked for the Vendor, Dr. Ivins wrote:

From B. anthracis Ames strain, Ames Iowa[7]

So, the belief held by Bruce Ivins and *everyone else* at USAMRIID was that the Ames strain came from the USDA in Ames, Iowa.

But, when the USDA was contacted by FBI investigators and by the media, no one there had ever heard of any "Ames strain" of anthrax. And the USDA had never sent anyone any "Ames strain," certainly not USAMRIID. No cows had died of anthrax in 1980 or 1981 in Iowa, so the information on the reports was clearly wrong.

The question became: If the Ames strain didn't come from the USDA in Ames, where *did* it come from?

For the FBI, the task became to figure out why everyone at USAMRIID believed the Ames strain came from the USDA in Ames. How did they get that false impression? Through the work of Paul Keim and his associates at Northern Arizona University, the FBI had tracked the attack strain to USAMRIID. But, that just made USAMRIID the starting point. Where USAMRIID had obtained the Ames strain wasn't the only question. For the FBI investigators, there was another, equally important question: Did *USAMRIID* distribute the Ames strain to anyone? Any sample of the Ames strain - *up* the chain of labs with samples or *down* the chain - should theoretically be identical to the attack anthrax.

For the media, however, accuracy wasn't as important as immediacy. They had deadlines and impatient editors and producers waiting for the latest "news," whether it was accurate or not.

The assumption for the media appears to have been: If it didn't come from the USDA, obviously the "Ames strain" came from some other lab in Ames, Iowa. After all, it was called "the Ames strain."

A little research found that the US Department of Energy (DOE) *also* had a lab in Ames. It was called the "Ames Laboratory," and it was a government owned, contractor operated research facility of the DOE run by Iowa State University in Ames. That *must* be it.

According to October 11 issue of *The New York Times*,

> The Miami Herald reported on Wednesday that investigators had linked the anthrax to a strain that was harvested from Iowa in the 1950's, and NBC News reported on Wednesday evening that the F.B.I. was beginning to conclude that the anthrax was stolen from a Department of Energy laboratory in Ames, Iowa.[8]

The FBI was *not* beginning to conclude that the Ames strain had been *stolen* from a DOE lab. Later in the article, a very likely source for the misinformation was identified:

> Kevin Teale, a spokesman for the Iowa Department of Public Health, said today that the Ames strain was discovered in the 1950's at Iowa State University, in livestock that had died of anthrax. It has since been sent to laboratories across the world for research purposes.

It's totally false information, probably just guesswork and speculation. In reality, in October of 2001, absolutely no one in the entire world knew for certain where the Ames strain had come from. No one knew how widely it was distributed. No one even knew *when* it was discovered, although the facts seemed to indicate it was around 1981, since there was no record of the Ames strain being used anywhere prior to 1981.

The CDC told reporters that the news reports about the source of the Ames strain were "premature," since the investigation had found nothing solid. But, newspapers and the other media were continuing to claim the Ames strain was made in the 1950's and was commonly used in laboratories all over the world.

"This is a standard laboratory strain worldwide," Dr. Norm Cheville, dean of the Iowa State University College of Veterinary Medicine told the San Francisco Chronicle.[9] "Most labs working on anthrax would have it in their stocks." According to another source:

An Unexpected Mystery

> Newsday (NY) reports that a team of microbiologists at Lawrence Livermore National Laboratory tested the Florida anthrax strain and found that, despite denials from health officials, it was the Ames strain that was developed in Iowa in the 1950s.[10]

The media had descended upon Iowa State University in a feeding frenzy looking for anyone willing to speculate further.

Destroying "Evidence"

The anthrax collection at Iowa State University consisted of a drawer full of dried material inside hundreds of test tubes. The last time anyone had even looked in the drawer could have been in 1978 when a sample stored away on January 13, 1928 was uncorked and tested to see if the spores were still viable. They were.

As a result of the media attention, two members of the Iowa State University's environmental health and safety unit went through every test tube in the drawer looking for anything labeled "Ames." While some labels were incomplete or too cryptic to decipher, they found nothing labeled "Ames Strain." They also found nothing from 1980 or 1981, when scientific reports say the Ames strain was first isolated.

Clearly, the ISU collection had nothing to do with what killed Bob Stevens. But, the University was being told by the State that they were going to have to spend $30,000 a month to guard the collection 24 hours a day. The University preferred to spend the money on its students, so they decided to autoclave the collection.[11]

To make sure it was okay, the ISU officials contacted the FBI, the CDC and the USDA. All approved.

To the FBI, the collection was just something the media was interested in. Even if there was some original sample in the ISU collection, the strain was supposedly in labs all over the world, so it would be like going to the Colt Firearms Company in Hartford, Connecticut to investigate a shooting in Florida.

At 5:30 p.m. on the evening of October 11, 2001, every strain in the ISU collection was tossed into pink plastic autoclave bags and then thrown into an autoclave which was left to run all night.

A Crime Unlike Any Other

They had destroyed a collection of anthrax that had absolutely nothing to do with the killing of Bob Stevens, but they had created fodder for a conspiracy theory that would still be argued about over a decade later.

The FBI's Investigation

FBI investigators were focusing on USAMRIID, and they were questioning anyone who had actually worked with the Ames strain. One such person was Dr. Bruce Ivins. And others at USAMRIID and people in the media were also seeking information from Ivins, since he seemed to be the top expert at USAMRIID.

Early in the morning of October 12, 2001, someone at USAMRIID sent Dr. Ivins the following email:

> We have a tasker to report to whom we may have sent the Ames strain in the past several years. Do you, or someone else in BACT, have any records relating to such information? If so, could you please provide me with that information?[12]

The response from Ivins later that day clearly showed his annoyance with being questioned on the subject, along with his own belief about the source of Ames strain:

> I can tell you to whom I have sent this so-called "Ames" strain. Please keep in mind that a) it is apparently 50 years old; b) that USAMRIID received this strain 20 years ago; c) that it is a USDA strain, not a USAMRIID strain, U.S. Army strain, or Department of Defense strain; d) the individuals primarily responsible for determining the location of the strain are located in Ames, Iowa, not in Frederick, Maryland; e) that of any U.S. labs having human pathogenic strains (including B. anthracis), none have higher security than USAMRIID, f) that if we are the only recipients of this "tasker," it is transparently evident that we are being harassed by our regular detractors simply because we are DOD researchers. It is not within the purview of USAMRIID researchers to ascertain where the USDA has sent its strains of Bacillus anthracis or any other organism.[13]

An Unexpected Mystery

In his response, Ivins included a list of laboratories to which he'd sent the Ames strain. He was absolutely certain that the USDA had furnished USAMRIID with the Ames strain, even if the USDA didn't have any record of any "Ames strain." To open up other possibilities for the source of the anthrax that killed Bob Stevens, he also suggested in an email that someone might have *assembled* a sample of virulent *Bacillus anthracis* Ames bacteria by taking versions that had been modified to make them less deadly and biologically rebuilding the original bacteria.

The FBI, meanwhile, was learning that *no one* had a sample of the Ames strain that hadn't been obtained from USAMRIID.

Chapter 12

More Victims & Found Letters

On Friday, October 12, 2001, the world learned of another victim of the attacks. Unlike previous victims, this victim was not in Florida. Although her name wasn't initially publicly released, the victim was Erin O'Connor, a 38-year-old assistant to NBC anchorman Tom Brokaw in New York City.

On September 25th, O'Connnor had noticed a raised lesion on her chest, near her collarbone. Over the next three days, the area around the lesion turned an angry red and began to swell up. By September 29, she was starting to feel sickly and had developed a persistent headache. The lesion itself wasn't painful, but, on October 1, O'Connor paid a visit to a clinic where the doctor prescribed oral ciprofloxacin, also known as Cipro. Over the next several days, the lesion developed a dry, black scab. Growing more concerned and suspicious, the doctor performed a biopsy and sent the sample to the CDC in Atlanta for testing.[1]

On the 12th of October, the results of the biopsy came back. It was the cutaneous or skin infection type of anthrax.

Everyone began to search for the letter, but Tom Brokaw's office always received "tons and tons" of mail, a lot of it from angry nut cases.[2] O'Connor, however, specifically recalled a hate-filled letter that recently arrived from St. Petersburg Florida. The letter was soon found and sent to the New York City Department of Health (NYCDOH) for testing. Although the letter was postmarked in the right timeframe to have caused O'Connor's infection, September 20, it tested *negative* for anthrax.

90

While everyone at NBC, particularly those who may have handled Tom Brokaw's mail, started getting tested for exposure to anthrax, the search for the anthrax letter that caused O'Connor's infection continued. The next day, Saturday, October 13, it was found inside a larger envelope. The anthrax letter and its envelope had been stapled together, and the powder had evidently been poured out. The envelope had been postmarked at a Trenton, New Jersey postal facility on September 18. The envelope and letter were transported to the NYCDOH, where they tested positive for anthrax. It was definitely the source of O'Connor's infection. And it was quickly realized that the powder was a lot more dangerous than people had been thinking.

The process of transporting the Brokaw letter to the NYCDOH resulted in several new exposures, demonstrating just how unprepared people were for handling such a dangerous substance. Nasal swabs showed that the police officer who transported the letter had been exposed to anthrax spores. And two technicians at the NYCDOH laboratory who received the letter also tested positive. All were put on antibiotics to help prevent any actual infection.[3]

And, it was learned that the anthrax letter had actually been opened by another of Brokaw's assistants, Casey Chamberlain, before it was turned over to O'Connor for filing. Tests showed that Chamberlain also had symptoms of cutaneous anthrax in the form of a lesion on her leg. She had not only been exposed, she had been infected.

Presumably, everyone was much more careful when the NYCDOH shipped the anthrax letter to the CDC in Atlanta for further examination and testing.

False Alarms

On Sunday, October 14, the media was reporting on an anthrax letter found at the Microsoft offices in Reno, Nevada. That same day, *The New York Times* briefly evacuated its Manhattan offices after Judith Miller, a reporter who had written about Osama bin Laden and bioterrorism, opened an envelope containing a white powder. Like the letter that Erin O'Connor originally thought to be the anthrax letter, the envelope sent to Miller was postmarked in St. Petersburg, Fla. And, as with the O'Connor letter, tests for anthrax turned out to be negative.

A similar scare occurred at the *Columbus Dispatch* in Ohio, where the newspaper building was evacuated when a Halloween card was opened and found to contain powder, which proved to be harmless. Other false alarms were reported from a suburban Denver hospital, the State Department's Foreign Service Institute in Arlington, Va., a Burbank, Calif., television station and the Microsoft office in Reno, Nev.

The Microsoft letter, in particular, generated scary news reports as some tests gave "false positive" results and others gave negative results. The letter was from Malaysia, but it didn't contain any specific threats of any kind. Apparently, after spitting on a check that Microsoft had sent him, an angry Microsoft customer in Malaysia had returned the check to Microsoft, and he included in the same envelope a few pornographic images, which seemed to make it particularly suspicious to Microsoft's clerks. The bacteria from the spit may have triggered the "false positives."[4]

The Daschle Letter

On Monday, October 15, 2001, at around 10:30 a.m. in the morning in the Hart Senate Office Building in Washington, a staff member working in the offices of Senator Tom Daschle of North Dakota opened a letter postmarked in Trenton, NJ, and discovered a powdery substance inside. Since nearly everyone in the country was now greatly concerned about anthrax powders being sent through the mails, the woman immediately set down the letter, backed away, and sounded the alarm.

The first to respond were members of the Hazardous Devices Unit of the United States Capitol Police. More experienced with handing bomb threats than bioweapons, they were uncertain which letter contained the powder and simply placed the several letters that were in the described area into a plastic bag until other first responders with the right knowledge arrived.

The FBI's Joint Terrorism Task Force (JTTF) and their Hazardous Materials Response Team (HMRT) were the next to arrive.

The HMRT tested the powder in the envelope by putting a swab of it into a test liquid. The liquid turned milky white, indicating that the powder did indeed contain *Bacillus anthracis* spores or something very much like it. The plastic bag of letters was put inside a second plastic bag, the sealed tube of milky test material was dropped into the bag with it. While the HMRT team set about cleaning up the area, the bag of letters was turned over to a Metropolitan Police Department officer who was a member of the JTTF. The officer was instructed to transport it to the nearest laboratory qualified to handle such dangerous bacteria.[5]

The only laboratory in the area fully equipped to deal with deadly anthrax was USAMRIID, about 55 miles away.

To Err Is Human

The plastic bag of letters arrived at USAMRIID's Building 1425 at 2:01 p.m. on the 15th. The Daschle letter was carried into the building through the same doors Ivins had used to take it out of the building ten days earlier. Instead of turning left at the entrance, however, it appears the letter was taken toward the opposite corner of the building from Ivins' lab - to the Diagnostic Systems Division (DSD) which occupied a suite of laboratories within the Animal Assessment Division.

Ivins was probably unaware that one of his letters had just reentered the building, but DSD scientists were anxiously waiting, as was Darin Steele, an FBI agent who was also a microbiologist and who had been dispatched to USAMRIID to photograph the envelope and the letter it contained.[6]

Once the chain of custody procedures had been followed and documents signed, senior scientist Dr. John Ezzell had official custody of the letter. Ezzell's first task was also to photograph the letter and envelope. While he was doing that, others on his team would be further testing the powder to verify that it was indeed dried *Bacillus anthracis* spores. They were going through steps they had followed many times before when examining powders in suspected anthrax letters which had all turned out to be hoaxes. This time, however, all indications were that the Daschle letter was not a hoax.

A Crime Unlike Any Other

They began the examination work inside a biosafety cabinet in a Bio-Safety Level 2 lab.

Wearing protective masks and gloves, and further protected by years of anthrax vaccine shots, Dr. Ezzell examined the envelopes that were still inside the plastic bags. Using just his sense of touch, he located the envelope that contained the powder simply by feeling it and observing how the powder inside shifted from one side of the envelope to the other. It was clear there was a detectable quantity of actual powder inside the envelope, and it was not just the crunchable bulge of a badly folded letter.

Ezzell could also see tiny particles floating in the air inside the plastic bags. That observation, plus the way the letter felt and the way the powder moved convinced Dr. Ezzell that they needed to change to a BSL-3 environment before proceeding any further.

The first step was to put the letter into a pass-through box built into the walls between the BSL-2 and the BSL-3 lab. The box could only be opened from one side at a time. FBI agent Darin Steele stood guard on the box while Ezzell made the transition.

Entering a Bio-Safety Level 3 laboratory meant that Dr. Ezzell needed to change into disposable lab clothes, and enter an entire lab that was under negative pressure.

Once inside the BSL-3 lab in his green "scrubs" of the type a surgeon might wear, plus a filter mask and wearing lab shoes, Ezzell removed the Ziplock bag from the pass-through box and took it to one of the biosafety cabinets. Meanwhile, the empty pass-through box was being sterilized with ultraviolet light.

Ezzell began by thoroughly cleaning the cabinet with a bleach solution to eliminate any chance that the contents of the letter might be contaminated by something already in the cabinet. He then laid out a layer of bleach-soaked paper towels on the desk-top surface inside the cabinet to catch any powder that might accidentally spill from the letters.

Lastly, wearing multiple layers of latex gloves and sleeve protectors, Dr. Ezzell removed the Daschle envelope containing the letter from its plastic bag and carefully propped it against the rear of the cabinet so he could photograph it. He put the bottom of the envelope into a groove in the desk top to hold it steady.

As he was focusing the camera, he noticed something: *a liquid was soaking into the bottom of the envelope!* The groove in the desktop *was filled with bleach,* and the bleach was being absorbed by the envelope - and probably also by the letter and powder inside!

Oh my God, what have I done? Ezzell thought.[7] He quickly moved to lift the envelope from the desk surface and to remove the letter inside. Yes, it, too, was slightly wet with some of the bleach, but not enough to get to the bulk of the powder inside. Ezzell quickly coaxed the powder out of the letter and back into the plastic bag. As he worked, he could see tiny particles floating around in the air within the cabinet. He put the unfolded letter inside a fresh plastic bag and the envelope inside another and took them both to a window in the wall that separated the BSL-2 and BSL-3 labs, where Darin Steele was able to photograph them through the glass.

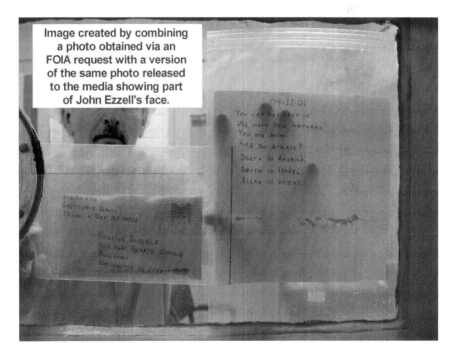

Image created by combining a photo obtained via an FOIA request with a version of the same photo released to the media showing part of John Ezzell's face.

Exhibit #12 - The Daschle letter and envelope.

His photographs showed that the accident with the bleach had caused the ink in the last line of the address on the envelope to run and smear. And the Daschle letter also showed signs of where the bleach had discolored the paper.

While Dr. Ezzell and his staff continued to work with the Daschle letter and its contents, news broke that a 7-month-old child who had attended a party at the ABC offices had been diagnosed with cutaneous anthrax. Because of the child's young age, the lesion on his arm could be life-threatening.

Chapter 13

When Nothing Goes Right

On Tuesday, October 16, 2001, Pat Fellows sent an e-mail to Mara Linscott stating that "Bruce has been an absolute manic basket case these last few days." [1]

Ivins' mental state is easy to understand. A plan that wasn't supposed to harm anyone had killed Bob Stevens, who shouldn't have been anywhere near the letter. And a mail clerk from the same building was also suspected of having contracted inhalation anthrax. Meanwhile, in New York City, two employees of NBC had cutaneous anthrax lesions. And, Ivins had mailed *three other* letters to New York.

It was becoming all too clear that the letters hadn't merely been ignored and thrown away. At least *some* had been opened, and innocent people had been exposed to the contents. But, because anthrax was such a rare infection, doctors were not correctly diagnosing those who had been exposed.

When word was received from the geneticists that the strain that had been found in New York was also the Ames strain, Ivins had to accept that the anthrax letter he had mailed to the *National Enquirer* had somehow killed Bob Stevens, an employee of the *Sun*, a sister magazine to the *Enquirer*.

To make matters worse, the Ames strain was supposed to be very common and in use all over the world, yet, no one seemed to know where the Ames strain came from or who possessed it besides USAMRIID and labs to which USAMRIID scientists had sent samples. Instead of looking overseas, the FBI was sniffing around USAMRIID as if it had some direct connection to the anthrax letters.

A Crime Unlike Any Other

Probably unknown to Ivins, science writer Richard Preston had been interviewing USAMRIID scientists for a new book he was writing (*The Demon In The Freezer*), and he was able to get descriptions of some of what happened after the letter's arrival. Plus, he also persuaded two scientists to give him descriptions of what they were *thinking* while they examined the Daschle letter and its contents. He was talking with virologist Dr. Peter Jahrling and electron microscope expert Dr. Tom Geisbert.

By the morning of October 16th, the news of the Daschle anthrax letter had spread throughout USAMRIID Building 1425. According to Preston, "Top Institute scientists were yelling in the halls about an unknown bioterrorist weapon." [2] Tensions were high. It was the first true anthrax attack in the history of the United States, and there was great danger that the envelope might contain *even deadlier agents than anthrax* - biological agents which could cause total and unprecedented havoc.

That morning, Jahrling, a "gregarious and excitable" [3] retired Army Captain now working in USAMRIID's Virology Division as a civilian, expressed his growing concern to John Ezzell. Jahrling was worried that the spores might be laced with *smallpox* viruses, and he felt a sample should be given to Tom Geisbert to examine under an electron microscope as soon as possible.

Two samples in small test tubes and double-wrapped in plastic bags were soon provided to Geisbert. One sample was the small tube of white, milky liquid containing anthrax spores from the tests done by the HazMat unit which had removed the letter from Daschle's office. The second sample was a bit of the actual powder that was in the envelope.

Tom Geisbert immediately got into a biosafety suit and took the samples into a Biosafety Level-4 containment room they called "The Submarine."

Oozing Goop & Nonsense

Once inside the "Submarine", Geisbert went through a routine procedure to prepare the spores in the liquid for examination. First he put a small drop of the milky liquid onto a slip of wax. Then, using tweezers, he placed a tiny copper grid atop the droplet.

He waited a few minutes while the droplet dried into a crust on the grid. The next step was to make certain the spores were dead by putting the grid into a test tube of lethal chemicals.

When the preparations were completed, Geisbert was in possession of a safe sample to work with. He left "the Submarine", got back into his normal clothes and took the sample upstairs to USAMRIID's eight foot high transmission electron microscope (TEM).

Under the TEM, "The view was wall to wall spores." To Tom Geisbert, "The material seemed to be absolutely pure spores".[4]

With ten thousand times the magnification of a standard microscope which uses glass lenses and a beam of light to image a sample, the TEM uses electromagnetic lenses and a thin beam of electrons. (Unlike a scanning electron microscope (SEM) which can only see the outer surface of an object, the TEM can also penetrate objects to view the internal structure - much like an X-ray machine. But that only works if the specimen is thin enough, less than 100 nanometers. The spores were 10 times that thick, so Geisbert was using a TEM to look at the outside of the spores.)

Geisbert turned a knob and zoomed in, searching for smallpox viruses which are roughly one fifth the size of an anthrax spore. As he searched, he didn't find any smallpox, but he began to notice something else. He noticed some kind of goop clinging to the spores. It was a kind of "splatty stuff."

Geisbert then turned up the power to get a closer look and crisper image. "As he did, he saw the goop begin to spread out of the spores. Those spores were sweating something."

Peter Jahrling came in to see how things were going, and Geisbert demonstrated the phenomenon for him. "Watch," he told Jahrling. He then turned the power knob, there was a hum, and "The spores began to ooze." According to Richard Preston:

> "Whoa," Jahrling muttered, hunched over the eyepieces. Something was boiling off the spores. "This is clearly bad stuff," he said. This was not your mother's anthrax. The spores had something in them, an additive, perhaps. Could this material have come from a national bioweapons program? From Iraq? Did al-Qaeda have anthrax capability that was this good?" [5]

A Crime Unlike Any Other

Photographic images of the goop oozing from the spores were taken via the TEM. Jahrling then showed the phenomenon to General John S. Parker from the Army's Medical Research and Materiel Command, which had authority over USAMRIID, and Colonel Ed Eitzen the commander of USAMRIID.

General Parker began issuing orders, putting USAMRIID into emergency 24-hour operations and summoning in outside experts to help.

In reality, of course, the "goop" was of their own making. It had to do with the chemicals in which the spores had been soaking, and the chemicals that Geisbert had used to destroy the DNA inside the spores. When the power was turned up on the TEM, the electron beam heated the interiors of the spores, and the dissolved material inside began to ooze out through pores. The "additive" they were seeing were their own additives and the effects of applying heat and pressure.

But, in the tensions of the moment, none of this was clear. And it wouldn't become clear for a long time. It was just more bad information resulting from scientists seeing what they expected to see instead of what was really there.

Samples were dispatched to the Hazardous Materials Research Center at the Battelle Memorial Institute in Columbus to get a second opinion.

Peter Jahrling, meanwhile, had a different expert in mind to examine the spores in the Daschle letter.

The next day, the 17th of October, without getting permission from Dr. Ezzell or Ezzell's boss, much less from the FBI, Jahrling gave an assignment to a bacteriologist he trusted: Bruce Ivins. He asked Ivins to get another sample in order to determine the concentration density of the spores within the Daschle letter.

Everyone at USAMRIID was evidently still in the same kind of trusting mood that had allowed a quirky scientist to work alone and unsupervised at night with deadly pathogens for months on end. Thus, on the afternoon of the 17th, when Ivins asked one of John Ezzell's aides, Stephanie Redus, if he could perform density tests on spores in the Daschle letter, Redus unlocked the refrigerator where the Daschle letter was stored and turned the letter over to Ivins.[6]

Ivins analyzes his own work

Ivins took the bagged letter to the pass-through box to Suite B3 and then walked back around to enter via the B301 change room. Once he was in his lab clothes, he went to room B304 and retrieved the letter from the pass-box. .

As he opened the bag inside the biosafety cabinet in his lab, he could see tiny particles drifting away into the air inside the cabinet! Just *touching* the envelope caused more spores to aerosolize! A simple touch caused the tiny amount of air trapped within the envelope to puff out through pores in the paper, and spores inside the envelope and inside the paper became aerosolized. Spores getting through paper that way was something that had never occurred to Ivins - and it hadn't occurred to very many others, either.

On a microscopic level, the paper wasn't like a sieve. It was more like a maze of paper and cloth fibers, and the maze was fifty or sixty times thicker than a single spore. So, when the paper was handled, the pressure would move the air, which in turn would move the spores in among the paper fibers and gradually to the outside, first through the letter and then through the envelope.

The letters were handled by postal employees and equipment at the post office. They were jostled in mail bags and tossed into trucks and carried across bumps in roads. It must have taken time and force to enable the spores to work between the paper fibers. That's why he hadn't noticed any such effects when he originally prepared the letter he was now holding.

Ivins undoubtedly realized it was possible that people could have been infected with anthrax *even if a letter was never opened!*

As tense and excited as he was, Ivins nevertheless set about analyzing the powder in the Daschle letter. His report described how he'd received the sample from Stephanie Redus, and, since there was insufficient actual powder in the letter, Ivins had to scrape some from the envelope. The powder he was able to extract weighed just 0.013

grams. He added 987 microliters of sterile water to get a total of 1 gram (and approximately 1 milliliter) of suspended spores.[7]

He then shook the container of spores and liquid to evenly distribute the spores into the liquid, and he divided the combined material into 10 equal parts, plating each of the ten parts onto Tryptic Soy Agar (TSA). The 10 plates were then incubated overnight.

Opinions

That evening, the news shows were again talking about anthrax, as they had for several days. On the PBS *NewsHour* with Jim Lehrer, Richard O. Spertzel, a retired Army colonel and former deputy USAMRIID commander was stating his opinion. Spertzel had served from 1994 to 1999 as a supervising inspector for the United Nations, searching for biological weapons in Iraq. He was known to have strong opinions and totally believed that Saddam Hussein was concealing an active bioweapons program. He saw a very clear and definite connection between the anthrax attacks and Saddam Hussein.

"I find it far too coincidental that a series of letters, both fake ones ... and actual letters would go out, that is actual letters containing anthrax spores, in a very narrow time frame in mid, late September. That's coincidence far too much." [8]

On the morning of the 18th, Ivins counted the number of visible colony forming units on the ten plates he had prepared the previous day, and he determined that the concentration was 2.1 X 10 to the 12th, or 2.1 trillion spores per gram, which is about the theoretical limit for purified spores. In then "Interpretations and conclusions" section of the report he wrote:

> These are not "garage" spores. The nature of the spore preparation suggests very highly that professional manufacturing techniques were used in the production and purification of the spores, as well as in converting the spores into an extremely fine powder.[9]

He had done a very professional job of analysis, but he was also stating an "opinion" when he wrote that "professional manufacturing techniques" had been used. There was no scientific reason to suggest that the tiny sample required any kind of "manufacturing" facility. So, his "opinion" was really *an outright lie.* The spores were no more pure than spores he created every day in his own lab, and similar spores could have been produced in any of thousands of other microbiology labs around the world by almost any experienced microbiologist.

But, the scientist who had asked for the computations, Peter Jahrling, wasn't a microbiologist. And, while almost any experienced microbiologist may have been able to make anthrax spores of equal purity, very few had. So, Ivins began giving his "opinion" to anyone who would listen, telling that the powder was the most pure material he had ever seen.

He told his supervisor, Jeffery Adamovicz, "I've never seen anything like this before." Adamovicz, the head of the Bacteriology Division later told reporter David Willman, "He said the stuff was incredible. I mean, he wouldn't, couldn't, stop talking about it. He said he'd never seen anything like that before ... It was like smoke. That's what he said it looked like. That's exactly how Bruce described it. He said it was just hovering in the air." [10]

And, as always, everyone trusted Dr. Bruce Ivins.

Chapter 14

October 18 & 19

John Ezzell and the FBI were attempting to establish and enforce protocols for the handing of the evidence from the attacks. Understandably, Ezzell was thoroughly upset over the fact that Ivins had been allowed to take the Daschle envelope to his own lab, a lab which was notoriously a mess, with dirty countertops and floors. Worst of all, it was an area where Ivins routinely worked with other spores, and there was the risk of contamination.

Fortunately, however, nearly all of the loose powder from the Daschle letter had been preserved in Ezzell's lab, so if there was ever a question of contamination, there was material which should help resolve the question.

The Tom Brokaw letter had also arrived at USAMRIID, but John Ezzell had put it in locked storage until protocols could be established and the best minds could be put to work to determine the most secure and effective way to handle all this evidence.

NBC, ABC, CBS

On the 18th, a clear pattern began to emerge when Claire Fletcher, a pretty 27-year-old assistant to Dan Rather was diagnosed with cutaneous anthrax in the form of two black lesions on her left cheek.[1] Fletcher's infection meant that all three major TV news networks had been targeted. Although no letter was found at ABC where the 7-month-old infant son of a news producer had contracted anthrax, and Fletcher couldn't recall seeing any letter containing powder arriving at CBS, their cases clearly weren't random. The offices of the three TV news networks were a mile or more apart, and no one in between had contracted anthrax.

There seemed to be no doubt that envelopes containing powdered anthrax had been delivered to offices of the three news organizations. And, when Teresa Heller, a 45-year-old mail carrier in New Jersey, became the seventh known victim of the attacks, the pattern of mailed letters became even more clear. Heller first noticed the lesion on her right forearm on September 28, but she wasn't officially diagnosed to have cutaneous anthrax until the morning of October 18.[2]

There could no longer be any doubt that it was not necessary to open a letter in order to become infected. Just handling the envelope, or being near where it was handled, as Heller apparently had, was enough.

And to end any doubt that news organizations had been targeted, there was word of yet another case of cutaneous anthrax in New York City, probably from another letter. And this case had occurred in the building that housed the FOX TV news network, although it wasn't FOX that was targeted, possibly because FOX had no evening news anchor the way the other networks did. The new case involved another news organization in the same building.

The Index Case

Joanna Huden, an editorial page assistant at the *New York Post*, had first observed an itchy, red bug-bite-like bump on the last joint of her right middle finger almost a month ago, on Saturday, September 22nd while she was at a wedding on Long Island with her boyfriend, Joe Cunningham, a reporter for the *Post*. The lesion gradually got worse, turning her finger almost black. After a week without any improvement, she'd gone to a walk-in clinic for treatment, and she'd been given a strong antibiotic, Augmentin, but it didn't seem to help. She was no longer able to bend the finger.[3]

So, Huden went to the emergency room at Beth Israel Hospital where doctors poked at her finger and looked puzzled. But, they didn't seem to be certain about what they were seeing. Finally, tired with waiting, Huden just walked out and went home.

The problems became worse. She was feeling achy and feverish, and she showed her finger to her boss, Bob McManus who insisted she be taken to New York University Medical Center right away. In their emergency room, a decision was made to cut away the infected part of her finger.

That didn't stop the infection, either. The lesion continued to get worse, making her weak and nauseous. She was at her desk on Friday, October 12, when the news broke that Tom Brokaw's assistant had cutaneous anthrax.

Huden was immediately certain that anthrax was the cause of her infection, too. The symptoms were identical. And she worked for another news organization.

She rushed to Mount Sinai Hospital where they did a chest X-ray, nasal swabs were taken, and a biopsy was taken directly from the lesion. And, just to be careful, she was put on Cipro, which was the best known antibiotic treatment for anthrax.

The next morning, she was a bit alarmed when she was asked to return to Mount Sinai. But, it turned out that they just wanted to do some more tests.

The Cipro seemed to work. For a week she waited while her condition seemed to improve. Then, she was called in again. More blood was needed. She'd been on antibiotics for so long it was difficult to make a diagnosis. Finally, on Thursday evening, October 18, she received a confirmation call from Mount Sinai. Yes, she had cutaneous anthrax. And, she'd shown symptoms on September 22, weeks before Bob Stevens had first shown symptoms. For the epidemiologists, she was now the "index case," the first person to show symptoms of anthrax infection as a result of the letter attacks. Others had been *diagnosed* with anthrax weeks before Joanna Huden was correctly diagnosed, but epidemiology involves sorting through panicky reports, sheer stupidity, simple human errors, and medical misdiagnoses based upon what was common instead of what was real, to find out what truly happened.

Looking for a source

The Wall Street Journal for October 18 contained an opinion piece by former CIA Director R. James Woolsey, which wildly overstated the situation with the anthrax letters, claiming thirty congressional staffers were "infected" by "professionally prepared and precisely-sized anthrax spores." Woolsey suggested that Saddam Hussein was most likely behind the anthrax letters.[4]

It wasn't part of Bruce Ivins' plan to start a war with Iraq. He'd assumed that Iraq would already have started a war with America by utilizing anthrax and other bioweapons they were known to possess. Nevertheless, he was very upset.

Very little was going according to his plans. And, most bizarre of all, people were still coming to *him* to try to find out where the Ames strain came from. It was like being asked where test tubes originated. The Ames strain didn't originate with him. Like test tubes, the Ames strain had been around for a long time. Yet, no one else at USAMRIID seemed to have any idea of its source. And Ivins was viewed as *the* Ames expert.

When someone sent Dr. Ivins another email about the Ames strain on October 18, 2001, Ivins testily responded:

> The "Ames" strain of Bacillus anthracis was sent to us in the late 1980-early 1981 time frame from the United States Department of Agriculture, Animal & Plant Health Inspection Services, National Veterinary Services Laboratories, Ames, Iowa. We were told it came from a dead cow. We were not told the specifics of the strain, specifically where it was isolated, or when it was isolated. Basically, we were told it was Bacillus anthracis that had been isolated from a clinical veterinary case. I've read that the strain was originally isolated in the 1950s at Iowa State University, but we were not given that information when we got the strain. I have also read that the strain is very common in veterinary labs, clinical labs, university bacteriology labs and research institutes all over the country, and that doesn't surprise me. From the literature, it seems that many places have the "Ames" strain or its derivatives. The proper place to find out the details of the strain is the USDA, not us. They sent it to us. It's their strain, and it's their responsibility to know the details about it. Thanks![5]

It appears that Ivins was just reading and repeating the total nonsense that was being printed in the media. The last thing in the world he wanted was for people to come to him to explain where the Ames strain came from. The facts, however, were beginning to indicate very clearly that the Ames strain didn't come from the USDA and never had anything to do with Iowa State University. Worst of all, *no one* knew where the Ames strain came from, but a lot of people - including FBI investigators - were trying to find out.

Peter Jahrling, meanwhile, just like Richard O. Spertzel, seemed convinced that the material in the Daschle letter was weaponized in some very sophisticated way by some foreign government. The "goop" Jahrling and Tom Geisbert had seen oozing from the spores was still unexplained. But, Jahrling may have been picking up suggestions or questions that the "goop" might have had something to do with the fact that the spores had been soaking in liquids before they arrived at USAMRIID and the spores were killed with other liquids by Tom Geisbert. And, microbiologists who had actually worked with weaponized anthrax were starting to tell everyone that all known weaponization additives could be clearly seen on the outside of the spores.

Early on the morning of October 19, Jahrling put on a Level 4 biosuit and went into the Submarine to retrieve the sample of dry powder that Geisbert had been given four days earlier. Jahrling put two small tubes containing dry spores into a cobalt irradiator which bombarded the DNA of the spores with sterilizing radiation, rendering them harmless. He then gave one of the irradiated tubes of spores to Tom Geisbert to examine under a Scanning Electron Microscope (SEM).[6]

Geisbert had problems almost immediately. As he was preparing the SEM, the spores vanished. Shocked, he examined the tube and tapped it with his finger. The spores had somehow gotten stuck under the cap, and the tapping caused them to drop again to the bottom of the tube.

Minutes later, after he finished preparing the SEM, he looked at the tube again, and the spores were gone again. They had again moved by themselves into the cap. He tapped the tube, causing the spores to drop to the bottom once more, and this time he watched as the spores seemed to crawl up the side of the plastic tube heading back toward the cap. He and his assistant, Denise Braun, shook their heads in wonder over the phenomenon. The spores were obviously charged with static electricity. Was it some kind of weaponization trick executed by the scientists who had created the spores and put them into the envelope?

He had further problems when he tried to coax the spores out of the tube and on to a piece of sticky black tape that would hold the spores in place while inside the SEM. The spores wouldn't stick to the tape and floated away into the air currents inside the hood to become sucked into the filters. At least eighty percent of the spores from the tube were lost before he could figure out what sort of action he need to take to stop it.

Finally, he managed to get some spores to stick to the tape, and he raced back upstairs to the scope room to see what this mysterious "jumping bean" powder looked like.

He was stunned by what he saw. The image in the SEM was pure spores, and some of the spores inside the vacuum chamber of the SEM seemed to move. There were clusters of spores, but the clusters seemed to be breaking down into smaller pieces as he watched. Large chunks became smaller chunks, which in turn were becoming individual spores. Geisbert concluded that this powder was designed to fall apart in the air, to self-crumble into the most potent and deadly form - individual spores which would be readily absorbed into the lungs.

Feeling excited and even a bit shaky, Geisbert called Jahrling in the Virology Division. Jahrling raced up the stairs to the scope room to take a look. They were both convinced they were looking at some kind of highly sophisticated weapon that no one at USAMRIID had ever seen before. Could this stuff have been made in Iraq? Or was it some kind of secret *new* American product?

Jahrling left the room shaken, and he went directly to a "Secure Room" where he could study secret documents of weaponization processes that were known to have existed or which might currently exist in laboratories around the world.

Geisbert, meanwhile, was also very concerned that the anthrax had come from an Iraqi bioweapons program, and that if he reported what he thought he had seen and what he believed, he might start a war with Iraq. He didn't sleep that night, and he hoped that the others with more experience who were also examining the anthrax powder might find something less alarming.

The *New York Post* Letter

When *New York Post* reporter and op-ed editor Mark Cunningham was told that his girlfriend, Joanna Huden, had cutaneous anthrax, he joined the hunt for the letter that had infected her. The letter was found late in the evening of October 19th in a bag of trash on a freight elevator.[7]

It had never been opened.

It had been postmarked in Trenton on the same day as the Brokaw envelope, September 18, and it was addressed to "Editor" at the *New York Post.*

The sealed envelope was turned over to FBI HazMat agents at 11:45 p.m. The HazMat experts opened the envelope and removed the letter. It was another Xerox-type copy of the same letter that had been sent to Tom Brokaw. Testing the powder confirmed that it contained anthrax. But, unlike the light-colored, very fine powder found in the Daschle letter, the *New York Post* powder was brown and granular.[8]

The HazMat experts transferred the powder from the envelope into a sealable tube and placed the letter, the envelope and the tube containing the powder in three separate plastic bags, which were then all sealed within yet another plastic bag.

At 2 a.m. on the morning of Saturday, October 20, the bagged *New York Post* envelope and contents were handed over to scientists at USAMRIID.[9]

Meanwhile, although no one yet realized it, two more *New York Post* employees had gotten spores into open sores or cuts on their bodies as a result of their hunt for the letter, Joanna Huden's boyfriend Mark Cunningham and mailroom worker William Monagas. The spores in the cuts were in the process of germinating. Cunningham and Monagas would soon become additional victims.

Chapter 15

Two More Deaths

Sometimes, the world seems to be divided between a lot of people who love to talk about unsolved puzzles and a few people who do not talk until they have solved a puzzle. That means that there is a lot of speculation and talk about possibilities before there is any talk about actualities.

At USAMRIID, protocols were still not in place to allow a thorough examination and testing of the powder in the newly found *New York Post* letter, so it too was placed in storage.

But, a third letter postmarked at the Hamilton Township mail processing facility near Trenton meant that the facility was shut down and more than 300 workers at the facility were offered antibiotics to help fight any possible exposure to spores. The West Trenton Post Office was also closed while environmental tests were done there.

Meanwhile, the media was finding numerous "experts" willing to speculate on who may have been responsible for the anthrax letters, as well as who was almost certainly not responsible.

While many were pointing at Saddam Hussein and Iraq as the most likely culprit, on October 19, the British newspaper *The Guardian* published an authoritative piece explaining why Iraq was almost certainly *not* behind the attacks.

> Under the most stringent on-site inspection regime in the history of arms control, Iraq's biological weapons programmes were dismantled, destroyed or rendered harmless during the course of hundreds of no-notice inspections. The major biological weapons production facil-

ity - al Hakum, which was responsible for producing Iraq's anthrax - was blown up by high explosive charges and all its equipment destroyed. [1]

Furthermore, Iraq had used the Vollum strain of anthrax in its work with bioweapons. There was absolutely no evidence that Iraq had ever possessed the Ames strain. In the opinion of the editors of *The Guardian*, "Based upon this information, it would be irresponsible to speculate about a Baghdad involvement."

Meanwhile, *The Atlanta Journal-Constitution* had rounded up a gaggle of "experts" to explain why it was unlikely that the attacks were the result of any kind of "domestic plot."[2] Their "experts" didn't believe that the anthrax mailer was any kind of typical right wing extremist. Right Wing extremists didn't have laboratories for making and weaponizing anthrax spores. And the targets weren't typical Right Wing targets. Thus, according to *The Journal-Constitution's* "experts," it was "far more likely" that the culprit was "foreign rather than domestic."

Of course, the anthrax mailer might actually be someone who didn't neatly fit into either of those two categories.

FBI Director Robert Mueller announced that a 1 million dollar reward was being offered to anyone with information that led to the arrest and conviction of the anthrax mailer - regardless of whether the culprit was foreign or domestic.

Morris & Curseen

On Sunday, October 21, Thomas Morris, Jr., a 55-year-old postal worker at the Brentwood mail facility in Washington, D.C., was admitted to a hospital with a suspected case of inhalation anthrax. He'd first reported symptoms three days earlier and visited his primary physician. Noting that the patient already suffered from Type-2 diabetes and sarcoidosis (a chronic swelling in various parts of the body), his doctor decided the problem was just some sort of minor virus and sent Morris home.

When Morris was admitted to a hospital on the 21st, it was clear to everyone that he was deathly ill. He suffered from fatigue, muscle pain, a tightness in the chest, chills, nausea, vomiting and shortness of breath. He died later that evening.[3]

Meanwhile, 47-year-old Joseph Curseen, another employee of the Brentwood mail facility had been suffering from progressive fatigue for 5 days. When nausea and vomiting started, he visited an emergency room doctor. After a series of tests, no specific cause for his symptoms could be found, and he was released.

The next day, Monday October 22, when Curseen went back to a hospital with worsening symptoms, the death of Tom Morris was known, and it was evidently suddenly clear to everyone that Curseen was also showing symptoms of inhalation anthrax. But, it was too late. Curseen died later that same day.[4]

Two new deaths from of inhalation anthrax in two days, and both victims were employees of the Brentwood mail facility.

Scientists vs. Scientists

On the 22nd, the head of the FBI laboratories, Allyson Simons, called a meeting to see if there was anything that could be passed on to the Centers for Disease Control (CDC) in Atlanta about the anthrax so that the CDC would be able to give appropriate advice when concerned doctors and first responders from around the country called them. But, the meeting turned into arguments between scientists. The scientists from USAMRIID were saying that the powder was extremely pure and extremely dangerous, and scientists from Battelle reportedly disagreed.

A week earlier, to get a second opinion after USAMRIID scientists reported an additive "goop" oozing from the Daschle spores, the FBI had asked that a sample to be sent do Battelle Memorial Institute for evaluation. At the meeting, Battelle's expert, Michael Kuhlman, reportedly claimed that the powder was ten to fifty times less potent than the army was saying. And one Army Official from USAMRIID reportedly shouted back, "Goddamn it, you stuck the anthrax in an autoclave, and you turned it into hockey pucks!"

A woman from the Department of Health and Human Services agreed. "It was one of the most screwed-up situations I've ever heard of. The people at Battelle took the anthrax and heated it in an autoclave, and this caused the material to clump up, and then they told the FBI it looked like puppy chow. It was like a used-car dealer offering a car for sale that's been in an accident and is covered with dents, and then the dealer is trying to claim this is the way the car looked when it was new." [5]

What the FBI was learning was that there just weren't many scientists around who were knowledgeable about powdered anthrax, but there was no shortage of scientists willing to experiment and give conflicting opinions.

And the CDC didn't have the information it needed to tell postal authorities whether or not it was safe to keep open the facilities through which the letters had passed. Each case was being handled as a unique case. Testing of 300 people at NBC didn't result in any positive nasal swabs for anyone. And swabs around the NBC building turned up only a few spores. Nevertheless, rugs were torn out and replaced in any office where the letter might have traveled, and a massive cleaning operation was still underway. At ABC and CBS, the situation was even less ominous. No one tested positive, and no spores were found anywhere. The cleaning operations were therefore far less intense.

Since the typical period for showing symptoms of cutaneous anthrax is between 1 and 7 days, it appeared that there weren't likely to be any more cases at the three networks or at the *New York Post* from the letters postmarked September 28. It was an incorrect judgment call, but no one was thinking about what may have been stirred up when people went hunting for the missing letter at the *Post* just a day or two ago.

The Daschle letter was something else again. No one was certain what might yet show up as a result of that letter. All six Senate and House office buildings had been closed for testing. The workers who had been in the vicinity when the Daschle letter was found were given Cipro, and thousands of others were subjected to nasal swabs to see if they had been exposed. So far, 31 had tested positive.[6]

And there were more victims. Another postal worker at the Brentwood facility in Washington, where Morris and Curseen had been infected, was hospitalized with inhalation anthrax. 56-year-old Leroy Richmond had suffered symptoms for three days before going to a hospital.[7] His prognosis was good, and he was expected to recover. In New Jersey, meanwhile, Jyotsna Patel, a 43-year-old postal worker at the Hamilton Township mail center had also been hospitalized with inhalation anthrax. Her prognosis was also good.[8]

Anywhere from 20 to 500 anthrax spores were also found at the White House mail opening facility operated by the Secret Service on property shared by the Anacostia Naval Station and Bolling Air Force Base about three miles from the White House[9] Mail deliveries to the White House itself had been stopped shortly after it was confirmed that someone was sending anthrax through the mails.

Handwriting Opinions

On Tuesday, October 23, the FBI put photographs of the Daschle, Brokaw and New York Post letters on its web site.

Forensic experts were telling the media that it was clear that the handwriting on the letters and envelopes was all from the same person. And he or she didn't appear to be doing any of the typical tricks for disguising handwriting (writing using the wrong hand, tracing someone else's writing, writing upside down, etc.), so it was likely that the writing was the writer's natural style - when writing in block letters. But, it was also clear that the writer did things that weren't typical for an experienced writer - such as constructing characters with more than the normal number of strokes - using 3 pen strokes to create an "N" instead of 1 or 2 strokes, and using 4 strokes to create an "M" instead of fewer strokes.[10]

As always, there was no shortage of opinions about what those particular characteristics indicated, particularly from people who analyzed handwriting to determine the personalities of the writers. To professional forensic handwriting experts there weren't enough examples in the three letters and three envelopes to come to any solid conclusions.

Analyzing the *New York Post* powder

The entirety of Suite AA3 in the Animal Assessment Division within Building 1425 at USAMRID had been turned into a forensic analysis and processing center. It was the place where all the samples from the letters were stored along with swabs and samples from the buildings through which the letters had moved and/or were found. About 200 forensic samples were arriving every day. Helicopters were arriving day and night at the helipad located at the far end of a field across the street from the PX entrance to Building 1425.

Each sample was potential evidence and had to be treated accordingly. Each sample had to have a green federal chain of custody form associated with it. And each form had to relate to an evidence tracking folder. And each evidence-tracking folder would eventually have over a hundred sheets of paper in it. Hallways in the Animal Assessment Division and elsewhere within Building 1425 were becoming lined with filing boxes filled with the evidence folders.[11]

On October 23, the *New York Post* letter was taken out of storage and examinations began.

To John Ezzell, the *Post* powder looked very different from the fine, light tan Daschle powder. The *Post* powder was not only

Exhibit #13 - NY Post powder - low SEM resolution - courtesy Sandia National Laboratories

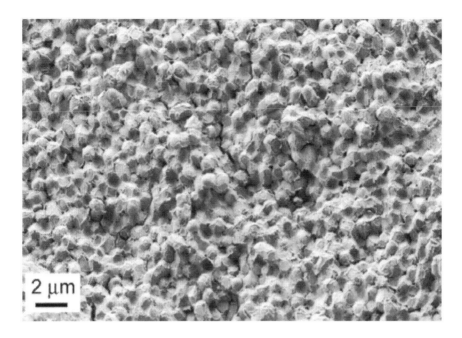

Exhibit #14 - NY Post powder - high SEM resolution - courtesy Sandia National Laboratories

granular in appearance, it was also multi-colored. That indicated it had been centrifuged to separate the water from the rest of the material, the layer of water had been removed, and the remaining multicolored layers were then dried. When thoroughly dried, the material may have been ground or chopped up, possibly with something as simple as a razor blade. The mostly brownish powder contained black bits among other colors. It was clearly a non-homogenous material.[12]

Low resolution SEM images showed broken concrete-like chunks. High resolution images showed individual spores imbedded in dried slime.

When a concentration evaluation was needed, Bruce Ivins wasn't allowed to take the letter or envelope with him to his own lab. He was only given a tiny, representative sample of the *Post* powder to analyze.

The next day, Ivins produced his report. He concluded:

A Crime Unlike Any Other

> If this is a preparation of bacterial spores, it is a relatively
> pure preparation. This preparation did not appear to be as
> pure as the material (SPS02.57.03) previously examined on
> October 17, 2001. The SPS02.57.03 preparation contained
> spores in a concentration of 2.1 X 10 [to the 12th] per
> gram. The SPS02.57.03 spores were thus approximately
> 15.8 times "hotter" or more concentrated than the
> SPS02.88.01 spores examined here.[13]

Other testing and examinations by other scientists produced
roughly similar findings. While Ivins calculated the Daschle powder
to be 15.8 times more lethal than the *Post* powder (i.e., 15.8 times
more spores per gram) the general number used during the investigation was 10 times as lethal. I.e., there were ten times as many spores
in a gram of the Daschle powder than there were in a gram of the
New York Post powder.

Any powdered anthrax will also contain the very small particles and single spores which have to get deep into the lungs in order
to cause inhalation anthrax. So, even at one tenth the lethality of the
Daschle powder, the *Post* powder was still plenty dangerous. An
identical powder had evidently killed Bob Stevens. There was nothing that said a single anthrax spore couldn't kill a particularly suscepti-
ble person.

A Day of Meetings

Early in the morning of October 24, 2001, Major General
Parker at USAMRIID received a phone call from Cabinet member
Tommy Thompson, the head of the Department of Health and Hu-
man Services (HHS). Thompson felt "out of the loop" on the prog-
ress in tracking down who had sent the anthrax letters, and he asked
Parker for a personal update.

Parker agreed, and he asked Peter Jahrling to come along.[14]

Out of all the people at USAMRIID who could have been
asked, including many bacteriologists with years of experience working with anthrax, why was virologist Peter Jahrling picked? Evidently, it was because of the bond that had been established when
Jahrling asked Parker to view the strange happenings when they had
watched the goop ooze out of the spores a week earlier. And, too,

the bacteriologists may all have been extremely busy with the work that was coming in day and night.

Whatever the reason, Parker and Jahrling went to meet with Thompson. Jahrling brought along some talking materials he'd accumulated during the past weeks. The two men were surprised to find the meeting was to take place in a large conference room at HHS headquarters, and in addition to several other HHS executives, there were some CIA and FBI officials in attendance, including Director Mueller.

Jahrling did most of the talking, passing around the photographs Tom Geisbert had taken of the "goop" oozing out of the spores. He also had a plastic bag containing vials of anthrax simulants, such as *Bacillus thuringiensis* (*Bt*), a spore forming bacteria that is used to kill caterpillars in gardens and growing fields. One of the vials was a sample of *Bt* that had been weaponized with bentonite, a gray clay primarily used in the oil industry as a lubricant for drilling pipes. The weaponized *Bt* didn't look anything like what was in the photos of the Daschle anthrax.

The HHS meeting went so well that General Parker suggested that he and Jahrling go to the Pentagon and brief some of the assistant secretaries of defense. Those meetings also went well.

As Parker and Jahrling were returning to Ft. Detrick, the General received a phone call. People at the White House wanted to hear Peter Jahrling's talk. A meeting was scheduled for 7:30 p.m.

The White House

As they headed to the White House, they agreed that it wouldn't be a good idea to take the materials from Iraq in with them, so Jahrling left them in the car when they arrived.

The meeting was held in the Roosevelt Room, where there was a long conference table surrounded by leather covered chairs, and a circle of additional chair lining the walls.[15]

Everyone was advised that the meeting was to be classified "secret." FBI Director Mueller and Tommy Thompson were again in attendance, as was Attorney General John Ashcroft, and a cluster of FBI officials. The newly appointed Director of Homeland Security, Tom Ridge, presided over the meeting, but John Ashcroft was the first to speak. The first subject he wanted to discuss was why the CDC hadn't realized that the anthrax in the letters was "weapons grade," and why no one had taken any action to close the Brentwood facility where two people had just been killed by these "weapons grade" spores and another was badly infected.

It was clear that whoever had sent the anthrax through the mails could also use it in other, more lethal ways, such as a massive release inside some government offices or transportation terminals. What was being done? Where did the communication breakdown occur that allowed the postal employees to be murdered with a bioweapon?

Ashcroft's questions seemed to be directed toward Mueller, but Mueller could only say that it wasn't clear how dangerous the anthrax powders really were, nor did they have any idea who had mailed the letters or why. But, Mueller had to agree that the spores had been used as a weapon, and people were dead, but that didn't technically qualify the powder as a biological weapon in the military sense of the term.

After some debate about what was a "biological weapon" and what wasn't, Ashcroft ended the discussion with, "Okay, okay!" And he said all the discussion about what is a biological weapon what is not is like arguing over the number of angels who can dance on the head of a pin. He wanted to hear what the "professor" had to say.

It took a moment for Jahrling, who is not a professor, to realize Ashcroft was referring to him. Evidently, the talks he'd given earlier in the day had worked their way to Ashcroft's ears, and now Ashcroft want to hear the whole story for himself.

Jarhling once again passed around the photos that Geisbert had taken. He pointed out the "goop" and stated that it was probably an "additive."

Someone wanted to know if the attack anthrax could have been made by Iraq.

Jahrling could only say it was possible, but the samples they had of materials from Iraq's bioweapons programs didn't look anything like what was in the letters. Iraq used bentonite to keep the spores from sticking together, and there didn't appear to be any bentonite on the spores in the letters.

Jahrling was stunned as the meeting suddenly went off on a tangent with discussions about what other "state actor" could have been behind the attacks.

He tried to reign in the discussions by pointing out that the letters only contained a few grams of powder, and some of it was very crude. Almost any microbiology lab in the world could have produced such a small quantity. There was nothing in the letters that indicated that a "state actor" was involved. He told them, "This anthrax could have come from a hospital lab or from any reasonably equipped college microbiology lab."

The FBI wanted to know if there were any "signatures" in the powder that might point to a specific lab or a specific country or anything else specific.

Jahrling didn't know. But there were other tests that could be done. Earlier discussions had brought to mind some critical tests that might be done tomorrow.

The meeting ended with Ashcroft telling the FBI, the Army and Homeland Security that they needed to get their acts together and start communicating with each other and with the CDC more effectively. They all served at the pleasure of the President, and that pleasure could cease in an instant.

Seven years later, Peter Jahrling would admit to David Willman at the *Los Angeles Times* that he had been totally out of his realm during that meeting at the White House. He was a virologist, not a bacteriologist, and should never have even opened his mouth. He wasn't an expert on weaponization, and should never have even mentioned the subject of possible additives.[16]

There were *no additives* in the powders.

Chapter 16

AFIP, Silicon & Bentonite

The morning after the "secret" White House meeting, leading newspapers seemed to know almost everything that had been said. And the subject of "weaponization" was front and center.

The *Washington Post's* front page headline was: *Additive Made Spores Deadlier,* and the sub-headline: *3 Nations Known to Be Able to Make Sophisticated Coating.* The opening paragraph:

> The anthrax spores that contaminated the air in Senate Majority Leader Thomas A. Daschle's office had been treated with a chemical additive so sophisticated that only three nations are thought to have been capable of making it, sources said yesterday.[1]

According to the *Post,* the three nations were The United States, the former Soviet Union and Iraq.

The article made it clear that their "experts" were in direct dispute with the government's official experts on nearly everything. The only point of agreement seemed to be that it was very difficult to accurately define the terms that were being used, like "weaponized," "military quality," and "highly refined."

According to the *Post,* however, the source was "almost certainly a state-sponsored laboratory," and the only real question was whether the spores had been stolen from that laboratory or supplied directly to the terrorists who mailed the letters.

AFIP, Silicon & Bentonite

William J. Broad's article in *The New York Times* that same morning, October 25, was titled, *Contradicting Some U.S. Officials, 3 Scientists Call Anthrax Powder High-Grade.*

There was clearly little agreement among scientists on how dangerous the powders were. Most scientists who had actually seen the powders were saying the powders were "ordinary," while those who only knew about the powders from what reporters had told them were saying the powders were highly exceptional, weaponized and extremely lethal.

Weaponized or not, the spores in the letters had already killed three people and infected nearly a dozen others.

AFIP

That same morning, Thursday, October 25, 2001, in response to the FBI's stated request that the spores be further examined for some kind of "signature," Tom Geisbert was sent with an irradiated sample of the Daschle anthrax to the Armed Forces Institute of Pathology (AFIP) in Northeastern Washington DC. The tiny sample he carried in his beat-up station wagon was already specially mounted on a cassette, thus eliminating any need for preparation by the AFIP technicians.[2]

None of USAMRIID's Scanning Electron Microscopes had the capability to test which specific elements were contained within a sample. AFIP had such an instrument, an Energy Dispersive X-Ray Spectrometer or "EDX."

By lunchtime, the results were clear. The powder did *not* contain any detectable aluminum, which would be part of the EDX signal for the aluminum rich clay known as bentonite.

There was *no* bentonite in the Daschle powder.

But, mysteriously, the EDX showed that there was an element in the spores that *did* fit with theories of weaponization: Silicon. There was Oxygen, too, of course, since Oxygen would be expected in any biological specimen. But, the presence of Silicon *and* Oxygen suggested to some of the doctors and technicians at AFIP that the common mineral silica was present in the spores. Silica, or silicon dioxide is one of the most common substances on earth and is the primary ingredient of glass. More significantly, silica was known to be a weaponization agent used to reduce static electricity in milled spores created by America's bioweapons programs back during the Cold War.

The SEM images didn't show any silica particles on the outside of the spores, and the EDX couldn't determine whether the Silicon was combined with Oxygen in the form of silica, or in the form of silcates (clays) or if it was combined with the Oxygen at all. However, the presence of Silicon, and the possibility that it was in the form of silica, was enough to excite almost everyone, including and specifically Tom Geisbert.

Geisbert asked for the use of a secure telephone to call USAMRIID. He told Peter Jahrling about the Silicon and the possibility that it could be proof of weaponization using silica particles. Neither of them had any idea what a spore weaponized with silica would look like, but they envisioned it as looking like an orange speckled with sand, tiny particles which might go unresolved in the standard resolution of an SEM image.

They were looking for signs of weaponization, and they believed they had found signs of weaponization.

Bentonite

Inexplicably, the next day, on Friday October 26, *ABC News* began telling America that the attack spores were weaponized with bentonite, which was the one substance all the people involved in analyzing the spores could say with absolute certainty was definitely *not* present in the spores.

ABC evidently checked with the White House before going ahead with their story, but that only resulted in ABC news reporting that White House spokesman Ari Fleisher "flatly denied" what ABC's sources were saying. The story said:

> ABCNEWS has been told by three well-placed and separate sources that initial tests on an anthrax-laced letter sent to Senate Majority Leader Tom Daschle have detected a troubling chemical additive that authorities consider their first significant clue yet.

> An urgent series of tests conducted on the letter at Ft.
> Detrick, Md., and elsewhere discovered the anthrax spores
> were treated with bentonite, a substance that keeps the tiny
> particles floating in the air by preventing them from stick-
> ing together. The easier the particles are to inhale, the more
> deadly they are.
>
> As far as is known, only one country, Iraq, has used ben-
> tonite to produce biological weapons.[3]

The "three well-placed and separate sources" were not identified in the report. But, once again there was no shortage of "experts"
willing to speculate on what the bogus finding meant:

> "It means to me that Iraq becomes the prime suspect as
> the source of the anthrax used in these letters," former
> U.N. weapons inspector Timothy Trevan told ABCNEWS.

Timothy Trevan was never a U.N. weapons inspector. From
1992 to 1995 he was a political advisor and spokesman for the chairman of the United Nations Special Commission on Iraq. Trevan's
information was all hearsay, second and third hand information obtained mostly from people he knew at Ft. Detrick.[4]

ABC News, and specifically reporter Brian Ross would continue with the bentonite story for days. On the 28th, Ross reported
that the bentonite finding had been bolstered by a "second set of
tests." On ABC's Sunday morning public affairs show *This Week,*
Ross reported that despite continuing White House denials, there
were now *four* well-placed and separate sources confirming the finding of bentonite in the Daschle letter. He made a similar claim on
that evening's nightly news show.

On the Monday the 29th, on ABC's *Good Morning America,*
Ross stated, "Former U.N. weapons inspectors say the anthrax found
in the letter to Senator Daschle is nearly identical to samples they re-
covered in Iraq in 1994... And under an electron microscope, trace
amounts of telltale additives are matching up, according to at least
four well-placed sources, although the White House denies it."

On that same ABC show, co-host George Stephanopoulos
questioned the information, stating his sources were saying that there

was no test which confirmed a finding of bentonite in the Daschle powder. Ross acknowledged that he was going mostly on hearsay, and that his sources had no direct knowledge about the Daschle powder, but he was confident his information was correct.[5]

And, so were officials at ABC. Jeffrey Schneider, an ABC News spokesman told *USA Today* that their sources were saying that the Daschle powder was indistinguishable from samples taken out of Iraq in the early 1990's, and *ABC News* was "confident" in its reporting.

On November 1, Brian Ross was questioned by Peter Jennings on *World News Tonight*, and Ross changed his story. He stated that, while initial tests had shown the presence of bentonite in the Daschle powder, a trademark of the Iraqi bioweapons program, "a further chemical analysis has ruled that out." He didn't explain why that new test was more conclusive than all the other tests he claimed had been performed, nor did he explain why he was suddenly backing off the story he had been loudly promoting for days.

Evidently, the lack of any aluminum in the Daschle spores finally made an impression on Brian Ross. But not on everyone. It was on that same day, November 1, 2001, that Gary Matsumoto at *ABC News* reported in an article on their web site that ABC had located two companies in Europe which manufactured "aluminum-free bentonite." [6]

A day after that, ABC corrected their on-line story by adding a final paragraph stating that one of the European companies ABC had contacted had contacted *ABC News* after their story went on the air and told them that, while their process "does remove some aluminum from bentonite, it does not remove all aluminum."

The bentonite issue was finally dead.

Ari Fleischer would later state that the *ABC News* story about bentonite was "what I view as the most worrisome, inaccurate story of my time in the White House." [7]

Chapter 17

The Last Anthrax Victims

More victims of Bruce Ivins' anthrax letters were showing up in hospitals. In October 22, another employee of the Brentwood mail center in Washington D.C., 56-year-old George Fairfax, was confirmed to have inhalation anthrax. His prognosis was good.[1]

That same day, a 34-year-old mail room employee at *The New York Post*, William Monagas, was confirmed to have cutaneous anthrax in the form of a raised spot of swelling on his left forearm. He was given Cipro and was expected to fully recover.[2]

On October 24, Linda Burch, a 51-year-old bookkeeper in an office near the Hamilton Township mail facility in New Jersey was diagnosed with cutaneous anthrax in the form of a lesion on her forehead. She worked as a bookkeeper and had never been in the Hamilton facility, nor had she been to any post offices in recent weeks. Although she was expected to fully recover, the case was worrisome, since it seemed to indicate that she had somehow become infected by cross-contamination, possibly a letter she received had touched one of the anthrax letters, causing a transfer of spores to an otherwise normal letter. If so, it was the first indication that spores could be spread that way, and it opened nearly the entire world to possible infection.[3]

On October 25, 59-year-old David Hose, an employee at the State Department mail facility in Sterling, Virginia, was diagnosed with inhalation anthrax. His prognosis was very good, but his case also opened up the matter of cross-contamination.[4] No known anthrax letter had passed through the State Department facility. So, cross-contamination seemed a possibility. Yet, cross-contamination didn't seem likely since it implied that the cross-contaminated letter had dispersed enough spores into the air near Mr. Hose for him to inhale the 8 to 10 thousand required to overcome his immune system and cause infection. The other, more likely possibility was that there was another anthrax letter in the system somewhere that had not yet been found. It might be in a mail bag or on someone's desk somewhere waiting for the time when people would feel it was safe to begin delivering and opening mail again.

On the 28th, Joanna Huden's 38-year-old boyfriend, Mark Cunningham of *The New York Post* was diagnosed with cutaneous anthrax in the form of a lesion on his forehead.[5] Like William Monagas, the infection evidently hadn't resulted from the delivery of *The New York Post* letter, it had resulted from the *search* for the letter that had ensued weeks later, after Joanna Huden had been diagnosed with cutaneous anthrax.

Kathy Nguyen

On October 31, 2001, Bruce Ivins' anthrax letters claimed another life and created another mystery.

Kathy Nguyen, a Vietnamese immigrant who worked in the stockroom at the Manhattan Eye, Ear & Throat Hospital had become ill on the 25th, feeling weak and achy. She didn't go to an emergency room for treatment until the 28th when she was having a difficult time breathing. She was immediately sent to intensive care where she soon required mechanical ventilation to help her breathe.

She died on Wednesday, October 31st, of inhalation anthrax.

Nguyen lived alone, she had no family in the United States, and none of her few friends could explain how she might have contracted inhalation anthrax.[6] The ensuing investigation found no spores in her apartment in the Bronx, there were no spores where she worked, and there were no spores in any mailbox or on any mail route which might have resulted from the delivery of a cross-contaminated letter.[7]

The official thinking was that she must have been exposed to a piece of mail cross-contaminated by the Daschle letter[8] The data, however, indicated a different scenario.[9] (1) Her case fell into the time frame as the Monagas and Cunningham cases which were conclusively known to have resulted from the first mailing and the search for the *New York Post* letter. (2) There were other cases of exposure in New York City as a result of the mishandling of the Brokaw letter. (3) Nguyen worked in central Manhattan, about 1¼ miles (as the crow flies) from the ABC news studios near Lincoln Center and the NBC news studios at Rockerfeller Center, and about 1½ miles from CBS news studios and the offices of *The New York Post.* The chances of a cross-contaminated letter from the second mailing infecting *by pure chance* someone within that tiny portion of the planet Earth was infinitely small compared with the odds that Nguyen was somehow infected by spores from the one of the letters sent to the New York media organizations.

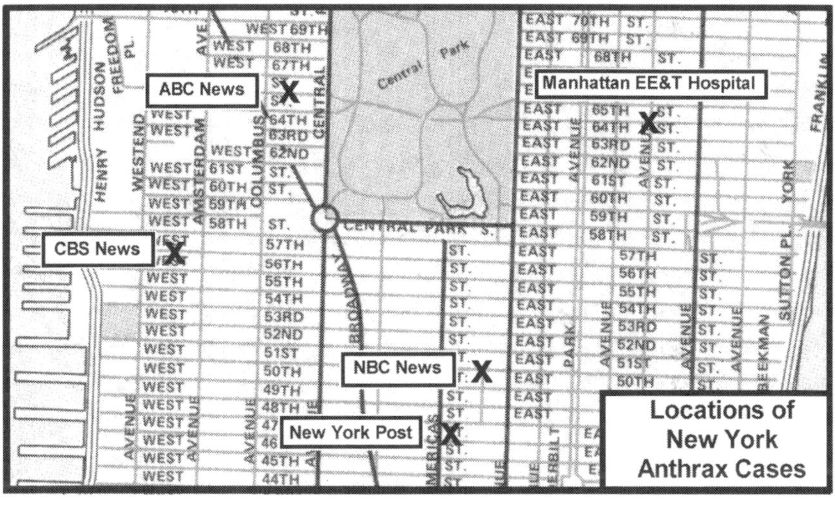

Exhibit #15 - Location of New York City anthrax cases

The real mystery was exactly *how* Nguyen had become infected. Did someone who had been hunting for the missing *Post* letter go to the MEE&T hospital for antibiotics while covered with spores, and by pure chance pass Nguyen in a hallway? Did Nguyen stand next to a Post or NYCDOH employee who had spores on his or her clothing while she was traveling home by subway? We'll almost certainly never know.

The one thing that seems very evident, however, is that it probably didn't take 8 to 10 thousand spores to kill Kathy Nguyen.

Age	Location	Type	Name	Onset
7 mos	ABC-NY	C	child	Sept. 29
23	NBC-NY	C	Casey Chamberlain	Sept. 29
27	CBS-NY	C	Claire Fletcher	Oct. 1
30	NY Post	C	Joanna Huden	Sept. 22
32	NJ PO	C	Teresa Heller	Sept. 27
34	NY Post	C	William Monagas	Oct. 19
38	NY Post	C	Mark Cunningham	Oct. 23
39	NBC-NY	C	Erin O'Connor	Sept. 25
39	NJ PO	C	Richard Morgano	Sept. 26
61	NYC	I	Kathy Nguyen	Oct. 25
63	AMI-FL	I	Bob Stevens	Sept. 30
73	AMI-FL	I	Ernesto Blanco	Sept. 28

And it probably didn't take anywhere near that many to kill Bob Stevens in Florida, either. The above list of the 12 victims of the first mailing in order by their age shows that all the inhalation anthrax victims were over the age of 60. Age clearly seemed to play a role in who would most likely get inhalation anthrax.

It's undoubtedly no coincidence that the 1979 Sverdlovsk outbreak in Russia, which took at least 70 lives, didn't kill anyone under the age of 24, even though there were many children in the danger area.[10]

Ottilie Lundgren

The final victim of the anthrax attacks of 2001 was a 94-year-old Connecticut widow whose husband had died in 1977. Ottilie Lundgren almost certainly handled a cross-contaminated letter resulting from the October 9 mailing. The local mail processing center at Wallingford, CT, which distributed mail to Lundgren's mail route was found to have spores on several of its sorting machines. And, postal inspectors were able to determine that a letter addressed to someone on the same mail route as Lundgren had gone through the postal machines in New Jersey shortly after the anthrax letter addressed to Senator Tom Daschle was processed.

The person who received the letter was not infected, but Lungren was infected - possibly by only a few spores. People remembered that Ottilie would tear up junk mail before throwing it away, a process which conceivably would throw spores into her face.

Lundgren started showing symptoms similar to pneumonia on November 14, and sought medical care two days later. She was diagnosed with inhalation anthrax by the hospital on the 19th. The diagnosis was confirmed by the Connecticut Department of Health on the 20th and by the CDC on the 21st, the same day Lundgren died.[11]

Lundgren's death would bring the total number of known victims of Ivins' letters to 22, including 5 deaths. Two of the dead were postal employees, two were totally innocent women who were infected by pure happenstance, and one was a victim who worked for a magazine owned by the same company as the magazine to which a letter had been sent.

None of the dead were the addressees of the letters, so by any measure, none were intended victims.

During this time, Bruce Ivins was also a source for an article written by Peter Boyer for the November 12 issue of *The New Yorker*, *The Ames Strain: How a sick cow in Iowa may have helped to create a lethal bioweapon*. The error-filled article explained how USAMRIID obtained the Ames strain:

> The National Veterinary Services Laboratory in Ames serves as the diagnostic center for the entire nation; it is a repository for all manner of germs and diseases that afflict American livestock. That is why the U.S. Army wrote to the N.V.S.L. in late 1980 requesting a sample of an anthrax culture. The Ames lab made a subculture of the anthrax and sent it to the Army's Medical Research Institute of Infectious Diseases-USAMRIID-at Fort Detrick, near Frederick, Maryland, along with the information that the isolate had come from a dead cow. The Army named it the Ames strain.
>
> ....

A Crime Unlike Any Other

> The Ames strain's reputation among laboratory scientists
> created a demand for it, and the demand was handily met.

Very little of what was in the article was true. It was all based upon beliefs and memories. By this time, the FBI may have learned the truth, but, if so, they weren't sharing.

Chapter 18

The *Rare* Ames Strain?

In mid-November of 2001, no one knew for certain that the last victim of the anthrax attacks of 2001 had been identified. Although there hadn't been any more deliveries of anthrax-laden letters for a month, there was always the possibility that a new mailing could occur at any time - or an entirely new batch of lethal spores might be delivered via some other, more devastating technique.

On Tuesday, November 14, Ivins must have been feeling confident that he would never be found out, since he took pictures of himself working in his lab and sent the pictures to friends and former colleagues around the country, including Nancy Haigwood.

Two days later, the Leahy letter was found.

Undelivered mail that was still at the Brentwood mail facility in Washington, D.C., when it was shut down had been put into 280 barrels for shipment to Ohio for sterilization via irradiation. Investigators did tests of each barrel before its contents went into the irradiation process, and one barrel tested so high for anthrax that it was a virtual certainty that it contained another anthrax-laden letter.

As investigators went through the barrel letter by letter, they found one addressed to Senator Leahy that looked very similar to the Daschle letter. It sent their testing equipment off the charts. It had similar handwriting, it was postmarked in Trenton on October 9, just like the Daschle letter, it had tape on the back just like the Daschle letter, and it had the same return address as the Daschle letter.[1]

A Crime Unlike Any Other

The ZIP code on the envelope's address had been read incorrectly by machines at the Hamilton facility in New Jersey. Because the writer used serifs on his 1's, and because he wrote the ZIP code at a slight slant, the machine had interpreted the 1 as a 2 and sent it to zone 20520 instead to 20510. It went to the State Department mail sorting facility, where it had undoubtedly infected postal employee David Hose before the ZIP error was corrected and it was redirected back to the Brentwood facility, and then into a barrel for storage awaiting irradiation.[2]

The letter was, of course, unopened. And it was decided that it should remain unopened until all the equipment and protocols were in place to get maximum information from this new find. It was placed in refrigerated storage at USAMRIID to await that day.

Meanwhile, the government had upped the reward for information leading to the arrest and conviction of the anthrax mailer to $1,125,000.

And, it was becoming more and more certain that the culprit was very likely *not* a foreign terrorist. He or she was an American scientist with some unknown agenda. There were simply no facts which pointed to al Qaeda or any other outside state or entity. As facts were gathered, they all pointed *away* from Iraq and al Qaeda. The letters did indeed contain Muslim-type threats, but it was becoming more and more likely that the perpetrator simply wanted his letters to *appear* to have been mailed by Muslim terrorists. There were things about the letters which did not agree with all the past letters from Muslim terrorists. For example, there was no Arabic writing in the letters, which past letters tended to include. Also, the term "Allah is great" is almost always expressed in Arabic: Allahu Akbar, which means "Allah is the greatest" or "God is great." Past terrorist attacks show it to be *extremely* unusual for a Muslim to use the English translation in such a declaration.[3]

The fact that there hadn't been a follow-up attack was another indicator that it wasn't a foreign terrorist, as was the fact that the culprit seemed to have taken some very unusual precautions to avoid harming anyone. That certainly didn't fit the normal pattern for Muslim terrorists - or typical terrorists of any kind.

And, the fact that the Ames strain was used in the letters was the primary indicator that the culprit was an American scientist. No one could find *any* evidence to suggest that Iraq or any Middle-East country had ever obtained a sample of the Ames strain. In fact, it was difficult to find any American lab that possessed the Ames strain, even though it was believed to be possessed by countless labs.

Ames - Beliefs vs. Facts

There was absolutely no evidence that the spores had been "weaponized," in any military sense of the term. And USAMRIID was certainly not making "weaponized" spores for its vaccine tests on animals.

Bruce Ivins was becoming so angry at any suggestion that powdered anthrax was being made at USAMRIID for animal testing or any other purpose, that he began occasionally signing his name as "Bruce (We don't make anthrax spore powder at USAMRIID) Ivins." And he continued to insist that the Ames strain was a common strain used in labs all over the world.[4]

However, it was slowly becoming very clear that the Ames strain wasn't the "common" strain that everyone believed it was, and a November 25, 2001 article in *The Washington Post* titled *Deadly Anthrax Strain Leaves a Muddy Trail* described the new understanding:

> Once thought to be accessible to thousands of researchers, the strain now appears to have circulated in only a small universe of laboratories. One of its main distributors, according to scientists, was the U.S. Army Medical Research Institute of Infectious Diseases (USAMRIID) at Fort Detrick, Md., which used Ames to test vaccines that could protect U.S. troops in case of a biological attack.
>
> ...
>
> When the attacks began, there was speculation that thousands of labs might have had access to Ames, but that number has been knocked down by anthrax experts. Philip C. Hanna, a microbiologist at the University of Michigan, said: "I'd put it . . . between 10 and 24."
>
> Paul Keim, who has done genetic mapping of anthrax strains at Northern Arizona University and is reportedly

assisting the FBI with the investigation, said he was uncertain of the number of labs with Ames but described it as "a pretty small list" that he thought was "very discoverable."

Paul Keim's collection of over 2,000 anthrax samples was undoubtedly key to the realization that the Ames strain was *not* widely distributed and that USAMRIID did most or all of the distribution of the Ames strain. All the samples of the Ames strain in Keim's extensive collection came directly or indirectly from USAMRIID. So, scientists at USAMRIID seemed to be in a position to know everyone - or almost everyone - who had the Ames strain.

The *Washington Post* article also showed why the focus was shifting to USAMRIID:

> Martin Hugh-Jones, an anthrax expert at Louisiana State University who maintains a global database of anthrax outbreaks for the World Health Organization, concurred that it was relatively simple in the past to obtain anthrax cultures from USAMRIID.
>
> "They kept the stuff there, and if you needed a culture, you called up Art" -- Col. Arthur Friedlander, USAMRIID's senior military research scientist, Hugh-Jones said.
> ....
> "Basically, if some guy's got this culture on his dirty clothes or on his bench top, he'll have some explaining to do," said Hugh-Jones. "It's like owning a pistol that was used in a homicide."

That last comment by Hugh-Jones was very prescient. However, at that same time (and in the same *Washington Post* article), it is made clear that the media (and possibly the FBI investigators) still believed the Ames strain originally came from somewhere around Ames, Iowa:

> Only a few facts have been clearly established. The strain of Bacillus anthracis that became known as Ames was first isolated decades ago from a diseased cow near Ames. A natural or "wild" strain, Ames was recognized relatively early for its virulence and for its ability to resist vaccines.

The Rare Ames Strain?

USAMRIID scientists didn't know what they didn't know about the Ames strain. They also didn't know what the FBI was doing. But, they knew the FBI was checking out people who worked for USAMRIID.

On Monday, November 19, 2001, two FBI agents had visited Bruce Ivins in his office in Building 1425 to get information about a scientist who had been formerly employed by USAMRIID.[5]

Joseph Farchaus had been one of the co-inventors of the new anthrax vaccine, and Ivins had known him well. The FBI interview seems to have prompted Ivins to view Farchaus as the person he should concentrate upon when talking with the FBI. If the FBI suspected Farchaus, Ivins was more than willing to help promote that suspicion. During that first interview, however, Ivins could only tell the FBI that he didn't know if Farchause was right wing or left wing, and he mentioned how Farchaus would treat him like a child, giving him "noogies" and bullying him.

Meanwhile, the name of another former USAMRIID employee, virologist Dr. Steven Hatfill, had been furnished to the FBI by scientists and others outside of USAMRIID as being a very likely suspect in the case.

Chapter 19

Birth of a Conspiracy Theory

The fact that the Ames strain was a strain used in a U.S. Army lab, and the fact that the evidence showed that anthrax mailer clearly wanted to do minimal damage while at the same time trying to appear to be a Muslim terrorist making a threat of much greater damage to come, made the anthrax letters seem highly suspicious to people who were already highly suspicious of the U.S. government's involvement with bioweapons. As a result, it didn't take them long to come up with a conspiracy theory.

The lead theorist was Dr. Barbara Hatch Rosenberg, and the seminal event was the Biological and Toxic Weapons Convention (BTWC) which took place in Geneva, Switzerland in November of 2001.

Barbara Hatch Rosenberg

Dr. Rosenberg had impressive credentials to make many people listen to her theories. At the time of the attacks, she was in her early 70's and a co-founder of the Scientists Working Group on Biological and Chemical Weapons at the Federation of American Scientists (FAS). In 1990 she had been hired as a Research Professor of Environmental Science at the State University of New York at Purchase, where she is able to devote most of her time to biological weapons issues. Dr. Rosenberg had also been a member of a panel of scientists that advised President Clinton, the Secretary of Defense and the Secretary of Health on biological weapons issues in 1998, and she had been an Advisor to the U.S. Congress's Office of Technology Assessment's study of Weapons of Mass Destruction in 1993-4. She was also an officer of ProMED-mail, the global electronic rapid reporting system for outbreaks of emerging diseases, which was launched by the Working Group in 1994 as a prototype and later became an independent entity.[1]

It was also clear that she did not trust the U.S. government when it came to biological and toxic weapons development.

Controlling Biological Weapons

The United States started developing biological weapons in the spring of 1943 when President Franklin Delano Roosevelt signed an order to begin research. The research continued after the end of World War II, and the U.S. continued to build up a large stockpile of biological agents and weapons. The official policy of the United States was first to deter the use of bio-weapons against U.S. forces, and secondarily to retaliate if that deterrence failed. There is no evidence, however, that the U.S. ever used any biological weapons against any enemy troops on any battlefield.

In 1969, President Nixon ended all non-defensive aspects of U.S. biological weapons programs. In 1975, the U.S. ratified both the 1925 Geneva Protocol and the 1972 Biological Weapons Convention (BWC), which were international treaties outlawing biological warfare.

According to many nations, however, those treaties suffered from a very serious flaw: they provided for no way to confirm that treaty members were actually adhering to the protocols. The United States was one of the nations concerned about that flaw, particularly since Iraqi weapons discovered during the 1991 Gulf War had showed that the BWC had failed to stop Iraq from developing such weapons. So, for seven years a multi-nation committee had worked to develop a new version of the 1972 BWC treaty that would authorize laboratory inspections and require signatory nations to make public which sites could be used to develop biological weapons.

But, in mid-2001, it was becoming clear that the United States had a change of mind and was not ready to ratify such a treaty.[2]

A Crime Unlike Any Other

On June 5, 2001, Barbara Hatch Rosenberg expressed her concern about this at a Congressional Hearing on The Biological Weapons Convention Protocol: Status and Implications. She stated,

> Unless it can be seen by the end of the remaining four weeks of negotiation that agreement is near, there is sure to be a contentious row at the fifth BWC Review Conference in November, with quite likely a lack of agreement on what to do next. The United States is certain to receive most of the blame. We led the chorus in citing the danger; if we turn down an international step toward prevention that is almost within our grasp, it will tell potential proliferators that the international community is not prepared to enforce the ban on biological weapons. As citizens of the lone superpower, Americans would be a prime target if these weapons were used either strategically or as an instrument of terror.[3]

Her concerns became reality when the United States rejected the treaty on July 26, 2001. Government negotiators stated that they had "long-standing concerns" and would not support the current draft of the treaty because the treaty posed a "serious risk" to U.S. national interests. The treaty or protocol would open U.S. laboratories to inspection by foreign scientists which would give them information needed to counter U.S. biological weapons defensive programs. It also would open the door to industrial espionage. The Bush Administration also felt the protocol would endanger existing export controls, which they saw as the strongest defense in stopping bio-weapons proliferation.[4]

The protocol also didn't include any penalties that would deter countries from manufacturing bio-weapons. What good is a law if there is no penalty for breaking the law?

However, the U.S. was willing to continue to negotiate to develop a treaty that would satisfy their concerns.

For most other nations, however, it meant that the seven years of work to develop the protocol were for naught. They'd have to start from scratch again.

Birth of a Conspiracy Theory

And to American scientists who had worked on the protocol and supported its development, it meant that the U.S. government was unreasonable, and the Bush administration's rejection of inspections *could* even mean that they were hiding some secret and illegal bio-weapons program that was currently in progress.

It was irresistible fodder for conspiracy theorists.

That was the situation when America was attacked by al Qaeda terrorists on 9/11, and a month later the anthrax attacks started making headlines.

Suspicions were seemingly confirmed when it was soon learned that an American strain - the Ames strain - had been used in the attacks, and that it was a strain primarily used by the United States Army at their labs at Ft. Detrick in Maryland. Fort Detrick labs had been front and center during the 1940's and 1950's when bioweapons *were* being developed by the U.S.

"A Rogue CIA Agent"

Shortly after it was learned that the Ames strain had been used in the anthrax attacks and that the primary source for the Ames strain appeared to be Ft. Detrick, conspiracy theorists began discussing via emails which USAMRIID employee or former USAMRIID employee would *most likely* have been responsible for the attacks.

The name Steven Jay Hatfill came up, possibly from an angry co-worker at Hatfill's current place of employment, Science Applications International Corporation (SAIC), where Hatfill and the co-worker had clashed over issues. Hatfill had left USAMRIID to go to work at SAIC in January of 1999.

A year earlier, Hatfill had cooperated with a reporter for *Insight* magazine, and in the magazine's January 26, 1998 issue Hatfill was featured in a brief article titled *Cooking Up The Plague At Home*, which included a photo of him demonstrating how "a determined terrorist could cook up a batch of plague in his or her own kitchen using common household ingredients and protective equipment from the supermarket." The recipe had been published by Louis Pasteur in the late 1800's, but in Hatfill's demonstration, he left out the key ingredient: plague bacteria.

141

That article seemed to anger some of Rosenberg's growing group of theorists (which apparently never numbered more than five) because they felt it was irresponsible. Others saw it as an indicator that Hatfill sided with the Bush Administration's implication that treaties were a waste of time, since treaties couldn't stop terrorists who operated outside of any government's control.

Hatfill was also known to have Right Wing political beliefs, which made him suspicious to Left Wingers like Rosenberg. Dr. Hatfill, who was an MD, had gotten his medical training at the Godfrey Huggins Medical School in Rhodesia in the late 1970's,[5] around the time of a major anthrax outbreak there which killed hundreds and sickened thousands. Hatfill claimed to have worked with the Rhodesian army and a group called "the Selous Scouts" during the time of the anthrax outbreak. The Scouts were an all-white elite army unit that specialized in tracking and killing enemy units in remote areas, and there was talk that they may have somehow been responsible for the anthrax outbreak, since it mostly affected Rhodesia's native population.

There was more talk, too. Steven Hatfill was a friend of a retired and leading figure in America's old bioweapons programs, William C. Patrick III. The theory was that Hatfill could have learned bioweapons manufacturing secrets from Patrick.

Furthermore, because of all the hoax anthrax letters which had been in the news for years, shortly after going to work for SAIC, Hatfill and SAIC vice president Joseph Soukup had commissioned Patrick to write a report on the threat and possible effects of a terrorist actually sending live anthrax spores through the postal system.[6]

After the anthrax mailings of 2001, conspiracy theorists saw the 28-page report as a "blueprint" for the anthrax attacks. Rosenberg claimed that the report was commissioned "under a CIA contract to SAIC," but it had been commissioned internally and had nothing to do with the CIA.

So, there were many reasons for Rosenberg and her group to choose Dr. Steven Hatfill as their prime suspect, but they had no true evidence of any kind. It was all just rumor and innuendo. But, rumor and innuendo are all that conspiracy theorists need.

Rosenberg's comments indicate that she and others informed the FBI of their suspicions in late October of 2001. And they waited for the FBI to do something.

The FBI checked out Dr. Hatfill and found no foundation for the suspicions. Hatfill wasn't even a microbiologist. He'd been another USAMRIID virologist, working with viruses, not bacteria. He didn't have the shots that would have been necessary to protect him from anthrax. He even had a reasonably good alibi for one of the mailings, when he was attending a wedding and sleeping off a night of drinking afterward. Plus, at SAIC he had no known access to the types of equipment needed, nor the privacy needed to have created the powders. And, Hatfill had left USAMRIID 2 years before the attacks.

The conspiracy theorists then suggested that Hatfill may have made the anthrax at a CIA "safe house" located in the Maryland mountains not far from Ft. Detrick. The FBI checked the specified location and found that it was an elegant and expensive condominium owned by a friend of Hatfill's, and Hatfill had only visited the location a few times to attend parties.[7]

The tip that Hatfill was taking Cipro to prevent infection from anthrax also turned out to be false. He was taking Cipro in an attempt to rid himself of a lingering sinus infection.

The fact that the tips from the conspiracy theorists hadn't resulted in Hatfill being arrested was clear evidence that the FBI wasn't seeing what the conspiracy theorists were seeing. Perhaps, the FBI hadn't taken them seriously, and had done nothing. Or the FBI was helping the Bush Administration to cover up the secret and illegal bioweapons program that the conspiracy theorists were certain the U.S. government was running at Ft. Detrick. Whatever the explanation for the FBI's lack of action, it only made Rosenberg and her group more determined. If the FBI wouldn't listen, there were other people who *would* listen.

The Biological Weapons Convention

Perhaps it was just a coincidence, but Dr. Hatfill attended a seminar at the Porton Down laboratories in England in November of 2001, and it was while he was there that someone mailed a hoax anthrax letter from London to Senator Daschle that appeared to be written in a style very similar to the actual anthrax letter received in October.[8]

When the conspiracy theorists learned of the letter, they were even more certain that Hatfill was the culprit. But, to the FBI and others it was highly suspicious that Barbara Hatch Rosenberg had gone to Europe at that time to attend the 4-week long Biological and Toxic Weapons Convention in Geneva, Switzerland. So, there were suspicions that one of her cronies could have mailed the letter in an attempt to help *frame* Dr. Hatfill.[9]

It was during the BTWC that Dr. Rosenberg went public with her theories.

Representatives from nongovernmental organizations were supposed to sit quietly in the gallery as the convention delegates debated how to strengthen the Biological and Toxin Weapons Convention protocols. But the rules didn't stop Dr. Rosenberg from taking a seat on the main floor.

Members of the U.S. delegation to the convention forced her to move back to the gallery.

According to *Science* magazine, Rosenberg's supporters and detractors already knew she was a hard-nosed and vocal activist who's unmovable once she takes a stand. "Barbara obviously makes no bones about her views," says Stephen Morse, an epidemiologist at Columbia University in New York City and a longtime friend. A government scientist who's battled Rosenberg for years puts a sharper edge on his description of her: "What she brings [to discussions] is an attitude." [10]

U.S. Undersecretary of State for Arms Control, John Bolton, also brought an "attitude" to the convention. At a formal session, Bolton shocked the assembled delegates by accusing a number of identified states of "flatly violating" the BWC. Then, in a press conference on November 19, he elaborated that "simply putting one convention on top of another is not going to solve the problem that the rogue states that we are talking about are prepared to violate the underlined prohibitions in the BWC."

He went on, "The draft protocol that was under negotiation for the past several years is dead in our view. Dead, and it is not going to be resurrected. It has proven to be a blind alley."

Meanwhile, Dr. Rosenberg was talking with anyone who would listen, telling them that "[The U.S. was] accusing everyone else of having bioweapons, when the attack was coming from our program. ... I felt that it was necessary to point out."

She felt that the FBI had a suspect (who she and others had pointed out to them) but was reluctant to pursue that individual because "the suspect knows too much and must be controlled forever from the moment of arrest." She didn't claim there was any conspiracy but said, "I can only speculate as to why" the FBI hadn't been more aggressive.

In the end, it was Barbara Hatch Rosenberg who made all the headlines with her speech to the convention on November 21, which was also released via emails and Internet web sites at the same time. One American delegate to the convention reportedly walked out while Rosenberg was speaking.

"I'm a New Yorker," she told the convention. "My city has just been attacked, first by foreign terrorists, then by an American using a weaponized biological agent - anthrax, that was derived, almost certainly, from a US defense laboratory." And she planted the idea that a covert CIA program could have been behind the attacks:

> Douglas MacEachin, former Deputy Director of the CIA and current CIA consultant, testified last week in Congress that: The principal concern today, the thing (he said) that I would be most worried about if I were back at the CIA, would be a covert state program using a terrorism mechanism to deliver it. The state could get the terrorist group to make the delivery and then deny any connection with it. ... That, I believe, is the threat -- the next one that is going to hit us.[11]

That wasn't the end of it. It was just the beginning. On December 3, 2001, after Dr. Rosenberg had returned to the United States, she published a paper on the Federation of American Scientists' web site titled *A Compilation of Evidence and Comments on the Source of the Mailed Anthrax*. Some of her comments:

A Crime Unlike Any Other

The perpetrator is an American microbiologist who has access to recently-weaponized anthrax or to the expertise and materials for making it, in a US government or contractor lab. He does not live in or near Trenton, which is a stop on the Amtrak line that runs along the East coast. If he is smart enough to handle anthrax he is smart enough not to mail it from his home town. ...

The anthrax in the letters was made and weaponized in a US government or contractor lab. It may have been made recently rather than in the US BW program before Nixon terminated the program in 1969. ...

The recent anthrax attack was a minor one but nonetheless we now see that it was perpetrated with the unwitting assistance of a sophisticated government program. It is reassuring to know that it was not perpetrated by a lone terrorist without such support. However it is not reassuring to know that a secret US program was the source of that support.

She then continued her campaign to point the finger at Dr. Hatfill and the Bush Administration with lectures and talks with members of the media to advance her theories about who was responsible for the anthrax attacks of 2001. Eventually, even politicians would be listening to her and nodding their heads in agreement.

Chapter 20

Discoveries

Bruce Ivins was more than willing to jump on a conspiracy theory bandwagon, as long as the theory pointed at the USDA or Iowa State University and away from USAMRIID.

Three days after reading the article in the November 25 issue of *The Washington Post* about how it was beginning to appear that the Ames strain was not such a common strain after all, and that the strain seemed to come primarily from USAMRIID, Ivins wrote an email to a long list of recipients:

> In view of recent comments by [redacted - probably Martin Hugh-Jones] and [redacted - probably Paul Keim] to the press about the supposed ease of getting anthrax strains (especially the Ames strain) from [redacted] and USAMRIID, perhaps it should be pointed out to people that neither of the above individuals got the strain from us. The Ames strain was sent to Porton Down in the mid 1980s. From there, the Brits sent the strain to [redacted] who, in turn sent it to [redacted]. Also, it should be pointed out that this is not a "Fort Detrick strain." It was a strain from the USDA National Veterinary Service Laboratory in Ames, Iowa. Neither they, nor Iowa State University (which conveniently autoclaved all of its B. anthracis strains in October) are able (or willing) to provide a record of all the individuals and institutions that received the Ames strain from them. We know EXACTLY who received the Ames strain (and other B. anthracis strains) from us:

A Crime Unlike Any Other

1) Porton Down, mid 1980s
2) 1992, Dugway Proving Ground
3) 1998, DRES (Canada)
4) 2001, Battelle (Columbus, Ohio)
5) 2001, U. of New Mexico Health Science Center
(Albequerque)

The assertion that we basically just provided that strain and other strains willy-nilly to whoever asked for them is incorrect.

Perhaps it should also be pointed out that the biosecurity here at USAMRIID (keycard access to specific biocontainment suiets [sic] by specific individuals) has historically been very stringent. In contrast, the biosecurity at the labs of [redacted] and [redacted] have only recenly been tightened.[1]

So, from Bruce Ivins' perspective, Iowa State had "conveniently" destroyed all of their anthrax samples, and neither they nor the USDA in Ames were able or "willing" to provide lists of the labs to which they'd sent the Ames strain. And, that was why everyone was focusing on USAMRIID - the last place in the world where Ivins had expected or planned for the investigation to focus.

Ivins was also starting to point to his fellow workers at USAMRIID as being better potential suspects than he. Ever since his first formal interview with the FBI on November 19, 2001, Ivins had been pointing at former colleague Joseph Fairchaus as being a good potential suspect. Fairchaus had all the skills, he could have taken a sample of Ames with him when he left USAMRIID, and he currently lived near Trenton, NJ, the area in which the anthrax letters had been mailed.

Paul Keim & Jacques Ravel

Scientists were trying to determine if there was any scientific way - utilizing DNA - to tell one Ames sample from another. Paul Keim at Northern Arizona University painstakingly extracted the DNA from the sample of Ames USAMRIID had obtained in 1981.

Then, he did the same with a sample taken from the spinal fluid of the first victim of the anthrax attacks, Bob Stevens. The two samples were sent to microbiologist Jacques Ravel, Ph.D., at The Institute for Genomic Research (TIGR). Ravel was the head of a group that was mapping out the sequence of the individual building blocks in a DNA sample for comparison to other samples

They thought it would be a slam dunk. A sample from a dead cow found in Iowa in 1981 compared to a sample taken from the first known human victim of an anthrax attack in 2001, twenty years later? To the scientists, it seemed like there would almost *have* to be differences in the DNA.

But, there were *no detectable differences.* The two samples were identical twins. There was no known way to tell one sample from the other.[2]

Everyone was very disappointed. The hope of using DNA extracted from the attack spores to track down the anthrax mailer appeared to be a dead end.

Terry Abshire Notices Something

Terry Abshire had worked for John Ezzell for about 20 years, although she generally worked in Building 1412 while Ezzell worked in Building 1425. After the anthrax attacks, Abshire and Ezzell had assisted the FBI in developing the protocols for making certain that incoming evidence was properly handled and recorded. Abshire had been spending day after day testing powders from hoax letters and from the anthrax letters, a very tedious process.

Sometime in late November - possibly as a result of near exhaustion - she forgot to clear out some plates that had been left in the incubator overnight. Then, when she needed to use the incubator again the following day, she noticed the plates she'd forgotten about. The colonies on the plates had been allowed to grow for at least double the normal standard time.

When she looked at the plates, the colonies were larger than normal, as would be expected since the colonies had been allowed to grow longer than normal. But, she also noticed that some of the colonies were different in appearance. Ames Anthrax colonies typically looked like little rounded mounds of ground glass. The vast bulk of the colonies on the plates did indeed look like those little ground glass mounds, but that made the other colonies stand out. A few colonies were less regular in shape, some were a slightly different color, a yellowish gray, and others looked like little donuts with the centers showing less growth than the edges, just the opposite of normal colonies. And, most interesting of all, the plates she'd left in the incubator for a day longer than normal were plates that had been inoculated with spores taken from the Daschle letter.[3]

She called her boss and asked him to come take a look. John Ezzell rushed over from Building 1425, changed into BSL-3 scrubs and joined Abshire in her lab. Initially, he was skeptical. There could be some simple explanation for the oddly shaped and colored colonies, a simple explanation that just didn't come instantly to mind. But, the strange colonies *might* also be significant.

He asked Abshire to repeat the process using more spores from the Daschle letter, and to also repeat the process using spores from the *New York Post* letter so they could compare results. And, to do the same thing with some other Ames samples from their collection, specifically the frozen bacteria from the original 1981 sample USAMRIID had supposedly received from the USDA.

Two days later, they had the results. When they looked at the plates inoculated with Daschle spores, the odd shaped colonies were there again. About three or four spores in a hundred seemed to create the odd colonies, just as with the first sample. And, even more significantly, the plates inoculated with spores from the *New York Post* letter showed the same thing. The plates inoculated with frozen bacteria from the 1981 sample didn't have the odd colonies, but another sample from USAMRIID stocks did.

That certainly seemed to indicate that, although the attack powders were very different in their levels of purification, they originated from the same source.

John Ezzell shared the finding with the FBI microbiologists working with them in Building 1412, Darin Steele and Scott Stanley. The odd colonies were undoubtedly all Ames anthrax colonies, not contaminants nor other strains, so they could be morphological variants, mutations slightly different from the basic Ames strain.

It was clearly possible that there might be a detectable DNA difference. If so, there could be some way to compare the letter spores to potential sources at USAMRIID and at other labs that possessed samples of the Ames strain. The FBI agents needed to discuss the finding with headquarters. Meanwhile, Abshire took photographs of the plates for future reference.

The Leahy Letter

On December 5, after experts spent two weeks devising a plan for opening the Leahy envelope that would make certain any evidence involving fibers, fingerprints, human DNA would be reliably contained, the envelope was finally taken out of storage, opened and the contents inspected. The envelope contained 0.871 grams of very fine powdered anthrax spores.[4]

No one had any idea how many spores might have escaped the sealed envelope during its passage from Trenton to the State Department mail facility and then back to the Brentwood mail center in Washington. There could have been a gram or more of powder in the letter when it was dropped in the mailbox. But, the fine powder was estimated to contain 2.1 trillion spores per gram, which meant the letter still contained about 1 trillion, 829 billion spores, enough to kill vast numbers of people if the method of delivery had been different.

The degree of sophistication needed to produce the spores was still a matter of heated debate. U.S. Air Force Col. (Ret.) Randall Larsen, an instructor and specialist on homeland security at the National War College, argued that the powder would require expertise in engineering, microbiology and aerosol physics. "I do not believe that a single individual -- I don't care how smart he is, Ted Kaczynski or whatever -- can make a sophisticated biological weapon," Larsen said. "It takes a team of people." He hadn't examined the spores, of course. He was only commenting on what he read in the newspapers.[5]

Other experts were telling the media that the culprit could have made the anthrax powders alone in his basement with no more than $2,500 worth of equipment.[6] The powder in the envelopes could have been made by any microbiology graduate student with lab experience. Purifying other kinds of *Bacillus* spores was almost a requirement for graduation.[7]

A Crime Unlike Any Other

The FBI was repeatedly stating that the person who sent the anthrax letters was almost certainly an American scientist, not some Muslim terrorist.

And Ivins was alternately telling people in public that no one at USAMRIID had the capability to make powdered anthrax, while telling the FBI in private that numerous people at USAMRIID could easily have done it.

A *TIME*/CNN poll of 1,037 Americans found that 63% of Americans thought it very likely that bin Laden was responsible for the anthrax attacks, 40% thought it very likely that Saddam Hussein was to blame, and only 16% picked "U.S. citizens not associated with foreign terrorists" as the likely suspect.[8]

Microbial Forensics

FBI scientists were busy consulting with other scientists regarding what Terry Abshire had found and what it might mean. Tests were underway to see what detectable DNA differences there might be between "normal" Ames anthrax bacteria in "normal" colonies and the Ames anthrax bacteria that had formed the unusual or "morph" colonies. It had already been determined from observation that spores from a morph colony would produce more morph colonies, not normal colonies, and not some combination of normal and morph colonies. So, there was almost certainly a fixed, repeating DNA difference involved.

Another issue was also clear: there was no existing science for doing what they needed to do in order to develop *evidence* that would be useable in court. A new science had to be developed, tentatively named *Microbial Forensics*, which would have to be formalized, verified and scientifically accepted. That meant the developmental work that needed to be done couldn't just be about what they'd found in a few samples, it had to be about what those samples represented in the entire universe of Ames anthrax samples.

It was like a fingerprint. How often did identical fingerprints occur? How unique were the odd shaped morphs? How unique were the odd colored morphs? Did they appear together? What caused the morphs to appear, and how frequently would they appear?

Discoveries

No one had any answers. Until they did, the FBI had nothing that could be used in court. In a 1993 decision, *Daubert vs. Merrell Dow Pharmaceuticals*, the Supreme Court had demanded that forensic testimony not simply meet the existing standard of "general acceptance" in its field, but also address some of the hallmarks of scientific inquiry -- testing, peer review and rates of error. The Court created the strict "Daubert standard," which held that trial judges "must ensure that any and all scientific testimony or evidence admitted is not only relevant, but reliable."

Microbial forensics currently met no standard at all.

Probably as a result of rumors, Bruce Ivins became aware that some kinds of DNA studies were underway to determine if that avenue might identify the anthrax mailer. It appeared that, if the Ames strain was really a rare strain and not the common strain that everyone had believed, the possibility of some kind of DNA breakthrough was a definite possibility, even if it was widely known that *Bacillus anthracis* was a highly stable bacterium, and mutations occurred only about once per billion generations, on average.[9]

On December 16, 2001, Ivins sent out an email mentioning "ongoing genetic studies" and evidently fishing for new information about what may have been learned:

> I've heard about the ongoing genetic studies to identify the source of the Ames strain. I have "Dugway Ames" spores that were made by Dugway and sent to us in 1997 for challenge studies. (We have a hard-copy record of them, when we got them, how much of them has been used (and when). All of the spores are accounted for.) I also have frozen down the "USAMRIID Ames" seed stock from the early 1980s. If needed for genetic analysis or sequencing by whomever, my lab could provide both "Dugway Ames" strain material as well as "USAMRIID Ames" strain material.[10]

A few days after Ivins sent the above email, it was learned that the packaging for the original shipment of Ames supposedly from the USDA had been found, along with a letter that had been enclosed.[11]

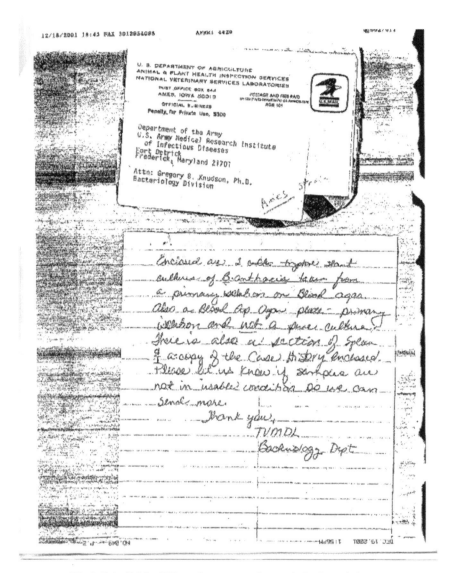

Exhibit #16 - The Ames package label and letter

At first glance, the address label seemed to confirm that the strain came from the USDA. Their prepaid label had been used on the package. There was no other return address.

And, while the enclosed letter was less clear about who had sent the samples, the letter didn't provide any specific individual's name, nor did it clearly identify which division or office at the USDA in Ames had sent the package to Gregory E. Knudson at USAMRIID who was known to have been the first person to use the Ames strain.

The only "signature" on the letter was "TVMDL Bacteriology Dept."

Was that some kind of an in-house acronym or misspelling for the USDA's National Veterinary Services Laboratories (NSVL)?

The FBI also began mentioning to scientists at USAMRIID that they would like to have everyone working on evidence related to the anthrax investigation take a lie detector test. That would include Bruce Ivins, even though his handling of the evidence had been relatively minor.

Ivins quickly decided it was time to attempt to destroy any possible evidence that might connect him to the attack spores.

The December Cleanup

In late December, Ivins spent an evening using bleach to decontaminate areas in his office and laboratory. He specifically cleaned the desk of Kristie Friend, who had replaced Mara Linscott as Ivins' lab technician. Ivins would later claim that he cleaned her desk because she had expressed concern over the way the Daschle letter had been handled and that people may not have removed their gloves after handing the letter. Plus, Friend's desk seemed to be covered with dust, which might hide the stray spores.[12]

Later, Ivins would tell the FBI and USAMRIID officials that he had also tested about 20 areas on Friend's desk for anthrax spores, including her telephone and computer. He plated the swabs on Tryptic Soy Agar (TSA), let them set in an incubator overnight, and the next day, he found that approximately half the plates showed indications of *Bacillus* colonies consistent with anthrax contamination.

Without verifying that the growths were truly anthrax colonies, Ivins autoclaved all of the plates and swab materials, and he placed Friend's keyboard and mouse pad in the B-3 pass box to decontaminate them with ultra-violet light.

Two days after the cleaning, he mentioned to his supervisor Patricia Worsham what he'd done and what he had found. Ivins explained that it was probably best to not mention it to lab officials or other scientists, since they were busy handing samples for the FBI's investigation of the anthrax attacks. He didn't want to "Cry Wolf!" and alarm anyone unnecessarily. After all, he'd cleaned up the area and it no longer presented any danger.

At the time, no one found it suspicious that Ivins claimed to have done all this cleaning and testing because of concerns expressed by his associate Kristie Friend, yet he never told her that he'd thoroughly cleaned her desk and other areas, and that there was no longer any need for her to be concerned.[13]

Chapter 21

January 2002

In his column in the Editorial/Op-Ed page of the January 4, 2002 issue of *The New York Times*, Nicholas D. Kristof provided America and the world with a *Profile of a Killer* as evidently described to him by Barbara Hatch Rosenberg. Kristof wrote:

> I think I know who sent out the anthrax last fall.
>
> He is an American insider, a man working in the military bio-weapons field. He's a skilled microbiologist who did not aim to kill anybody or even to disrupt the postal system. Rather, he wanted to sow terror. Like many in the bio-warfare field, he felt that the government was not sufficiently attuned to the risks of anthrax, so he seized upon the opportunity presented by Sept. 11 to get more attention and funding for bio-terror programs like those that have been his career.
>
> How do I know all this? Well, I don't exactly. But talk to the people in the spooky world of bio-terror awhile, sop up the gossip and theories, and as you put the clues together -- as bio-terror experts and F.B.I. officials are now doing -- a hazy picture seems to come into focus. It's not a certainty but an educated guess, circulating among many who know their business.

It was the first in a series of columns Kristof would write describing "educated guesses" and aspects of what he and Rosenberg apparently saw as a lack of will on the part of the FBI to investigate the person who Kristof would soon begin calling "Mr. Z."

Meanwhile, an FBI official in Florida felt that not enough attention had been paid to the fact that 9/11 terrorists had stayed in Florida and that the first anthrax victim lived and died in Florida. The official wrote a two page memo to Tara O'Toole and Thomas V. Inglesby at Johns Hopkins University and asked them to look into a possible case of cutaneous anthrax on the leg of 9/11 hijacker Amed Ibrahim Al Haznawi that had been treated by a Florida physician. The physician, Dr. Christos Tsonas, acknowledged to O'Toole and Inglesby that the infected gash he'd treated *could have been* an anthrax lesion, even though it was in the right place for a gash resulting from bumping into the sharp corner of a suitcase, which was what Al Haznawi had claimed and Tsonas had recorded. The Johns Hopkins' scientists quickly found "experts" and "officials" who agreed that it *could have been* a cutaneous anthrax lesion. And, no one could prove otherwise.[1]

At this same time, conspiracy theorists were focusing on rumors and stories about samples of anthrax that had gone missing from USAMRIID in 1991 or 1992. Also, someone had mailed a letter to the military police in Quantico, VA., claiming that a former USAMRIID scientist named Ayaad Assaad was a "potential terrorist." On October 3, 2001, Assaad had been questioned by the FBI, and they found no reason to suspect him of anything. Then, after the anthrax letters started arriving, the *Hartford Courant* and other newspapers started looking into the lax security procedures at Ft. Detrick. In January, 2002, Assaad was in the news again, in a report he had been racially harassed when he worked at USAMRIID.[2] Some started suspecting Assaad of being the anthrax mailer. Assaad, in turn, was convinced that whoever sent the letter about him was the anthrax killer. At least one newspaper agreed with his theory.

Ivins' Lie Detector Test

In an attempt to make certain that no one working with the evidence at USAMRIID was also involved in the crime, critical USAMRIID personnel - including John Ezzell, Pat Worsham, Terry Abshire, Bruce Ivins and a few others were given lie detector tests in early January. Ivins was extremely agitated and nervous prior to his test. According to John Ezzell, Ivins "was bouncing off the walls."[3] Ezzell and everyone else tried to get him to calm down. Ivins may have taken Valium just before it was time to take the test, since he had an assortment of anxiety-relieving drugs available to him. It appears he'd also researched ways to beat a lie detector.

Whatever the reason, Bruce Ivins passed the test.[4]

Ivins' Opinion

After Ivins passed the lie detector test, making it okay to trust him, Terry Abshire dug out two photographs she'd taken of Ames strain plates in November, and she emailed the photos to Ivins on January 10 to get his opinion. Like so many others, she considered him to be an expert on the all things related to the Ames strain.

Ivins pondered the photos for nearly two weeks trying to figure out what was in them that interested Abshire so much. The first photo showed some odd-shaped colonies, the second showed only normal colonies. On January 22, Ivins sent the FBI an email with the two photographs, to which he'd added his own descriptions of what was in the photos. He also sent a crudely drawn chart describing what the photos represented.[5]

Agents interviewed him in his office the next day.

The mutations evidently meant nothing significant to Ivins, since he believed as nearly every other microbiologist believed at the time: because anthrax mutated so very slowly, it was virtually impossible to tell one batch of anthrax from another.

Ivins explained to the agents that he did not use the process Abshire must have used to create the odd shaped cultures in the first photo. He *never* "passaged" the same culture material over and over by transferring it from plate to plate. The Ames source material he used was "just a slant away from the cow," and when he used that source material, he created only a single culture from it. He seemed to believe that the variations in the photos were contamination or effects resulting from Abshire transferring a culture from plate to plate. Ivins *never* did that, thus, in his view, he would never produce a growth that contained the variations that could be seen in the first photograph he'd received from Terry Abshire.

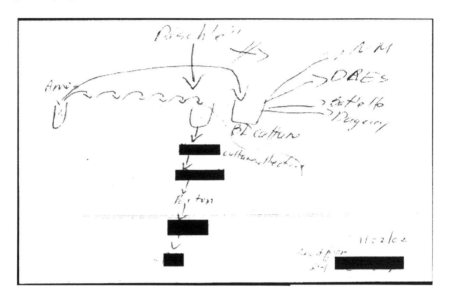

Exhibit #17 - Ivins' drawing describing "passaging"

The FBI agents listened patiently and wrote a report about the meeting. The agents almost certainly knew that Ivins was wrong in some of his beliefs, but, when a supposed "expert" is telling you things that you know to be untrue, FBI agents generally just smile and say, "Thank you."

Ivins had also taken the opportunity to finger John Ezzell and Gregory Knudson as potential suspects. Since the photos showed that Terry Abshire had a sample of the original Ames, that made her boss, Ezzell, a very good suspect. Ivins told the FBI that Ezzell also had all the knowledge and the right type of character to have been responsible for the mailings. The same with Knudson, who had been the first person to use the Ames strain at USAMRIID.[6]

Amanda's Suicide Attempt

Sometime in January, Ivins' adopted daughter Amanda tried to commit suicide by overdosing on Tylenol and painkillers. Diane found her in time, and Amanda was rushed to a hospital for emergency treatment. The high-school senior was then taken to a hospital in Rockville which specialized in treating adolescents. Bruce Ivins visited her every evening. She admitted to attempting suicide and indicated that it had to do with the way she was treated by "mean girls" at school.[7]

The FBI Flyers

On January 23, 2002, the FBI upped the reward for information leading to the arrest and conviction of the anthrax killer. They sent out about a hundred thousand flyers to residents in Central New Jersey and the Philadelphia area offering a "Special Reward up to $2.5 million" to for information. The flyer showed pictures of the four envelopes that had been recovered and stated that the person responsible for the five anthrax deaths "Likely has a scientific background/work history which may include a specific familiarity with anthrax" and he "Has a level of comfort in and around the Trenton, NJ area due to present or prior association."

The evidence the FBI had at the time was still pointing to someone who lived and worked in New Jersey. It didn't seem likely that someone from a distant location would travel *twice* to the Trenton area in New Jersey to mail the letters, although it was certainly possible. Ted Kaczynski, the Unabomber, had lived in Montana and had traveled long distances to mail his packages from Chicago and different cities in California. But, Kaczynski was an *exception*, not the rule.

So, the FBI and Postal investigators were focusing their field investigation on Central New Jersey where there were hundreds of medical, industrial and university labs with equipment capable of making the attack anthrax. They also tested hundreds of copy machines, looking for the one used to make letters.

A Texas Strain

It's not known exactly when federal investigators discovered the true source of the Ames strain, but it was definitely long before the news broke in the media on January 29 that the so-called "Ames strain" actually came from Texas, not from Iowa.

The Washington Post was the first to break the news. According to the *Post*, federal investigators had learned that the sample came from the TVMDL, the Texas Veterinary Medical Diagnostics Laboratory at Texas A&M University in College Station, Texas. TVMDL had sent the sample to USAMRIID in 1981 using a USDA pre-paid mailing label in order to save shipping costs.[8]

Ivins disbelieves

Ivins learned of the news about the true source of the Ames strain early on the morning of January 29. Someone at the Homeland Security office in the White House had emailed someone high in the command structure at USAMRIID, advising that they'd received a "Heads Up" that both the *Washington Post* and *The New York Times* were about to report that the Ames strain came from Texas and had nothing to do with Iowa or any lab in Iowa.[9] The official at USAMRIID was looking for some way to counter or dispute the claim - if it was untrue. If it was true, it would make USAMRIID officials look like fools for falsely telling everyone that the Ames strain came from Iowa.

Ivins had read the *Washington Post's* article by that time and thought it *must* be wrong. He was sending out emails before 7:30 a.m., arguing against what the media was finding and reporting:

Everyone,

We most certainly DID get the "Ames strain" from the USDA, Animal and Plant Health Inspection Services, National Veterinary Services Laboratories, P.O. Box 844, Ames, Iowa 50010. We have a Xerox copy of the original mailing label from them. Also, to our good fortune, we ([Redacted] actually) [Redacted] We can supply you with the actual strain number (put on it by the NVSL labs) if desired. I have tried repeatedly, without success, to talk to [Gregory R. Knudson] about this. He is at AFRRI [Armed Forces Radiobiology Research Institute] and has failed to return my calls. He can be reached at [Redacted].

...

> About the same time that we received the Ames strain, we
> received the "Texas" strain from [Redacted] at Texas A&M.

Ivins was just making assumptions (or stating his hopes and
beliefs) when he claimed to have received samples from both Iowa
and Texas at the same time. Nine minutes later, Ivins sent out
another email:

> Again, we have a copy of the mailing label from the
> USDA. A few days ago I went back to the USAMRIID
> library and USAMRIID Library archives and looked
> through everyone of [Gregory Knudson's] notebooks.
> Unfortunately, he never mentions writing for the strain or
> receiving it in any notebook. The first mention of the
> strain is in September, 1981, when he also says he looks at
> the Sterne, Vollum (probably Vollum 1B), Colorado, Ames
> and Texas strains. Hope this helps. [10]

And a couple hours later, after what was undoubtedly a
frantic search for additional information to support his beliefs, Ivins
sent this:

> I just spoke on the phone with [Gregory Knudson] at
> AFRRI. He is going to FAX me whatever information he
> has on the Ames strain. He told me that the strain was
> definitely sent to him from the NVSL in Ames, Iowa. He
> also said that it is possible that the actual case (dead cow)
> may have been in Texas, and that the strain may have then
> gone from Texas to Ames, Iowa, and then to [Knudson].
> If that is the case, then USAMRIID is third in line as far
> the origin of the "Ames strain," and we have no idea as to
> where the Texas lab or the NVSL in Ames sent the strain.
> I will keep everyone informed on this as soon as I get
> more information from [Knudson]. [11]

However, there was more information coming that would
end all doubt that the source of the Ames strain was in Texas -
except, for Bruce Ivins who must have been stunned to find that

facts upon which he had so thoroughly depended were turning out to be totally *false* beliefs.

Testimony & New Facts

A *New York Times* article published on January 30th provided many more details from FOIA responses - including the names of the veterinarians and scientists involved and explanations of how and why events unfolded the way they did.[12]

The history of the strain began in late 1980 when Gregory Knudson, who then worked at USAMRIID, wrote to Texas A&M's veterinary officials asking for samples of any unusual strains of anthrax that they might come across.

"Unfortunately, I have discarded all my pathogenic cultures," Texas A&M's Howard W. Whitford replied to Knudson in January 1981. But he said warmer weather would probably bring new outbreaks.

And the prediction came true. In May of 1981, Michael L. Vickers, a veterinarian in Falfurrias, Texas, found a sick cow in a herd of 900. "The heifer in excellent flesh was found in the morning unable to rise," Vickers wrote in his case report. "By noon she was dead." As part of established protocols, Vickers sent specimens to the Texas Veterinary Medical Diagnostics Laboratory at Texas A&M.

And a scientist at the TVMDL, remembering the request from Knudson, sent part of the iced sample to USAMRIID using a prepaid USDA label which caused all the confusion. The TVMDL frequently sent shipments to the USDA using pre-labeled boxes with prepaid postage. Since it would save shipping costs, and USAMRIID was another government agency, TVMDL scientists simply used one of those boxes and slapped another label over the address for the shipment they sent to Greg Knudson at USAMRIID.

The only signature on the letter that was sent along with the sample from Texas was "TVMDL," and Knudson evidently assumed that TVMDL was a division of the US Department of Agriculture in Ames, Iowa. Thus, the strain became forever known as "the Ames strain."

And, of course, the Ames strain never had anything to do with any bioweapons programs from the 1950's, regardless of what the "experts" at various agencies in Iowa believed when they spoke to the media back in October.

Ivins' reaction was another example of how he tried to make the facts fit his beliefs or his wishes. The FBI would use it as an example of "Consciousness of Guilt." If Bruce Ivins had been innocent of the crimes, it shouldn't have mattered one bit to him whether the Ames strain came from Iowa or Texas or Afghanistan, nor whether it was a rare strain or a common strain. But, because the facts were now saying that the common, untraceable strain he thought he had used in the anthrax letters was actually a *rare*, very *traceable* strain used primarily by USAMRIID, he was desperately looking for ways to make the facts fit with what he wanted others to believe.

Looking for Leads

On the 30th of January, the day after the news broke about the true origins of the Ames strain, the FBI sent out emails to 40,000 members of the American Society for Microbiology, looking for tips about who may have sent the anthrax letters.

"It is very likely that one or more of you know this individual," the email said, and it went on to describe traits an FBI profiler thought the mailer might have which people should look for. The FBI email asked for "all relevant information, no matter how insignificant it may seem."

One person to respond was Nancy Haigwood, who named Bruce Ivins as someone who would likely have committed such a crime.[13]

But it was just one name among hundreds - or thousands - since everyone seemed to have a theory. And, Haigwood's message was simply filed away to await a time when some other information might make it worth reading again.

Chapter 22

Rosenberg Advances Her Theory

In early 2002, Barbara Hatch Rosenberg was talking with any reporter who was willing to listen. On January 23rd, the Scripps-Howard News service published an article which included this:

> Barbara Hatch Rosenberg, a professor of molecular biology at the State University of New York and chair of the biological weapons panel at the Federation of American Scientists, says she has shared her ideas on who is the likely culprit with the FBI, and now posts updates regularly on the Internet. "I get a lot of calls _ some with very elaborate theories, although some people do not know the simple facts," she said. She believes the culprit is going to turn out to be a middle-aged American, who is a government insider with a doctoral degree in biology and knowledge of sophisticated U.S. bio-defense programs, which he would need to make the anthrax.

> In order not be made sick from the bacteria, he must have an up-to-date vaccination, and may be employed by a government contractor in the Washington, D.C., area, she said. That's a small enough group that the FBI should be zeroing in on a possible suspect, and she believes the FBI has already interviewed the culprit.

> "Whoever knows this knows an awful lot _ it's going to be very embarrassing information that's going to come out in a trial," she said. [1]

At no time did she actually identify her suspect to any reporter. She'd given the FBI his name, and it was up to the FBI to find the evidence that Rosenberg believed was there to be found.

On February 5th, Rosenberg produced another article for the FAS site, this one titled *Is the FBI Dragging Its Feet*. In the article she accused the FBI of knowing who sent the anthrax letters, but doing nothing about it. The article also tied in a lot of material which appear to have been provided by Professor Donald Wayne Foster, another conspiracy theorist who also believed he had evidence showing Steven Hatfill to be the anthrax mailer.

Foster was a professor of English at Vassar College who had gained some fame in promoting his theories related to the dedication of Shakespeare's sonnets and some other works by Shakespeare. Some articles about his efforts had referred to him as a "forensic linguist," and he gained genuine fame when he helped identify Joe Klein as the anonymous author of the sensational best seller *Primary Colors* in 1996.

Foster's "evidence" in the anthrax case involved analyzing handwriting, the writer's choice of words and phrases, and Hatfill's location at the time of various mailings of hoax letters, which Foster believed must also have been sent by Hatfill.

Rosenberg at the podium

On February 18, 2002, Rosenberg spoke to about 65 students, faculty members and others at the Woodrow Wilson School of Public and International Affairs at Princeton, New Jersey. Among the others in attendance at her speech were reporters from New Jersey newspapers.

The Trenton Times for the 19th reported that Rosenberg claimed that "the Federal Bureau of Investigation has a strong hunch about who mailed the deadly letters," but the FBI was "dragging its feet and not pressing charges because the suspect had knowledge of secret activities that the government would not like to see disclosed."

She told her audience that the government has known about the suspect since October, and had interrogated him more than once, but they still weren't doing anything about arresting him.

A Crime Unlike Any Other

"We know that the FBI is looking at this person, and it's likely that he participated in the past in secret activities that the government would not like to see disclosed," Rosenberg said. "And this raises the question of whether the FBI may be dragging its feet somewhat and may not be so anxious to bring to public light the person who did this.[2]

A reporter from *The Daily Princetonian* also wrote about Rosenberg's speech:

But according to Rosenberg, the government may not want to prosecute this person because he is a government insider. Taking this insider to court might require making aspects of America's secret bioweapons program public.[3]

Rosenberg told her audience that the weaponization process used by the anthrax mailer was more advanced than anything known to Russian or Iraqi bioweapons scientists. It was a process that would only be known to someone who had worked for a current U.S. bioweapons program.

The British newspaper *The Guardian* headlined that a *"US scientist" is suspect in anthrax investigation*, but claimed the FBI was dragging its heels because the unidentified suspect was familiar with "state-sponsored" bioweapons research.[4]

FBI Denials

On the 20th, the *Trenton Times* printed another article on the same subject, this one titled *FBI says no prime anthrax suspect*. Several FBI sources had told the *Times* that Rosenberg was "flat wrong." [5] Sandra Carroll, an FBI spokesperson based in Newark, said, "Ms. Rosenberg has made these comments before. She, and I'm sure many others, may have their ideas or opinions about the investigation." Congressman Chris Smith of New Jersey had also questioned the FBI about Rosenberg's claims, and the FBI "was pretty upset at the accusation that the FBI would be hiding a suspect."

Rosenberg Advances Her Theory

The New York Times got into the act a week later, on February 26, when an article by Judith Miller and William J. Broad declared *U.S. Says Short List of 'Suspects' Is Being Checked in Anthrax Case.* According to *The New York Times*, the FBI had identified a "short list" of 18 to 20 people who had the means, opportunity and possible motive to have sent the anthrax letters. The list had been compiled mostly from tips given to the FBI by scientists, plus an analysis by investigators of which people had the necessary skills to make the anthrax powders.

White House press secretary Ari Fleisher had also said that the FBI had several "suspects" in the case, but the FBI disagreed. The FBI was still sorting through the clues, and "It would be inaccurate to say that these people are suspects in the classic sense." The so-called "short list" had been whittled down in recent weeks from a larger group of 35 to 40 researchers and technicians with the necessary expertise.

On the 21st of February, the *Trenton Times* contained an article headlined *Anthrax expert stands by her claim.* Rosenberg said she had been besieged by phone calls after her speech on the 18th. She called upon the public and the FBI to "keep up the pressure on the FBI," because some of her sources were saying that the FBI "might attempt to deal with the suspect discreetly, out of the glare of public scrutiny." Rosenberg and her associates knew that the FBI had interviewed one particular person more than once, and that person was clearly a "main suspect" in the case.

Congressman Chris Smith was making a formal request to FBI Director Robert Mueller for a detailed briefing on the progress of the investigation. And, he was going to ask for a detailed response from the FBI to Rosenberg's claims.

The world was learning just how much noise a 70-something woman with no direct knowledge of the investigation or the attack anthrax could make if she was fired up over a cause, if she had a few supporters, and if she and her followers knew how to get the media and politicians fired up as well.

Chapter 23

Ivins & the FBIR

There were very heated discussions at USAMRIID after it became certain that the source of the Ames strain was in Texas, not at the USDA as USAMRIID employees had been claiming for twenty years. And Texas A&M had sent the so-called "Ames strain" to only one place - USAMRIID.

A strain that had once been thought to be very common was now known to be very rare, and USAMRIID had distributed "Ames strain" samples to only a few other labs. An area of investigation that once seemed hopeless now seemed straightforward and critical.

TIGR & the FBIR

Patricia Worsham was asked to help repeat and clarify what Terry Abshire had noticed. Worsham took samples of spores from the *Post*, Daschle and Leahy letters and inoculated hundreds of plates. After two days of incubation, every one of the plates seemed to show a small number of mutations. Then she took spores from the original 1981 slant and inoculated hundreds of additional plates, each of which had to be carefully examined for the mutations. *None* showed the morphs. Not a one.[1]

The premise had been verified. There were mutations in the attack powders that weren't in the original 1981 sample of the Ames strain. Therefore, it seemed very possible that the attack spores could be traced to a lab stock somewhere within the known-universe of

Ames samples, a universe which currently seemed to include less than two dozen labs around the world.

Worsham was regularly providing her test results to FBI microbiologist Scott Stanley who was at USAMRIID almost daily. When Worham's work began to show consistent results, Stanley discussed the findings with Jacques Ravel at The Institute of Genomic Research, a non-profit research facility in Rockville, MD. In 1995, TIGR had been the first group to sequence the genome of a free-living organism, the bacterium *Haemophilus influenzae*. Stanley explained that merely looking at plates wouldn't provide the kind of scientific proof needed in court. The question was: Could TIGR genetically sequence the *Bacillus anthracis* morphological variants that Worsham and Abshire had found? Judges and juries understood DNA, and they'd understand DNA evidence that showed the source of the anthrax powders.

Ravel advised Stanley that TIGR was fully prepared to sequence the DNA of the morphs, the DNA of the original Ames sample and the DNA of any other samples the FBI would send them.

After discussion with other scientists, FBI scientists agreed that it was time to start building an FBI repository (FBIR) of samples taken from every known flask, vial, test tube, plate or beaker containing the Ames strain in every lab known to possess the strain.[2]

FBIR sample 053-070

Ivins still could not believe that he could have been so wrong about the Ames strain, and he still felt the FBI didn't know what they were doing in trying to trace anthrax spores via their DNA. In early February, 2002, Terry Abshire asked Ivins for a sample of the "Dugway spores" to use as the "gold standard" in future DNA tests. Ivins couldn't see how anything could be traced to him, since he hadn't actually used material from flask RMR-1029 in the letters, he'd used spores grown on agar plates. So, he did as requested and supplied a sample from flask RMR-1029 to Abshire.[3]

Without realizing it, Abshire's plan was to compare all Ames samples to a standard that was the actual source for the attack spores. But, before she could begin her work, the FBI stopped her and instructed her to wait for an official procedure to be developed.

A Crime Unlike Any Other

Abshire set aside the sample Ivins had given her and simply forgot about it. Later, it would be found again by the FBI and given the repository number FBIR 053-070.

On February 7, someone sent an email to Bruce Ivins asking a technical question. Ivins responded with an email that clearly indicated that he'd been warned to stop disputing the findings about the source and rarity of the Ames strain. The email began with:

> I'll be happy to give you my personal opinion, but it can't be posted because "we speak with one voice" here, and I am not that voice.

And Ivins signed the email:

> Bruce (We don't make anthrax spore powder at USAMRIID) Ivins[4]

Ivins had made a *huge* error in believing that the Ames strain could not be traced because it was such a common strain used by countless labs all over the world. But, he still didn't understand all the implications of the mistake he'd made. And, as February progressed, he began to see indications that he'd made another major error in believing that no one could ever distinguish between two different samples of the same strain.

On the same day as the above email, the *Wall Street Journal* published an article which stated that "scientists believe careful analysis will reveal slight genetic differences between the specific Ames variant used in the terror attacks and the variants kept by different laboratories around the world. Scientists could then create a kind of family tree showing which labs hold strains that are most closely related to the one used in the terror attacks."

The article also said that while the scientific investigation was continuing with the goal of determining how far science could go in identifying an exact source for the attack anthrax, the FBI was also about to begin questioning every scientist with access to the Ames strain, including lie detector tests, handwriting tests, and checks into personal backgrounds.[5]

Within USAMRIID, it was well-known that Pat Worsham was assisting the FBI in figuring out how to use DNA techniques to locate the source of the attack anthrax powders. And, it was about this time that Pat Worsham found a note stuck to her office door with the words "FBI RAT" on it.[6]

Ivins plan to have Muslim extremists blamed for the attacks seemed no longer even open to discussion by "experts" on the Internet and in the media. The focus was now mostly on American microbiologists who had access to the Ames strain and who were also capable of making the powders in the envelopes.

Generations

Somewhere around this time, Ivins learned of another very serious incorrect belief he'd held for decades. His "single colony pick" method of selecting bacteria to grow new cultures didn't have any real affect on whether or not mutations would form. He believed that if he scooped up a tiny sample of bacteria from a "normal" colony grown from a single spore, the new growth from that culture would be virtually free from morphological variants because mutations only occur about once in a billion generations.

The first problem with his belief was that he didn't seem to realize that "one mutation in a billion generations" could apply to the *very first* division of bacterial cells, which, in theory, could mean that *half* the growth would be genetic deviations. Or the mutation could occur during any division between the 1st and the 1 billionth.

The second misunderstanding he may have had was thinking that bacterial generations were somehow counted the same way as human generations, where a couple (1st generation) has one or more children (2nd generation) which can each have one or more children (3rd generation), etc. When figuring the time it takes to produce ten human generations, an average of 20 years per generation is typically used, so it would take 200 years to produce 10 human generations. If counted that way, it would 20 minutes to produce a new "generation" of *Bacillus anthacis* bacteria, and it would take well over a thousand years to produce a billion generations.

A Crime Unlike Any Other

But, *B anthracis* generations cannot be counted that way. First of all, *B anthracis* bacteria are asexual, which means each bacterium is capable of reproducing all by itself. No sex is necessary. And the number of "children" doesn't vary the way it does with humans. A bacterium absorbs nutrients and grows to nearly twice its original size, then it divides in two equal parts. The "mother" produces *two daughters, either or both of which could be mutations.* Totally unlike human generations, neither of the two daughters can be referred to as the "mother," because the original "mother" may not have had the mutations which appeared in one or both of the daughters. So, for generation counting purposes, the "mother" numerically and biologically *ceased to exist.* Thus, with *Bacillus anthracis* bacteria, one cell division is the same as one generation, except for the fact that the very first division produced two generations.

Since it takes about 20 minutes for an anthrax bacterium to grow and divide, you can theoretically have a million generations in roughly 7 hours, and a billion generations in just over 10 hours. [7]

Thus, there could be mutations in virtually any culture allowed to grow overnight. But, another very critical fact about mutations is that they don't all reproduce at the same rate as the original "mother." And, many might be incapable of reproducing at all or may die almost immediately because the mutation prevented the absorption of nutrients.

Ivins may have believed that "passaging" affected the number of "generations" and increased the chance of mutations. In reality, mutation creation appears to be purely a matter of statistics, and statistically you get a mutation about once per billion divisions regardless of whether the divisions occurred in one flask or were passaged many times onto many plates.

While Bruce Ivins tried to appear be his normal self, he was well aware that the FBI was preparing to put together a repository of Ames samples with the hope that they would be able to use genetics and other sciences to find the anthrax mailer.

The FBI was still consulting with microbiologists on how to make certain that there would be no chance of contamination or invalidation of any collected samples. A list of requirements for the creation of each sample was assembled and would be sent out along with the subpoenas. Every sample of Ames sent out by USAMRIID during the past twenty years was being tracked down by investigators, and if the receiving lab sent samples to a third lab, subpoenas would go to that lab, too - and to any other lab if further distribution had taken place.

Eventually, they would determine that 15 laboratories in the United States had received samples of the Ames strain, plus three labs outside of the United States, one each in Canada, Sweden and the United Kingdom. Eighteen labs was a far cry from the "countless" labs that everyone a few months earlier believed had the Ames strain.[8]

Sandia & Silicon

Meanwhile, the FBI was also checking another angle. It was becoming very clear that the anthrax mailer wasn't going to be caught by simply interviewing possible suspects. Science was going to have to play a large role in narrowing down those suspects.

To get a better feel for exactly what the spores consisted of chemically, the FBI sent samples of the attack powders as "blind samples" to Sandia National Laboratories in Albuquerque, NM, to see what their world-renowned experts in material composition could determine. Sandia had no capability to handle dangerous bacteria, so the samples had to be radiated and certified harmless before Sandia would accept them.[9]

The first thing Sandia's experts Joseph Michael and Paul Kotula determined was that no chemical compounds had been added to the spores to help them aerosolize more easily. When comparing the spores to examples of weaponized spores, there was no sign of any additives on the outside of the spores, where all such additives would logically be. And, the reality of coating a spore with silica wasn't at all like the sand on an orange image Peter Jahrling and Tom Geisbert had imagined after their visit to AFIP in 2001. It was more like covering the orange with popcorn. There was no way you couldn't see such a coating via an electron microscope.

The primary "weaponization" process used by the United States during the Cold War involved freeze-drying a pellet of billions

Exhibit #18 (top) - A single spore coated with fumed silica

Exhibit #19 - Cluster of spores with fumed silica particles
(Photos courtesy of Dugway Proving Grounds)

of purified spores and then grinding the pellet in a mill to break the pellet down into individual spores. Milling generates static electricity, which would cause the spores to cling to the walls of the mill and to just about anything else they might touch. So, tiny particles of fumed silica were added during milling. The fumed silica particles would cling to the spores due to the static electricity, producing an electrically neutral particle of just the right size to cause inhalation anthrax. The coated spore wouldn't cling to surfaces and would float freely in the air to be inhaled by soldiers on a battlefield. Inside the soldier's lungs, water would neutralize the static electricity, and the spore would be free to do its damage.[10]

Russian Cold War weaponization techniques didn't involve the coating of individual spores but involved the *mixing* of the tiny silica particles with the spores after the static electricity had been removed by chemicals during spray drying.[11] In both cases, the silica particles would be clearly visible. No silica particles were visible in any of the attack powders.

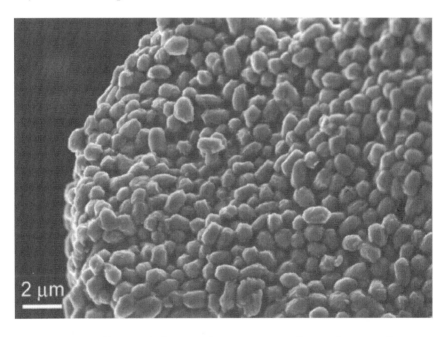

Exhibit #20 - A clump of pure spores from the attacks
(courtesy Sandia National Laboratories)

Also unlike Tom Geisbert's external examination of the spores, the Sandia scientists had ultramicrotomed the tiny spores, slicing them into thin wavers barely a few nanometers thick so they could examine the internal structure of the spores. What they found was that the silicon that had been detected by the EDX machine at AFIP was definitely *not* on the outside of the exosporium, the flexible outer coating on a spore, it was accumulated inside the inner spore coat as the spore was being formed inside the mother germ. That meant it was natural silicon from the agar or blood used in the growth nutrients. (*Bacillus anthracis* bacteria may have evolved to utilize silicon as protection against the UV rays from the sun. Other theories suggest silicon helps harden the spore coat. Either way, it appears that silicon is only utilized by the bacterium if temperatures are lowered and the biological processes are slowed down to the "natural" levels found outdoors or in a room, instead of the warmer temperatures and hastened processes achieved in incubators.)

Furthermore, the purpose of such additives was to keep the spores from sticking together, thus allowing single spores to float easily in the air and to be absorbed deep into the lungs. The sample powders examined by Sandia had many single spores and small clumps, but there were also large clumps containing thousands of spores. When Michael and Kotula put a clump between a pair of tweezers, it would resist breaking until enough pressure was applied and the clump would shatter like a tiny piece of concrete.

When Sandia reported its findings to the FBI, someone suggested that Sandia check to see if a spore could be found that was still inside the mother germ and already contained the protective shield of silicon in the spore coat. It took a long time for Sandia to locate a spore that was still inside the mother germ, but when they found one, it did indeed already have the silicon in the spore coat. That made it clear beyond any doubt that the silicon was absorbed as a natural function of spore creation and was not added afterward as an additive.

And another finding made it even more certain that the spores had not been deliberately weaponized. Only *some* of the spores actually contained silicon. Each spore in the attack powders tended to either have a complete sphere of silicon particles within the spore coat, or it had no silicon at all.[12] No weaponization technique would only be applied to a percentage of spores. Sandia scientists were able to determine that

76% of 124 spores from the Leahy letter contained silicon.
66% of 111 spores from the Daschle letter contained silicon.
65% of 141 spores from the NY Post letter contained silicon.

The findings were evidence and confidential. As a result, the mistaken theories about weaponization persisted for many years.

Ivins' First FBIR Submission

The FBI's subpoenas started going out in mid-February, one to each company or institution known to have possessed a sample of Ames at some point in time. USAMRIID formally received their subpoena on February 15.

The three main groups examining the samples were led by Paul Keim of Northern Arizona University, Paul J. Jackson of the Los Alamos National Laboratory and Claire M. Fraser of the Institute for Genomic Research in Rockville, Md. John Ezzell's lab was primarily responsible for the cataloging of samples. Catalogued samples would be sent out to a different set of labs for testing as "blind samples" with no information as to the actual source of the sample. FBI scientists working at USAMRIID would analyze the results.

On February 27, Ivins called an FBI agent working in the FBI repository and told him that he was sending over the slants created from his Ames samples "per subpoena" that day.[13] The subpoena required the slants be standard Remel prepared media tubes. Two slants were to be prepared for each sample. Instructions for labeling the slants, the growth temperatures, the growth time, and the wrapping procedures for mailing were also in the subpoena. And, to make certain that no one used the "single colony pick" method that Ivins typically used, the subpoena said:

> A representative sample of each stock shall be used for inoculation of the TSA slants. If the stock is an agar culture, do not use a single colony, but rather use an inoculum taken across multiple colonies. Thawed frozen stocks or other liquid suspensions shall be well mixed prior to transfer of inoculum to the TSA.[14]

A Crime Unlike Any Other

Ivins had his assistant Patricia Fellows hand-deliver the slants he had created to John Ezzell's lab in the FBIR area. He'd created two slants each of the four samples of Ames he claimed to have in his possession.

He sent two slants made from his sample of the original 1981 Ames ancestor material.

He sent two slants made from a sample identified as "7800a" and created in 1985 from the original 1981 ancestor material.

He sent two slants made from a sample identified as "7800b," also created in 1985 from the original 1981 ancestor material.

He sent two slants made from the contents of flask RMR-1029. He identified that sample as "7737 - Dugway Ames Spores - 1997."[15]

Very likely intentionally, but possibly by mistake, none of the slants were made according to the protocols defined in the subpoena. And, as a result, they would be unusable in court, since they couldn't be reliably compared to the other samples in the FBIR collection.

Most significantly, Ivins mixed his own growth media to pour into his own test tubes to create the slants, instead of using the standard pre-prepared Remel slants required by the subpoena. In time, his slants would stand out like oranges in a collection of apples.

He also had Patricia Fellows hand-deliver the slants, which violated chain of custody protocols.

Bruce Ivins had been making slants for 35 years, and he knew the importance of making certain that protocols were followed when creating samples for analysis. However, since the FBI Repository wasn't yet officially up and running, Terry Abshire accepted the slants without thoroughly examining them. She marked each tube in a pair as #1 and #2 and sent the four even numbered slants to Paul Keim at Northern Arizona University for strain typing. The remaining four odd-numbered slants went into the repository for safekeeping and to wait for the time when everything was set to begin the hunt for similarities to the attack anthrax.

Chapter 24

Consciousness of Guilt

News accounts from early March, 2002, contain another good example of how wrong the media can be when they use "experts" who have no real information but just put two and two together and come up with conclusions which the media then report as fact.

On March 4, the *Hartford Courant* reported that the FBI had asked "dozens of labs" to send samples of the Ames strain to Ft. Detrick for analysis. They then asked "knowledgeable outside observer" and "renowned forensic expert" Dr. Henry C. Lee his opinion about the progress of the investigation. According to Dr. Lee and the *Hartford Courant*:

> "These last two months, [FBI agents] have probably interviewed everyone at Fort Detrick and didn't find a suspect," he said. "They don't want to publicly rule anyone out, but their actions suggest that's what's going on. They don't think it's anybody who currently works at Detrick." [1]

The Frederick News-Post then jumped on the comments by Lee and reported on March 6:

Anthrax Story: Detrick cleared.

No Fort Detrick scientist, past or present, is probably a suspect in the anthrax letter case, according to the Hartford, Conn., Courant.

A Crime Unlike Any Other

It was totally untrue, of course. The FBI hadn't ruled out anyone at Ft. Detrick, except, perhaps, for a few who were known to be in foreign countries, in jail or hospitalized during the times of the attacks. The FBI simply had no choice but to rely on John Ezzell, Terry Abshire, Patricia Worsham and a few others in handling the samples. Those USAMRIID scientists had all been checked out as thoroughly as possible, including taking lie detector tests, but there was still no guarantee that the new scientific techniques they were about to implement wouldn't eventually point to one of them as a potential suspect. That possibility was hopefully covered by making certain that at least one FBI scientist was always present when the USAMRIID scientists were working with evidence.

Bruce Ivins, meanwhile, was not yet a suspect of any kind, and on March 11 he was asked to test the Leahy powder to determine its spore concentration. The report Ivins released the next day stated that the powder was slightly off-white or "eggshell" in color. When suspended in liquid, no visual clumps were seen with the naked eye. Under phase contrast microscopy, the spores appeared to be 99% viable, with no visible debris and just a slight amount of clumping.[2]

The spores were just as pure as the spores in the Daschle letter, and, although he didn't say so, as pure as the spores he'd created countless times in his own lab.

The investigation's progress was a big issue in the media, and, according to a *Wall Street Journal* article from March 26, "The biggest problem was that nobody knew at the beginning how to analyze the murder weapon itself to narrow down the list of repositories it might have come from -- and therefore the list of suspects. 'Every step we take, we're writing a new page in the book,' one official said."[3]

The FBI had convened a panel of about 20 experts from the American Association for the Advancement of Science, the National Science Foundation, the national laboratories and other research groups. The group produced a flowchart of all the different tests that should be attempted in order to find out how the powders were made, where were they made, how old the spores were, etc.[4]

Once they settled on which tests to perform, FBI microbiologists developed surrogate samples of harmless bacteria to conduct dry runs. "All the analyses and protocols had to be vetted and proven to withstand the legal challenges that we could anticipate," one of the officials said. They even irradiated the harmless bacteria to see if that step would confound the tests.

USAMRIID also had to construct two secure storage facilities for the FBIR samples, one a backup in case of a fire or other catastrophe. Constructing secure facilities, of course, took resources, material, money and approval and authentication, all of which added to the time involved in getting ready.

The new construction involved closing down labs and rooms for remodeling, and moving people into other labs and rooms, often requiring scientists to share labs when they previously had labs all to themselves. The remodeled areas were turned over to scientists assisting the FBI in the investigation.

Meanwhile, during the six months since the attacks, the FBI had conducted approximately 5,000 interviews, issued 1,300 subpoenas and amassed more than 100 computerized databases of potential suspects and leads, including detailed lists of people vaccinated against anthrax, visitors to certain Web sites, and employees of public and private laboratories with access to anthrax.[5]

It was still an individual-by-individual process of elimination. There'd been no breakthrough. Nothing had been found that would give investigators a clear way to eliminate large segments of the tens of thousands of microbiologists who, in theory, could have made the anthrax powders.

The official start of the FBIR analysis was March 28, 2002.

Sometime shortly before March 28, Terry Abshire noticed that Bruce Ivins' February 27 submissions to the FBIR collection looked different from the others. After examining them, she notified Ivins and Fellows that the submissions did not use the pre-prepared Remel tubes as specified in the subpoena. Dr. Ivins was told that he must resubmit the culture samples using the appropriate slants.[6]

Although Ivins was probably very upset because his attempt at deception had been found out, he ranted to others over how insulting it was that his slants weren't accepted as being equivalent to Remel slants. And he declared that he could point to numerous studies which showed that his home-made slants met the same requirements as Remel slants.[7]

A Crime Unlike Any Other

It was a silly argument, because using non-standard slants would mean that a prosecution "expert witness" would probably have to testify in court that the slant that showed Ivins to be guilty was really created the same way as the other slants used for other samples, while Ivins' defense lawyers would bring in their own "expert witnesses" to testify that the non-standard slants might possibly account for whatever differences the prosecution claimed pointed to the defendant. If everyone used identical slants, there would be no need for a courtroom battle over slant preparations between "expert witnesses" in front of the jury.

Ivins undoubtedly knew this, but he made a show of being indignant, anyway. And, at the same time, he had to figure out a different way to make sure the replacement set of slants couldn't be used as evidence against him in court. In legal terminology, that is called "consciousness of guilt."

The March 29, 2002 Meeting

Pat Worsham didn't want any of the scientists working under her supervision to improperly prepare their samples for the FBIR. So, on March 29, 2002, she summoned together Bruce Ivins and everyone else in Suites B3 and B4 who would be creating FBIR samples and, with FBI scientist Scott Stanley sitting in and taking notes, she explain the correct process.

Worsham made it clear that the task was to make certain that samples would cover a selection of spores as wide as possible for a given sample, since they were hunting for morphological variants that were only a relatively small percentage of the attack spores. Only 1 in 50 - or perhaps 1 in 100 spores were morphs. So, to be certain of getting whatever morphs might be in a given sample, it would be required that everyone use methods that would be certain to get the widest possible selection. That meant that using the method known as "single colony pick" - where spores or bacteria were gathered only from a single colony - would be totally unacceptable. Worsham explained that anyone creating samples that way would be in violation of the subpoena. The correct way to gather spores from a liquid sample was to thoroughly stir and/or shake the sample before extracting spores for the FBIR. With a slant or plate, everyone was to make certain that spores from the widest possible selection of colonies were sampled.[8]

As Ivins listened, it became a near certainty that there was something in the attack powders that just might pinpoint his lab as the source for the attacks.

The April Slants

On April 10, 2002, Dr. Ivins set about preparing the eight replacement slants which were supposed to represent the four different Ames cultures in his possession. This time he would have to use the appropriate Remel slants, but he could take other measures to make certain the slants couldn't point to him.

The facts indicate that Ivins was becoming aware that he had previously misunderstood the cause of mutations in *Bacillus anthracis* bacteria, and he had vastly underestimated the frequency that such mutations could occur. That newly learned lesson specifically applied flask RMR-1029, which he referred to as "The Battelle spores."

When that collection of spores had been created, it contained *30 trillion* spores. If mutations were strictly a numbers game, that meant flask RMR-1029 almost certainly contained vast numbers of mutations. That meant, in turn, that there just could be something about flask RMR-1029 that could incriminate him or point the investigation toward him. Ivins had no way to know for certain, but he wasn't about to let it happen.

All the plates he'd used to collect the spores for the letters were plates from diluted aliquots taken from flask RMR-1029. He couldn't destroy the flask or replace the remaining contents without creating even more suspicion, so he would have to mislead the investigators in some other way.

He prepared the slants for the other three samples properly. But, he made certain the sample from flask RMR-1029 would not include whatever it was that RMR-1029 might contain to incriminate him. There's no way to know exactly what Ivins did, but he very likely either used a sample from another flask of Ames he found in the cold storage room or he did a "single colony pick" to make certain that none of the mutations would be included in the slant.

Perhaps to further annoy the FBI agents and the group of people in the Diagnostic Systems Division who were helping the FBI, Ivins only put his name on one of the labels and omitted other relevant information.[9] He personally took the 8 slants to Dr. Ezzell's lab to maintain chain of custody. He must have felt some satisfaction when they were accepted into the FBIR. If Abshire noticed the incomplete labels, she said nothing. After Ivins was gone, Abshire destroyed the original four slants Ivins had submitted in February and replaced them with the four new slants, sending the duplicate four to Paul Keim.

Resentment

In early 2002, Patricia Worsham was formally put in charge of Bacteriology Suites 3 and 4.

Although Ivins couldn't tell anyone, he had been responsible for the rejuvenation of the entire anthrax vaccine program and for bringing the attention of the world on the work USAMRIID was doing to develop vaccines to protect Americans and American troops overseas. Ivins had almost single-handedly brought in millions of dollars in new funding. The place had never been busier. New people were being hired every day.

Yet, a woman who came to USAMRIID nine years after Ivins had been promoted over him. Worst of all, Pat Worsham was working closely with the FBI to help find the person who sent the anthrax letters. They were buddy-buddies, holding meetings, following each other around in the hallways and in and out of labs, talking about things to which Ivins wasn't privy.

Ivins evidently felt he had to strike back at Worsham somehow, just as he'd stuck back at other women who had wronged him over the years.

The April Cleanup

When Ivins had done the unauthorized cleaning and testing in December, he'd cleaned and checked Kristie Friend's desk and a few things from atop her desk. He had evidently handled the letters there in a way that he felt might have left behind some tell-tale spores. By the beginning of April, however, he was becoming concerned that there were other places where spores from the letters might have landed. He needed to do a more thorough cleanup.

An incident that occurred in one of Pat Worsham's labs gave Ivins the excuse he needed.

Around 9 a.m. on Monday, April 8, a scientist working in room B306 noticed that there was dried material on the outside of a couple flasks of anthrax and growth media she was about to remove from a rotary shaker. The scientist alerted the other scientists working in the room, since the dried material meant that spores probably seeped out of the flask with the media. When the liquid evaporated, the air-dried spores could have aerosolized.[10]

The flasks were taken to a biosafety cabinet where their exteriors were carefully cleaned and disinfected with bleach.

Both scientists working in B306 visited the medical division to get tested. After their nostrils are swabbed, they were given the antibiotic Cipro to help ward off any infection, even though both were up-to-date on their anthrax vaccinations. Later, the swab test results showed that one of the two scientists had indeed been exposed to aerosolized dry anthrax spores.[11]

On Thursday, April 11, Dr. Worsham and other USAMRIID scientists tested lab areas near room B306, and they found anthrax contamination in several of the areas, including on the inside handle of the passbox in room B304. A thorough cleaning was performed on the infected areas, and the matter was considered closed.

But, Ivins wanted to clean a much larger area. And, since the incident had happened in the lab area supervised by Pat Worsham, he evidently wanted to make certain that the incident didn't pass unnoticed by higher authorities.

Ivins informed Worsham that he believed there should be a much larger search performed for anthrax spores, including locations far outside of the immediate area around room B306 - like the Diagnostic System Division where the evidence was being handled. Worsham saw no reason for such a large cleaning and instructed Ivins to get official permission from the head of the Bacteriology

Division, Gerry Andrews, before he did any more swabbings or cleaning like he did without permission in December.

After thinking about it over the weekend, on Monday, April 15, Ivins decided to ignore the instructions from Worsham, and he proceeded to do another cleaning and swabbing. It was another unauthorized cleaning in violation of established protocols, yet, even though it was done during normal work hours, no one questioned what Ivins was doing or why. Ivins swabbed areas in the men's locker room, the molding around the passbox between the hallway and room B304, and areas in his own office in room 19. He used the swabs to inoculate Petri dishes and then put the dishes into an incubator in room B304 overnight.[12]

The next morning, when cultures from about 25 percent of the swabs showed positive results, Ivins did more swabbing and cleaning around the passbox molding and around the outside of the women's locker room. Then, after inoculating new plates with that day's swabs and putting the cultures into an incubator, he notified Worsham about what he'd done.

Needless to say, Worsham wasn't pleased. But, the fact that Ivins had gotten positive results from his swabbings - and the fact that Worsham had been informed of Ivins' findings - meant that a much more comprehensive cleaning and testing was needed. And that meant that people all the way up to Fort Detrick's Commanding General Maj. Gen. Martinez-Lopez needed to be informed.

Labs were shut down. Ivins' office was sealed off. Safety experts swarmed over the building taking samples nearly everywhere. Everyone involved was formally interviewed by USAMRIID safety personnel, and the Q&A sessions were recorded and transcribed. When Ivins was interviewed, he not only talked about his actions on April 15 and 16, but also about his earlier cleanup work in December, which he described as another example of people working with the FBI tracking spores around the building. On April 24 and 25, FBI agents also interviewed Ivins about the incident, producing a 4-page report about the interview.[13]

The possibility of contamination meant that there was a possibility that spores had escaped the USAMRIID area, and the Mayor of Frederick, Jennifer Doherty, had to be notified. There was also the possibility that lab clothes sent to a laundry had been contaminated, so the laundry had to be checked for contamination.

"Town hall" -style meetings were held with all USAMRIID employees to instruct them of proper procedures for handling and reporting mishaps. When the final "Anthrax Contamination of Bldg. 1425" report was completed in mid-May, it was 361 pages long.

The major fuss Bruce Ivins had created didn't seem to do Pat Worsham any harm, however it seems to have put an end to Ivins' concerns about cleaning up evidence he may have left behind in September and October.

He didn't know that the spores that had leaked from the flask in room B306 were one from of the mutations, and no matching spores had been found anywhere in the building. Non-mutated Ames spores were found in Ivins' office, but no other office. They were also found in the B301 men's locker room, but not in the women's locker room. No lab in the Diagnostic Systems Division tested positive for Ames. The only places where Ames spores were found by investigators were places around where Ivins had previously cleaned.

It was almost as if Ivins knew exactly where to clean.

Chapter 25

Lynch Mob

Dr. Barbara Hatch Rosenberg seemed to be absolutely certain that the anthrax powders sent in the letters were very sophisticated, weaponized spores. The fact that Silicon had been detected in the powders seemed to be concrete proof of that.

Although bioweapons experts who had actually seen the attack spores were repeatedly stating that the spores showed no indications of weaponization, Barbara Hatch Rosenberg, her group of conspiracy theorists and others remained convinced that the U.S. Government was hiding a secret and illegal bio-weapons program, and that the FBI was covering up for the actual perpetrator of the attacks.

Rosenberg differed from the others, however, in that she had the ways and means to do extensive rabble rousing in order to form a quasi lynch mob to demand that the person who she thought was or might be the culprit was brought to justice. More than once, the FBI had checked out the "suspect" Rosenberg wouldn't publicly name, and they found nothing that pointed to him more than anyone else, and they found plenty that indicated he was *not* the anthrax mailer. But, to conspiracy theorists, investigations that aren't done in front of the public aren't real investigations. And, it could be all lies with nothing being done at all.

On February 26, 2002, the FBI flatly discounted Rosenberg's claims. Bill Carter, an FBI spokesman told the media, "There is no prime suspect at this time." White House spokesman Ari Fleischer told the media that the claims about a suspect were false, and that the FBI wasn't even close to identifying a suspect in the case.[1]

In the March 11 issue of *The New Yorker*, Dr. Rosenberg was interviewed by Nicholas Lemann, who described Rosenberg's claims as "a conspiracy theory," but he nevertheless explained every element of her theory as if they were the words of a prophet.[2]

In some ways, though, Rosenberg was correct. She was just pointing at the wrong person. According to Lemann's article, "All of the anthrax letters were sent by one person, a middle-aged man." But, Rosenberg believed he no longer worked for USAMRIID. And she believed he'd gotten his training in weaponizing anthrax from William Patrick III, "the long-time head of bioweapons research at Ft. Detrick." She believed the culprit now worked for a sub-contractor in the Washington area. She believed him to have suffered some kind of career set back which left him "confused, upset, depressed, angry." So, he decided to retaliate with the anthrax attacks to prove two things: (1) how good he was, and (2) to get the government to invest more in bioweapons research, which would mean a budget increase for his employer.

She believed that the culprit prepared the anthrax during the summer, and, when 9/11 occurred, he saw the perfect opportunity to strike and to cover his tracks.

A lot of this fits Bruce Ivins very well, but then Rosenberg gets off track by claiming that a letter sent to the military police at the Marine base in Quantico, Virginia, pointing the finger at Egyptian-born scientist Ayaad Assaad was part of the same scheme. *The New Yorker* article ends with this:

> Is Rosenberg's theory right? At the very least, she is persuasive in arguing that sending the anthrax letters required not just access to the "Ames strain" of anthrax but also knowledge of the weaponization technique developed by Bill Patrick. If the government is saying that the perpetrator was probably an American, it's hard to imagine how it couldn't have been an American who worked in a government-supported bioweapons lab.

So, *The New Yorker* reporter was part of the mob that believed the attack spores were weaponized in some special military way. And

A Crime Unlike Any Other

Rosenberg might just be right about all the other details of her theory, too.

On March 15, a UK newspaper, *The Scotsman*, printed an article titled *Anthrax attacks may have been a CIA test gone wrong*. It cited Rosenberg as the source behind that idea. She speculated that the CIA could have ordered a "field trial" on the possible effects of sending letters through the mails, and "Some expert field person would have been given this job, and it would have been left to him to decide exactly how to carry it out." The result might have been a project gone badly awry. He could have decided to use the anthrax for his own purposes and target the media and the Senate for his own motives, not some reason intended by the government project.

On March 20, Glenn Beck's web site picked up the article and distributed the idea to his followers.[3]

On March 26, the head of the Washington Field Office and the Amerithrax investigation, Assistant Director Van A. Harp told *USA Today*: "We have made substantial progress in our investigation, but unfortunately we have not identified the perpetrator. I'm confident that in the long run, we will be able to do so." [4]

A month later, on April 29, *The Weekly Standard* and *The New York Post* printed an article by David Tell which again used Dr. Rosenberg as an authority on the attacks.[5] Rosenberg claimed that "the FBI has known the anthrax mailer's precise identity for months already, but has deliberately avoided arresting him -- indeed may never arrest him -- because he 'knows too much' that the United States isn't very anxious to publicize." She repeated her theory that the attacks were a CIA project gone wrong and that the FBI was working very hard to NOT discover what the CIA did.

On May 24, Rosenberg's most powerful ally, Nicholas Kristof of *The New York Times*, produced another one of his columns about how the FBI knows who the anthrax mailer is but won't arrest him.[6]

Not every newspaper was going along with Rosenberg's theory. On June 3, *The Wall Street Journal* tried to point the finger at foreigners and declared that the FBI's "lone wolf" theory was "evidence of the Bureau's ineptitude." They listed the Bureau's mistakes in failing to prevent 9/11 and provided a laundry list of nonsense pointing to al Qaeda or Iraq as being responsible for the attacks. They laughed at the "lone wolf" idea and suggested that the FBI might be in need of a thorough overhaul.[7]

There was other talk at the time of merging the FBI into the Department of Homeland Security in some way in order to force the FBI off its theories that an American was behind the attacks instead of some Muslim terrorist.

So, the FBI was getting pressure from two directions, from those who felt the anthrax mailer was an American scientist who they couldn't arrest because he "knew too much," and from Right Wingers who felt that the FBI was mindlessly following some lamebrain theory about an American scientist when all the facts clearly showed that foreigners were behind the attacks - probably al Qaeda, and if not them, then Saddam Hussein.

What the FBI knows

On June 13, 2002, Dr. Rosenberg published another one of her articles on the Federation of American Scientist's web site. This one was titled, *The Anthrax Case: What the FBI knows.* She adopted Don Foster's theories and suggested that some hoax letters sent around the same time as the real letters were mailed *before* anything was known about the real letters, and the "likelihood that the hoax letters were coincidental is therefore small."

According to Rosenberg, "nearly everyone who has followed the situation closely -- knowledgeable biodefense insiders, investigative reporters (who have turned up a great many pertinent facts that have not yet been reported), and interested outsiders like myself -- knows who a likely perpetrator is." She explained that "a number of inside experts (at least five that I know about) gave the FBI the name of one specific person as the most likely suspect."

In spite of all this, the FBI continued to claim that it had no suspects and few clues.

The she proceeded to list aspects of her theory, the making of the spores in a "CIA safe house," how the person got his expertise at USAMRIID, how "The Suspect is part of a clique that includes high-level former USAMRIID scientists and high-level former FBI officials. Some of these people may wish to conceal any suspicions they may have about the identity of the perpetrator, in order to protect programs and sensitive information."

And the key lynch mob logic: The FBI was insisting on "100% proof before making an arrest." Why was there such a stringent requirement in this specific case?

Three days later, on June 16, *The Scotsman* declared *FBI "guilty of coverup" over anthrax suspect.* And they added, "Dr. Barbara Hatch Rosenberg says she knows who the terrorist is." [8]

Political Support

Dr. Rosenberg sent her article "*What the FBI knows*" to the senators who had been sent the anthrax letters, Senators Daschle and Leahy. And, very quickly she had the support of staffers working for those senators. On Tuesday, June 18, 2001, Rosenberg was granted an audience with the staffers. Assistant FBI Director Van Harp was summoned to attend the meeting and to listen to Professor Rosenberg's theory on who committed the anthrax attacks.

According to documents filed in Dr. Hatfill's lawsuit against the government,

29. In this meeting, Professor Rosenberg, who had no official authority, no investigative experience, and most significantly no access to the forensic tests conducted on the anthrax letters or the FBI's investigative file, made clear to the Daschle and Leahy staffs that her suspicions rested on Dr. Hatfill as the person most likely responsible for the mailings.

30. Assistant Director Harp was openly skeptical of Rosenberg's claims during their meeting, so much so that a Senate staffer later instructed him to call Professor Rosenberg and apologize, which he did. Harp and his superiors were anxious to placate the senators because at that time many senators had made it publicly known that they were displeased at how the FBI had handled terrorism investigations generally and the Amerithrax investigation in particular. Some had remarked that it was time to think about revoking the FBI's responsibility in investigating domestic

terrorism and to consider turning those responsibilities over to another government agency.[9]

However, other documents indicate that Rosenberg didn't actually identify Steven Hatfill by name. A June 20 article on Salon.com stated,

> The meeting, which was requested by Rosenberg, lasted about 90 minutes. After Rosenberg left, Senate staff talked to FBI representatives for an additional 45 minutes.
>
> "They discussed her letter, which has been online for sometime," said one Senate source, referring to writings posted on the FAS Web site. "She answered questions from the staff members and the FBI, but she was not asked, and did not identify, any individual in conjunction with her letter." [10]

While Rosenberg was succeeding very well in getting many influential people interested in her "suspect," Steven Hatfill's name had not yet appeared anywhere in the media. But, the media was starting to explain how, if her "suspect" was not soon arrested, *everyone* could be in great danger.

On Monday, June 24, 2002, the British newspaper *The Guardian* published an article titled *Anthrax killer "could grow more bacteria."*

And, on that same day, *USA Today* printed an article titled, *FBI mystified by anthrax attacks*, which said,

> "Without a swift arrest, and the message it sends, the nation risks a future threat that could dwarf 9-11," Rosenberg warned in a critique prepared for the Web site of the Federation of American Scientists.

In other words, if they didn't catch the anthrax mailer soon, he could do something that would totally devastate the entire county. And, the FBI would be totally responsible, since they had been told repeatedly who the anthrax mailer was, but they hadn't arrested him because he had information about making secret and illegal biological weapons that higher-ups in "the government" couldn't afford to let be made public.

Steven Jay Hatfill

The next day, June 25, 2002, the FBI conducted a search of Steven Hatfill's apartment that turned out to be a media circus. There's no solid information about how the media learned of the pending search, but the best guesses seem to be that it came from attorneys at the Department of Justice who were frustrated that the FBI investigators didn't appear to be taking seriously all the tips they'd been getting from scientists, including scientist Barbara Hatch Rosenberg. When the FBI search team reached the apartment, there were already media helicopters circling overhead.

Inexplicably, almost no one in the media seemed to remember that Dr. Rosenberg had been pointing at some specific person for *eight months*. Almost no one made the connection. When Dr. Hatfill's name was mentioned in the news, it was mostly by journalists who had never heard the name before and assumed that *the FBI's investigation* had determined that Hatfill was their prime suspect. Nothing could have been farther from the truth, yet that same belief would persist among journalists for many years to come. According to most in the media, Hatfill had been identified as the prime suspect by the FBI, and that was the only reason they were investigating him publicly. Barbara Hatch Rosenberg had nothing to do with it. According to *The New York Times*,

> Dr. Hatfill, 48, had been the subject of Web site gossip among scientists, journalists and other professionals about possible domestic suspects in last year's anthrax attacks. After reporters pursued him, he was fired in March from his job at Science Applications International Corporation, a contractor for the Pentagon and the Central Intelligence Agency that helps the government with germ defenses. From 1997 to 1999, he worked at the Army's biodefense laboratory at Fort Detrick.[11]

In an interview with the *Times*, Dr. Hatfill said he had been the victim of a "witch hunt." A better term might have been "a lynch mob." According to the *Times*:

> "I've got a letter from the F.B.I. that says I'm not a suspect and never was," he said. "I just got caught up in the normal screening they were doing, because of the nature of my job."

The Hartford Courant made the connection between Rosenberg's campaign and the search of Hatfill's apartment, but that may only be because they had their own suspect and disagreed with Rosenberg's theory.[12]

Brian Ross at ABC, however, considered the search to be "a raid," and wrote:

> The FBI obtained a copy of the secret anthrax report last week just before agents raided Hatfill's home in Frederick, Md., and a storage facility he maintains in Ocala, Fla.
>
> The report describes a hypothetical anthrax attack, specifying an amount and quality of anthrax that is remarkably similar to what was sent to the offices of U.S. Sens. Patrick Leahy and Tom Daschle last October.[13]

ABC called Dr. Hatfill before airing Ross's story to see what his reaction would be. Hatfill called the story "completely inaccurate, scandalous and libelous."

And other reporters were also suggesting that the report William Patrick had written was a "blueprint" for the attacks.

The FBI kept telling one reporter after another that Dr. Hatfill was *not* a suspect, but the TV images of the search were saying just the opposite. If he wasn't a suspect, why was his apartment being searched? The answer was very likely that the FBI needed to demonstrate that Dr. Hatfill didn't have anything in his apartment that could be more devastating to America than 9/11. The search found nothing more "devastating" than a container of harmless anthrax simulant that Hatfill used in lectures to show what powdered anthrax looked like.

A Crime Unlike Any Other

On July 2, Nicholas Kristof admitted in his *New York Times* column that he'd been writing about Hatfill since January, and, thus, when he'd written "I think I know who sent out the anthrax," he had been referring to Hatfill. If Hatfill were an Arab, "he would have been imprisoned long ago," Kristof declared. And he went on to state that Hatfill had "connections to the biggest anthrax outbreak among humans ever recorded, the one that sickened more than 10,000 farmers in Zimbabwe in 1978-80." Kristof declared that there was evidence that the anthrax had been released by the "white Rhodesian Army fighting against black guerrillas," and that Hatfill had "participated in the army's much feared Selous Scouts." [14]

So, Hatfill was not only most likely the murderer of 5 Americans, he had very likely participated in the murder of 10,000 Africans.

And, that was just the beginning of the public lynching of Steven Jay Hatfill by the media and others.

Chapter 26

FBI vs. DOJ

On Sunday, July 28, 2002, the *Pittsburg Tribune-Review* printed an opinion piece titled, *Slowness in tracking down anthrax killer is intolerable*. According to the unidentified British journalist who wrote the opinion, "'non-suspect' Hatfill has been so deeply involved in U.S. secret operations related to biological warfare that the possibility of him 'telling all' has terrified the Justice Department -- and *not* the FBI -- into immobility."

More than a few people across the country and around the world were totally buying into the nonsense preached by Barbara Hatch Rosenberg. True, there were also news stories stating that, according to the FBI, Dr. Hatfill was *not* a suspect, and he was *not* on any list of suspects, but *The New York Times* was saying that was because everyone was afraid of what Hatfill might spill about secret operations by the U.S. government.

Contrary to the beliefs of many True Believers and nearly all conspiracy theorists, the Federal Bureau of Investigation and the Department of Justice are *not* organizations where everyone believes as everyone else believes, where everyone knows what everyone else knows, and when anything new is learned, it is learned immediately by everyone.

Like every other organization, the FBI and DOJ are groups of individuals, each with his own point of view, his own skills, his own strengths, his own weaknesses.

And, if an agent is actually out gathering evidence, his view can be very different from other agents in offices who are just reading summaries and daily reports.

A Crime Unlike Any Other

With so many people pointing at Dr. Hatfill, there were some in the FBI and more than a few in the Department of Justice who believed that where there is so much smoke there must also be fire. There just might be something to what everyone was saying about Hatfill, even if no one could find any solid proof of it. Besides, the FBI investigators didn't have a better suspect than Dr. Hatfill. And there was no solid, undeniable proof that Dr. Hatfill was *not* the anthrax mailer.

The Assistant Director of the FBI who was also the head of the Washington Field Office and the head of the Amerithrax investigation, Van A. Harp, was initially largely uninvolved in the case and left it to Special Agents Robert Roth and Dave Dawson to supervise. But, the June 18, 2002, meeting with Senator Daschle's and Leahy's staffers where the staffers seemed to believe a conspiracy theorist's opinions instead of the FBI's findings - even to the point of demanding that Harp apologize to Dr. Rosenberg - didn't allow Harp to keep his distance from the case any longer.

Bringing in the Bloodhounds

The part of the Hatfill saga that involved the use of bloodhounds began on July 31, 2002.

A few days earlier, Dr. Hatfill had driven down to Baton Rouge, Louisiana, in his black, 2000 Chevrolet Camaro, with his Malaysian girlfriend Peck Chegne at his side. They went to look over the area. On July 1st, Hatfill had been hired into a $150,000 per year position at Louisiana State University to teach first responders, a job funded by the Department of Justice. He had been offered the job in March, before all the notoriety had started. But, Hatfill had been assured that the new position was considered secure, which meant he needed to do some apartment hunting and the other chores one does in preparation for a move to a new city far away from Maryland.[1]

The FBI didn't know who sent the anthrax letters, but they knew they had no evidence of any kind that showed Dr. Hatfill did it. In fact, all the evidence they'd accumulated so far said that he *couldn't* have done it. Yet, none of the FBI's contrary evidence would have mattered one bit if there was another anthrax attack while Hatfill was

200

being allowed to wander around the country without any kind of surveillance by the FBI. The FBI was still on the defensive because they hadn't stopped the 9/11 hijackers. A new anthrax attack while the world's prime suspect was being ignored by the FBI would be an intolerable situation that could damage the FBI's reputation beyond any hope of repair.

The FBI had absolutely no choice but to put Steven Hatfill under 24-hour close surveillance seven days a week.

However, that didn't mean that Dr. Hatfill would enjoy leading a parade of FBI vehicles around Baton Rouge.

On the morning of July 31, 2002, Hatfill and Chegne were ready to return to Maryland. They led the parade of FBI vehicles to a Denny's restaurant in Baton Rouge for breakfast. The facts indicate that the FBI agents also used the occasion to use the toilets, to have breakfast or at least to get a cup of coffee to go.[2]

Then, as the FBI agents were in the toilets or ordering, Steven Hatfill and Peck Chegne *vanished*. Rushing into the parking lot, the agents found that Hatfill's Camaro was gone.

FBI vehicles were sent in various directions in attempts to find the Camaro and the missing couple, but to no avail. There was no sign of Hatfill or his companion. It must have appeared to the FBI agents that they had been deliberately ditched. (In late 2003, when I asked Dr. Hatfill about this incident, he said that, if he had lost the FBI tail, "it wasn't intentional.")

Intentional or not, it was a mighty embarrassment to the FBI, and countless wheels were put in motion to prevent the mistake from turning into a total disaster. Some FBI agents evidently also saw it as being nearly the same as a suspect escaping from FBI custody - it could easily be construed as *evidence of guilt*.

What do you do when you lose a tail on someone? One option, if you have the ability - and the FBI did - is to bring in bloodhounds to find the trail again.

Since the human scent detected by the dogs comes from dead skin cells which people constantly shed, the bloodhounds can often tell their handlers which way the person went and if that person passed over a given spot - although not with anything approaching 100% reliability. In theory, a dog might even be able to find a scent on a highway and pinpoint a specific turnoff used by the missing person. Even if the windows are closed on a car, the skin cells can still be transferred into the environment via air vents.[3] Bloodhound handlers have dozens of such stories to tell.

The FBI quickly brought in three bloodhounds from California: Tinkerbell from the South Pasadena Police Department, Knight from the Los Angeles County Sheriff's Office, and Lucy from the Long Beach Police Department.[4] The facts also indicate that the FBI obtained items of Hatfill's clothing from his home to prepare the dogs by providing them with the scent they needed.

The trail began at the Denny's in Baton Rouge. The first objective was to find which way Hatfill had gone. After being given Hatfill's scent, the dogs sniffed around the restaurant booth where Hatfill had last been seen, then the trail to the car. Then the hounds did their best to try to figure out which way Hatfill had gone. It's a game to the dogs. They get a treat if they play they game well.

There are reports that at least one bloodhound was also sent to Florida to sniff around a storage locker Hatfill kept there near the home of his parents.[5] Although the locker had been searched by the FBI, there was always a possibility that there was something in the locker that had been missed.

There's not much in the way of a public record of exactly how the dogs tried to find Hatfill's trail, where they went, or what the results were, except for a visit to William Patrick's home. It's known that the dogs sniffed around the driveway but gave no indication that Dr. Hatfill had recently visited the bioweapons expert who some conspiracy theorists considered to be the true mastermind behind the attacks.[6]

On August 1st, the FBI learned that Hatfill had returned to his apartment in Frederick and was in the process of tossing out junk in preparation for moving to Louisiana.

When Lucy the bloodhound was brought out of an FBI car on the street in front of Hatfill's apartment, she immediately started barking and giving signs that she'd picked up Hatfill's scent.[7]

But, the facts indicate that by that time someone within the FBI had changed tactics.

Over nine months earlier, on October 26, 2001, whatever scents - human or otherwise - that might be on the *New York Post* letter were extracted and put onto a scent pack. A month later, at 11 a.m. on the 9th of December of 2001, an FBI agent had transferred whatever scents might be on the Leahy letter onto a scent pack.[8] Of course, no one knew what kind of scent or exactly whose scents might be on the letters. The skin cells of postal workers could very likely be on the letters. Moreover, if Hatfill had handled the Leahy and Post envelopes and letters as anyone would do if concerned about leaving behind fingerprints, the paper would probably never have been physically touched by uncovered hands.

But, there was nothing to lose by attempting to capture and preserve the scents from the letters. And the FBI had done so.

On August 1, 2002, someone in a high position within the FBI had decided it was time to use those scent packs - or at least the scent pack from the Leahy letter, since the Post letter had also been handled by employees at the Post and numerous other people before the scent pack could be applied.

It appears that the FBI performed an experiment when they entered Steven Hatfill's apartment, this time with a criminal search warrant. They asked Hatfill to go into a room and sit on a chair. Then they had Lucy sniff the Leahy scent pack, and they let Lucy go. Lucy went directly to Hatfill. Unaware of what the "game" was all about, Hatfill scratched Lucy behind her ears and petted her.[9]

Was Lucy still following the scent she'd been given in Louisiana and followed across half the country? There's no way to know. Was there any kind of scent on the scent pack which could also be on Hatfill? There's no way to know. But, the FBI now had an explanation for why they used the bloodhounds. It wasn't to help find the person who had inexcusably escaped their 24/7 surveillance; it was to find a match to the scent on the Leahy letter. No mention was ever made to anyone about losing the tail on Hatfill. It's only what the facts say.

The facts also say that top officials in the FBI - at least within the Washington Field Office - were tired of having their plans turned over to the media. The media was there at Hatfill's apartment again when the FBI arrived on August 1. So, someone with access to key information was definitely talking to the media. It didn't appear to be anyone within the FBI. The FBI was being embarrassed by the leaks. That left only the lawyers at the Department of Justice who were constantly proclaiming that the FBI needed to find better evidence to indict someone - anyone - for the anthrax mailings. Some of them wanted or even believed that Hatfill was the culprit. Otherwise, why would so many influential people be pointing at him?

The FBI decided to use the scent pack story as part of an old fashioned "sting" operation sometimes called a "canary trap" to try to find out who might be behind the leaks. Such a "sting" required that they use different variations on the story when discussing the search warrant application with different lawyers at the Department of Justice. One version was told to the Chief of the Criminal Division in the United States Attorney's Office for the District of Columbia, Daniel S. Seikaly.[10] And, it appears that Seikaly promptly told Daniel Klaidman of *Newsweek* and Allan Lengel of *The Washington Post*, since that was the version that was printed.

The "sting" worked. The FBI knew the name of at least one of the leakers. But, in the process of executing the "sting," they'd also given *Newsweek* and *The Washington Post* a totally bogus story about the bloodhounds tracking a scent from the Leahy letter to Dr. Steven Jay Hatfill.

No one at *Newsweek* bothered to ask why the FBI would take the bloodhounds to a Denny's restaurant in Louisiana to match a scent on a scent pack to Dr. Hatfill. And Daniel Seikaly evidently didn't ask either.

The FBI impounded Hatfill's Camaro in hopes that it might help show where he'd been during the time he hadn't been under FBI surveillance. It was over 1,100 miles from Baton Rouge to Frederick, so there hadn't been any time to make any significant detours, but the Camaro had to be checked anyway.

The second search of Hatfill's apartment on August 1st appeared to many to be solid evidence that Dr. Hatfill was truly a prime suspect - and, very likely, the *only* suspect. After all, no one else had been in the news because their apartment was being searched by FBI agents investigating the anthrax attacks of 2001.

On August 2nd, the day after the FBI search, Louisiana State University cited "current circumstances" and put Hatfill on paid "administrative leave" for 30 days. His status would be reviewed and reevaluated at the end of that time. The next day, news reports were saying that many people at LSU were "shocked" to learn that Steven Hatfill was coming to work there, and a few researchers at LSU told the media they wouldn't even allow Hatfill into their research facilities, guilty or not.[11]

That same day, the media was reporting that the FBI had interviewed Dr. Barbara Hatch Rosenberg and questioned her to see if some scientists might be trying to *frame* Dr. Hatfill for some reason. Rosenberg immediately told the *Washington Times* about the interview.[12]

Hatfill Speaks

On Sunday, August 11, *The Washington Post* printed an exclusive interview with Dr. Hatfill in the office of his lawyer, Victor M. Glasberg. The *Post* reported:

> "I went from being someone with pride in my work, pride in my profession, to being made into the biggest criminal of the 21st century, for something I never touched," Hatfill said. "What I've been trying to contribute, my work, is finished. My life is destroyed." [13]

Against his lawyer's advice, Hatfill also talked to a crowd of reporters waiting when he exited his lawyer's office. He read a lengthy statement which began by declaring that

> I am a loyal American, and I love my country. I have had nothing to do in any way, shape or form with the mailing of these anthrax letters, and it is extremely wrong for anyone to contend or suggest that I have.[14]

He identified Dr. Barbara Hatch Rosenberg as the cause behind all that was happening to him, describing the meeting Rosenberg had had with Leahy and Daschle staffers, then stating, "I don't know Dr. Rosenberg, I have never met her, I have never spoken or corresponded with this woman, And to my knowledge, she is ignorant of my work and background except in the very broadest of terms." And, "I am at a complete loss to explain her reported hostility and accusations. I don't know this woman at all."

That same day, on August 11, Rosenberg published another article on the Federation of American Scientists where she proclaimed that whatever was happening to Hatfill was the FBI's fault, not hers:

> I have never mentioned any names in connection with the anthrax investigation, not to the FBI, nor to media, nor to Senate Committees or staffs, not to anyone. I have never said or written anything publicly that pointed only to one specific person. Anyone who sees parallels is expressing his own opinion.
>
> It is the FBI that has gone out of its way to make one suspect's name public. I presume they must have had some good reason for doing that; only time will tell. But if the publicity was not an important part of their investigative strategy, I think it was reprehensible.[15]

Inexplicably, it seemed that most in the media had already come to that same conclusion. It was *the FBI* who was pointing at Dr. Hatfill. Barbara Hatch Rosenberg was just a little old lady who taught school in upstate New York. Who cared what she thought?

And, to many in the media, Dr. Hatfill's declaration was just his lawyer's pathetic attempt to get the public on Hatfill's side - even though it was abundantly clear to the entire world that Hatfill was the anthrax mailer.

The only newspapers which didn't seem accept that Hatfill was probably the anthrax mailer were those who thought al Qaeda or Saddam Hussein did it.

Chapter 27

Searching For Leads

At some point in early 2002, someone realized that if the anthrax letters had left a trail of spores through post offices, they might also have been left in the mailbox used to mail the letters.

Every possible mailbox which provided mail to the Hamilton mail processing center had to be eliminated before it could be conclusively stated that the mailbox on the corner of Nassau Street and Bank Street in Princeton, directly across from Princeton University, was the only mailbox which showed anthrax contamination.[1]

The next step was to see if anyone near the mailbox might have seen Dr. Steven Hatfill in the vicinity. No one had. All the FBI accomplished was to tell the world that Hatfill was still the only serious suspect the FBI had. Meanwhile, those with knowledge of courtroom procedures knew that the act of showing Hatfill's picture around would have invalidated any evidence found, since *only* Hatfill's picture was shown, meaning they were putting Hatfill's image into the memory of potential witnesses instead of presenting those potential witnesses with an array of faces and asking them to pick out any whom they recognized.[2]

"Person of Interest"

On August 6, 2002, Attorney General John Aschroft had appeared on two morning television shows. On CBS's *The Early Show* he had described Steven Hatfill as a "person of interest" in the anthrax investigation. That same morning, on NBC's *Today Show*, Ashcroft described Hatfill as "a person that - that the FBI's been interested in" in its investigation.

On August 22, during a press conference at the Peter Rodino Federal Building in Newark, NJ, Ashcroft again described Hatfill as "a person of interest to the Department of Justice." [3]

Ashcroft and his aides would later try to explain that using that term was an attempt to show that Hatfill was *not* a suspect.[4] He was just someone whose name kept coming up in the investigation, and therefore he was someone who might have information or who might have some connection to the case, even though there was no proof of any kind to link him to the case. But, to the public and many in the media there was no difference between a "suspect" and a "person of interest."

Hatfill is Fired

In mid-August, 2002, the media was filled with stories about how Hatfill had written an unpublished novel about a terrorist attack upon Washington. The villain in the novel used a wheelchair to spray bubonic plague bacteria around the White House during a tour, turning the White House into a "house of death." [5] It was nothing like what happened in reality, but to those who believed that Hatfill was the anthrax mailer, it was "proof" that he had been thinking about such a crime. And, the fact that countless other scientists had worried about such a crime meant nothing, since planning a crime and worrying about a crime are very different.

On September 3, 2002, Steven Hatfill was fired from his new position at Louisiana State University. LSU didn't notify Hatfill directly, instead they contacted his lawyer and let his lawyer break the news. Dr. Hatfill issued a statement saying, "My life has been completely and utterly destroyed by John Ashcroft and the FBI. I do not understand why they are doing this to me. My professional reputation is in tatters. All I have left are my savings and they will be exhausted soon because of my legal bills." [6]

On September 11, 2002, without giving any explanation, the FBI performed a third search of Hatfill's apartment. It wasn't even Hatfill's apartment any longer. He'd moved out after he'd returned from Louisiana, because he expected to be moving there to work at his new position in Baton Rouge. But, then he was fired from that job before he could even start it, and he ended up moving in with his girlfriend, Peck Chegne.

On the positive side, some media reporters were beginning to ask why the FBI was hounding someone endlessly without making an arrest. Even Senator Charles E. Grassley (R-Iowa) asked for an explanation for why Ashcroft was going around describing Hatfill as a "person of interest," when normally the policy of the Justice Department is to keep secret the names of people who are under investigation unless he is under arrest or wanted for questioning.[7]

And the media was beginning to question the bloodhound story, too. Article after article told of how unreliable bloodhounds could be in certain situations.[8]

In early October, Hatfill went on the offensive and talked with reporters about plans to sue John Ashcroft and the Department of Justice for defamation of character.

Ivins & Mara Linscott

During the month of September, 2002, Bruce Ivins may have been thinking a lot about all the news reports stating that FBI investigators had identified the exact mailbox that had been used to mail the letters. It was something else he never believed possible that was suddenly proved to be *very* possible because of another of his mistakes: believing that anthrax spores could not escape through a carefully folded letter inside a sealed envelope. It was as if his stop to look over the KKG office had caused Fate to step in and alter what was possible and not possible.

He evidently felt a need to discuss this latest quirk of Fate with someone without actually talking about the anthrax mailing. And, the only person he felt he could really talk with was Mara Linscott. We don't know everything he said, but we know he told her about his decades-long obsession with KKG and about the burglary of at least one KKG sorority house he'd committed many years ago. Mara promptly told Pat Fellows about it via an email which included this comment: "He broke into a sorority house, while no one was there, to get the code book."[9]

A Crime Unlike Any Other

It was also during that same September that Ivins drove nearly 600 miles round trip *twice* to where Linscott was staying with her parents at the time, first to merely scout the location, the second drive to leave a bottle of Kahlua (Mara's favorite liqueur) on the porch of her parent's home.[10]

Lab Work

By late June of 2002, USAMRIID had provided the FBIR with 606 samples of the Ames strain, any or all of which could be the match to the material in the anthrax letters. Other labs had turned over a total of 115 samples of Ames, and more were still coming in. Any or all of those could also be a match. The testing procedures for the samples had just begun.[11]

The FBI had enlisted the aid of private and government laboratories to assist in the scientific investigation. A semi-weekly report describing activities and advances by the various labs was being distributed by the Washington Field Office to FBI and Postal Inspection Services executives, team leaders and others with "a need to know."

At NAU, Paul Keim and his team had been trying for months to determine what factors caused the mutations and where they occurred in the DNA. The general thinking was still what Ivins had believed: transfers or passaging had something to do with the probabilities of creating mutations. NAU used a sample of the original 1981 ancestor strain and stepped through 10 transfers or passages from plate to plate, and calculated that the result was equivalent to "25,000 generations." They found two mutations, but it was too early to determine the significance of the mutations.[12]

The Institute for Genomic Research was trying to locate "hot spots" in the Bacillus anthracis DNA where mutations occurred, in order to reduce the search time when looking for the mutations. They were also trying to determine to a scientific certainty that there was no difference between the strains used in the New York letters, the senate letters and the bacteria that had killed Bob Stevens. They were also doing a study of mutation rates to compare to the work being done by NAU.[13]

210

Woods Hole Oceanographic Institute was trying to determine the age of the attack anthrax using methods akin to Carbon-dating. They'd already determined that the spores and the growth media that had been used to create the spores appeared to be no more than two years old. That further rule out the conspiracy theories claiming that the attack anthrax had come from weaponized stocks created back in the 1950's and 1960's during the Cold War, stocks which were supposed to have been destroyed, but which the conspiracy theorists believed were still available for use.[14]

Dugway Proving Grounds (DPG) was trying to determine what specific process caused the silicon signature found in the attack spores. They were going through every published procedure they could find, trying them all, and testing the results. As with most of the testing being done by these outside laboratories, it was a "blind" test. The scientists at Dugway didn't know what the results would be measured against; they were only trying each known procedure and quantifying the results. (They were *not* trying to "reverse engineer" the attack anthrax, as some would later claim.) The DPG results would be compared to the attack anthrax by other labs, again in blind tests to avoid any kind of bias. Only the FBI would be able to compare test results and match them to specific samples.[15]

Los Alamos National Laboratories were attempting to determine if any kind of genetic engineering had been done to the attack anthrax. It seemed clear already that there was no genetic engineering involved, but there wasn't enough data to be scientifically certain that the attack anthrax hadn't been somehow modified. It was a matter of testing a large number of samples and thereby reducing the probability that the effects of genetic engineering would only show up in a few samples.[16]

The FBI laboratory at Quantico, which had no capability to handle live spores, was examining radiated spores and trying to determine if any kind of solvents were used in the drying process.[17]

The University of Maryland (UM) was attempting to determine whether the attack spores were grown on agar or in liquid. Tests done so far were showing positive for growth on agar plates, but the results weren't conclusive.[18]

A Crime Unlike Any Other

Scientists at Sandia National Laboratories in New Mexico were continuing their analysis of chemical elements found in the spores.[19]

The University of Utah was trying to analyze isotopes in the attack anthrax with the hope of being able to locate a water source used to make the attack anthrax. The initial results were showing that Dugway could probably be ruled out as a source for the water that was used to make the spores because of unusual isotope ratios in the water there, but there didn't appear to be any isotope ratio evidence that ruled out any East Coast laboratory.[20]

USAMRIID scientists were analyzing samples from Steven Hatfill's apartment and his car. They were also extremely busy analyzing samples taken from a new survey of the interior of the AMI building in Boca Raton to help investigators determine with greater certainty exactly how the anthrax entered the building and where and how it traveled from place to place within the building.[21]

USAMRIID and the Armed Forces Institute of Pathology had tested the remains of the hijackers who went down with United Airlines flight 93 in Stonycreek Township, Pennsylvania. 17 of 17 samples had tested negative for anthrax.[22]

Commonwealth Biotechnologies, Inc. in Richmond, VA, was doing some of the same work being done at NAU and TIGR with the plan of being able to confirm the results from those laboratories by using alternative procedures.[23]

The CDC was largely left out of the investigation because their computer systems were not secure enough to process evidence for use in court. But, they had the capability to do certain kinds of blind tests, and they were also testing tissue samples from the 9/11 hijackers who died in Pennsylvania.[24]

Theories Without Facts

On October 28, 2002, the *Washington Post* published an article titled *FBI's Theory On Anthrax is Doubted*, by Guy Gugliotta and Gary Matsumoto,. It was subtitled *Attacks Not Likely Work of 1 person, Experts Say*.

The article stated that a "significant number of scientists and biological warfare experts" were "expressing skepticism about the

FBI's view that a single disgruntled American scientist prepared and mailed the deadly anthrax letters that killed five people last year."

One of the "experts," Richard Spertzel, opined that only "four or five people in the whole country" could have made what was in the letters - even though Spertzel had never actually examined the attack powders. The other identified "experts" were equally uninformed: an executive for a company that made spray dryers, a pharmaceutical scientist at the University of Maryland, a chemical engineer at Sandia (who was not involved in the investigation), and a chemical engineer from Harvard. All seemingly agreed that hundreds of thousands of dollars worth of equipment would have been needed, and that the spores would have had to have been coated with fumed silica to make them do what they did.

Sandia scientists had determined beyond any doubt that there was no fumed silica mixed with the spores. But, their work was still confidential. It was left to two well-known bioweapons experts who had seen electron microscope photos of the attack powders to respond to the Post article. Matthew Messelson from Harvard and Ken Alibek from George Mason University (who had made powdered anthrax in the Soviet Union before defecting) sent a letter to the editor of the *Washington Post* stating that particles of fumed silica would be clearly visible under an electron microscope. There were no "balls or strands" of fumed silicon in the powders. The silicon that had been detected appeared to be something that was *naturally* concentrated into the spore coats, instead of something that was artificially added.[25]

The information from actual experts who had seen actual photographs of the powders failed to persuade the skeptics who felt that the powders *must* have been weaponized, and those skeptics were endlessly busy stating their opinions to anyone who would listen, while the real experts just stated the facts and went back to work.

Chapter 28

Interviewing Ivins

In mid-December of 2002, apparently as a result of something Dr. Steven Hatfill had written in his unpublished novel, but also very likely the result of "tips" from conspiracy theorists, the FBI embarked on one of the more unbelievable searches for clues in the Amerithrax investigation. They began poking around a pond in the City of Frederick Municipal Forest in the Catoctin Mountains, about 8 miles north of USAMRIID. The FBI explained to the media only that they were looking to see if there were any traces of anthrax in the area. But the media knew it was all about Hatfill.[1]

Tom Connolly, Hatfill's new lawyer, told the media that any connection Hatfill might have to the search was "far-fetched" and that Hatfill was totally innocent of any connection to the anthrax attacks.[2]

Ivins the Volunteer

Bruce Ivins learned about the search when he was contacted by the Red Cross asking if he would volunteer to help provide canteen services for the FBI, serving coffee and donuts to the weary searchers. Ivins certainly knew it would be totally inappropriate for him to be at the scene of a search involving the anthrax attacks while he was among those who might turn out to be a suspect in the case, but he volunteered anyway.

On a cold, rainy Saturday, December 14, 2002, Ivins was driven to the Red Cross tent near the pond. He was there for less than an hour before an FBI agent recognized him. Ivins was asked for his identification, the backpack he'd brought along was searched, and he was ordered to leave the area as soon as transportation could be arranged. He feigned confusion and told the FBI that he'd been asked to come to the scene, and he'd assumed that everyone knew he was coming, but he obeyed orders and left.[3]

Three days later, apparently having thoroughly enjoyed his time in the Catoctin Mountains, he formally applied to be a member of the Red Cross's local disaster response unit, telling the Red Cross, "Perhaps, I could help in case of a disaster related to biological agents."

The search of the pond went on for several days, but then ended as suddenly as it had started.

Late the next month, in January of 2003, the search began again. The pond was frozen, so holes had to be cut into the surface to allow divers to search beneath the ice. Roadblocks had been set up, and restrictions were put in place to prevent news helicopters from hovering over the pond and the small town of tents that had been erected nearby.

Ivins' February 12, 2003 Interview

Meanwhile, another team of FBI agents was still trying to sort through its list of possible suspects at Ft. Detrick, and on Wednesday, February 12, 2003, they talked with Bruce Ivins.[4]

Ivins had been waiting for the FBI to interview him, and he had a packet of materials ready to hand over to them. The packet included a list of individuals that the FBI might want to question, statements regarding his work on the Daschle and *New York Post* letters, a spore calculation form for the Leahy letter, and his "Hoover Statement," in which Ivins described his work analyzing the contents of the anthrax letters, provided explanations for the swabbing incidents in December of 2001 and April of 2002, and stated his concerns that other people at USAMRIID weren't taking sufficient precautions when handling dangerous pathogens such as anthrax.

The "Hoover Statement" had been prepared in April 2002 in response to an informal investigation performed by an Army colonel from the Walter Reed Army Institute of Research, Dr. David L. Hoover. Hoover had collected statements under oath from all witnesses to the infamous April contamination incident.[5]

During the February 12, 2003, interview with the FBI agents, Ivins endlessly complained about the way the Daschle letter was handled by others before it was turned over to him. Ivins didn't approve of the Daschle letter being handled in the Diagnostic Systems Division (DSD). He had no idea who might have handled the Daschle letter before it was given to him or whether someone in DSD may have opened the Ziplock bag when it was not inside a biosafety cabinet in that area.

Ivins explained that when he quantified the spore contents of the Daschle letter, Peter Jahrling had watched from outside of Room B313, looking in through the glass in the door. The biosafety cabinet is just inside the door. One of Ivins' assistants was also in B313 while Ivins worked.

Because Ivins didn't have a scale accurate enough to weigh very finite amount, when he weighed the spores he'd extracted from the Daschle letter during his October 17, 2001, quantification tests, he had to first weigh the empty vial in a BSL-2 lab in another part of the building, then he added the spores to the vial in his BSL-3 lab in Room B313, and then he carried the closed vial and its contents back to that same accurate scale to measure the weight of the vial *and* the spores. It was one of the problems encountered daily at USAMRIID as a result of having inadequate funding.

Ivins also complained about the latex gloves they were forced to use, claiming that they were "bargain gloves and sometimes had holes or were torn."

Ivins volunteered his opinions about the attack anthrax, suggesting that the attack spores were probably grown in broth in fermenters, not on agar plates. They seemed too clean to have been agar grown. His lab had no fermenters. He stated that agar growth produces spores which are far dirtier than the spores from the anthrax letters. When growing spores on agar, he said, it seemed that no matter how many times you washed them, you'd never get them as clean as spores grown in broth in fermenters.

The FBI interview report shows that considerable time was spent on discussing flask RMR-1029 and how it was created in 1997 by combining spores grown at Dugway with spores grown at USAM-

RIID. Flask RMR-1029 had been kept in the cold room in Bacteriology Suite 3 since it was created, and a record had been kept of every aliquot removed from the flask. It was clearly not possible for someone to have used spores taken directly from RMR-1029 to dry and then put into the letters. That would have required a large quantity of material that he would have noticed as being missing.

The agents requested any documentation Ivins might have about the trip he took to Covance research facility in Pennsylvania on the morning of September 18, 2001. They also wanted copies of any emails he had regarding the Red Cross request that he volunteer to do canteen work during FBI in the search of the pond areas in the Catoctin Mountains. And they wanted to see his lab notebooks from 2001.

The FBI agents had done a check of Ivins' computer and were concerned that he didn't have any emails or electronic calendar information from prior to May 2002, which seemed very odd. Ivins' explanation was that there had probably been some kind of upgrade of computer systems at around that time, thereby eliminating all old email records.

The interview took place in Ivins' office, but the agents were also given a limited tour of Suite B3, merely looking through the window next to the passbox and the window in the "crash door" at the rear of the suite to see how things were laid out.

At the end of the session, as the FBI agents were preparing to leave, Ivins volunteered a suggestion that the silicon that had been found in the attack spores could have come from purifying and drying spores by the use very fine sand, the way he'd read that they do things in Iraq.

Ivins Provides Information

Ivins evidently felt that the February 12 interview had gone very well for him. On Friday, February 21, Ivins called one of the agents who had interviewed him to say he'd found the documents about the trip to Covance on September 18, 2001. Plus he had some other documents about what he was working on in the fall of 2001, which he described as mostly "desk work."[6]

A Crime Unlike Any Other

On the following Monday, February 24, Ivins supplied the FBI with more information about what he'd been doing in the fall of 2001, plus a copy of the reference sheet on which all details and usage of spores from flask RMR-1029 were recorded.[7]

ALL FBI INFORMATION CONTAINED
HEREIN UNCLASSIFIED
DATE 12-08-2008 BY 60324 UC BAW/RS/LJC

U.S. Army Medical Research Institute of Infectious Diseases

Reference Material Receipt Record

Date Received at USAMRIID: 22 Oct 97

Received by: Bruce Ivins / Bruce E. Ivins

Description: Highly purified Ames spores, ~3x10¹⁰/ml, 1000ml total, in polycarbonate flasks

USAMRIID Part No.: 1029   Lot No.: Not Applicable

Supplier: Bacterial / Dried Mycotoxin +USAMRIID, Bacteriology Division   Quantity: 1000ml total

Expiration Date: 31 Dec 2002   Storage: 2-8°C in Isopropanol 33 cold room in Bldg 1425

Vendor: From B. anthracis Ames Strain, Ames, Iowa

Condition: Very good

Intact Container: Y   N

Temperature upon arrival: 2-8°C

Comment: See USAMRIID Notebook 4010. These spores are highly purified. They are >95% unclumped, single, refractile spores.

Reference Material Inventory:

Amount In	Amount Used	Date	Balance Left	Init.
1000 ml	1 ml	9/17/98	999 ml	BEI
	1 ml	3/16/99	998 ml	BEI
	1 ml	2/23/99	997 ml	BEI
	2 ml	5/5/99	995 ml	BEI
	1 ml	5/11/99	994 ml	BEI
	6 ml	2/22/00	988 ml	BEI
	8 ml	3/22/00	980 ml	BEI
	75 ml (5243)	4/3/00	905 ml	BEI
	1 ml	6/29/00	904 ml	BEI
	40 ml (5272 a)	7/7/00	864 ml	BEI
	40 ml	7/28/00	824 ml	BEI
	100 ml	12/14/00	724 ml	BEI

Exhibit #21 - RMR-1029 Reference Material Receipt - page 1

RMR 1029 - page 2

from previous page

Amount In	Amount Used	Date	Balance Left	Init.
624 ml	60 ml	6 Apr 01	564 ml	BA
564 ml	90 ml	1 May 01	474 ml	BA
474 ml	50 ml	15 Jun 01	424 ml	BA
424	50 ml	9 Jul 01	374 ml	BA
374 ml	5 ml	27 Aug 01	369 ml	BA
369 ml	10 ml	4 Oct 01	359 ml	BA
359 ml	12 ml	2 Nov 01	347 ml	BA
			358 ml	BA
358 ml	1 ml	14 Nov 01	357 ml	BA
357 ml	10 ml	15 Nov 01	347 ml	BA
347 ml	40 ml	10 Dec 01	307 ml	BA
307 ml	8 ml	21 Dec 01	299 ml	BA
299 ml	2 ml	14 Jan 02	278 ml	BA
278 ml	1 ml	18 Mar 02	277 ml	BA
277 ml	5 ml	2 Apr 02	262 ml	BA
262 ml	20 ml	22 Jul 02	242 ml	BA
242 ml	50 ml	5 Aug 02	192 ml	BA
192 ml	35 ml	17 Sep 02	157 ml	BB
157 ml	3 ml	1 Nov 02	154 ml	BA
154 ml	50 ml	Nov 02	104 ml	BA
		29 Nov 02		
104 ml	26 ml	18 Feb 03	78 ml	BA
78 ml				

Exhibit #22 - RMR-1029 Reference Material Receipt - page 2

On March 3, 2003, Bruce Ivins was again formally interviewed at USAMRIID by FBI agents. Ivins supplied the agents with another list of people he felt the FBI should interview regarding the attacks, people who Ivins implied had the capability to make the attack powders and the temperament to send them through the mails.

He also turned over emails showing that it was Peter Jahrling who had asked him to do the spore concentration test on the powder from the Daschle letter. Ivins explained that he didn't have any idea of who had custody of the Daschle letter at that time, so even if Jahrling had simply told him to go get the letter, Ivins wouldn't have known where to go unless Jahrling told him. And, without approval from someone else, Ivins was certain that Stephanie Redus would never have given the letter to him.

Ivins again stated that, in retrospect, after he saw how easily the spores floated around inside the hood when he merely touched the letter, he felt that the letter should have been handled only inside an enclosed glovebox, and not merely under the hood of a standard biosafety cabinet. But, there were no gloveboxes in Suite B3.

Ivins told the agents that the "scuttlebutt" was that the people in the Diagnostic Systems Division who had originally handled the Daschle letter had all been put on Cipro because of the careless way they handled it. But, if Ezzell made a mistake, the most he'd get would be a slap on the hand. If the same mistake were made in other labs - specifically in B3, there would be much more severe penalties.

Ivins gave his opinion that the Daschle letter shouldn't have been carried around in a Ziploc bag, it should have been in a can. It should never have been in the Diagnostic Systems Division, since that is a BSL-2 lab. And, Ivins had been advised by higher authorities that he should never have examined the letter in his lab, either. He'd been given a large, new Standard Operating Procedure manual describing how evidence would be handled in the future. No evidence was to be handled in B3 or anywhere in the Bacteriology Division in general.[8]

But, no one in high authority at USAMRIID seemed to be particularly upset with Bruce Ivins over the handling of the letter evidence or his unauthorized cleanings in December of 2001 and April of 2002. On the 14th of March, 2003, in a formal ceremony at the Pentagon, Army Secretary Thomas White presented Bruce Ivins, Patricia Fellows, Dr. Louise Pitt and Steven Little with the Exceptional Civilian Service Award -- the highest award given to Defense Department civilian employees -- for helping solve technical problems in the manufacture of anthrax vaccine.

"Awards are nice," Ivins said in accepting the honor. "But the real satisfaction is knowing the vaccine is back on line."[9]

Ivins' plan to use the anthrax letters to restart the efforts to develop a better anthrax vaccine had succeeded beyond his wildest dreams.

Exhibit #23 - Dr. Bruce Ivins at 2003 Awards Ceremony
(Photo courtesy of USAMRIID)

Chapter 29

Interviews & Lawsuits

Until the science being used in the Amerithrax investigation could provide some solid leads - which might possibly never happen - the FBI and USPIS investigators were forced to rely on age-old police procedures, which mostly consisted of interviewing people and checking backgrounds, police records and alibis in order to narrow down the list of potential suspects.

It had been learned via tracking documented transfers of the Ames strain that there were three laboratories outside of the US which had received samples of the Ames strain from USAMRIID. Needless to say, it wouldn't have been easy for personnel at the labs in England, Canada and Sweden to make the trip to Princeton to mail the letters *twice* without leaving a trail. But, everyone still had to be checked out.

To a somewhat greater degree, the same held true for personnel working at Dugway Proving Grounds in Utah, which was 2,300 miles from the mailbox in Princeton. Plus, the tests performed by the University of Utah on water-related isotopes in the attack powders appeared to show that Dugway could be ruled out as the source of the attack anthrax.[1]

Battelle Memorial Institute, which had become a favorite target for conspiracy theorists because they did work with anthrax for the CIA, eventually turned out to be the only lab beside USAMRIID that had a stock of the Ames strain with the same morphs that were in the attack anthrax. But, Battelle was very different from USAM-

RIID in the way they did business, making it much easier to rule out people as potential suspects.

Records showed that only 42 people physically accessed the area where the Ames sample was stored from the time it arrived on May 21, 2001 until after the mailing of the second batch of letters. That list was cut down to just 20 who had the technical knowledge to create the powders. Then there were the Battelle operating policy factors which were different from USAMRIID: (1) Every minute of every person's lab time at Battelle was billed to someone, so there was no such thing as spending hours at night in a lab for unexplained reasons. (2) During normal business hours (7:30 a.m. to 4:30 p.m.), Battelle scientists never worked alone. A "two person rule" had been in effect in 2001. And, (3) on the one 4-evening instance during the critical September-October-2001 time period where scientists did work after normal hours, there were still always two scientists in the lab where the Ames material was stored, and on every one of the four evenings it was a different pair of individuals.[2]

For people not actually involved in the investigation, al Qaeda would remain a top suspect for years. However, the FBI had managed to recover 22 pounds of body parts from the 4 hijackers who had died in the crash of Flight 93 in Pennsylvania. One of the bodies was that of Al Haznawi, who theorists believed had had an anthrax lesion on his leg. Testing of the body parts found no trace of anthrax.[3] The same was true of a small lab in Afghanistan which intelligence agents had identified as a possible site for bioweapons development. Three swabs resulted in tentative positive matches for the Ames strain on the outside of an unopened medicine dropper package, on a sink and on a drain hose. But, when the entire sink, hose and other items were removed from the lab and brought to the US for additional testing, 1,254 samples found no trace of anthrax at all. There were absolutely no anthrax spores or live anthrax bacteria in the lab.[4]

Ivins' April Interviews

There is no public record of how specific individuals at USAMRIID were eliminated as potential suspects, but it's clear that nothing was being found that would eliminate Bruce Ivins. FBI agents interviewed him again on April 15 and 17, 2003, both times by telephone while Ivins was at work.[5]

On the 15th, Ivins was questioned about the VirTis lyophilizer (a freeze dryer) that was kept in Suite B5, a BSL-2 suite. Years ago, Ivins had arranged for its purchase. He'd used the refrigerator-size device to make "monophosphoryl lipid A protective antigen vaccine," a non-specific immunity booster that doesn't offer protection against any specific disease, but it can be added to many other vaccines to improve their effectiveness.[6]

Ivins was also asked about the procedures for preparing spores for the animal aerosol challenges that were performed in Building 1412. He explained the process to the agents. When asked about plates in autoclave bags, Ivins said he had no idea how long the autoclave bags might remain in the basement before they were actually put into the autoclave and sterilized.

It appears to have been clear to Ivins that the FBI was very carefully considering the idea that the attack spores could have come from the inoculated plates in the trash that were allowed to accumulate before autoclaving. No doubt feeling uncomfortable with that line of discussion, Ivins mentioned once again that growing spores on plates produced dirtier spores than growing in broth, and the spores in the attack powders looked to him like they were grown in broth.

Two days later, on the 17th, when Ivins was again interviewed via telephone. The questions were about parties celebrating promotions, new jobs, births and marriages held at USAMRIID and if guest lists were ever maintained. Ivins used the opportunity to express how bad he felt because someone could have used some product from his lab to make the anthrax powders sent in the mailings. He claimed it was particularly distressing to him to realize that someone could have used the trash he generated from aerosol challenge preparations to collect the spores that were in the anthrax letters.

The Mountain Pond

Van Harp, as the head of the Washington Field Office, had hoped to see the case solved before he retired. That was not to be.

Harp announced on April 18, 2003 that he would be retiring from the FBI in May. Inspector Richard L. Lambert was put in direct charge of the Amerithrax investigation.[7]

By all accounts, Inspector Lambert appeared to be focused on Steven Hatfill as the prime suspect.[8] And, the media was equally or even more intensely still focused on Hatfill. Harp's replacement as head of the Washington Field Office was Michael Mason, who began his time in that office by expressing regret over the leaks which seemed to continually point to Steven Hatfill as the prime suspect in the case.[9]

One specific pond in the Catoctin Mountains was still viewed by some as a possible source for evidence against Hatfill, probably because a pair of cloth work gloves had been found at its bottom. The public and city officials worried that anthrax in the pond might somehow contaminate the water supply for the town of Frederick, particularly after CNN mistakenly stated on May 11 that traces of anthrax had been found in the pond. The statement was retracted the next day, after the finding was determined to be merely another "false positive."[10] The pond was only about an acre in size, and no more than 10 feet deep at its deepest point, but cutting holes in the ice in December and January and sending down divers had found nothing but the gloves.

In early May, divers had been sent back down into the cold waters of the pond, and they'd stumbled upon a plastic box or tub of unknown purpose. It had two holes cut into its opposite sides, and speculation was that it could have been a makeshift glovebox used by the anthrax mailer. Some even suggested the glovebox - if that is what it was - might have been used underwater to prevent the escape of any spores while the culprit poured the spores into the letters and sealed them. Holding an air-filled box of any significant size under water was next to impossible and seemed totally impractical, but it was not *im*possible, and there was simply no way to claim that there was no other potential evidence or anthrax at the bottom of the pond unless the pond was thoroughly and exhaustively tested and searched. And, the only way to conclusively do that would be to actually *drain* the pond to allow investigators to poke around at what was left at the bottom. In May of 2003, the decision was made to do that. It would cost about a quarter million dollars.[11]

A Crime Unlike Any Other

Late in May, Steven Hatfill became angry over the way he was being followed so dangerously close by two FBI vehicles. After he'd stopped to park at a curb, Hatfill got out of his car and approached the nearest FBI vehicle to complain about the "tailgating" and to take the agent's picture. The agent tried to move his vehicle away from Hatfill, and, in doing so, accidentally ran over Hatfill's foot. Hatfill fell to the ground and banged his head. Paramedics were called to the scene and treated Hatfill for a head abrasion and a severely bruised foot, but he refused to be taken to a hospital. As if to pour salt on his wounds, during the brouhaha, the police ticketed Hatfill for "walking to create a hazard" (a.k.a. jaywalking), which involved a $5 fine. The FBI employee who had driven the car over Hatfill's foot was not cited.[12]

In June, the mountain pond was drained. Tests were done on the mud at the bottom of the pond, and on every piece of junk found in the pond - including a bicycle, some coins, fishing lures, a hand-gun, sodden logs and a street sign.[13]

Before very long, it was clear that there was no anthrax in the mud or anywhere else in the pond. The plastic box was most likely nothing more sinister than a makeshift turtle trap. And, of course, the handgun had no connection to Dr. Steven Hatfill or the Ameri-thrax investigation.

The "Mobile Bioweapons Lab"

In July of 2003, a battle was going on which pitted Barbara Hatch Rosenberg and *The New York Times* against Dr. Steven Hatfill. Rosenberg started claiming that Dr. Hatfill had built a functional mo-bile bioweapons lab for the government, and *The New York Times* printed a totally bogus report about it. The report by William J. Broad, David Johnston and Judith Miller began with this:

> Three years ago, the United States began a secret project to train Special Operations units to detect and disarm mobile germ factories of the sort that Iraq and some other coun-tries were suspected of building, according to administra-tion officials and experts in germ weaponry.

> The heart of the effort, these officials said, was a covert plan to construct a mobile germ plant, real in all its parts but never actually "plugged in" to make weapons. In the months before the war against Iraq, American commandos trained on this factory.[14]

The article stated that the FBI had examined the "mobile germ plant" as possibly being where Steven Hatfill had made the attack anthrax, but they found no trace of anthrax spores and no indication that it had been used to make the attack powders. As part of his work at SAIC, Hatfill had helped in its construction, which was done in a government contractor location in Frederick, not far from where Hatfill lived, and construction had been underway at the time of the attacks. The article suggested that the mobile plant could be in violation of international treaties.

The next day, *The Washington Post* printed an article by Marilyn Thompson which supported many of the claims in *The Times*.[15] But, on that same day, *The Baltimore Sun* published an article by Scott Shane which made it clear that the lab was *not* a functional bioweapons lab.[16] And the *Frederick News-Post* also published an article on the same subject.[17]

On July 17, Barbara Hatch Rosenberg posted a lengthy *Hypothesis regarding US trailer lab* on the Federation of American Scientist's (FAS) web site. After receiving a phone call from Hatfill, FAS executive Ivan Oelrich made a public statement via a web site:

> In the past, she [Rosenberg] has used her FAS affiliation when speaking about Mr. Hatfill. FAS takes no position regarding Mr. Hatfill. We have a disclaimer to that effect on our website. In two cases in which Rosenberg's FAS affiliation has been noted in newspaper articles, we have written letters to the editor disavowing her speculation (although the letter was published in only one case).[18]

The so-called mobile lab was actually just a hollow shell containing absolutely no scientific equipment of any kind, nothing except an air-conditioner. Its purpose was to show troops and pilots what such a vehicle looked like so they wouldn't blow them up on a battlefield.

A Crime Unlike Any Other

Hatfill's lawyers had warned Rosenberg more than once that she was treading on litigious grounds, but she seemed to take the warnings as proof that she was doing the right thing, and she just forged ahead.

Lawsuits

On August 15, Steven Hatfill contested the $5 fine he received for jaywalking, but after the hearing examiner looked at the video the FBI employee had taken of Ivins standing in the street to take photographs and approaching the FBI vehicle, instead of remaining on the sidewalk, the hearing examiner agreed that Hatfill was the one at fault and ordered that the $5 fine be paid.[19]

Eleven days later, Hatfill and Connolly were in court again. On August 26, Hatfill filed a lawsuit accusing Attorney General John Ashcroft and other government officials of violation of Hatfill's constitutional rights. The lawsuit claimed that, since August of 2002, Ashcroft and the FBI had been conducting "a coordinated smear campaign," following him around, wiretapping his telephone and demanding that he be fired from his job at Louisiana State University, all because the FBI needed to appear to be actively working on solving the anthrax murders of 2001.[20]

On September 3, Maureen Stevens filed a lawsuit against the government for carelessly allowing deadly bacteria from their labs to be used to kill her husband. The claim was that samples of anthrax were known to have gone missing from Ft. Detrick as far back as 1992, but the government never instituted adequate security measures to keep anthrax spores from falling into the wrong hands. Judge Daniel T. K. Hurley would first have to determine if the U.S. District Court for the Southern District of Florida had jurisdiction in the case, and the government was claiming that the lawsuit could jeopardize the investigation. But, legal experts were saying that Stevens should have a viable case.

"The Pursuit of Steven Hatfill"

There were many in the media and academia who seemed absolutely convinced of Hatfill's guilt. Marilyn Thompson of the

Washington Post wrote a long article for their September 14, 2003, Sunday magazine titled *The Pursuit of Steven Hatfill.* The article conjured up more fanciful connections between Hatfill and the anthrax attacks, including the "mobile germ lab" and the fact that Hatfill had attended medical school in Harare, Zimbabwe, which was not far from a suburb named "Greendale." There was no "Greendale School" anywhere in Zimbabwe, but the implication was it couldn't be just a coincidence that the return address on the senate letters was "Greendale School." The article dug into Hatfill's background with various government agencies and repeated the old claim Hatfill had been in Africa when one of History's deadliest anthrax outbreaks occurred. (The outbreak was a natural phenomenon, not the work of any government agency or sinister force.[21])

And, Hatfill had dated a Malaysian woman for several years, which seemed to connect to a "hoax letter" sent from Malaysia to the Microsoft offices in Reno shortly after the anthrax attacks.

In reality, the Reno letter was not a "hoax letter," it was just an angry letter from a man in Malaysia who had some kind of dispute with Microsoft. And the anthrax reading was merely another "false positive."

To cover all bases, Marilyn Thompson dutifully pointed out that Hatfill seemed to have a good alibi for the time of the crimes, plus he worked with viruses, not bacteria, so he wasn't really an expert on anthrax.

"The Message in the Anthrax"

In their October 2003 issue, distributed in mid-September, *Vanity Fair Magazine* published an 11-page article titled *The Message in the Anthrax* by Donald Wayne Foster.

Much of the *Vanity Fair* article is about Foster himself, as he first paints himself as being on call to the FBI as an expert on the writings of hoaxers, terrorists and the anthrax case. The editor's description of the article says, "Frustrated with the FBI's anthrax task force, he [Foster] unseals his investigation of a most intriguing - and disturbing - suspect."

That "suspect," of course, was Steven Jay Hatfill.

A Crime Unlike Any Other

Foster started the article by connecting Dr. Hatfill to the anthrax attacks using the same material Marilyn Thompson used - the anthrax epidemic in Africa, the fact that there was a town in Africa called "Greendale", etc. Then he added his own theories about connections to various hoax letters. The implication was that, if Hatfill even mentioned a hoax letter or if a hoax letter was every mailed from anywhere near Hatfill, he could have been responsible. In a 1997 interview about biological preparedness, Hatfill had mentioned the B'nai B'rith hoax letter that was in the news at the time. It had contained a Petri dish of harmless *Bacillus cereus*, an anthrax simulant. Foster seemed to imply that Hatfill could he have sent the B'nai B'rith hoax letter. Otherwise, why would he have remembered or mentioned it?

Foster described his attempts to bring such things to the attention of the FBI, but no one at the Bureau seemed interested. So, Foster persisted, going on and on in the article, developing other tenuous connections between Hatfill and the anthrax letters of 2001, including a connection to a flood of hoax letters sent from Lafayette, Louisiana, in March of 2002, after Hatfill had supposedly moved to Louisiana. Foster's implication was that Hatfill sent them. In reality, Hatfill never moved to Louisiana, he wasn't in Louisiana when the hoax letters were mailed in April - not March - and the person who had mailed the letters had been identified as a mentally ill man named Stephen Michael Long, who'd been arrested for the crime in August.

Chapter 30

Ivins Under Scrutiny

Of course, there were still those who believed that al Qaeda must have been behind the attacks, since the attacks followed so closely after 9/11, and the first person to die was a man in Florida, where some of the 9/11 hijackers had stayed and had taken flight school training. In October of 2003, a book titled *The Anthrax Letters*, written by Leonard Cole was published. It pointed to al Qaeda as being behind the anthrax attacks and suggested that the so-called J-Lo letter was the "holy grail" in the evidence confirming Cole's hypothesis.

And, there were still those who solidly believed that the attack anthrax was weaponized with silica and that it came from some secret and illegal U.S. government bioweapons program. On November 28th, *Science* magazine printed an article by Gary Matsumoto titled *Anthrax Powder: State of the Art?* in which Matsumoto promoted a theory by Dr. Stuart Jacobsen, an expert in silicon microchips, that the attack powders were weaponized with tiny particles of fumed silica to overcome van der Waals forces which he believed caused clumping. It was nonsense from beginning to end, but because it was printed in *Science* magazine, it would be viewed by many as valid and would be cited for years in other scientific articles related to the weaponization of anthrax spores.

On December 2, Maureen Stevens lawsuit was officially accepted by Judge Hurley as being within his jurisdiction and it was entered on his docket for trial.

While this was going on, it was becoming clear to some FBI and Post Office investigators in the field that there were only a very few scientists who they weren't able to eliminate as suspects. And one of them was Dr. Bruce Edwards Ivins.

More Ames Samples

On September 5, 2003, the FBI contacted Dr. Ivins by telephone and asked about the locations of various freezers and cold rooms, and who used them.[1]

While Patricia Worsham and her assistants shared Suite B3 with Ivins, Ivins explained that Worsham used a different cold room. She used the one in Suite B4. All other USAMRIID scientists working with Ames strain anthrax used a cold room in Building 1412. The only freezer in B3 was a movable freezer that stood in the hallway outside of the cold room. Worsham and her people used a similar freezer in B4.

During the course of the conversation, the FBI agent mentioned anthrax researcher, Perry Mikesell, who had left USAMRIID in the mid-1990's. Ivins acknowledged that Mikesell had left samples of Ames anthrax behind that were still in the cold room used by Ivins. And, after the agent asked, Ivins further acknowledged that there were also samples in the same cold room that had been left behind by Gregory Knudson when Knudson left.

None of these items had been included in the samples that Ivins sent to the FBI repository in April of 2002 because they weren't samples belonging to Ivins' or his associates. The subpoena had only asked for samples that belonged to him and his team, and he'd never even thought about the old samples which might have been left behind by others and might still be in the cold room. The cold room was a clutter of hundreds of samples, some of them without any real identifying markings explaining their origin.

Ivins' sloppy lab procedures were being highlighted again. But, he deflected some of the fault by explaining that he had no way of knowing if someone else hadn't sent in slants from the Mikesell and Knudson materials. After all, Dr. Worsham and her people had access to the cold room, and so did almost everyone else at USAMRIID with access to Building 1425.

The FBI agent explained that an FBI scientist would be sent around in due course to pick up the samples left behind by Drs. Mikesell and Knudson and to look over the other materials in the B3 cold room.

Before the end of the day, Ivins had gone through his own notebooks to see what he may have missed of his own that could still be in the cold room, that he'd missed when he sent the samples to the FBIR in April of 2002. He then sent the FBI agent an 18 page FAX containing 17 pages of from his lab books plus a typewritten note indicating that there were indeed other Ames samples in the B3 cold room which had not been included in the material Ivins had turned over to the FBI repository in 2002.

The notes showed that, in the mid-1980's, Ivins had re-grown several samples of Ames using the original 1981 sample as seed stock. Most of those samples were probably still in the B3 cold room.[2] Ivins had simply forgotten about those old samples, and that's why he hadn't sent slants from them to the repository. By telling the FBI about them, Ivins was showing how cooperative he was with the investigation. If the FBI was going to be going through his cold room, they would almost certainly have found the unreported samples, anyway.

On October 21, Ivins provided slants from four containers of Ames he had long ago created and forgotten about. One of them was flask RMR-1030.[3]

Ivins explained that, even though it had a higher reference number, flask RMR-1030 had been created from ancestor Ames seed stock before flask RMR-1029. It had been created from 13 separate runs over a period from November 1995 to November 1996. It definitely should have been part of the April 2002 submission. And, the same held true for three other samples identified as 7739a, 7739b and 7739c, which were also apparently created from the original ancestor Ames sample.

More Interviews

On December 12, 2003, FBI agents paid Ivins a visit in his office at USAMRIID and interviewed him about the cold room and the samples he'd submitted to the FBIR. They asked for names of everyone who could have had access to that cold room in 2001 or a couple years before.[4]

Ivins listed all the names of people he could remember who had worked in Suites B3 or B4 during the years in question.

The agents questioned Ivins about foreign visitors to USAM-RIID who may have had unescorted access to cold room. Ivins had met some of the foreign visitors, but knew nothing about any access they may have had to other people's labs or cold rooms.

The agents also asked about other Ames samples of interest, samples obtained from other countries and other parts of the U.S., but Ivins knew nothing about them. But, Ivins could provide a long list of American scientists who had worked at USMARIID who might have taken samples of Ames out of Building 1425. He also provided the agents with gossip about conflicts between Mikesell and Knudson, explaining that there was friction because Mikesell had only had a Masters Degree, while Knudson had a doctorate.

One of the agents accompanied Ivins into Suite B3 for a look at the cold room and freezer. The B311 cold room was about 7 feet wide and 11 feet deep. It contained a work bench covered with samples, plus two shelves on the wall which were also covered with samples. And, there were also hundreds of samples simply stored in boxes or just setting on the floor of the room. Looking around at the labels on other samples, the agent found the word "Ames" on dozens of them. Some had Perry Mikesell's name on them, but most had no indication of who may have created them.

In the hallway outside of the cold room, Ivins showed the agent to a freezer that contained boxes of Ames bacteria samples. There were 15 freezer tubes marked "Ames" inside the freezer, and 18 more freezer tubes in a box marked "Ames spores" with information indicating the tubes contained materials extracted from the original Ames ancestor slant and diluted.

Clearly, Ivins had sent in slants from only a tiny fraction of the Ames samples he had. He'd assumed that all the tubes containing materials from the same source would have identical contents, and there would, therefore, be no need to send dozens of assumed duplicates to the FBI repository.

Before leaving, the agents asked for all of Ivins notebooks, explaining that copies would be made and the notebooks would be returned. Ivins turned over 15 notebooks, each with a unique USAMRIID number, since the notebooks were government property and issued to scientists and employees for the official recording of lab notes.

RMR-1030

On January 29, 2004, the FBI made a request of Bruce Ivins. The FBI needed to irradiate a sample of spores from flask RMR-1030, and they asked for Ivins' help in checking to make certain that the spores were truly dead after irradiation.[5]

A portion of the irradiated sample was sent to Sandia National Laboratories for testing to see if the silicon signature that had been detected in the attack spores was also present in the spores from flask RMR-1030. The results showed that there were indeed some spores in flask RMR-1030 which contained the same silicon signature that was present in the attack anthrax. But, only about 6% of the spores in flask RMR-1030 contained the silicon signature, where 65% to 75% of the attack spores contained the silicon signature.[6]

Since flask RMR-1030 was a combination of 13 different growth runs, one might conclude that one or two of the 13 runs used the same processes as were used to create the attack anthrax. It would be pure speculation, but what was undeniable was the fact that there *was* a greater percentage of spores containing silicon in flask RMR-1030 than in most other samples that had been examined by Sandia. Since Ivins had created all the spores in RMR-1030, it indicated that Ivins sometimes used a procedure that resulted in creating spores with silicon in their spore coats, even if it seemed very likely that he didn't know he was doing it.

In March of 2004, the media was claiming that the FBI had "hit a wall" on the investigation,[7] but, in reality, things were actually starting to fall together - albeit very slowly.

Around this time, the government claimed that the investigation was at a critical stage, and they didn't want the Stevens lawsuit probing into confidential matters that might divulge the current focus of the investigation. The same was true with the Hatfill lawsuit. In response to confidential information Judge Reggie Walton was pro-vided, he delayed the Hatfill lawsuit for six months to give the gov-ernment time to work on the case. In April, Judge Daniel Hurley did the same for the Stevens lawsuit.[8]

Missing Emails

On March 18, 2004, FBI agents again interviewed Ivins in his office at USAMRIID.[9] The interview began with questions about the fact that all of Ivins' emails from 2001 were missing from the com-puter in Ivins' office. Ivins couldn't explain how it happened. He said he'd consulted with someone in Computer Services and had learned that emails could be retrieved for the past two years, but it was a very expensive process. However, they had told him that it was not possible to retrieve emails from more than two years ago. So, his emails from 2001 were not recoverable that way.

Ivins was asked if he traveled to New Jersey in 2001. His re-sponse was that he didn't travel to New Jersey in 2001, and he didn't recall traveling to New Jersey since he was a child, when his father took the family on a tour of various historical sites in New Jersey and Massachusetts.

Ivins was also questioned about his whereabouts during the periods September 17-18 and October 5-9, 2001. Ivins supplied pa-per copies of emails sent on September 17 and 19 and October 5. He also provided music lists for the times he performed at his church on September 16 and October 7. But, none of that provided an alibi for the times of the mailings.

When asked, Ivins claimed he'd never bought a packet of pre-stamped envelopes from a postal vending machine.

These are direct questions related to the anthrax attacks, indi-cating that the FBI was now in the process of determining whether or not Ivins could be the anthrax mailer.

On April 7, 2004, the FBI arranged for Bruce Ivins to create slants from 22 samples of Ames that had been found in the B3 cold room, but which had not been previously sent to the FBI repository because it was unclear who originally created the samples.[10]

On April 13, Ivins was interviewed via telephone to get his help in deciphering illegible or barely legible entries on the Reference Material Receipt Report for flask RMR-1029.[11] Ivins used the opportunity to state that he had no reason to suspect that anyone who worked or previously worked in the USAMRIID Bacteriology Division was responsible for the anthrax mailings. However he couldn't say the same about Building 1412, which Ivins characterized as a "black hole" for *Bacillus anthracis* spores. He'd sent trillions of spores over to Building 1412 that were never seen again. He claimed there was no reason to suspect anyone in Building 1425 had accessed flask RMR-1029 without approval, and there was no reason to be concerned that someone might get Ames material by rifling through the lab's trash to get to the growths on plates that had been used to test samples extracted from flask RMR-1029.

The questioning was becoming more intense and specific, but, it would be another year before the investigation would truly start to focus on Dr. Bruce Ivins.

Chapter 31

Collateral Damage

In mid-2004, 31 FBI agents and 13 postal inspectors were still working full time on the Amerithrax investigation, plus one U.S. Attorney and a "scattering" of support personnel.[1] There were also FBI scientists working part time on the case whenever the need arose. Their attention was focused on a list of between 12 and 20 individuals who were still considered to be potential suspects.

The head of the task force, Richard Lambert, considered Steven Hatfill to be the top suspect. Many of the agents working under Lambert disagreed and had favorites of their own, although none had any solid alternative to Steven Hatfill. The public focus on Hatfill meant that any alternative had to be an *obviously* better choice. There needed to be *convincing* and *undeniable* evidence to move someone else to the top of the list.

There was still no such evidence - not against Hatfill and not against anyone else.

In early-May of 2004, FBI agents were digging deeper into the lab records of the USAMRIID scientists who hadn't yet been eliminated from their list of possible suspects. One of those possible suspects continued to be Bruce Ivins.

At the same time, FBI agents were still trying to track down every known sample of the Ames strain and all the information that could be gathered on the different methods used to produce anthrax spores.

Although it was certain the silicon in the attack spores was not deliberately added for weaponization purposes, on May 7, two FBI agents questioned Ivins about the use of anti-foam, a substance which helps reduce the formation of foam in fermenters and was suspected in a 1980 scientific paper of causing silicon to appear in spore coats of another *Bacillus* species. But, Ivins never used anti-foam materials, and he almost never used fermenters. He primarily grew spores in shaking flasks, and shaking flasks didn't produce enough foam to cause a problem. He did countless tests with plates, but there were no foam problems with plates.[2]

The agents also questioned Ivins about the meaning of certain notations in his notebooks. And one of them pointed out a math error in the Receipt Record for flask RMR-1029. On Feb. 22, 2000, the record showed that 6 milliliters of material had been removed from the flask, but when subtracting 6 from the remaining 994 milliliters, the result was recorded as 888 instead of 988. Ivins was unfazed and just said that it meant there should currently be 100 additional milliliters of material in the flask than the record showed. The Receipt Record form wasn't a scientific document used for scientific work, it was a record that was kept to show where the material went and how much was left in the supply.

The agents also asked about what happened to serial dilution plates that had been used to determine spore concentrations and how Ivins went about disposing of the plates. Ivins explained the procedure to them once again.

On June 3, FBI agent/scientist Darin Steele accompanied Ivins into Suite B3 to retrieve 25 samples of the Ames strain.[3] All the necessary chain-of-custody documents were completed, and the 25 samples were transported by helicopter to Navy Medical Research Center in Silver Spring, Maryland, for analysis.

Sample #15 was flask RMR-1029.

When sample #15 was tested, it was found to contain the same mutations that were in the attack anthrax. But, the sample from RMR-1029 Ivins had supplied to the FBIR in April 2002 did *not*.

On June 29, the FBI agents interviewed Ivins again. This time, they were interested in every notebook Ivins had ever used at

USAMRIID that contained any information of any kind about the Ames strain, even if the strain was just used as a control and not as the object of some experiment.[4]

Shutdown

On Tuesday, July 20, 2004, the FBI closed down some of the labs at USAMRIID to do a comprehensive search for additional samples of the Ames strain that hadn't yet been provided to the FBI repository. Newspaper accounts indicate that the search continued for the remainder of the week and all weekend, finally allowing the labs to operate again on Monday, July 26.[5]

There's no public record of exactly which labs were shut down, but it's certain that Suites B3 and B4 were among them.[6]

On July 30, one agent wrote a report about a phone call Ivins made to the College Board in Ewing, New Jersey, to obtain registration ticket for their October 2001 tests. A check of Ivins' credit card purchases showed that he paid a fee to obtain a registration ticket.[7]

Ivins' adopted twins were 17 years old in October of 2001. If anyone could prove Ivins was in New Jersey at the time of the mailings, Ivins could claim he had driven to Princeton to check it out as a possible place for his children to go to college.

On August 4, Ivins called an FBI agent he'd talked with many times before to advise the agent of an abstract for a scientific report that someone had given him about "Bacillus spore suspensions in which the addition of silica to the spore coat was discussed." Ivins offered to send the abstract to the agent, and after he was given the fax number, he did so.[8] Presumably, this was the report from 1980 by Murray Stewart et al where silicon was detected in the spore coats of *Bacillus cereus* spores.

Ivins was almost certainly fishing for information while at the same time trying to appear helpful. If the FBI agents thought anything about the calls from Ivins at all, they may have thought it was just another aspect of Ivins peculiar personality and apparent lack of social skills. He was definitely an "odd ball," but he was in a profession where odd balls were common.

And, the head of the investigation, Richard Lambert, believed that Hatfill was the one. If the facts said that Hatfill couldn't have done it alone, then he must have had help.

Dr. Kenneth Berry

In August of 2004, everyone following the progress (or lack of progress) in the anthrax investigation was taken on a very puzzling side trip when newspapers and TV news shows suddenly started reporting on a possible suspect that no one had ever heard of before: Dr. Kenneth M. Berry of Wellsville, NY.

At the time of the anthrax attacks, Dr. Berry was an emergency room physician and Chairman of Emergency Medicine at Jones Memorial Hospital in Wellsville. And, at the time of the first anthrax mailing, Berry was on his honeymoon. He'd gotten married on Saturday September 15, 2001. He appeared as far removed from being a suspect as anyone could be.[9]

Yet, on August 4, 2004, FBI hazmat teams descended on Berry's home in Wellsville at about 8 a.m. in the morning, wearing full protective gear to begin searching the place in plain sight of all of his neighbors. Berry wasn't at home at the time. He was in Point Pleasant Beach, New Jersey, where he and his family were using his parents' summer home for a vacation. And, at 8 a.m., after Dr. Berry and his family had left to go to a local pancake house for breakfast, another swarm of FBI agents and postal inspectors descended on the red-shingled bungalow to search it and the small boat in the lagoon behind the home.[10]

When Dr. Berry and his family returned from having breakfast, they were not allowed to enter the search scene, and the FBI arranged for them to stay at the White Sands Ocean Front Resort and Spa nearby until the search was completed.

Later that same day, the FBI agents and postal inspectors searched an apartment in Wellsville where Berry had lived before he got married and another apartment in the Pittsburgh area where he had once lived. They searched a white Mercury Sable, the car he kept at the Connellsville airport in Pennsylvania, 223 miles from Wellsville, and they began a search through his flight records at the Connellsville airport, a search which would continue for several days.

A Crime Unlike Any Other

At least 50 FBI agents and postal inspectors were involved from the Washington Field Office, the Pittsburgh Field Office, the Buffalo Field Office, and even some from as far away as the Bahamas.

The FBI had asked Dr. Berry for permission to search his home in Wellsville, apparently in response to tips from the same people who were still pointing at Dr. Hatfill.

Dr. Berry had refused to give permission.

And Dr. Berry became wildly upset that the FBI was going ahead without his permission. He got into a public fight with his family in the lobby of the resort where the FBI had provided them with rooms. Authorities later said Berry punched his wife, Tana, and two stepdaughters, ages 17 and 18, and jeopardized his son, 3, during an argument that erupted over a cell phone. Berry's wife had given the FBI permission to check the cell phone. When Berry learned of it, he allegedly shoved his wife to the ground while she was holding their son, and after one of his stepdaughters hit him, he struck her and knocked her down.

What were the searches all about? The facts aren't clear, but there are several specific facts which stand out:

(1) In 1997, Berry founded the not-for-profit Planned Response Exercises and Emergency Medical Preparedness Training (PREEMT) Medical Counter-Terrorism Inc., an organization that trained medical professionals to respond to chemical and biological attacks. In a 1997 interview with *USA Today*, Dr. Berry "said military experts believe that a terrorist attack in a major U.S. city using a biological weapon is likely within five years."[11] On September 24, 1997, he presented a workshop on a hypothetical terrorist anthrax attack on San Francisco, which he warned would kill more than 1 million people.[12] To conspiracy theorists, this put him in the same category as Steven Hatfill: someone who was warning people about anthrax attacks before the anthrax attacks happened.

(2) In late 2000, Dr. Berry had persuaded William Patrick III to give him a two-day course on using pathogens - including anthrax - as weapons. Dr. Berry had paid for the course with a personal check, even though he had claimed to be (and was) a contractor for the Defense Threat Reduction Agency.[13] To conspiracy theorists, this connected Dr. Berry to William Patrick III, who was a biowea-

pons expert as well as a mentor and a good friend of their favorite suspect: Steven Hatfill.

(3) Dr. Berry owned a private airplane. In October 2001, around the time the anthrax attacks became headline news, Dr. Berry resigned his position at Jones Memorial and began commuting 273 miles to work at the University of Pittsburgh Medical Center in McKeesport, PA. Using his own plane, he would fly down to MPMC McKeesport, work for four or five shifts in a row, and then he'd fly back to Wellsville to spend five days with his family before flying back to McKeesport again.[14] To conspiracy theorists, owning a private airplane and using it so frequently meant that Dr. Berry could have played a role in transporting the letters to Princeton for mailing.

(4) In October 2000, Dr. Berry filed a provisional patent for a system he touted as an effective way to respond to bioterrorism attacks. The system consisted of a computer program that combined weather data with information about various chemical and biological agents to determine how they would affect a certain location. He filed the actual patent application on Sept. 28, 2001, ten days after the first anthrax letters were postmarked but weeks before the first letters were actually found.[15] To conspiracy theorists, this meant that Dr. Berry could profit from the anthrax attacks which he seemed able to predict.

There was no "official story" of what the searches were all about. One source said that the FBI was just "tying up loose ends."[16] Another source believed that Dr. Berry could be a "material witness."

Dr. Berry was a doctor, not a scientist. He had no known lab skills. He had no known access to anthrax. He had no known experience with anthrax. He just had a brief connection to William Patrick III, and Patrick had a connection to Steven Hatfill.

And it all seemed to end about as quickly as it started. Dr. Berry's life was changed forever and nearly destroyed, but no one seemed to think he was the anthrax mailer. He was just someone who could have had information about the case but refused to allow the FBI to do a search of his home to help clear him. He appeared to be "collateral damage" in the investigation of "person of interest" Dr. Steven Jay Hatfill.

Chapter 32

Hatfill or Ivins

Bruce Ivins undoubtedly read about the destruction of Dr. Kenneth Berry's life with puzzled fascination, possibly with a feeling of horror. Berry lost his job as a result of the incident, and he'd been arrested for assault as a result of the public fight he had with his wife and children.

Although the Berry story only lasted for a few days, those few days would have still been fresh in Bruce Ivins' mind when he found his *own* name mentioned in the newspapers.

On Saturday, August 21, 2004, Ivins called the office the FBI had set up in Frederick and talked with the Supervisory Special Agent, telling him that the *Los Angeles Times* had printed a story on Friday about the environmental swabbings Ivins had done in December of 2001 and April of 2002.[1] Ivins complained that he'd done the swabbing to help the FBI, and now it was being mentioned in an article about sloppy researchers and disorganized labs. The article by a *Times* staff writer, Charles Piller, was titled *Anthrax Leaks Blamed on Lax Safety Habits*. It blamed "cavalier attitudes" for the safety breach, and, although it was clearly based upon the Containment report produced in May of 2002, to Ivins it also seemed to disclose confidential FBI information. But, it was the portion of the article that mentioned his role in the contamination report that bothered Ivins the most:

> The breach was discovered by Bruce Ivins, an institute researcher.

> He detected an apparent anthrax leak in December 2001, at the height of the anthrax mailings investigation, but did not report it. Ivins considered the problem solved when he cleaned the affected office with bleach.
>
> "I didn't keep records or verify the cultures because I was concerned that records might be obtained under the Freedom of Information Act," he said in a sworn statement included in the Army report.
>
> "I was also afraid that reporting would have raised great alarm within the institute, which at the time was very busy" working on the anthrax mailing samples.
>
> Ivins could not be reached for comment.[2]

While Bruce Ivins hadn't been available for comment, it was clear that many others at USAMRIID were reachable. One after another in the article, they talked about researchers having inadequate training, about dirty counter tops and floors, and how the place was like a "rat's nest."

The *LA Times* article made all of USAMRIID look like a bunch of careless researchers who didn't care about safety. But, it was the mention of his name that upset Ivins the most, and it wasn't something the FBI could do anything about.

On September 8, 2004, agents of the FBI again interviewed Ivins at USAMRIID.[3] The discussion began with questions about how Ivins created the anthrax samples he used. Then the agents asked about flask RMR-1030. Ivins told them that the flask just contained a "bunch of spores" he'd grown at various times in 1995 and 1996. Most of it had been used up. Whatever remained had been turned over to the FBI.

After creating the contents of flask RMR-1030, Ivins calculated how long it would take to create all the spores needed for some upcoming vaccine work and determined it would take about two years. That's when it was decided to contract with Dugway to help produce the large quantity identified as RMR-1029.

The agents then went through the RMR-1029 receipt record and asked for details about nearly every sample taken from the flask.

At one point in the interview, the agents asked for a copy of the form used to record the shipment to Dugway in 1997, and Ivins escorted them to the Safety Office where the records were kept.

The interview went on all morning, and they then took a break for lunch. While the agents were eating lunch, Ivins was doing research, and after the break he provided them with more documents about how flask RMR-1029 had been created.

The interview continued through the afternoon and concluded with Ivins advising them that it would take a large amount of time to get all the other records the FBI was requesting. He demonstrated that by doing a search for the word "Ames" in his email files, he came up with over 1,200 emails mentioning the subject.

On Friday, September 10, he sent the FBI a diagram he had drawn which showed the sources of various samples of spores sent to Dugway.[4]

On Monday, September 13, Ivins called to clarify once again that he never took flask RMR-1029 to Building 1412, he would only take diluted aliquots.[5]

A week later, an FBI agent stopped by to ask Ivins more questions about past versus current lab procedures.[6]

Hatfill Files Another Lawsuit

On October 4, 2004, it was announced that Steven Hatfill was suing Don Foster, *Vanity Fair* magazine and *Readers' Digest* for defamation. The lawsuit stated that Foster's article would leave no doubt in any reasonable reader's mind that Dr. Hatfill was not only the perpetrator of the anthrax attacks of 2001 but had also been behind numerous hoaxes. The lawsuit ridiculed Foster's theory of "literary forensics" and demanded ten million dollars in damages.[7]

On November 29, 2004, U.S. District Judge Claude Hilton dismissed the lawsuit Hatfill had filed against the *New York Times* because he believed the columns by Kristof didn't defame Hatfill but accurately reflected the state of the FBI's investigation in which Hatfill was labeled "a person of interest" by Attorney General John Ashcroft.[8]

246

Hatfill or Ivins

Disagreement at the FBI

It was becoming clear to some in the FBI's Amerithrax task force that there was at least one person being investigated who made a far better suspect than Steven Hatfill. One big reason for the shift in thinking was that it was becoming certain that no primary supply of the Ames strain had ever been stored in Building 1412, and Hatfill had worked exclusively in Building 1412. Try as they might, there was no way the FBI could make any kind of connection between Hatfill and a supply of the Ames strain. And, even if they could, it was clear that Hatfill didn't have the expertise to make the powders that were found in the letters.

Hatfill's lawsuit against *Vanity Fair* may have been another factor that caused people to start changing their minds. The lawsuit showed how idiotic some of the theories about Hatfill truly were. Don Foster had tried to implicate Hatfill in at least one hoax that had already been solved and an arrest made. And there was no reason to believe that Hatfill had been involved in any hoax anywhere.

Although Richard Lambert seemingly remained convinced that Hatfill was the best suspect in the case, investigators working under him were beginning to look seriously at Bruce Ivins. One of them was Special Agent Lawrence Alexander.

SA Lawrence Alexander

Alexander had joined the Amerithrax task force a year earlier, in January of 2004. He was a former Marine Corps officer and a graduate of Virginia Military Institute with a degree in biology. He had problems seeing Hatfill as the culprit from the very beginning. As soon as he started going through all the files on the case, he saw Hatfill as nothing but a loud-mouth and a braggart who could easily antagonize others, and Hatfill clearly lacked the skills to make the powders that were found in the anthrax letters. Gradually, Alexander became convinced that Hatfill had nothing to do with the attacks.[9]

It was also clear to agent Alexander that there were many other agents on the task force who also didn't see Hatfill as a viable suspect. But, there was someone in the files who was clearly a very good suspect: Dr. Bruce Edwards Ivins.

Dr. Ivins had no alibi for the times of the mailings.

Dr. Ivins had worked alone in his lab at night during the critical times when the anthrax powders could have been made, and his journals showed no explanation for those unusual hours.

Dr. Ivins' emails indicated he had mental problems.

Dr. Ivins was being too helpful and seemed to be trying to insinuate himself into the case to keep track of what was going on.

Dr. Ivins was viewed as harmless and socially inept by others at USAMRIID, and his quirks were viewed as "Bruce being Bruce," which meant that none of his fellow workers was ever alarmed by strange things he did.

In Amerithrax task force meetings, Alexander would voice his thoughts about Ivins. Others who also felt Hatfill was the wrong man started agreeing. Thomas Dellafera, the top postal inspector on the case was one of those who saw Ivins as a definite possibility, and together Alexander and Dellafera went though the files to see what they might have missed. They found emails from the period after the letters were mailed but before the letters were found in which Ivins seemed to predict what was about to happen. He seemed to be hopped up with excitement as he waited for something to happen.

Alexander worked for Supervisor Special Agent (SSA) Robert Roth. Roth tended to agree with Lambert that Hatfill was the most likely person to have sent the letters, but he encouraged Alexander to look for evidence that might point elsewhere. The AUSA on the case, Kenneth Kohl, was stating that there was no way he could try to get an indictment of Hatfill with the evidence available.

And then there was the genetic evidence. The tests done thus far on the thousand-plus samples in the FBI repository were showing very clearly that there was a genetic connection between the spores in the letters and the flask known as RMR-1029 which Bruce Ivins controlled. Yet, a sample from RMR-1029 that Ivins sent to the FBI repository in April of 2002 didn't match what FBI scientists found when RMR-1029 was sampled by others. That suggested to Alexander and others that Ivins may have deliberately falsified the April 2002 samples to mislead the investigation. That could be "consciousness of guilt." Ivins knew the real evidence would point to him, so he had submitted false evidence.

When questioned about the sample, Ivins said that it had been prepared by one of his assistants. But, the handwriting on the labels seemed to belong to Ivins -- possibly indicating additional "consciousness of guilt."

To see what else he might find, Alexander evidently arranged interviews with about 20 USAMRIID employees, but *not* with Ivins. When Ivins learned of the interviews and that he wasn't on the list, his paranoia may have been activated. Ivins called his lawyer, Richard P. Bricken, to tell him that that FBI might be looking at him.[10]

Alexander vs. Lambert

In mid-March, 2005, Lawrence Alexander decided to take a less confrontational approach with Richard Lambert. He met with Lambert one-on-one in his office and explained that unless they could clear Ivins, there could never be a legal case against Hatfill, since Hatfill's lawyers would learn of all the suspicious circumstances surrounding Ivins when it would come up in discovery. And they'd be presenting those suspicious activities to a jury to give them reasonable doubt of Hatfill's guilt. Ivins was clearly a viable suspect who had never been cleared by the FBI investigation.

The result of the meeting, however, was something that Alexander hadn't anticipated: Lambert decided he wanted to personally question Bruce Ivins as quickly as it could be arranged.

That decision set off a furor as Alexander and others protested that such a meeting without full preparation could do more harm than good.[11]

Lambert seemed to think that Ivins might be a good witness against Hatfill, if it could be shown that Ivins had given a sample from RMR-1029 to a USAMRIID scientist known by Hatfill.

Alexander argued that Lambert should wait for a week or two. If Ivins became spooked, he could throw away critical evidence. Such a confrontation should be coordinated with a hazmat team and others to perform a simultaneous search of Ivins home, and that would take at least a week to arrange.

But, Lambert wasn't willing to wait. A meeting between Lambert and Ivins was arranged for Thursday, March 31, 2005.

A Crime Unlike Any Other

The March 31, 2005 Interview[12]

On the morning of the 31st, Lambert arrived with FBI agent Ann Colbert. The agents began by having Ivins sign a non-disclosure agreement that he wouldn't talk about what they were going to discuss. Once that formality was over, Lambert asked about the environmental samplings Ivins did in December of 2001 and April of 2002. Ivins explanations merely repeated what he'd said in earlier interviews: He did the swabbings and cleanups because he was concerned that the anthrax letters hadn't been properly handled, since they were initially examined in a BSL-2 lab in the Diagnostic Systems Division. Plus, Kristie Friend had repeatedly expressed her concern about how anthrax from the letters was being handled and how easily things could be contaminated.

Why didn't Ivins tell anyone when he found spores in his office and in the change room? Because it wasn't enough to be concerned about, and he didn't want to create a fuss.

Lambert then explained to Ivins that the flask of anthrax spores Ivins controlled, RMR-1029, had been identified as the most likely source for seed material for the attack powders. This had been done by DNA testing of morphological variants found in the attack anthrax, which were also found in flask RMR-1029 and nowhere else except in samples that originally came from RMR-1029. And there was only one exception to that rule: the sample Ivins had supplied to the FBIR in April of 2002 did not have the mutations that other tests showed were definitely in the flask.

Ivins responded that he had no explanation for why the sample he submitted in April 2002 didn't have the mutations.

Lambert then shifted to asking about who might have had access to the contents of RMR-1029. Although Lambert didn't name Hatfill, it was clear that he was trying to figure out how someone could have gotten spores from RMR-1029. They knew Hatfill worked in Building 1412, and Lambert showed Ivins an early copy of the original Reference Material Receipt Record which indicated that the flask was stored in Building 1412.

Ivins stated that the record was wrong. It was thought at the time that the material was created that it would be stored in Building

1412, but it was never actually stored there. So, the person Lambert was talking about it could never have had access to the flask itself. However, aliquots - which would have had all the morphs - were frequently carried to 1412 for use in animal aerosol tests. This seemed to please Lambert, since it left open the possibility that Hatfill could have gotten the right material somehow.

Then the FBI agents turned their attention to the unusual hours Ivins spent alone in his lab during the weeks just prior to the anthrax attacks. Ivins explained that he worked long hours at night because of problems he had with his home life. Working kept his mind off of difficulties at home.

When asked about what happened to spore cultures that were discarded, Ivins explained that between 1 in 5 and 1 in 10 cultures is typically contaminated or spoiled in some way to make it unusable. So, it is autoclaved. No records are kept, since it's a routine part of the work and they don't record ever step of every process.

The agents asked about emails they'd found that he'd sent to Mara Linscott telling her about his "paranoid personality disorder." Ivins shrugged away the comments by saying he was feeling better now. He was no longer taking the anti-depressant Celexa. When agent Colbert asked if his psychological condition ever caused him to do something he wouldn't ordinarily do, Ivins shook his head and replied in the negative, adding that he wasn't the type of person to "act out." And he certainly has never hit his wife.

The agents asked Ivins about a time described in his emails when he drove 10 or 11 hours to secretly place a bottle of Kahlua on the doorstep of his former assistant, Mara Linscott. Ivins admitted that he done it on a day when his wife wasn't home. And he'd never done anything like that before or after.

The agents then asked if Ivins ever made such a trip to Princeton. Ivins responded by saying, "No, I was not involved," meaning the anthrax mailings. However, he acknowledged that he once drove to Gaithersburg, Maryland, to mail a package to Mara Linscott. He used a phony return address so she wouldn't realize the package was from him until she opened it. And Ivins went on to explain that he sometimes drove to Flintstone, MD, where some friends lived, but didn't visit his friends while there. He just drove there for the same reasons people go for a long walk.

A Crime Unlike Any Other

Ivins also explained that his father graduated from Princeton University, but Ivins had never visited there -- except when he was a kid when he and his family passed through the town on a tour of historic sites in 1956 or thereabouts. When asked why the anthrax mailer picked Princeton to mail the letters, Ivins suggested that the mailer might have been a Princeton professor.

Still trying to figure out why all the emails from 2001 were missing from his computer at work, the two FBI agents pointed out that immediately after 9/11 everyone was instructed to make backups of their hard drives in case the base was attacked. Ivins didn't recall the order, so he didn't make the backups. When agent Colbert showed him an email he'd sent telling someone else about the order and the need to do backups, Ivins couldn't remember sending the email, but he agreed to look for any backups he might have taken home after 9/11.

Later in the day, they went across the street to Ivins home where Ivins allowed FBI specialists to copy the hard drive on his home computer. While there, Ivins also searched unsuccessfully for backups to his work computer.

Ivins asked about what the FBI did if they found child pornography on someone's computer. The agents responded that they would turn it over to FBI specialists in such matters.

When the interview was coming to a close, Ivins evidently seemed very depressed, and SA Colbert asked him if he was okay. Ivins responded that he was fine, but it was devastating "to learn that someone may have used his Ames material to commit a crime and that people were dead because of it."

Later in the day, Ivins sent SSA Richard Lambert a one-page email letter titled *New Thoughts and theories on the Anthrax Letter Attacks* with comments about eight issues that had been discussed during that day's interview. The comments pointed to a long list of people at USAMRIID or formerly at USAMRIID who could have been behind the attacks. He listed possible motives and described their expertise. He also stated that he never knew Hatfill.[13]

When calling to mention he was sending the FAX, he talked with agent Ann Colbert. She asked if he was going to be all right over the weekend. He seemed depressed.

Ivins indicated that he was probably going to resume taking his anti-depressants. Then he added, "Well, I'm not going to jump off a bridge or anything like that." [14]

Late that evening, aware that guilty people who learn that they are under suspicion sometimes throw away incriminating evidence soon after being interviewed, FBI agents collected Ivins trash for examination. It contained nothing of value to the case.

Later it would be learned that, as a result of the Lambert interview, Ivins had decided to destroy all of his materials related to the KKG sorority. He had kept them in his office. He dumped everything into an autoclave bag, took the bag to Building 1412 and tossed it into the incinerator. [15]

On Monday, April 4, 2005, Richard Lambert called Ivins at work to ask a few more questions. Ivins advised Lambert that, because of the personal focus of many of the questions asked in the March 31 interviews versus the scientific focus of prior interviews, Ivins wanted his attorney, Richard P. Bricken, to be present during any future interviews. [16]

Lambert's questions were left unanswered.

Chapter 33

Focusing on Bruce Ivins

On April 5, 2005, FBI agents began checking Ivins' family history going back four generations, just to make sure Ivins was who he said he was.[1]

Meanwhile, Bruce Ivins was busy on the Internet doing research into subjects *not* mentioned during his meeting with Richard Lambert. He printed out many scientific documents about chemical analysis and nutrient analysis, and information about laboratories which would do trace contaminant testing for a fee. He researched companies which would do forensic chemical analysis for hire, possibly thinking that he might need such work to challenge whatever the FBI thought it might have against him.[2] His ego would tell him that he could out-evidence the FBI's experts on any subject related to anthrax.

On April 10 he also researched handwriting experts and articles about whether or not handwriting analysis was a legitimate science and could hold up in court. He researched "levels of proof and the reliability of handwriting analysis." He researched handwriting experts who could testify as expert witnesses in court. Although the subject of handwriting doesn't appear to have come up during the meeting with Inspector Lambert, it was apparently viewed by Ivins as a vulnerable area for him. It's possible he could have been doing the research to find experts who would testify that his handwriting didn't match the handwriting on the letters and envelopes. The articles questioned whether any handwriting analysis could be considered undeniable proof of anything. Handwriting analysis was an art, not a science. And many handwriting experts were more like fortune tellers than scientists.

Nancy Haigwood Revisited

While digging through the FBI files for anything that might pertain to Ivins, FBI Agent Robyn Powell came across another agent's notes from two years earlier, when Nancy Haigwood had sent a letter to the FBI and was then interviewed by phone by an agent regarding her suspicion that Bruce Ivins could be the anthrax mailer.

The agent's notes include comments about the fraudulent letter justifying hazing that Ivins had sent to the *Frederick News-Post* using Haigwood's name. And the only reason for such a vile act seemed to be Ivins' obsession with the Kappa Kappa Gamma sorority. That obsession had shown up before in the investigation of Bruce Ivins, but previous thinking was that it didn't seem to have any connection to the case.

That changed when Agent Powell Googled "Princeton" and "Kappa Kappa Gamma" and found that the KKG office in Princeton was at 20 Nassau Street.[3] The mailbox used by the anthrax killer was at 10 Nassau Street. A little additional research showed the mailbox wasn't next door to the KKG offices as the address seemed to indicate. It was a block away. But, it was a short block and the mailbox the culprit used was the *closest* mailbox to the KKG offices. It was about 175 feet away.

The Greendale Connection

Powell told Lawrence Alexander about what she'd found, and they both saw it as a connection between Ivins and the mailing location. The information was added into the FBI database and shared with other field agents. The agents dug further into Ivins background with Internet searches, and they also dug through FBI files where they found another previously unseen connection.

Bruce Ivins' wife, Diane, had served as president of a local anti-abortion group and was strongly committed to the American Family Association (AFA). Bruce and Diane had subscribed to the *AFA Journal* until March of 2005, the month when Ivins was confronted by Richard Lambert. Donations were made to AFA in the name of Mr. and Mrs. Bruce Ivins 11 times between 1993 and 1997.[4] After a long period without making any donations, another donation was made in 1998, one month after an article appeared in the *AFA Journal* about "the Greendale Incident."

The Greendale Baptist Academy incident involved a ten-year-old female child who had received corporal punishment at the school in the form of a spanking using a wooden paddle. The child came home bruised from the spanking, and the parents had to complain repeatedly to Bureau of Milwaukee Child Welfare.

Greendale Baptist Academy was referred to as Greendale School and Greendale School had been part of the return address on the anthrax letters sent to Senators Daschle and Leahy. Furthermore, the child who had been spanked was in the 4th grade, and that was also part of the return address on the Senate letters.

Ivins Evening Hours in B3

These findings prompted Lawrence Alexander to put together all the information from the In-Out logs for Ivins and all of his co-workers in the Bacteriology Division. With the help of another agent, he produced bar charts for the evening work hours for all of those scientists. The chart showed Ivins work hours were not only unusual for everyone at USAMRIID, but his work hours just prior to the attacks were also unusual for Bruce Ivins.

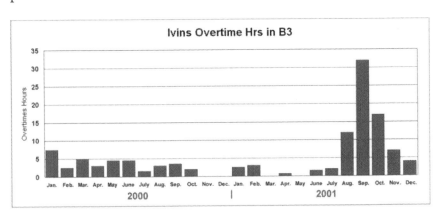

Exhibit #24 - Ivins' overtime hours in Suite B3 for 2000-2001

Focusing on Bruce Ivins

Day by day charts also seemed to indicate that between mailings, as if he had been waiting for the effects of what he'd done, Ivins didn't have any reason to go into Suite B3. It was intriguing evidence, but, for the moment, the charts just went into the file that Alexander and others were compiling about Ivins.

Contradictions

On May 24, 2005, a new 27-page report was placed in the Bruce Ivins file.[5] It appears to have been written by Lawrence Alexander, with copies sent to Richard Lambert and others in the Washington Field Office. The report showed that the reasons Ivins gave for performing the unauthorized "surveys" were contradicted by what he actually did. I.e., his actions didn't match his explanations. Regarding his December 2001 cleaning:

> 1.   Ivins stated he was concerned about contamination from the Daschle letter getting outside of the confinement suites, and his swabbings found contamination to confirm his concerns. So, why didn't he tell someone about it?
> 2.   Ivins said he didn't tell anyone because he didn't want to cause any unnecessary alarm. But why do the survey in the first place if you're not going to raise alarm if the results are positive?
> 3.   Ivins said he did it because Kristie Friend was worried. But when he found spores on her desk, he didn't tell her what he found.
> 4.   Ivins explained that he didn't think the amount of contamination was worth raising an alarm, but he didn't tell Kristie Friend that, either.

The report provided evidence that Ivins was lying about why he performed the swabbings. His claims would make more sense if he was the anthrax mailer trying to clean up after himself.

Ivins' explanation for the April 2002 swabbings appeared to be similarly bogus.

1.   Ivins claimed that he swabbed the path that the Daschle letter took from the Diagnostic Systems Division to the passbox into B3. However,

2.   Ivins didn't check any areas near the Diagnostic Systems Division.

3.   Ivins didn't check the hallway leading to Suite B3.

4.   Ivins checked his own office, which wasn't on the path the letter took.

Again and again the report mentions that Ivins claimed the contamination resulted from improper handling of the Daschle letter in the Diagnostic Systems Division. But testing didn't find any contamination there, only in areas associated with Ivins.

On June 7, 2005, someone in the Frederick office of the FBI filed a report on the prescription drugs Ivins was purchasing. It stated in part:

> Ivins was attending group counseling sessions during 2000 as a result of depression. He appeared to have refilled the Celexa® presciptions before the supply was supposed to have been complete. Ivins received a 45 day supply of Celexa® on 6/27/01 when he had 33 days remaining on the supply filled on 05/02/2001. Additionally, Ivins filled a 90 day supply of Celexa on 7/31/01 when he had 11 days remaining on the 45 day supply filled on 6/27/01.

also

> Cephalexin®, filled 10.18.01 (10 day supply), is an antibiotic. On 10.6.01, Ivins cut his finger but did not seek medical attention. Ivins feared the finger was infected and in an electronic email to [Mara Linscott] on 10/16/01, Ivins mentions that he should "probably go see someone and start talking antibiotics."

> Doxycycline HYC, filled 10.29.01 (6 day supply), is an antianxiety drug containing Valium. No additional information has been obtained regarding this prescription.

> In an email to [Mara Linscott] on 7.30/01 Ivins discussed the fact that he was taking Zyprexa®. Zyprexa® is used

on patients diagnosed with Schizophrenia. No additional
information has been obtained regarding this prescription.[6]

The FBI also checked USAMRIID records showing when
Ivins took paid leave. He took 4 hours of paid leave on September
17, 2001.[7] It wasn't enough time to drive to New Jersey, but it may
have been time spent preparing for the trip. He also had a group
counseling session from about 5:30 p.m. to about 7 p.m.

The FBI also accessed the computer files maintained by the
U.S. Government Patent Office to check into Ivins' patents to see if
they might provide any leads or motives.

On July 18, 2005, an FBI agent from the Frederick office
wrote a 4-page report explaining that, since Ivins had stated that
reading the book *Arrowsmith* in early high school had inspired him to
become a scientist, the FBI agent read the book to see what insights
it might provide into Ivins' psyche and motivations.[8]

Lower level FBI agents, particularly those working out of an
office in Frederick, were clearly starting to focus on Bruce Ivins, even
though Richard Lambert back at the Washington Field Office still felt
Hatfill was a better suspect. Even Lambert would have had to see
that there was a lot more and better evidence pointing to Ivins. And,
they'd run out of ideas on where to find additional evidence that
might point to Hatfill, whereas they were still uncovering very interesting details about Bruce Ivins every day.

Although there was still a year of work left to go before the
scientific analysis of the samples in the FBI repository could be considered complete and usable as evidence in court, it was already very
clear that Ivins' flask RMR-1029 was the source for the "murder
weapon." And no one could find any way Hatfill could have
accessed it, much less any reason he would have chosen that particular anthrax sample to use in the anthrax letters.

On July 28, 2005, for no other reason than that Ivins hadn't
shown up for work on time, an agent was dispatched to see what was
going on. The agent reported that, at approximately 8:15 a.m., there
were no "unusual vehicles or unusual activity at the home." There
was nothing wrong. Ivins was just late getting to work that day. But,
the FBI was now very interested in anything he did that was unusual.[9]

Chapter 34

A Change in Management

While FBI field agents were checking into everything there was to know about Bruce Ivins, Dr. Ivins continued to point at others as being better suspects than he.

In June of 2005, Ivins sent an email to Pat Fellows with the subject "Hot News!" in which he pointed the finger at John Ezzell, implying he could be the anthrax mailer. Ivins claimed Ezzell had made an anthrax powder in the 1990's that "was virtually identical to the spore powder in the letters," but in reality there were big differences. The work was done for DARPA, the Defense Advanced Research Projects Agency, which did a lot of secret work. The spores were grown in broth, which made them almost pure white instead of the egg-shell tan of agar-grown spores. They were also irradiated while still wet, making them harmless. However, Ivins was undeniably right in that the project proved that Ezzell was experienced in making dried anthrax powders.[1]

On July 30, 2005, Ivins wrote to his lawyer Richard Bricken about how John Ezzell had supposedly *admitted* to a group of people at a two-day conference at Argonne National Laboratories near Chicago in November of 2004 that he was the anthrax mailer. (No one else at the meeting remembered things that way.) Ivins also described in the letter how Ezzell had benefited from the attack because a book was written about him - *The Anthrax Letters: A Medical Detective Story* by Leonard A. Cole, who just happened to be a professor of science at Rutgers University, not far from where the anthrax letters were mailed. (In reality, the book only mentioned Ezzell once.)[2]

Ivins also suggested that Ezzell's boss, Colonel Erik Henchal, could have been involved, since he also profited from the attacks, because the attacks definitely led to Henchal getting a promotion in the spring of 2002.

Ivins was clearly also contemplating pointing the finger at Mara Linscott and Pat Fellows. He compiled a lengthy speculation about them in the form of an email that he sent to himself - perhaps to see if the FBI was intercepting his emails, in which case they might question him about his theory.

Ivins stated in the email that Fellows and Linscott could have worked on the letters together or separately, but their motive for sending the letters, he felt, was some kind of revenge against him. They wanted him to be blamed for sending the letters.[3]

The logic behind his reasoning was mostly that they seemed to talk about him behind his back.

Ivins was definitely feeling the pressure of being a potential suspect, even though the FBI was rarely talking with him after he said he wanted his lawyer to be present during interviews.

In September of 2005, at an International Conference on *Bacillus anthracis* in Santa Fe, NM, Ivins attended a gathering on the third floor of the La Fonda Hotel where complimentary drinks and hors d'oeuvres were being served. When someone mentioned to Ivins that one of the people having drinks nearby was FBI microbiologist Douglas Beecher, Ivins walked up to Beecher and loudly complained that the FBI was harassing him.

Although Beecher was working on certain scientific aspects of the case, he had no idea where Ivins stood on the list of suspects. His only response was to say nothing and walk away, a bit stunned.[4]

In late 2005, Bruce Ivins returned to his obsessions, as if they gave him some kind of assurance that he understood the forces behind all the bad things that were happening to him. He started posting comments about the Kappa Kappa Gamma sorority on various Internet forums, and he updated Wikipedia's article about KKG to include some questionable matters which others deleted, resulting in disputes and threats by Ivins to have the other person banned if the deletions continued.[5]

He posted under various names, including "prunetacos" and "jimmyflathead," continuing his postings into the first months of 2006 and for the rest of his life.

Where the Envelopes were Sold

In late-2005, Post Office Investigators found evidence which further indicated that the person behind the attacks probably didn't live in New Jersey where the letters were mailed, nor in Utah at Dugway Proving Grounds, nor in Ohio at Battelle. The culprit most likely lived in Maryland where USAMRIID was located.

As a result of tiny blobs of dried ink that randomly came and went, there were tiny defects in the printing on the back of the envelopes which said "THIS ENVELOPE IS RECYCLABLE AND MADE WITH 100% RECYCLED PAPER, 30% POST-CONSUMER CONTENT." Postal investigators were able to determine that the four anthrax envelopes that had been found came from a single production run that took place on February 14 and 15, 2001. Two plates had been used to print the envelopes and both had detectable defects. That meant that every other envelope in the run had a different defect than the envelopes in between. The Daschle envelope had the same defects as the New York Post envelope, and the Leahy envelope had the same defects as the Brokaw envelope.

More importantly, envelopes from the production run that contained those particular defects were sold only in Maryland and Virginia.[6]

Completing the FBIR

In early 2006, the completion of the analysis of the samples in the FBI repository started coming into sight. No new surprises were being found. It was clear beyond a reasonable doubt that flask RMR-1029 was the seed material for the attack powders. The FBIR now contained over 1,070 samples, and the only samples which had three of the four key mutations found in the attack powders were either spores taken directly from flask RMR-1029 or spores that been regrown from seed material that originated with flask RMR-1029.[7]

Well over a dozen morphs had been found in the attack anthrax, but only four had been chosen by consulting scientists to use in the DNA comparisons. The four were those with the most pronounced differences and therefore the easiest to visually spot, plus they were the mutations that were most stable and unlikely to mutate further, and they were the morphs that seemed to occur most frequently in the powders.

Testing was complete for three of the morphs. The fourth was still in progress, but the results could be reliably predicted.

Except for one sample found at Battelle Memorial Institute in Columbus, all other samples containing the three matched morphs were found at USAMRIID.

Four matched samples, including flask RMR-1029, came from the samples collected from the B3 cold room.

One sample had been found in room B304 in Suite B3.

One sample had been found in the Diagnostic Systems Division's cold room in the Animal Assessment Division area

And two samples had been found in Building 1412, one in the first floor cold room and the other in a second floor lab. The sample found on the second floor also belonged to the Diagnostic System Division. It was a vial that had been sitting untouched since Ivins had given it to Terry Abshire in February 2002 when she said she needed a "gold standard" sample of Ames to use for comparison to other FBIR samples.[8]

The list of possible suspects in the case had dwindled down to a handful, and each had been very extensively investigated. The lack of new leads meant that agents were running out of things to do and needed to be transferred to other cases.

Auditing Amerithrax

By June of 2006, the number of agents working full time on Amerithrax was reduced to 17 and the number of postal inspectors had dropped to 10. That was the situation when a 200 member team from the FBI's Inspection Division descended on the Washington Field Office for a full-scale audit.[9]

A Crime Unlike Any Other

During the audit, agents were provided an opportunity to discuss their views on how to improve efficiency in the office. And Lawrence Alexander was one of those who felt that time and resources would be better spent on checking out Bruce Ivins than on an endless stream of fruitless investigations into details about Steven Hatfill's work habits and personal background. Hatfill had no known access to flask RMR-1029 or any sample taken from it, and that would cause reasonable doubt in the minds of any jury. He had no access to the murder weapon.

Bruce Ivins, on the other hand, controlled the murder weapon. He created it. He used it constantly. No one could get a sample unless they stole it or Ivins gave it to them. Plus, Ivins had no alibi, he worked alone in his lab at critical times and couldn't explain why, he was definitely mentally unstable, and he liked to take long drives at night, so driving to New Jersey in the middle of the night wouldn't have been unthinkable for him. Ivins had the means, the opportunity, and he probably had a half dozen possible motives.

And there were all these weird connections between Ivins and the location of the mailbox.

The findings of the Inspection Division were confidential, but in terms of efficiency, it would have been clear to them that it would be better if everyone was working toward the same goal. It was time for a shakeup.

Richard Lambert had been in charge of the Amerithrax investigation for almost exactly four years. When the position of Agent in Charge opened up at the Knoxville Field Office, he had put his name in the hat. For a family man, home prices and living expenses in Knoxville were about half that in the Washington area.[10]

On August 25, 2006, FBI Director Mueller's office sent out a press release announcing the transfer of Inspector Richard Lambert to become Agent in Charge of the Knoxville Field Office.

In every way it was a promotion, but the media saw it in a different light and reported on it as another indicator that the Amerithrax investigation was going nowhere.[11]

264

A Change in Management

Edward Montooth

It took a few weeks, but by mid-September Lambert's successor had been chosen. The new head of the Amerithrax task force was Edward Montooth, a 19-year veteran of the FBI with the look of a graying, reliable, knowledgeable physician. Montooth was well-known within the Bureau for successfully investigated cases ranging from uncovering illegal contracts involving Navy and Air Force supply officers to the arrest and conviction of a group of Indonesian rebels who had killed two American teachers in Papua Province, in eastern Indonesia.[12]

Also new to the Amerithrax team was Vincent Lisi, who was five years younger than Montooth, trained as an accountant, but he was skilled at developing informants and had made a name for himself in the Bureau with successful investigations of homicides in the D.C. area. Lisi had competed with Montooth for the top position on Amerithax, but he saw Montooth as the better choice and was fully content to be installed as Montooth's second in command. Together, Montooth and Lisi brought the number of agents working full time on Amerithrax to 19.

The media saw a change in command as further evidence that the investigation had gone nowhere and wasn't likely to get anywhere in the future, since a new leader would have to spend a lot of time just getting familiar with what had gone on before.

Many journalists chose the occasion to make a connection between Lambert's departure and the unexpectedly controversial findings recently reported by FBI scientist Douglas Beecher in the August issue of the scientific journal *Applied and Environmental Microbiology*. Although submitted in April and accepted in May, the article *Forensic Application of Microbiological Culture Analysis to Identify Mail Intentionally Contaminated with Bacillus anthracis spores* created a major furor among many conspiracy theorists because, in the article, Dr. Beecher stated:

> Individuals familiar with the compositions of the powders in the letters have indicated that they were comprised simply of spores purified to different extents. However, a widely circulated misconception is that the spores were

produced using additives and sophisticated engineering supposedly akin to military weapon production. This idea is usually the basis for implying that the powders were inordinately dangerous compared to spores. The persistent credence given to this impression fosters erroneous preconceptions, which may misguide research and preparedness efforts and generally detract from the magnitude of hazards posed by simple spore preparations.

Purification of spores may exacerbate their dissemination to some extent by removing adhesive contaminants and maximizing the spore concentration. However, even in a crude state, dried microbial agents have long been considered especially hazardous. Experiments mimicking laboratory accidents have demonstrated that simply breaking vials of lyophilized bacterial cultures creates concentrated and persistent aerosols.

The FBI and outside experts who had actually seen or examined the attack spores had been saying since November of 2001 that the spores were "ordinary" and could have been produced by any skilled microbiologist in almost any well-equipped lab. But, their quiet statements were generally drowned out by heated arguments from conspiracy theorists.

As a result, many in the media combined Lambert's transfer with the information from Beecher's article to declare that the FBI had changed its collective mind and no longer believed that the attack spores were weaponized with a special coating that would make them float more easily in the air. And, as a further indication that the case had been bungled from the start, Steven Hatfill was no longer the focus of the investigation. Instead, the FBI was "casting a wider net" and basically starting from scratch.[13]

The media had claimed the spores were coated with silica, politicians had believed it, now the media was saying the spores were *not* covered with silica, and politicians wanted to know why FBI had not learned this in days, instead of taking years. The media and politicians wanted the FBI to explain why they had believed a myth they had actually denied for nearly five years. And why had the FBI spent so much time investigating a man who politicians, many in the media and nearly everyone *except* the FBI had said was the anthrax mailer?

A Change in Management

The questions had no answers that anyone in the media or the political area wanted to hear.

Montooth & Lisi

Montooth and Lisi agreed with one thing being reported by the media. They were basically starting from scratch, and they so informed the Amerthrax task force. They had no directives from higher up about any favorite suspect, nor were they instructed to pursue any specific theory about who may have done it. They were instructed to come in with no preconceived ideas, and to be prepared to be deluged with facts about one of the most complex investigations in the entire history of the FBI. And deluged they were. Both men described it as being like drinking from an endless, raging stream gushing from a broken fire hydrant.[14]

They put out the word that they were open to whatever the evidence said. The two new leaders listened to the views of the agents who had been on the case for years, including Scott Decker who had been on the case from the beginning and was now overseeing the scientific investigation, and Postal Inspector Thomas Dellafera who had also been on the case from Day One. Decker explained the details about the morphs and how their DNA had invariably led to flask RMR-1029. Dellafera explained how print defects on the envelopes had shown that the envelopes were purchased in the Maryland-Virginia area, and all the envelopes that had been found came from two packets that went through the printing press in sequence.

Lawrence Alexander was also debriefed, and explained that he'd been researching Bruce Ivins via the Internet on his own time. He explained how the evidence pointed toward Bruce Edwards Ivins instead of toward Steven Hatfill.

Within just a few weeks, Montooth and Lisi and everyone else on the Amerithrax team appeared to be in agreement: Steven Hatfill was *not* the anthrax killer. And Bruce Ivins was the person most likely to have sent the letters, even though there wasn't yet anywhere near enough evidence to arrest or convict him. However, because of the shift of focus away from Hatfill, there would now be a lot more manpower available to find facts and evidence that had not yet been uncovered about Dr. Ivins.

And, almost immediately, some stunning *new* information was noticed when someone compared two lists of numbered evidence samples and found that the sample from flask RMR-1029 that Ivins had submitted to the FBIR in February was marked as destroyed on Terry Abshire's list, but not on Paul Keim's list.

Paul Keim at Northern Arizona University was immediately contacted. He rushed to open the locked cabinet used for chain-of-custody materials and found the slants that everyone had forgotten about.[15] For Keim's purposes, there was nothing wrong with the slants. The work at Northern Arizona University wasn't governed by the same protocols as the FBIR.

Evidence Against Ivins

DNA testing soon found that three of the four morphs were present in the sample. When FBIR testing was completed, the fourth would very likely be in there, too.

It was already known that flask RMR-1029 had the four morphs. And it was known that the replacement sample of the contents of flask RMR-1029 that Bruce Ivins produced in April of 2002 contained *none* of the morphs. Ivins had repeatedly told FBI investigators that he didn't know how that had happened. Now it was also known that the original sample taken from flask RMR-1029 by Bruce Ivins in February of 2002 *when he wasn't aware of what the FBI was looking for* contained three of the four morphs, and so did the "gold standard" sample given to Abshire. Yet, the replacement slant that Ivins prepared in April 2002 *after it had been explained to him what the FBI was looking for* did not contain *any* of the morphs.

It would be a simple matter for the jury to see that when Ivins didn't know what the FBI was looking for, he gave the FBIR a valid sample. But, when he knew what the FBI was looking for, he gave the FBIR a *false* sample. In a court room it be would further evidence of "consciousness of guilt." Ivins knew he was guilty and he took actions only a person aware or conscious of his own guilt would take. He tried to mislead investigators away from himself.

A Change in Management

Meanwhile, the media was reporting the news the way they saw it. And politicians did the same. An NBC report dated October 24, 2006, titled *Congress, FBI battle over anthrax investigation*, described how upset Senator Grassley was over the lack of progress in the case. The article said in part:

> Late Monday, Sen. Charles Grassley, R-Iowa, sent a damning six-page letter to Attorney General Alberto Gonzales requesting a briefing on the FBI investigation, now five years old. The letter faults the agency for its handling of the case, saying "the FBI has little in the way of results to show for its work."

Chapter 35

Ivins Before a Grand Jury

2007 began with mixed news about two of Steven Hatfill's lawsuits. First, his lawsuit against *The New York Times* was again dismissed by a federal judge because the judge considered Hatfill to be a "public figure," and public figures cannot sue for libel unless they can prove deliberate malice. Hatfill's lawyers would have to prove that Nicholas Kristof and *The New York Times* printed false information about Hatfill that they *knew* to be false. The judge decided that deliberate malice had not been proved.

It wasn't the end of the matter, since Hatfill could still appeal to the Supreme Court, but it was a definite blow.

That blow was eased for Dr. Hatfill somewhat when a settlement was reached in the lawsuit against *Vanity Fair* and *Readers' Digest*.

Perhaps worried by the endless setbacks in the suit against *The New York Times* and the endless delays in the suit against the Attorney General and the United States, it appears that Dr. Hatfill wanted to settle the *Vanity Fair* et al lawsuit.

Vanity Fair and *Readers' Digest* had been making settlement offer after settlement offer for a long time, clearly seeing that they would have almost no defense in court. Unlike Kristof's columns which didn't identify Hatfill by name until after the FBI began its public searches of Hatfill's home, Donald Foster's article in *Vanity Fair* named Hatfill and included disproved theories about hoaxes.

Unable to find work because of the media attention he'd been under, totally broke and dependant upon his friends for support, Hatfill may have seen the *Vanity Fair/Readers' Digest* settlement offers as a bird in the hand that was infinitely better than the birds in the legal bush that had not yet been grabbed.

The facts suggest that Hatfill's lawyer, Tom Connolly, wanted to wait until the case against the government was settled and it could be proved that Hatfill was innocent and that the *Vanity Fair* article was total fiction. And there was positive movement in that case. In late 2006, when Dr. Hatfill wanted to take a trip outside of the Maryland-Virginia area, Connolly had called Vincent Lisi, who Connolly knew well from the time when Connolly was a federal prosecutor. Lisi told Connolly, "Tommy, you don't need to tell me his travel plans ... We've been working on a lot of things here. Your guy's not a priority." [1]

But, there was no way of knowing how long the lawsuit against the government could take, and Hatfill didn't want to wait for it to be settled before settling the lawsuit against *Vanity Fair* and *Readers' Digest*. So, presumably with Connolly's permission, Dr. Hatfill changed law firms in the lesser lawsuit.

On February 27, 2007, Steven Hatfill's new lawyer in the lawsuit, Hassan A. Zavareei of the small firm Tycko & Zavareei issued a press release announcing the settlement. It said in part:

> Dr. Hatfill's lawsuit has now been resolved to the mutual satisfaction of all the parties. And Condé Nast and Donald Foster have issued the following statement: "In publishing the article 'The Message In the Anthrax' by Donald Foster in the October 2003 issue of *Vanity Fair*, neither Condé Nast Publications nor the article's author intended to imply that they had concluded that Steven J. Hatfill, M.D., perpetrated the anthrax attacks that occurred in the United States in the fall of 2001. To the extent any statements contained in the article might be read to convey that Condé Nast and Prof. Foster were accusing Dr. Hatfill of perpetrating these attacks, Condé Nast and Prof. Foster retract any such implication."

The amount of the settlement wasn't made public. The lawsuit documents had asked for $10 million. And since the magazines had been virtually pleading with Hatfill to settle, the amounts they had offered had almost certainly reached the millions by the time Hatfill agreed - perhaps even many millions.

Mostly the main-stream media ignored the settlement, but the *New York Sun* reported:

> It seems doubtful that the settlement announced yesterday delivered much, if any, money to Dr. Hatfill.[2]

Undoubtedly, there was substantial money involved, since Hatfill's new lawyer received enough to make his time on the case very worthwhile, even though Dr. Hatfill had held nearly all the cards on what the contingency fee would be.

For Steven Hatfill the settlement money must have brought a large measure of relief and a way to move on with his life after it had been so thoroughly destroyed by gossipy conspiracy theorists, careless members of the media and ignorant politicians.

"An extremely sensitive suspect"

Meanwhile, as things improved for Steven Hatfill, the opposite was true for Bruce Ivins. On February 1, 2007, the FBI opened "sub-files" for the investigation and surveillance of Ivins.[3] And material was being accumulated for a grand jury investigation, although it was not yet an investigation of Bruce Ivins.

FBI agents at USAMRIID asked Ivins to arrange a meeting where he and his lawyer could be present.[4] The meeting between Ivins, his lawyer Richard Bricken, and FBI agents Lawrence Alexander and Darin Steele took place in the conference room near Bricken's office on February 27, 2007. It was the first time Alexander had ever actually questioned Ivins, but, as a result of his research, he was probably the FBI's leading expert on USAMRIID's #1 anthrax spore expert. The purpose of the meeting was described as being an opportunity for Ivins to provide more details about his theories as to who could have sent the anthrax letters. In reality, it was more of a test to see how much Richard Bricken would allow his client to say.[5]

Ivins jumped at the opportunity to once again point the finger at Joseph Farchaus, who he said was at the top of his list of potential suspects. Ivins and Farchaus shared a patent together, and had worked together many years earlier. Farchaus could easily have stolen a sample of the Ames strain when he left USAMRIID to move to New Jersey. Ivins explained how a colleague had once mentioned taking samples home in paint cans, and Ivins made a point of explaining very clearly to Alexander that the security at USAMRIID was very lax, and just about anyone with access to suites B3 and B4 or the aliquots sent over the Building 1412 could have smuggled out a sample of Ames and used it in the letters.

The two FBI agents listened and nodded dutifully, while getting a feel for attorney Bricken and his methods. They kept things low key, and they asked no questions which might be interpreted as evaluating Ivins' guilt or innocence.

Ivins' new will

Although there was nothing in the February 27 meeting that should have alarmed Ivins, he may have seen some form of writing on the wall. For some reason he decided to revise his will about five days later. The new changes were mainly about what would happen to his remains after his death. His wife thoroughly opposed the idea of cremation, but Ivins insisted upon it. And, if his wife did anything to prevent his cremation and the scattering of his ashes, Ivins stated in his will that fifty thousand dollars should be taken from his estate and given to Planned Parenthood of Maryland, which was a direct attack upon his wife who was a firm opponent of abortion and the leader of the Frederick County Right to Life organization.[6]

Ivins fears were given more weight on April 6 when he received a grand jury subpoena requiring that 130 different notebooks be turned over, including some in Ivins' possession.[7]

Three days later, Ivins received a subpoena to testify before the grand jury in Washington. The subpoena was sent by AUSA Kenneth Kohl who told Ivins in the cover letter, "You are not a target of this investigation." If Ivins had doubts about the sincerity of that statement, they would have been calmed somewhat when he learned that a dozen others at USAMRIID had received similar subpoenas with the same assurance. However, his testimony to the grand jury would be under oath, which meant that if he was as evasive and deceitful as he'd been with FBI agents, his words could be held against him in an actual trial.[8]

The grand jury may not yet have been targeting Ivins, but the FBI definitely was. On April 11, 2007, the Washington Field Office formally requested periodic surveillance of a female witness who was willing to testify about Ivins and his lab practices. The request stated:

> Bruce Edwards Ivins is an extremely sensitive suspect
> in the 2001 anthrax attacks.[9]

The request went on to explain, "Human intelligence reporting on Ivins has been scarce; therefore, AMERITHRAX is examining the potential of gaining intelligence through" various techniques, probably including having the confidential informant tape conversations with the suspect in which leading questions are asked in an attempt to get the suspect to incriminate himself.

Before doing that, the FBI needed to know if the witness was reliable and if she had any quirks or credibility problems that might discredit her testimony in court. So, they asked for "a thorough description of her-home, workplace, habits, and associates."

The Grand Jury

AUSA Kohl also invited Ivins to meet privately with him at the FBI office in Frederick on April 30, a week before his grand jury testimony was scheduled to be heard.

Ivins went to the meeting without his lawyer. When it was over, Ivins told Bricken about what types of questions he would be asked by the grand jury. They weren't scientific questions. They were personal questions. He would be asked about his psychiatric condition, his co-invention of the new anthrax vaccine and how it might benefit him financially, and the anger he had expressed to fellow employees at USAMRIID over the delays Senators Daschle and Leahy had caused in the passing of the USA Patriot ACT shortly after 9/11.[10]

Ivins may not have currently been the "target" of the grand jury's investigation, but it appeared they were going to ask questions to see if he should *become* such a target. Nevertheless, when Ivins took the Metro into Washington on May 8 and 9 to give his testimony in the E. Barrett Prettyman Federal Courthouse on Constitution Avenue, just west of the Capitol Building, he went without his lawyer. Attorney Bricken wouldn't have been allowed in the grand jury room anyway, but it is common for lawyers to wait just outside the room so that, if needed, a witness can leave the room to consult with his attorney.

In addition to the subjects AUSA Kohl had advised Ivins would be brought up before the grand jury, in the jury room Kohl also pressed Ivins at length about the sample Ivins had submitted to the FBIR in April of 2002 which was supposed to have been taken directly from flask RMR-1029, but which didn't contain any of the morphs that were known with absolute certainty to be in abundance within that flask. Whatever Ivins' responses were inside the grand jury room, they were now on the record and made under oath.

When Ivins informed his lawyer of what had taken place in the grand jury room, Bricken decided it was time for Ivins to find a lawyer with more experience in federal courtrooms, and someone who didn't need to make the hundred-mile round trip to Washington every time it was necessary for Ivins to make the trip.

Richard Bricken recommended Paul Kemp be hired as Ivins' lawyer. Kemp had an office in Rockville, MD, which was 47 minutes from Prettyman Courthouse by Metro-rail.[11]

Ivins and Kemp met for the first time on May 12, 2007, when Ivins drove to Rockville to meet with him and to describe his view of the case.

Kemp listened to Ivins' views about the abundance of potential suspects due to the extremely lax security at Ft. Detrick and decided taking Ivins on as a client would be mostly a matter of "witness hand-holding," even though Ivins seemed very concerned about the course of the FBI's investigation. To Kemp, Ivins seemed like a harmless, absent-minded professor, someone who needed to be protected from his own bumbling.

His grand jury sessions haunted Ivins for weeks afterward. In a May 14 email to a friend, Ivins described his time before the grand jury as being "a dreadful experience." He claimed it destroyed all enthusiasm he had for science, and he said he would be equally satisfied

if he "worked the graveyard shift at WalMart. Probably more so."
He then added:

> I can see why and how some people just reach a stage in
> their lives that they just don't give a **** anymore, and I'm
> pretty much there.[12]

In a May 16, 2007 email with the subject "Last week was a
rough week" he sent to himself at KingBadger7@aol.com and carbon
copied himself at goldenphoenix111@hotmail.com, Ivins wrote:

> I'm just so beat. I was at the grand jury for five hours, 3
> hours on one day and 2 on the next. The questions were
> very accusatory, on so many fronts. There's so much in-
> formation that I've forgotten or can't find or can't look up.
> I'm so miserable.[13]

A week later, at 11:30 at night on May 23, Ivins sent Mara
Linscott an email with the subject "Grand Jury":

> Hi. I'm still recovering from my twin experiences before
> the amerithrax grand jury. The metro rides were the only
> enjoyable part. They asked 'gotcha!' type questions and
> very personal questions related to email conversations be-
> tween people. They know everything about the personal
> and professional lives [redacted]. Eventually, a trial will
> come, and we'll be dragged up to the witness chair to tes-
> tify, and that's when the other side will start dragging us
> through the dirt. It's a lawyer's job to sully the personal
> and professional reputations of witnesses on the other side.
> For me it means people finding out that I'm a slob, keep
> poor records, am lousy at math, and see a psychiatrist." [14]

On June 7, 2007, Ivins sent an e-mail to an unidentified scientist at USAMRIID discussing, among other things, the anthrax investigation. In the email, Dr. Ivins made the following barely-veiled
threats:

> Do you realize that if anybody gets indicted for even the
> most remote reason with respect to the anthrax letters,

something as simple as not locking up spore preps to re-strict them from only people in [the] lab – they face the death penalty? Playing any part, even a minor part such as providing information about how to make spores or how to make them in broth, how to harvest and purify . . . that could wind up putting one or more hapless persons on death row. Not pleasant to think about.

In one of your recent e-mails you said that it would all be over soon. If they indict someone, that means that inno-cent people are going to get dragged through the mud by both the defense and the prosecution as the pre-trial and trial procedures move forward.[15]

Ivins then listed in the email "a litany of what he thought of as embarrassing personal information about this scientist and others at USAMRIID." The FBI viewed this e-mail as Dr. Ivins trying to silence the USAMRIID scientist by threatening that private matters would be revealed if someone - anyone - from USAMRIID were to be put on trial for the anthrax mailings.

The FBI tried to determine what the scientist might know about Dr. Ivins that Ivins would consider potentially damaging. But, the scientist only expressed frustration over having no idea what in-formation it might be.

To the FBI, however, this seemingly "harmless" man who looked and acted like an "absent minded professor" was not too timid to threaten potential witnesses. And intimidating witnesses was definitely another act demonstrating "consciousness of guilt."

Chapter 36

Building a Case

In the second half of 2007, as the FBI continued to dig into Bruce Ivins' background and off-work hours, the media was focused on attempts by Steven Hatfill's lawyers to find out who in the government had been leaking information about him to the media. Three government employees had notified their media contacts that they no longer needed to keep their names secret. Two were Department of Justice lawyers: Roscoe C. Howard Jr., who from 2001 to 2004 served as U.S. Attorney for District of Columbia; and Daniel S. Seikaly, who served as Howard's criminal division chief. One was from the FBI: Edwin Cogswell, who had served as a spokesman for the FBI, and it was therefore his job to talk with the media.[1]

But, Hatfill's lawyers wanted more names. And U.S. District Judge Reggie Walton agreed that the names of any other government employees who illegally provided confidential information about the FBI's investigation of Steven Hatfill should be provided. Six journalists were on the spot, facing possible fines as much as $1,000 per day if they failed to comply: Michael Isikoff and Daniel Klaidman of *Newsweek*; Allan Lengel of *The Washington Post*; Toni Locy, formerly of *USA Today*; James Stewart, formerly of *CBS News*; and Brian Ross of *ABC News*.[2]

The intensifying investigation of Bruce Ivins wasn't on any reporter's radar. And that was the way it was supposed to be.

Building a Case

Ivins Takes a Vacation

In late July, Ivins even took time off and joined his brother Charles for a three day Caribbean cruise aboard the *Sovereign of the Seas*. The FBI sent two undercover female FBI agents to join the cruise and to chat with Ivins to see what he might tell them, but it appears that nothing of consequence was learned.[3]

On August 10, Ivins wrote a lengthy email responding to a series of questions from a Swedish couple he'd met on cruise. It may have been totally innocent, but the questions seem to be designed to get Ivins to talk about things the FBI was interested in. When asked about his work, Ivins responded:

> Work has been a drag for about 10 years! The vaccine work went down the drain, and the company that was supposed to pick up on it (the vaccine) made a mess of it. The scientists here can't talk to them about what they did wrong, because that would be a conflict of interests and a definite ethics violation, so I'm just basically putting in time here until I retire. It's a terrible attitude, and I['m] sorry I have it, but I'm just so beaten down.[4]

When asked if he's still sad because Patricia Fellows left USAMRIID, Ivins responded that he is still sad, even though they sometimes meet for coffee, and they still keep in touch via emails.

But the question that most clearly seems to be from the FBI is this one:

> I was really interested in that trivia you were telling me (the game you won on the ship!!) I really wish I was there for that and could have been on your team and been a BADG-ER too!!!! Can you make me an honorary one??? ;)

The question seems clearly designed to get Ivins to explain why he uses the address "kingbadger7@aol.com" when posting to forums on the Internet. And he'd also signed the "Queen of the Universe" email he'd sent to Patricia Worsham in September 2001, "Bruce Badger." Ivins provided the answer in his response:

You can CERTAINLY be a badger! It was one of our division chiefs that gave me that name. It was a guy named [redacted]. He came into the office one day in the 1990s and said, "I need to talk to King Badger!" That was very funny, and he just wanted to ask a question about the anthrax vaccine, but the name kind of stuck in our lab.

Bruce Ivins' personal explanation of the use of the King Badger name would be direct evidence connecting him to the AOL account and would help justify the search warrants to be issued later to access all records regarding the account Ivins used around the time of the anthrax attacks.

FBIR Final Results

On September 5, 2007, TIGR's work with the fourth morph was complete.[5] Flask RMR-1029 contained the fourth morph. So did seven other samples derived from flask RMR-1029. *None* of the other 1,200+ samples in the FBIR contained all four morphs. For the FBI and DOJ's legal case, the fourth morph fully *confirmed* what the other three morphs had only indicated: the original source of the attack anthrax was flask RMR-1029. It also confirmed that the only serious suspect they had left was Dr. Bruce Edwards Ivins, the person who controlled the flask and attempted to mislead investigators about its contents.

It was time to start thinking about the kind of confrontation that Richard Lambert had ineffectively conducted over two years earlier, on March 31, 2005. Only this time it would be done right.

The FBI had never searched Ivins' home. They had never searched his vehicles. They had never searched his safe deposit box. They never had a hazmat team check Ivins' home and vehicles for anthrax spores. All that would be done this time. But, it would take some time to plan and arrange. The right time would depend upon when all the elements could be brought together. And, unlike the public search of Steven Hatfill's apartment in 2002, this one had to be done with as much secrecy as possible.

They had also never talked with Ivins' psychiatrist. On September 6, FBI agents interviewed Dr. Allan Levy in his office and attempted to get information about Ivins' attendance at Monday group therapy sessions during August, September and October 2001. Dr. Levy stated that he was uncertain if he still had such records, but he'd check and get back to the FBI on the matter.[6]

On September 25 Ivins showed up at work with a black eye. Being unable to question Ivins without his lawyer being present, the FBI appears to have managed to get the explanation via Patricia Worsham.[7]

When Worsham asked about the black eye, Ivins first joked by saying that he'd run into his wife's fist. But, then he more seriously explained that it didn't have anything to do with alcohol, and that he thought he got it while sleeping. He believed he rolled over and hit his head against the nightstand next to his bed.

Worsham then asked Ivins why he had been at work around midnight the previous night sending her emails. She asked him if he didn't understand that it would likely send up "a big red flag" to investigators (which it apparently had). Ivins merely responded that it didn't used to be that way. Working long hours didn't used to be viewed as evil and suspicious. He explained that he'd walked to work last night, then walked home at around 1 a.m., took an Ambien and then slept until morning.

Ivins rambled on about how another employee at USAMRIID was taunting the FBI by sending people pictures via email of powdered sugar donuts which are supposed to represent anthrax spores. And, that person took a picture of himself standing in a pond with a Tupperware container. The caption for the photograph was "genuine FBI trap," presumably ridiculing the turtle trap that had been found in the pond search in the Hatfill investigation.

Ivins stated that he didn't want to become another Richard Jewell (who was wrongly described as "suspect" in Centennial Park bombing during the 1996 Olympics) just because it would let everyone else off the hook. He was afraid that the FBI might arrest him for allowing material from flask RMR-1029 to get into the hands of the person who sent the letters. He worried that he could get as much as a five year jail sentence for being negligent with U.S. government property. He compared his lack of tight controls on flask RMR-1029 to leaving the keys in a government car that is then stolen.

He listed several people who he thought made better suspects than he, including one who had connections to the area in Connecticut where the elderly woman had died of anthrax. And he mentioned how others were reacting to the interviews and to lie detector tests. It all made Ivins very depressed, and he looked forward to the time in September of 2008 when he could retire. He was only continuing to work now because he needed to have his health care costs paid by the government.

Getting Serious

As of October 12, Dr. Levy had not responded to the FBI's request for Ivins' attendance at Monday group therapy sessions. So, they sent Dr. Levy a FAX requesting whether group therapy sessions were held on all Mondays from August 6 through October 29, 2001, and what time the sessions were held.

Dr. Levy responded that he didn't retain records from that long ago, and his billing records for that time period had "crashed." [8]

On October 26, a confidential informant informed the FBI that Ivins had recently told her that he had appeared before a grand jury in Washington, D.C., and during the course of his testimony he'd "laid it all out," explaining to the jury why he thought former USAM-RIID employee Joseph Farchaus "had perpetrated the anthrax-laced letter mailings of 2001." [9]

At one time or another over the previous six years, Ivins had tried to implicate seven current or former colleagues in the anthrax attacks: John Ezzell, Joseph Farchaus, Patricia Fellows, Gregory Knudson, Henry Heine, Erick Henchal and Mara Linscott. But the FBI's investigation had determined than none of them had anything to do with the attacks. Instead, it was their accuser who appeared to be the anthrax mailer. And he'd evidently acted alone.

And, it was time that the FBI told him so and made sure he knew that they were going to leave no stone unturned in their search for evidence to take into court to prove it.

It was time for the long-planned confrontation.

Chapter 37

Confrontation

At 4 p.m. on the afternoon of Thursday, November 1, 2007, FBI agents Lawrence Alexander and Darin Steele entered the office of USMRIID commander Colonel George Korch. The agents advised Korch that they needed to have a long discussion with Dr. Bruce Ivins, and they wanted to do it in a way that would attract minimal attention. Ivins was known to be currently in his office, but if the FBI agents went there for the discussion, everyone would notice, and there was a good possibility it would be disruptive to the rest of the staff area.[1]

Korch understood and obligingly offered the conference area in his office for the meeting. When the agents agreed, Korch then picked up the phone and called Ivins to tell him that he had two visitors waiting in the conference room.

When Ivins entered the commander's conference room, Korch left.

Ivins then saw the two agents waiting for him, and he realized something was up. He asked, "Do I need my attorney?"

The agents explained that it wasn't necessary for him to have his attorney present. They weren't there to interview him or to ask questions, they were there to share important information with him. All they asked of him was that he listen to what they had to say.

Ivins agreed and took a seat at the conference table.

The agents knew that having the confrontation in the commander's conference room instead of in Ivins' office had additional

283

benefits besides confidentiality. It insured that Ivins couldn't receive any phone calls while they talked.

At the same time agents Alexander and Steele started their confrontation with Ivins, other FBI agents and postal inspectors were conducting surveillance on Ivins' wife and children, waiting for the right opportunity to confront them and take them to a hotel where they could be questioned and could remain overnight while their house was being searched.

Other FBI agents and a hazmat team were near Ivins home, waiting for the right moment when they could enter the home and remove Ivins' vehicles without attracting the attention of neighbors.

Laying out the Evidence

In Colonel Korch's conference room, FBI agents Alexander and Steele explained to Ivins in great detail why their investigation appeared to show that Ivins had deliberately falsified evidence when he submitted the April 2002 slants that were supposed to be samples representative of the contents of flask RMR-1029.

As he'd done numerous times before, Ivins offered up various other possible explanations for the apparent error, but this time the FBI agents made it clear they were buying none of it. And, he was there to listen, not to make statements.

The agents described how flask RMR-1029 contained a pure concentration of spores that was nearly identical to the concentrated spores in the senate letters, yet the FBI was never able to get a proper sample of it from Ivins until they seized flask RMR-1029 in April of 2004, resulting in a 2 year delay in identifying the source of the genetic material found in the anthrax letters.

They told Ivins of various other attempts it appeared he had made to try to mislead the investigation by providing information that later turned out to be false.

Ivins Takes the Fifth

The FBI agents then changed the subject in an attempt to catch Ivins off-guard. They asked him who Carla Sander was. It was a false name Ivins had used on a post office box, and a feminization and distortion of Carl Scandella, the man who was once engaged to Nancy Haigwood. Ivins refused to answer, claiming it was his Fifth Amendment right. If the FBI agents knew that Ivins had used the false name to rent a post office box, he had to wonder what else they might know. Ivins complained that the conversation was beginning to look like he should have his lawyer present, but he was told that he only needed to listen. If he talked, he was doing it because he wanted to say something, not because he'd been asked a question by the agents. The agents explained that they didn't see any connection between the name Cara Sander and the anthrax mailing, so that question didn't have anything to do with the investigation.

While Steele talked with Ivins, agent Alexander would occasionally leave the conference room to call Edward Montooth to see how everything else was going. They'd approached Diane Ivins as she was leaving work at the shopping center restaurant where she worked as a waitress, they'd confiscated her 1996 red Dodge Ram van, and they now had her at the hotel where they were questioning her. They had also presented Diane with the search warrant for the Ivins home. At 6:45, when it was starting to get dark, the FBI agents dressed as movers and maintenance men had knocked on the door of the Ivins' home. Bruce and Diane's son, Andy Ivins, was at home and answered the door. He was presented with the search warrant, and was told that he needed to vacate the house during the search. He would be taken to a hotel where his father and mother would meet with him later. Then, when Andy had gone, the agents began putting blackout material over the windows to prevent any neighbors from seeing what was going on inside.[2]

Bruce and Diane Ivins' adopted daughter, Amanda, was interviewed by two female FBI agents at her apartment in Hagerstown, MD, about thirty miles northwest of Frederick. Then she, too, was taken to the hotel.

Back in the confrontation with Bruce Ivins, agents Alexander and Steele talked about Ivins' expertise with anthrax. Ivins again claimed that he wasn't an expert, which the agents said was not a realistic claim, since he was not only widely recognized as an expert, he was able to do things with anthrax that few others could do.

Ivins just sat and shook his head in disagreement.

A Crime Unlike Any Other

At 8 p.m., the session was interrupted when Colonel Korch knocked on the door asking to come in to get a set of keys he needed. Ivins used the opportunity to tell the agents that he would not continue to talk with them. He'd said all he was going to say.

Ivins was told that it was important that he remain for five more minutes, since they had something else he needed to hear.

Ivins stated that he wanted Colonel Korch to remain in the office.

The agents advised Ivins that it would not be in his best interest to have Colonel Korch present when the agents told Ivins what they were about to tell him.

Since it was clear that his presence was not in Ivins' best interests, Korch took the opportunity to say he wasn't going to stay. He left the office and went home.

As soon as Korch had left, the agents advised Ivins that they had obtained search warrants for his residence, his vehicles, his office in room 19, and that he would not be allowed access to any of them until the completion of the search. They advised Ivins that the FBI and postal inspectors had taken numerous precautions to avoid attracting the attention of his neighbors, and they had waited until everyone in the vicinity of office 19 had left before they moved in to do their searches quietly and with the door closed.

Ivins was then advised that hotel rooms had been arranged for him and his family, and his family was already at the hotel. The agents apologized for the inconvenience, but it was a necessity, and they would do all they could to minimize the disruption to his family and his routines. The FBI would drive Ivins to the hotel, or, if he preferred, he could arrange other transportation, but he wouldn't be allowed to go home. If there were medicines or anything else that Ivins would need from his home for the overnight stay in the hotel, the agents would see that the items were brought to him.

Ivins said he needed some of his prescriptions, and he listed them for the agents. Agent Alexander then apologized and said Ivins had to be frisked, since he was known to own weapons. Ivins put his hands on the wall and accepted the pat down. When Alexander was finished, Ivins put his hands behind his back as if he expected to handcuffed, but it wasn't necessary.

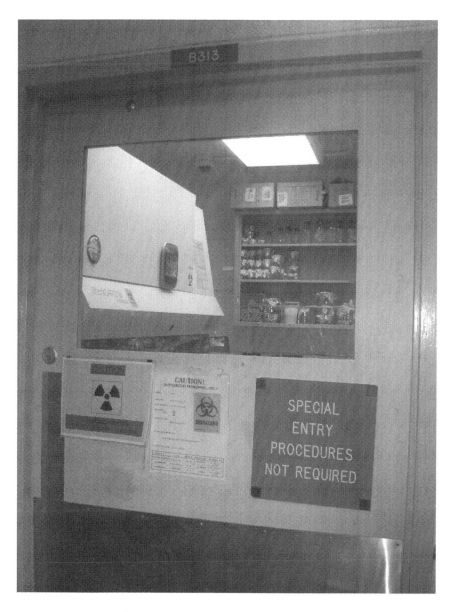

Exhibit #25 - The door to Ivins' lab in room B313
(Note that the door has no knob and that Ivins' biosafety cabinet can
be seen just inside the door.)

Exhibit #26 - The biosafety cabinet in lab B313
(The clock on the cabinet says the photo was taken at 1:37 a.m on the morning of November 2, 2007)

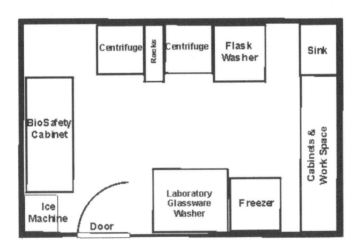

Exhibit #27 - Floor plan of Ivins' B313 lab

Confrontation

En Route to the Hotel

Ivins was then escorted out of the building to where FBI agent Scott Stanley was waiting behind the wheel of an idling Ford Explorer, and Postal Inspector Thomas Dellafera was standing next to the vehicle. Ivins climbed into the passenger seat beside Stanley, and Dellafera climbed in back, sitting in the middle of the seat in order to be able to study Ivins more carefully as they drove.

During the drive no one said anything for awhile, and then Ivins suddenly asked agent Stanley about a serious car crash he'd been in a few months earlier. Stanley asked where Ivins had learned about the crash, but Ivins just smiled and didn't answer. He clearly just wanted to let the FBI agent know that he knew things about his personal life that weren't common knowledge.

Stanley then asked if Ivins was concerned about the searches. Ivins replied that he was concerned, since the FBI was likely to find things about his personal habits that he didn't want others to know about, such as a bag of materials he sometimes used to "cross-dress."

The agents told Ivins that they weren't there to judge Ivins about his personal habits. They were only concerned with matters that directly related to the anthrax attacks of 2001. As long as his habits didn't hurt anyone, the agents didn't care about them.

Ivins was clearly worried and anxious, and Stanley asked if something else was bothering him. Ivins responded that he didn't want to be thought of as a "mass killer or a terrorist," and he couldn't believe that the FBI believed he was the anthrax mailer.

Stanley used the opportunity to try the age-old tactic of getting the suspect to confess by explaining how it appeared the crime was just an accident and not intentional. Stanley explained that he always thought the letter writer never intended to kill anyone, since the person who sent the letters taped the envelopes shut, he included medical advice in the media letters, and he told the recipients of the senate letters that the powder was anthrax.

"What kind of person do you think would have done this?" Stanley asked Ivins.

But Ivins just moved away from Stanley in his seat and didn't say another word for the rest of the trip.

A Crime Unlike Any Other

At the hotel, Ivins tried contacting his lawyer but got only his answering machine. A few minutes later, however, Paul Kemp returned the call. And within an hour, Kemp was at Ivins' side to help him through the ordeal. Inspector Dellafera explained the purpose of the search to Ivins' lawyer and wife. Neither Bruce Ivins nor his family were in custody. They were free to leave the hotel any time they wished. Kemp tried to calm down his panicked client by telling him that nothing was critical at that moment, and there would evidently be plenty of time to sort things out and to understand what the searches and other happenings that evening were all about.

Shortly before 10 p.m., an agent arrived with Ivins' medicines: Ambien, a sleep-aid; Celexa, an anti-depressant; and Valium, an anti-anxiety drug.

The Search

At the Ivins home, agents were taking hundreds of photographs and identifying 69 different items which needed to be examined in greater detail at the Washington Field Office. A written list of the items that had been taken and where they had been found in the house was prepared and left on the kitchen table. The items taken included three types of stun guns, a supply of pepper spray and several hand guns: an easy to conceal 40-caliber Glock 27; a long barrel, 9mm Glock 34; and a 22 caliber Baretta 21 Bobcat, which was another easily concealed weapon. Plus Ivins had an extra barrel for the Glock 27, which could be used to mislead ballistics if the weapon were used in a crime. And there was evidence that Ivins had used his basement as a target range, firing into old phone books.

At approximately 3:50 in the morning of November 2, when all the neighbors were sound asleep, members of the FBI's Hazardous Materials Response Unit and Homeland Security's Hazardous Materials Response Team arrived at the home in their protective suits to hunt for anthrax spores. That search lasted about two hours. At 5:50 a.m. on the morning, after the blackout materials had been removed from the windows and before the neighbors started going to work, the last of the FBI agents left the Ivins home.

The searches of both Diane Ivins' red Dodge van and Bruce Ivins' blue 1993 Honda Civic were completed and the vehicles had been returned at shortly past 1 a.m. They were parked in front of the Ivins home. The 2002 blue SL1 Saturn sedan was driven to the hotel where the Ivins had spent the night. It would be turned over to the Ivins there. At 622 Military Road, except for the missing Saturn, the scene was as it would have looked the previous morning at that time.

The search of Ivins' office in room 19 of Building 1425 had turned up a key to his safe deposit box.

At 9 a.m. on November 2, FBI agents presented a search warrant to the ranking official at PNC Bank. They had to wait until an assistant manager arrived at 9:37. After photographing the exterior of the box and where it was located, the key found in Ivins' office was used to open his safe deposit box, and the inner box was taken to a counter outside of the vault in order to inventory the contents of the box.[3]

In less than a half hour, all the items in the box were photographed, everything was put back, nothing was seized, and a copy of the search warrant was left inside the box when it was put back.

The End of the Beginning

The main part of the confrontation and search was over, but the analysis of what they had found was just beginning.

The tests for anthrax spores in the Ivins home had come back negative, so Bruce Ivins, his wife and son were allowed to return to their home on the afternoon of the 2nd.

And that set up the final part of the confrontation. The agents had taken everything they saw that they believed might be of value to the investigation. But, from past experience they knew that it was possible that they had missed something critical. As was done after Lambert's confrontation on March 31, 2005, the FBI would watch Ivins trash for a couple weeks to see what he might throw out that he wouldn't want the FBI to find if they should ever come back and perform another search.

Chapter 38

Direct Evidence?

The search of Ivins' home found a few interesting things in addition to his weapons. They found counter-surveillance equipment, including earphones, telephone equipment, a device for detecting transmitters and a CD labeled "white noise generator." The booklets with the equipment said it could be used to detect body wires, room bugs, telephone eavesdropping transmitters and concealed video cameras which transmitted images. It could also detect the "infinity bug" which allows an ordinary telephone to be used as a room bug even the phone is in its cradle.[1]

They found a bag with fake hair pieces such as sideburns, and a mustache; glue, putty mix, a fake bruise kit, fake blood, makeup and powder and a brush.

They found instructions printed off the Internet on how to get to Mara Linscott's parent's home. They found photocopies of nine of his lab notebooks. They found numerous spore preparation forms from July 2000 and April 2001 showing plate counts and other data related to various experiments.

They found paper copies of numerous articles about handwriting analysis that Ivins had downloaded on April 10, 2005, shortly after his meeting with Richard Lambert. There were also articles about forensic elemental analysis, mostly downloaded and printed on April 5, 2005.

They found a paper copy of an email Ivins had sent to himself on November 19, 2005, listing twelve reasons why Pat Fellows and Mara Linscott should be considered suspects in the anthrax mailings. They found paper copies of other emails Ivins had sent pointing to current or former USAMRIID scientists as being likely suspects in the Amerithrax investigation.

But, nothing they found was quite as interesting as what Ivins threw away a week after the searches.

BINGO!

On the night of November 7-8, 2007, FBI personnel were watching Ivins' home very carefully because it was a trash pickup night.

Just after 1 a.m. on Thursday, November 8, Ivins exited the front door of his home wearing long underwear. With the porch light making him clearly visible to the FBI agents trying to keep warm in their vehicle in the parking lot across the street, Ivins stood on the porch for a few minutes looking into the darkness. Then, he returned inside.[2]

A few minutes later, the Frederick municipal garbage truck pulled up in front of Ivins' house and took his garbage. As they'd done with the trash check after the Lambert meeting two years earlier, another group of FBI agents were waiting until the garbage truck had finished with the block and turned a corner, taking it out of sight of Ivins' home. There, the agents stopped the truck and retrieved Ivins' trash bags.

Meanwhile, seven minutes after his previous look around outside, Ivins again emerged from his front door and walked to the curb where the wheeled trash cart stood. He looked inside the cart to verify that it had been emptied, and he then pulled it back into the driveway next to the house. Unlike other trash nights, however, he didn't just return into the house. Instead, he walked toward his neighbor's house and stood in the street, apparently to get a better view of the parking lot and wooded area across from his house. He stood for about a full minute and just looked toward the area and the lot where part of the surveillance team was watching carefully, while taking precautions to prevent being seen by Ivins. Another agent, James Griffin, Jr. was just a few feet away, behind one of the evergreens that lined Ft. Detrick, standing with his arms close to his sides to avoid being spotted.

Then, apparently deciding there was no one watching him and nothing to be concerned about, Dr. Ivins returned into his house.

To the FBI, this was significant, since Ivins had never done anything like that on previous trash nights (and would never do anything like that again on the next dozen trash nights). He'd never even come out of the house in the middle of the night to check the trash cans. He'd always wait until morning.

When investigators went through his trash they found two items that they hoped might explain Ivins' unusual behavior. Ivins had throw out a dog-eared, abundantly underlined and heavily annotated paperback copy of one of his favorite books, the 1992 Pulitzer Prize winning tome by Richard R. Hofstadter titled *Gödel, Escher, Bach: An Eternal Golden Braid*. And, he'd also thrown out the November 1992 issue of *American Scientist*.

The first thing that attracted the eye when looking through these two items was that they both related to codes. Ivins was known to have a fascination with codes, but how did these materials relate? And why did he throw them out? And, why did he do it right after the FBI had thoroughly searched his home? The FBI had watched his trash because they hoped he would throw out some important evidence. The book and magazine could be it, but what did they contain?

It was FBI scientist Darin Steele who eventually figured it out. The first clue may have been the very peculiar list of 6 famous mathematicians on page 404 and the highlighted letters. Everyone had been wondering why certain characters in the anthrax letter sent to the media were darker than others. And here was a coded message that used darkened characters as part of the code.

Agent Steele had long ago noticed that the first three darkened characters in the media letter were TTT. He knew TTT was a code (called a "codon") for phenylalanine, an amino acid that is part of DNA. And, that now seemed significant since the other item Ivins had thrown away was an issue of *American Scientist* which contained an article by David Searls titled *The Linquistics of DNA*. It discussed, among other things, codons and hidden messages.

Direct Evidence?

When Agent Steele looked at all the characters that appeared to be darkened, he ended up with

TTTAATTAT

Nine characters, forming three codons for three amino acids found in DNA:

TTT = **P**henylalanine (single-letter designator **F**)
AAT = **A**sparagine (single-letter designator **N**)
TAT = **T**yrosine (single-letter designator **Y**)

The first letter in each of the amino acid names were PAT. Pat is short for Patricia. Patricia Fellows was one of the former female assistants with whom Ivins seemed to be obsessed. Could that be just a coincidence?

But, there was another way of translating the codon code, and the hidden message at the third level could also be decoded as FNY. Four of the first five anthrax letters were sent to media organizations in New York City. FNY seemed to stand for Fuck New York. Ivins was known to have a strong dislike for New York City. Could that be just a coincidence, too?

More likely, *neither* was a coincidence.[3]

The three levels described in *GEB* were *all there*. (1) The first and last characters in the first and last lines of the media letter were darkened, forming a frame for the hidden message. (2) The media letter consisted of three word sentences, there were three letters in a codon, and the A that didn't belong in "PENACILIN" was highlighted, all providing clues to how to decode the message. And (3) the solutions related to Ivins' obsessions. How could those all be coincidences?

There were just too many coincidences. When Agent Steele told the others on the Amerithrax team about what he'd found, they also saw it appeared to be a *direct* connection between Bruce Ivins and the first media letters. Any jury in the land would almost certainly see it that way - if it was properly explained by an able prosecutor.

Chapter 39

Ivins Explains

On November 19, 2007, Ivins' lawyer Paul Kemp and Kemp's colleague Thomas DeGonia III paid a visit to Amerithrax prosecutor Kenneth Kohl in Kohl's office in Washington.[1]

Kemp explained that he was very surprised by the November 1st search and everything else that had happened on that evening and the following day, when Ivins' safe deposit box was also searched.

At that point in time, Kenneth Kohl still wasn't convinced that Ivins was the anthrax mailer, and he wasn't fully up-to-date on the latest FBI findings. In fact, Kohl had been trying to slow down the pace of the investigation of Bruce Ivins, since he didn't want another Steven Hatfill-type situation, which he believed was the result of the FBI moving too fast with too little solid evidence.

As a result, Kohl could only tell Ivins' lawyers what he personally believed to be the situation. Ivins was not yet an official target of the investigation. However, the FBI was very concerned about Ivins' lack of truthfulness and his apparently deliberate attempts to mislead the investigation. Ivins' April 2002 submission to the FBIR was of particular concern, since Ivins had attended a meeting where it was explained to him how the slants were to be prepared, and he'd previously prepared incorrect slants in February. So, he should have been doubly careful in preparing the April 2002 materials. There didn't seem to be any reasonable explanation for why the slants Ivins prepared didn't contain the morphs -- other than he was deliberately trying to hide the fact that the anthrax powders originated with the flask he controlled.

Ivins Explains

The November 1-2 search was the result of Ivins' apparent deceit or carelessness. If it appeared to FBI investigators that Ivins was continuing to try to deceive the Amerithrax investigators, Ivins could expect more of the same.

More of the Same

At USAMRIID, Ivins was going around Building 1425 telling people about how the FBI was brutalizing government employees, and they appeared to be determined to find someone at USAMRIID who they could blame for the anthrax mailings. He bitched about how a "gay black guy" had frisked him before driving him to the hotel because they wouldn't let him go home. (In reality, African-American FBI Agent Lawrence Alexander was a heterosexual and the father of three children.[2])

Meanwhile, the FBI was interviewing everyone who knew Ivins, while at the same time trying to find out if Ivins had other places to store things or other places to use a computer. In an interview on December 6 and 7, agents tried to determine if Ivins kept a locker at a fitness club to which he belonged, but it appeared that Ivins never left anything in a locker there overnight. He gave some of the other members of the club the creeps, and once he almost got into a fistfight in the sauna room when some Navy seal or marine took offense at the way Ivins was suggestively applying oil to his legs.[3]

While the operator of the club claimed that Ivins had no access to the club's computer, the club would occasionally receive emails from Russian web sites that appeared to be addressed to Ivins at USAMRIID but were nevertheless delivered to the club manager's email address. The emails offered deals in pornography, Viagra, penis enlargement, etc. Most of the emails used the Cyrillic alphabet, but the club operator had run them through a translator program to figure out what they were all about. He'd also advised his Internet provider about the problem, but they'd never gotten back to him with any kind of explanation. The club manager managed to find three of the emails in his cache and printed them out for the FBI.

In a December 14 interview with a USAMRIID scientist, the agents were told about how their searches were creating friction within USAMRIID to the point where some people would not talk with Ivins anymore. The scientist insisted that he could not believe any suggestion that Ivins was behind the anthrax mailings, since Ivins seemed totally incapable of keeping his mouth shut about anything. He'd have told someone by now. Besides, Ivins was a good, reliable and consistent scientist, and his results and ideas were impeccable, even though the condition of his lab was often "horrible."[4]

Ivins was currently barred from entering his own lab, which was making life difficult for everyone -- particularly Ivins.

The interviews continued into January of 2008, and it appeared that the general consensus was that Ivins was an odd-ball, goofy, and a nutty professor type. It was very difficult for most people who knew Ivins to view him as a terrorist or killer. Ivins never talked much about his home life or his family. He had no social skills. He was awkward in situations that didn't involve his work, but his work was his life and he was good at it, good enough for people to overlook all of his awkwardness and goofiness.[5]

Ivins was very anxious to get back into his laboratory and to begin hands-on work again. He was constantly pestering his superiors to get permission. It was explained to him again and again that that was not possible until the anthrax investigation had blown over, but there didn't seem to be any reasoning that could stop Ivins from making request after request. More and more people at USAMRIID were beginning to feel that because of his long-term depression, the sloppy way he kept his lab, and unstable way he currently appeared, that he could be a definite safety problem.[6]

Ivins had talked of retiring in September 2008, when he would be eligible for additional benefits, but he was making no effort to instruct a replacement. He didn't use written protocols. He did everything from memory. When asked to show others how he did things, he'd go through the process so fast that no one could possible follow or keep up. And, when asked to repeat, he would explain things in a different way, further confusing the person being instructed. On occasion, Ivins would even flat out refuse to instruct someone. He claimed to want to retire, but he seemed to be trying to make it impossible for USAMRIID to replace him.

Ivins Explains

And on more than one occasion, Ivins would declare - seemingly out of the blue, "I could never intentionally kill or hurt anyone."

The January 16, 2008 Meeting

In the spring of 2007, Assistant U.S. Attorney Rachel Lieber had become part of the prosecution team. At that time, the case had begun to focus on people with access to flask RMR-1029, and she had to learn the science of the case as well as all the related details in what was a massive, multi-continent whodunit. Getting up to speed took six to eight months. By January of 2008, she was gradually taking over most chores from Kenneth Kohl, who had begun work on a different major case. Unlike Kohl, who was still urging the FBI to slow down on their investigation of Ivins, AUSA Lieber had started urging the investigators to move as fast as they could to maintain the momentum.[7]

Blonde, attractive, Rachel Carlson Lieber was a graduate of Villanova University and Georgetown law school. She had experience working homicides, and she worked hard to build good relationships between her office and the FBI investigators. Much to the pleasure of Edward Montooth and particularly Vincent Lisi, Lieber began to take the lead in the forming of a legal case against Ivins.

In early January, 2008, Lieber assembled together all the Amerithrax investigators, herself and Kohl, for a day-long meeting to review the status of the Amerithrax investigation. What areas of investigation were still open? What deadlines had been set? What deadlines needed to be set? Was there enough evidence for an indictment? If not, what else was needed and how could it be obtained? What would FBI agents and witnesses be able to say under oath about Bruce Edwards Ivins that would prove his guilt to a jury? If there wasn't enough evidence to get an indictment, did that mean that someone else could have done it? If so, who?

Steven Hatfill was no longer a suspect. The only official suspect in the case was now Bruce Ivins. And, before AUSA Lieber could set the wheels in motion toward an indictment, she needed to get a better feel for this man she only knew from the reports she'd read. She needed to meet this person who seemed like a harmless, goofy professor to some people, yet to others - like Nancy Haigwood

- he was an obsessed stalker who saw no problem in damaging property, lying, cheating and even using a grieving mother's cause over a dead son in a sick attempt to destroy Haigwood's career with a forged letter.

The on-the-record meeting was arranged for Wednesday, January 16, 2008, in the U.S. Attorney's office in Washington.[8] Ground rules were established with Ivins' attorney, and the stated agenda was to discuss certain aspects of Ivins' personal life that the FBI agents needed to better understand. FBI agent Vincent Lisi would do most of the talking, playing a variation on "good cop" in an attempt to gain Ivins' confidence. Edward Montooth would play "stern cop" and mostly just preside over the session, changing the subject when it seemed advisable. Except for reminding Ivins and his lawyers that Ivins' presence at the meeting was entirely voluntary, Kohl and Lieber would mostly just sit, observe and listen.

Ivins arrived with Paul Kemp and Tom DeGonia. After the introductions, which included listing some of the past cases solved by Montooth and Lisi to show that they weren't amateurs to mess around with, Lisi began with what he described as an attempt to clarify some problems with things Ivins had said in the past that Montooth and Lisi needed to fully understand.

Lisi started with the March 29, 2002, meeting where Patricia Worsham and FBI scientist Scott Stanley instructed Ivins on how the slants for the FBIR were to be prepared. Ivins acted like a defense attorney and disputed that he was even there. When he was shown a diagram agent Scott Stanley had drawn showing where everyone was sitting at the conference table, Ivins disputed its accuracy and wanted to talk with the agent who had drawn the diagram.

Another one of the subjects Lisi wanted to discuss was Ivins' unusual "interest" in the Kappa Kappa Gamma sorority. On this subject, Ivins was very animated and open. Ivins even corrected what Lisi had said. "You don't understand," he told Lisi. "It's not an *interest*. It's an *obsession*."

Ivins went on to explain his "obsession" in great detail, telling the people on the other side of the table about how it all began in the 1960s while he was at the University of Cincinnati. He had asked a KKG member for a date and she turned him down. That resulted in Ivins often walking past the KKG sorority house on Clinton Avenue just to look at it. Later, he began to compile a list of locations of "dozens and dozens and dozens" of KKG chapters throughout the eastern United States. After he'd moved east, he'd go to the Library of Congress to dig through phone books from around the country to find addresses of various chapters. While he was working at the Uniformed Services University in Bethesda, he utilized a directory of universities and colleges to further identify schools which might possibly have KKG chapters.

He had visited several sorority houses, such as the ones at the University of North Carolina in Chapel Hill, at the University of Virginia in Charlottesville, at the University of Maryland in College Park, the one at West Virginia University in Morgantown, and the one at the University of Tennessee in Knoxville. He thought he may also have visited the KKG chapter house at Duke University in Durham, North Carolina. He once planned to visit the chapter at the University of Pennsylvania, in Philadelphia, but he called them and found the chapter had closed.

Ivins then described how, sometime between 1976 and 1978 he'd broken into the KKG sorority house at the University of North Carolina and stole ritual materials and a cypher device used to decode the sorority ritual book.

Between 1978 and 1980, Ivins traveled to Morgantown, West Virginia, during a school break to visit their KKG house. While there, he broke into the house and stole their copy of the ritual book.

He never broke into a house if there was any sign the building was occupied. He only entered during school breaks when he was certain there was no one in the houses.

There was an exception to that, however. In 1979 or 1980, Ivins went to a job interview at the University of Tennessee in Knoxville, and, while there, he located the KKG office which was housed in a commercial office building. He went to the office, knocked and was allowed to enter. He recalled that there were four or five sorority members there, and when he started talking with them about KKG secrets and rituals, they called security and he was escorted out of the building.

A security officer at the University of Maryland had once called him and accused him of breaking into the KKG house and stealing their ritual book. Ivins denied it. He'd never broken into that particular house. And he'd already obtained a copy of the ritual book from West Virginia University.

Ivins claimed he had never been to Princeton, however, even though they had a KKG chapter. His father had attended Princeton, but Bruce Ivins denied any connection to the place.

When Agent Lisi moved on to Ivins apparent obsession with Nancy Haigwood, Ivins continued to confess. His lawyers evidently let him ramble on, apparently seeing no harm in Ivins talking about long-ago events that didn't directly relate to the anthrax attacks, mostly misdemeanor crimes which could no longer be prosecuted, and which showed the FBI agents and the AUSAs that Ivins was telling them everything and withholding nothing.

Ivins confessed to stealing Haigwood's notebook. He confessed to painting KKG on Nancy Haigwood's fence and car window. He confessed to using the name "Carla Sander" to open post office boxes which he used when he paid for advertisements in *Rolling Stone* and *Mother Jones* magazines. And he sold copies of the KKG ritual book via those PO boxes. He used Carl Scandella's name to open a PO box where he received bondage-type porn magazines. When asked, he confessed to being a subscriber to the *American Family Association Journal*, even though Lisi didn't explain why he wanted to know about that.

Ivins even confessed to sending the pro-hazing letter to *The Frederick News-Post* and signing Nancy Haigwood's name to it. It was part of his Kappa Kappa Gamma obsession. He felt that KKG had instituted a "fatwa" against him, and everything he did against them was self-defense, more or less.

Ivins also explained that his wife and family knew nothing of this obsession. When he needed to take a long drive to do something KKG related, he either did it when Diane was asleep or away, or he would do it while he was on a legitimate trip to the area.

Direct Evidence

The meeting was brought to a close when one of Ivins' lawyers stated that he had to leave for another appointment. But, they agreed to a follow-up session to take place sometime in February.

Ivins Explains

During those three to four hours, the FBI agents had covered a lot more territory than they could ever have hoped. And, while the FBI had suspected that Ivins did things because of his obsession with KKG, it was quite another matter to have direct evidence in the form of a confession from Ivins that he did those things and why he did them. In a 2011 interview with PBS, Rachel Lieber said,

> To us, this was kind of an "aha" moment in the investigation. We now have an ability to prove in the own words of Dr. Ivins — so, again, direct evidence, his own words — why the location of the mailbox is so significant. ...

> It is a way to connect Dr. Ivins to that crime, to the location where the letters were mailed. It's a very significant thing to be able to say: "Ladies and gentlemen, Dr. Ivins, he showed this pattern of driving three or four hours in any direction from his home essentially to surveil Kappa Kappa Gamma locations. How do we know this? Because Dr. Ivins told us. And here, ladies and gentlemen, you'll see this picture. Here's where the mailbox was; here's where the Kappa building is. It's completely consistent with his pattern of his behavior."

Lieber was also fascinated by the difference in what Ivins claimed he could remember, and what he claimed he couldn't remember. He could remember details of breaking into a KKG chapter house in the 1980s and the exact address of Nancy Haigwood's apartment in 1981, but he claimed he couldn't recall the meeting where he was told how to prepare samples for the FBIR and he would just rattle off one illogical explanation after another.

And, of course, they had direct evidence that taking a long drive to Princeton in the middle of the night would not have been unusual for him, nor would his wife have noticed he was gone. Ivins seemed to take pride in being able to do things that his wife knew nothing about. To Assistant U.S. Attorney Rachel Lieber, it would help make Ivins' lack of an alibi look more incriminating to a jury.

Chapter 40

Ivins Attempts Suicide

After the Jan. 16 meeting with Ivins and his lawyers, the investigators and prosecutors held long meetings at the FBI and DOJ where other members of the Amerithrax team were brought in to hear what had been learned, to discuss what should be done next, and to determine what should be asked in the meeting with Ivins planned for February.[1]

Agent Montooth also invited psychiatrist Dr. Gregory Saathoff to one of the meetings with the investigators and prosecutors to get his advice on how Ivins might react if asked certain questions.

Searls & Hofstadter

On January 18, FBI agents interviewed David Searls, the author of the article on *The Linquistics of DNA* that Ivins had apparently studied when he devised the coded message in the media letters. The agents couldn't mention Ivins by name, but they learned that Searls had no close associates in the Maryland or Virgina areas.[2]

Before meeting with the FBI agents, Searls had wondered if the highlighted characters in the media letter had represented something to do with DNA, and he'd thought it might have something to do with a TATA box, "a promoter region in DNA that serves as a binding site for transcription regulators." But, when the agents pointed out that the letters actually had TTTAATTAT highlighted, it was clear that his theory about a TATA box was less likely to be the answer than the FBI's explanation.

On February 8, the FBI interviewed Douglas Hofstadter, the author of *Gödel, Escher, Bach*. Hofstadter was shown a copy of the *New York Post* letter and asked if he noticed anything significant about the letter. His initial response was that he didn't see anything significant, but then, after studying the letter for a few minutes, he pointed out that there were a number of A's and T's that were highlighted. He had no idea why that would be so, but he saw the possible connection to DNA coding and pointed out that none of the C's and G's were highlighted. A, C, G and T were the letters used to represent key parts of DNA. He also mentioned the Italian word "attacca" which appears in *GEB*, and he explained that attacca means either to attach to or to attack. But there were no highlighted C's.

Hofstadter's comments seemed to be more about how the handwriting differed from his own handwriting. The E's in the letter weren't drawn the way he drew E's and he thought that might indicate some foreign-born writer. The same with the R's. And, when he was shown a copy of the Daschle letter, he thought the size and shape of the question mark in the Daschle letters was odd.[3]

The agents explained the code and how it represented the three levels described in *GEB*, but Hofstadter wasn't so sure. He looked for other explanations. He was apparently set on the idea that the letters were written by some who wasn't originally taught in English, someone who may have been more accustomed to writing from right to left. He found the R's to be of particular interest. Apparently, Hofstadter had been taught how to write in a Catholic school, since the public-school style of drawing R's seemed totally alien to him, as if he'd never seen it before.

Public School   Catholic School

R   R

The agents asked if they could look through his correspondence and emails to see if he'd received anything from certain individuals, and Hofstadter agreed. The agents left copies of the Brokaw and Daschle letters with him to peruse. But, it was clear that Hofstadter had his own theory about who sent the anthrax letters, and he was only looking for proof that would fit his theory.

The interview seemed to point out how difficult it might be to convince a jury that there was no other logical interpretation for the highlighted characters in the media letter. Hopefully, the jury selection process would eliminate any juror who already had a theory about who had sent the anthrax letters.

The February 13, 2008 Meeting

The meeting on Wednesday, February 13 began the same way as the January meeting, with Kenneth Kohl and Rachel Lieber making certain that Ivins understood that this was another "on the record" interview, that it was entirely voluntary on Ivins' part and that he was free to stop the interview at any time. Ivins understood and agreed.[4]

This time, agent Montooth would do much of the questioning, while Vincent Lisi would mostly listen intently and nod as if fascinated, to encourage Ivins to continue talking.

The session began with questions about the burglary of the KKG sorority house in Chapel Hill, NC. Ivins couldn't remember the exact date, but he described every detail of how the entered at night through a first floor bathroom window that was located out of sight behind a shrub. He spent about an hour in the house before leaving with the cipher and ritual materials. He hadn't gone there to steal the cipher. He didn't even know of its existence before he found it.

He realized the importance of the cipher afterward, and when he burglarized the KKG house at West Virginia University, he specifically hunted for the ritual book. And, he found it.

Ivins explained that the trip to Morgantown was his last burglary, because he now had what he had been looking for: the book of rituals and the method to decode the book gave him a sense of "power" which he could use to get back at KKG and the woman who had refused to go out on a date with him in 1966.

Ivins explained how he'd been stopped by local police in Ithaca, NY, for "driving nervously" after he'd left a bottle of Khalua on the doorstep of Mara Linscott's parent's home in Ithaca. He wasn't issued a ticket, and nothing came of being stopped. He had apparently convinced the police officer that he was harmless.

The trips to Ithaca were done at night. Ivins' wife was totally unaware that they had taken place. She just assumed Ivins was working late at the lab. His wife knew he would sometimes go on long drives as a way to relieve stress and as a form of therapy, but she never knew where he went and never questioned him about it. Additionally, since she would be asleep when he left and returned, and since the two slept in separate bedrooms, he could come and go without being noticed.

The agents also discussed Ivins attempts to have certain KKG members added to a Wikipedia article as "notable" KKG members. And they talked about his fascination with bondage, which Ivins attributed to something that began when he was five or six years old and would put blindfolds on stuffed animals and teddy bears. Later, the practice took on sexual connotations.

He explained that there was a time when he took long walks instead of long drives to relieve his anxieties. In order to be protected, he purchased two stun guns via the Internet. After he'd received the guns, he realized that he would have to actually touch the person to activate them, and he never wanted to get that close. So, he purchased a "Tazer" which would enable him to disable a possible attacker by shooting a dart at them from a distance.

Ivins acknowledged buying "Spectra Pro" software, which allowed him to monitor activity on his computer at home. And, he'd purchased a device to search for electronic monitoring devices or "bugs," and he'd used those devices in his home, but he'd never taken them to work.

Ivins denied ever seeing any copies of the National Enquirer at work, and he certainly never took any copies to work.

Ivins was asked what he meant in his October 18, 2001 report on the powder in the Dachle letter when he wrote, "These are not 'garage' spores." Ivins explained that he simply meant they seemed to be of professional quality created in a laboratory, not in someone's garage. Then he added that Pat Fellows was the "spore queen" at USAMRIID who could make the purest anthrax spores.

The final topic for the meeting was the diagram and the two photographs Terry Abshire had taken and Ivins had given to the FBI in January 2002.

Ivins was initially reluctant to discuss the photos and the diagram because he couldn't recall what was going on at the time, but he eventually explained what he'd seen in the photos. Technically, he hadn't been trying to mislead the FBI when he explained that morphs resulted from passaging. He was trying to get them to understand that the path that they were following was based upon wrong science -- and Ivins understood the right science.

But, it was Ivins who in January 2002 misunderstood the science behind the formation of the morphs.

In 2008, he wasn't as sure of himself as he had been in 2002.

March 2008

With the FBI getting more and more overt in their investigation of him, Ivins began to feel the strain of fearing that at any moment they might knock on his door and place him under arrest. Or they might even come to his place of work and march him out in handcuffs.

On March 5, a confidential informant working at USAMRIID advised the FBI and said that Ivins had been coming to work only sporadically, and he didn't even bother to call in to inform people when he was not coming in to work. When he was at work, he frequently seemed jittery, always talking to himself, and no longer the jokester he had been in the past. His sole focus these days is on his work with the non-lethal Sterne stain of Bacillus anthracis, which he could handle in Suite B5. He still wasn't allowed in any BSL-3 level suite. But, he was still "old Bruce" in one respect: He was still ingratiating himself with an attractive female scientist, acting like he was "going goo-goo over her." [5]

When asked, the informant stated that Ivins was still planning to retire in about seven months, but, because of his legal bills he couldn't totally stop working, so, he would probably have to take on another job after retiring. He hoped to get a part time job as a laboratory technician at a private company, and do work characterizing various strains of anthrax.

On March 17, Ivins showed up at work with another black eye. This time he said he'd fallen down the stairs while on his way to the bathroom in the middle of the night. He claimed he was wearing glasses at the time he fell, and part of his glasses hit the corner of his eye causing it to become discolored.[6]

The next day, on March 18, Ivins accidentally broke a flask of Sterne anthrax. Then, instead of reporting the accident to a safety officer as regulations required, he simply cleaned the spill and his lab clothes with bleach. And, then he went home to wash and dry his pants before returning to work.[7]

It wasn't long before he was called into Colonel Korch's office and reprimanded. Korch was furious that Ivins failed to follow existing protocols and wanted to terminate Ivins' employment at USAMRIID on the spot. But, Pat Worsham interceded on Ivins' behalf and saved his job. Instead of being fired, Ivins was told that he could no longer work in *any* lab at USAMRIID for the remainder of his employment -- until his retirement in September.

That evening, Ivins wrote Mara Linscott an email filled with hopelessness and self-pity: It said, in part:

> I'm sorry you have abandoned me. You were the one person I knew I could bare my soul to and tell everything to, and now you have abandoned me. You have put me on your dark list ... I lose my connections. I lose my years. I lose my health. I lose my ability to think. I lose my friends. What do I have left but eternity?

On the 19th, Ivins evidently took another one of his days off, since he was home when his wife returned from work at 2 in the afternoon. He was unconscious and unresponsive, but still breathing, when she called 911. Her training as a registered nurse enabled her to make a diagnosis, and she advised the dispatcher that she believed he'd probably taken too many Valium tablets and possibly mixed them with alcohol. He'd been very depressed lately and was on antidepressants, but she didn't see any suicide note anywhere.

A Crime Unlike Any Other

The paramedics rushed him to Frederick Memorial Hospital where he was evaluated. It was determined that he didn't require hospital treatment, and he was released into Diane Ivins' care later that evening.

Around midnight, Ivins was on his computer again, sending a flowery and melodramatic email to Mara Linscott and her sister Cheryl in which he complained how he missed the days when he was able to work on life-saving vaccines for soldiers.

"O, Healer!" he wrote, referring to Mara's current career as a medical doctor. "O devoter of your life to the lives of others! I can hurt, kill, and terrorize, but others place me with the vilest of the vile." He clearly wanted Linscott to view him as a victim of the government, since he wrote, "The state smells its carnivorous death-blood sacrifice. I look into the mirror and cry out who it is."

He didn't blame himself for what was happening. It was all the fault of others. He'd only wanted to do only good, but it now seemed that the government was out to destroy him just as the KKG sorority had been out to destroy him during past decades.

Chapter 41

Non-denial Denials

During March of 2008, Ivins showed signs of falling apart. He sent Cheryl Linscott, who was Mara's older sister and Diane Ivins' best friend, an email complaining about how Mara had abandoned him. She was overly dedicated to winning, Ivins wrote. "She isn't satisfied until she makes someone lose." And, "She has to make someone lose. ... That's why she's proud of hurting me." [1]

On April 21, the trash inspection that had become routine found that Ivins had thrown out his porn magazine collection along with a bag of soiled women's panties, perhaps so they wouldn't be found during the time he was planning to stay in a hospital.[2]

A day or two later, on the advice of a CCA counselor, Ivins entered an alcohol abuse treatment program at Suburban Hospital in Bethesda, less than 40 miles from his home. He was at home briefly after a week in the hospital. Then, on May 2, a female acquaintance noticed him waiting in his car in front of her home when she got out of work. When she asked him what he was doing there, he explained that he was having some mental issues and was going to spend the entire month of May at "Massie" in Cumberland.[3]

As he said he'd do, Ivins entered the state psychiatric hospital in Cumberland, MD, about 90 miles from his home. He stayed at "Massie" for over two weeks. The Joseph S. Massie Unit of the Thomas B. Finan Center describes itself as a "multiple-modality treatment facility for adults experiencing the devastating effects of alcoholism and other chemical dependencies."

A Crime Unlike Any Other

A Meeting With Paul Keim

Meanwhile, the FBI was moving forward. On Wednesday, May 14, evidently as Paul Keim was on his way to somewhere else, a meeting was arranged to have him talk with investigators and prosecutors at Dulles International Airport in Washington. When Keim entered the room where the meeting was to take place, he found he was going to be interviewed by no less than six people, Ed Montooth, Vincent Lisi, Scott Stanley and Jason Bannan of the FBI, plus Kenneth Kohl and Rachel Lieber of the Department of Justice.

To Dr. Keim, the meeting initially appeared to be about his work with differentiating between different strains of anthrax and tracing strains back to their origins. The government people wanted to know how many scientists in his branch of microbiology knew about his efforts to attempt to be able to distinguish one batch of anthrax from another via DNA. But, it also appears now that Kohl and Lieber were sizing Keim up to see how he'd appeared to a jury if and when it became necessary. After a brief break when the agents and prosecutors seemed to need to confer over what to ask him next, they returned and began asking out Bruce Ivins and what Keim thought of certain emails Ivins had exchanged with various scientists in late 2001 and early 2002, in which he seemed to be attempting to learn more about the Ames strain.

Keim was stunned to realize that the FBI seriously considered Bruce Ivins to be a suspect in the 2001 anthrax mailings. Paul Keim had only known Ivins as a valuable colleague who had assisted in arranging scientific meetings from time to time over the past decade. He'd never seen anything in any newspaper or heard anything in any conversation that indicated that Ivins might be a suspect. And the FBI and DOJ wanted things kept that way, since they asked that he keep their meeting strictly confidential.[4]

Proffer or No Proffer

By this time, Ivins had already spent about $100,000 from his retirement fund on legal fees. And his lawyer had evidently advised him that the Department of Justice was suggesting that he needed to think about making a proffer.[5]

Non-denial Denials

A proffer is an offer to make a deal. The government didn't offer to make a deal, however. Apparently, the government attorneys had only suggested that Ivins make an offer to confess his role in the attacks in exchange for some form of leniency in sentencing.

Ivins' lawyer undoubtedly explained to him that the problem they had was that, if Ivins were to make a proffer or offer to confess, and if the government didn't agree to what Ivins wanted in exchange for the proffer, the fact that Ivins had made an offer to confess would greatly undermine any claim of innocence. An unaccepted proffer cannot be used in court as evidence of guilt, but the government can use what is stated in the proffer as new leads to further their investigation and look for addition evidence.

So, if someone was going to make a proffer, he had better be absolutely certain that the proffer will be accepted. Since, if it isn't accepted, he could have done serious harm to his own case.

Ivins had until his next meeting with prosecutors to make up his mind.

Ivins on Tape

Meanwhile, over the years many people had told the FBI that they didn't think Ivins could be the anthrax mailer because, if he was, he wouldn't have been able to keep quiet about it. They believed Ivins was incapable of keeping a secret. He was a blabbermouth.

That naturally led to FBI agents wondering if they could get one of Ivins' female friends to have a long, supposedly-private talk with him in some setting where he might open up and confess to being the person behind the anthrax attacks of 2001. And the FBI would be there taping the conversation.

They tried persuading Nancy Haigwood to do it, since Ivins had been infatuated with her for decades and would probably talk his head off to get back into her good graces. She was probably the person who would the best bet to cause him to open up and confess. But, after initially agreeing, Haigwood backed out when a friend convinced her that it was a bad idea.[6]

And, evidently, Mara Linscott was either unwilling or deemed unapproachable on the subject.

313

A Crime Unlike Any Other

That brought investigators to their third choice: Patricia Fellows. Like Haigwood, Fellows wasn't one of Ivins' friends who thought him to be just a harmless absent-minded professor type. Fellows knew of Ivins' evil side. Since he was usually unable to keep a secret and tended to blab to everyone, she knew he'd managed to steal the password to her computer, and he had used it to read her emails. She also knew that Ivins had named her as a better suspect than he was in the anthrax mailings because of her proficiency at growing spores.

Pat Fellows agreed to meet with Ivins and to try to get him to talk about "Bad Bruce" who, in his emails, he blamed for most of the inappropriate things he did. Maybe she could get "Good Bruce" to acknowledge that "Bad Bruce" had sent the anthrax letters.

The meeting was arranged to take place over coffee at a restaurant in Frederick where the FBI could listen in with the aid of hidden microphones. It took place on June 5, 2008.[7]

The conversation evidently began with a discussion of how Ivins looked. He looked terrible. He talked about the weeks he'd recently spent in mental hospitals for alcohol dependency and depression. After a while, Fellows worked the conversation into the desired direction:

> Fellows: "I'm trying to be supportive and understanding. But I guess a part of what you had said before to me in response to that was that, you know, there kind of seems to be another person at times. And if you don't remember doing that, I mean [pause], don't get mad [laugh], are you absolutely . . .?"

> Ivins: "You were going to say how do I know that I didn't have anything to do with . . . ."

> Fellows: "Yeah."

> Ivins: "I will tell that, I will tell you that it's, I can't pull that up. And a lot of times with e-mails, I don't know that I sent an e-mail until I see it in the sent box. And it worries me when I wake up in the morning and I've got all my clothes and my shoes on, and my car keys are right beside there. . . . And I don't have it in my, in my, I, I can tell you I don't have it in my heart to kill anybody."

314

...
Ivins: "And I, and I do not have any recollection of ever have doing anything like that. As a matter of fact, I don't have no clue how to, how to make a bio-weapon and I don't want to know."

Ivins wasn't stating emphatically that he did not commit the anthrax killings. He appeared to be saying, *if* he did it, he didn't recall doing it, and he wasn't a killer at heart, so it would have had to have been something unintentional. Later, he said:

Ivins: "The only reason I remember some of this stuff, it's because there's like a clue the next day. Like there's an e-mail or, or, you know, when you're, when you're in bed and you're like, you're like this, you know, that's, that's not real fun. It's like 'oh shit, did I drive somewhere last night?'"

Fellows: "Right, yeah, yeah, that must be awfully scary."

Ivins: "It really certainly is. Uh, because I can tell you, I am not a killer at heart."

Apparently, as part of the game plan devised by the FBI, Pat Fellows then suggested that maybe Dr. Ivins should get hypnotized to help him remember. Ivins replied that he would be terrified of doing that:

Ivins: "What happens if I find something that, that is like buried deep, deep, deep, and you know, like from, from my past or I mean . . . like when I was a kid or stuff like that you know?"
...
Ivins: "Oh, but I mean, you know, that would just, that would just like, like, like make me want to jump off a bridge. You know, that would be . . ."

Fellows: "What's that? If you found out that . . . ."

Ivins: "If I found out I was involved in some way, and, and . . ."

Fellows: "And you don't consciously know?"

Ivins: "Have any, any clue. [pause] [groan] 'Cause like, I'm, I'm not uh, a uh, I don't think of myself as a vicious, a, a nasty evil person."

Fellows: "Oh no, no, me either, but I mean, unless there is a whole other side . . ."

Ivins: "Yeah."

Fellows: " . . . that is buried down in there . . ."

Ivins: "Yeah."

Fellows: ". . . for whatever reason."

Ivins: "Because I, I don't like to hurt people, accidentally, in, in any way. And [several scientists at USAMRIID] wouldn't do that. And I, in my right mind wouldn't do it [laughs]. . . . But it's still, but I still feel responsibility because it [RMR-1029] wasn't locked up at the time . . . ."

The FBI and the DOJ prosecutors listening to the tapes after the meeting between Ivins and Fellows looked upon the statements from Ivins as being "non-denial denials." And there was little doubt that a jury would view them the same way. Rachel Lieber even planned to play parts of the tape to the jury when the time came for her to make her opening statements in Ivins' trial.[8] Everyone would realize that Ivins never actually claimed he didn't send the anthrax letters, although he was given every opportunity to do so. He only said he was "not a killer at heart," and that he did "not have any recollection of ever ... doing anything like that."

In other words, it was all a horrible mistake that he could not admit to himself he was responsible for.

Chapter 42

Over The Edge

The FBI and the DOJ prosecutors arranged another meeting with Ivins and his lawyers for Monday, June 9, 2008. At the insistence of Ivins' lawyers, this meeting was to be "off the record," meaning that nothing Ivins said during the meeting could be used against him in a court of law.[1]

The meeting began with a discussion about when and from whom Ivins learned that the spores in flask RMR-1029 resembled the anthrax spores that were mailed in 2001. Ivins claimed to be 100% certain a fellow USAMRIID employee told him first, and he was 99% certain he was told before February 2002.

Of course, no one had any idea that the spores in flask RMR-1029 matched the attack spores until years later.

They then discussed Ivins' relationship with his two former assistants, Mara Linscott and Pat Fellows. Ivins once again made the point that he ranked Pat Fellows as the best spore maker who ever worked at USAMRIID. Then he talked of his fascination with Mara Linscott. He told her all of his innermost thoughts and fully confided in her. He was "quite taken" with her for various reasons, and he would sometimes drive past her apartment much like he would with KKG sorority houses. Ivins admitted that, on one occasion when Mara went into the hot suite to work, Ivins took her personal keys and had duplicates made for her apartment.

He explained that when Linscott left USAMRIID, he was not angry, but he was very saddened by her departure. He also admitted to naming Mara and Pat in a witness conference in March 2007 before he testified to the grand jury. However, he no longer believed that anyone at USAMRIID mailed the anthrax letters.

Ivins explained that his relationship with Fellows and Linscott was "very complex." At one point, he and Fellows had blindfolded Mara Linscott and led her into an adult sex novelty shop, but it was just a joke between friends.

When the conversation delved into all the people Ivins had named as likely suspects over the years, Ivins backed off some claims and continued to push others.

They talked about why Ivins disliked New York City. Ivins explained he disliked the New York Yankees baseball team "because they win too much." He disliked New York City because of the way he'd been treated there by waitresses and hotel clerks.

Vincent Lisi then provided Ivins with a copy of the letter sent to *The New York Post* and Tom Brokaw. Lisi asked if anything in the letter stood out to him.

Ivins responded that the writer "can't make R's," had a "problem with T's," and "can't spell penicillin." In Ivins' opinion, the writing looked like that of a second grader, and he questioned the need for writing "09-11-01" at the top of the letter.

It was pointed out to Ivins that the first three highlighted characters in the letter were "TTT," and that was a codon for an amino acid. Ivins merely shrugged and said he didn't know that the amino acids used in his lab had single letter designators. He claimed that he never used codons or sent any messages using codons. He claimed he had never read anything related to any "linguistic" meaning of codons.

When Ivins was shown a newly purchased copy of *Gödel, Escher, Bach*, his response was "*Gödel, Escher, Bach*, that's cool." He said he'd read about three quarters of the book and found it intellectually fascinating. He said it's about "truths that cannot be proven within the system you're trying to prove them in." When asked to turn to page 404, Ivins claimed he hadn't read that far.

Ivins again claimed to not remember any meeting in March where he was told how to prepare the FBIR samples.

In summary: Ivins didn't remember much, didn't have any opinions, and he didn't currently think that anyone at USAMRIID sent the anthrax letters - although he felt some former employees could have done it.

On-Line with Ivins

On the evening of June 20, 2008, posting as "KingBadger7," Ivins had a long interactive chat on AOL with an unidentified friend. He complained about how tired he was, and how he'd stayed home from work that day because he wasn't feeling well. He talked about maybe becoming a greeter at Wal-Mart after he retired from USAMRIID on September 2.[2]

The next evening, on the 21st, Ivins was at it again, but only for a few minutes as he said, "I have to look for a place to work soon." [3]

Facing the Death Penalty

On June 25th and 26th, a confidential informant called the FBI to report that Ivins had talked about he'd spent a lot of money - "about six-figures" - on his attorney and would have to get another job after retirement. Also, Ivins' attorney had informed him that an indictment is coming and that Ivins should be prepared to face the death penalty.[4]

The Hatfill Settlement

In late June 2008, the government settled the invasion of privacy lawsuit filed by Steven Hatfill. Hatfill would receive 2.82 million dollars right away, and he would receive a tax-sheltered annuity of $150,000 per year for the next 20 years.[5]

The way was cleared to formally indict Bruce Ivins as the anthrax mailer.

The Mole

In early July, "Bad Bruce" seemed to be taking over Ivins' thinking. His barely-controlled rage seemed to be focused on a woman who had appeared on a reality TV series called *The Mole*. The program had been cancelled in 2004 after 4 seasons, but it was then brought back in June 2008 for a fifth season. And, at the same time, Season 1 was being rebroadcast on a cable network. It was the Season 1 reruns that seemingly enraged Ivins.[6]

The premise for *The Mole* was a competition in which contestants had to work as a group to add money to a pot that only one of them would eventually win. However, among the contestants was one person who wasn't really a contestant, but was instead a "mole" planted in the group to sabotage the group's money-making efforts. The task was to try to find the mole, i.e., the person sabotaging the group's efforts.

For some reason, Bruce Ivins became fixated upon a 1st season female contestant named Kathryn Price, and, using the screen name of "bruceivi," he began posting increasingly violent messages on an Internet blog site dedicated to the series. For example, he posted: "Steve had a great chance to kill Kathryn that would go down as the primo moment in reality TV." And later, "with that he should have taken the hatchet and brought it down hard and sharply across her neck, severing her carotid artery and jugular vein. . . . The 'Blind' mole is dead and Steve is a hero among heroes. I personally would have paid big money to have done it myself." Ivins also posted, "maybe something truly dreadful will happen to Kathryn Price. If so, she will richly deserve it! The least someone could do would be to take a sharp ballpoint pen or letter opener and put her eyes out, to complete the task of making her a true mole!"

Ivins seemed to almost immediately realize that what he'd written wouldn't be viewed kindly by others, since "Good Bruce" quickly posted, "Sorry if my comments offended people. This occurred several years ago. It was meant as a macabre twist to a pretty lame reality show."

It is not clear why Dr. Ivins fixated on Kathryn Price and *The Mole*. However, in one particular episode, Price was blindfolded, which is a self-admitted fetish of Dr. Ivins, who also belonged to online groups that shared images of blindfolding, and Ivins had literally hundreds of photos of blindfolded women on his computer when it was seized in November 2007.

Ivins' DNA

The women's panties seized in the November 1-2 search were apparently being pondered by the Grand Jury, since on July 2, 2008, a Grand Jury directive was issued for a DNA sample from Ivins. Ivins' attorney was contacted and eventually arrangements were made to obtain the DNA sample on July 21.[7]

It was all getting to Bruce Ivins.

Late on Sunday night, July 6, 2008, FBI agents observed Ivins wandering around the streets of Frederick, Maryland, behaving erratically, and appearing to be talking to himself. The next day, a coworker at USAMRIID informed agents that Ivins was in his office, again behaving erratically and talking to himself.[8]

On July 7, Rachel Lieber called Ivins' lawyer Paul Kemp to alert him to Ivins' erratic behavior and how she feared that he might be on the verge of suicide.

On July 8, Ivins sent an e-mail to Kathryn Price using KathrynPriceFan@yahoo.com as his email address, saying he was Price's biggest fan, and hoping for an opportunity, such as a book signing, to meet her. Ivins signed the email "Cindy Wood." Ivins also established another e-mail address around this time, stanfordhawker@yahoo.com, which he used to join a list-serve forum related to "The Mole." Ivins was evidently researching Price much in the same way he had researched Nancy Haigwood. The email address indicated that he'd learned that Kathryn Price had attended college at the University of Kansas - home of the Jayhawks - and went to law school at Stanford University.[9]

Ivins' Final Group Therapy Session

On the evening of Wednesday, July 9, Ivins attended a regular weekly group therapy session at CCA. He'd rejoined the sessions after his stays in alcohol dependency hospitals in May.

In earlier sessions, counselor Jean Duley had established some rapport with Ivins. Ivins would talk about the anthrax investigation in the sessions. He'd discuss scientific details and how he believed a certain colleague was the anthrax killer. And, Ivins also displayed clear suicidal thoughts. In one session, he showed Duley a piece of paper on which he'd calculated how much alcohol and pills he would need to kill himself. Ivins was generally cheery and affable at the sessions, but in one group session where Dr. Allan Levy was also present, members of the group went through role-playing exercises where they would first play the role of their father talking with themselves as a child, with another patient playing the child. Then the roles would be reversed, and Ivins would play himself talking with another patient playing his father. In that session, Ivins had unleashed his anger against his father to such a degree that Duley had to touch him on the arm to bring him back to reality.[10]

The therapy session on July 9 involved about a dozen patients and two counselors, Jean Duley and Wendy Levy, the psychologist wife of the owner.[11] Ivins arrived early, as he normally would. But, not much else was normal about him that evening. He even snapped at the receptionist as he handed over the check to pay for the session. The receptionist alerted Duley to Ivins' mood, telling her, "There's something wrong with Bruce."[12]

When the session began, Ivins was noticeably anxious and upset as the other members of the group talked about their personal problems. When one of the counselors asked Ivins if there was anything he wanted to say, Ivins started talking about suicide. When asked if he had a plan, Ivins told the group that he'd recently spent time walking about in Frederick's "ghetto" late at night. He'd hoped to lure someone into attacking him by calling out, "Come on, Nigger boy," so that he could stab the person with the sharp tip of his pen, the same instrument he'd written about using to stab TV contestant Kathryn Price. In the therapy session, he held out the pen and insisted that Duley touch it to see how sharp it was.

Obviously, Ivins wasn't just looking to get into a fight, he was looking to get himself *killed*. When someone asked what Ivins was so upset about, that really opened up the gates to his inner fury.

He started telling them details he hadn't previously disclosed about the Amerithrax investigation. He was about to be indicted, he angrily declared. He was furious with the government investigators who were after him. He was angry at the system that had allowed it to happen. And, he was tired of all the pressure he had been under for *years*. He planned to exact revenge on those who had helped the

FBI, primarily his colleagues at USAMRIID. He had obtained a bulletproof vest, and he was going to get his son to loan him the Glock semi-automatic he owned. He was going to take the Glock to work and open up on a list of people he had prepared. Killing the co-workers on the list would take care of all his problems.[13]

It was clearly a "suicide by cop" scenario. One of the patients in the session, a veteran who was there trying to deal with post-traumatic stress disorder got up and left. Another patient asked Ivins why he planned to do such things if he was innocent.

Ivins responded that he planned to go out in a blaze of glory. "I'm not going down for five capital murders," he declared. "I'm going to get them all."

Throughout his rant, Ivins' face was that of a furious maniac grinning over the revenge he would wreak.

When the session was over, the counselors had a discussion about what had just happened. Ivins' psychiatrist, Allan Levy, was out of town. The matter certainly couldn't wait until he got back, so, Jean Duley contacted Ivins' attorneys, Paul Kemp and Tom DeGonia, and described to them what happened and how she believed that Ivins might harm himself or others.

Kemp suggested that a session be arranged between Ivins and Dr. Levy.

But, there evidently wasn't any way to contact Dr. Levy that evening, so the matter continued over into the morning.

July 10, 2008

In the morning, Duley conferred with Dr. Levy by telephone. There was nothing Levy could do over the phone, and the matter was too urgent to wait for him to return. So, Duley contacted the Frederick Police Department.

Meanwhile, Ivins had reported to work as if nothing he'd said the previous evening would matter to anyone. But, it was clear that he was also still furious. When a long-time colleague, Dr. Arthur O. Anderson, tried to start a conversation with him to see how things were going, Ivins went into a rant about how the investigators had told his daughter Amanda that he was a "murderer." Amanda had been subpoenaed to appear before the Grand Jury a few weeks ago. Anderson saw Ivins as being visibly very angry.[14]

Yet, later in the day, another friend of Ivins, Jeffery Adamovicz saw him in a meeting honoring USAMRIID researchers who had made progress toward developing a vaccine against plague. At that meeting, Ivins seemed to be his normal, jovial self.

It wasn't until 2 p.m. that the Wheels of Justice had turned sufficiently to allow a team of officers from the Frederick Police Department to show up at USAMRIID with an Involuntary Commitment Order to take custody of a federal employee as a result of an emergency petition for psychological evaluation. Since the nature of the threats Ivins had made in the therapy session related to an investigation of Ivins by the FBI, the FPD had notified the Bureau that they were about to take Ivins into custody.

Ivins was angry but did not resist when he was quietly put under arrest in a conference room. Detective Bruce DeGrange of the Frederick Police Department searched Ivins and found no weapons, only a wallet which seemed to be about an inch and a half thick and contained not only Ivins' driver's license, credit cards, business cards, but also "numerous pieces of paper with what appeared to be handwriting." [15]

A few USAMRIID employees watched as DeGrange escorted Ivins out of the building to a waiting ambulance.

Before reaching the ambulance, Ivins must have realized that he'd never be allowed back into USAMRIID again. He began raging loudly against "the government" and what "the government" had done to him. When he spotted people standing and watching in the distance, he assumed them to be FBI agents and he yelled at them, "Identify yourselves! I know you're here!"

Chapter 43

Ivins Locked Up

Bruce Ivins was allowed to use the telephone while he was kept for overnight observation at Frederick Memorial Hospital. So, at 4:25 a.m. on the morning of Friday July 11, he called the office number for his counselor Jean Duley and left a message on her answering machine in a calm but menacing tone, " Hello, Jean. This is Bruce. And I want to thank you for getting me arrested at Fort Detrick and roughed up, threatened with being handcuffed, guarded by two police officers with guns in the room and incarcerated. And also I want to thank you for your destroying the client-patient relationship. So, now the FBI can come and get all the information from you and from Dr. Levy and you can't do anything about it because it's already been made available." [1]

As soon as he'd hung up, he realized he had more to say and, at 4:28 a.m., Ivins called again to add a few additional thoughts: "Yes, in my last phone call I forgot to tell you that I'm going to be leaving both you and Dr. Levy as therapist and psychiatrist and be seeking help from a preferred provider for Blue Cross and Blue Shield. Thank you very much."

But, Duley didn't check her messages that Friday morning. She was too busy dealing with the aftermath of the Wednesday evening session. She was still unaware of the messages when the FBI paid her a visit later in the day at the CCA offices. Duley and Wendy Levy were questioned about exactly what Ivins had said at the therapy session. Wendy Levy confirmed what Duley had told the police was true.

A Crime Unlike Any Other

Later on Friday, July 11, Bruce Ivins was transferred to Sheppard Pratt, a psychiatric hospital in Towson, MD, fifty-six miles from Frederick.

More Searches

At 6:15 a.m., on Saturday, July 12, 2008, the FBI began initiating another series of searches of Ivins home, his office and various lockers at work. They also searched his personal possessions at Sheppard-Pratt, specifically his wallet, where they went through the "numerous pieces of paper with what appeared to be handwriting" to see if the list of people he'd planned to kill at USAMRIID was among them. It wasn't.[2]

The search of Ivins office lasted until 1 in the afternoon, when the searchers moved to Ivins lockers, taking photographs of everything before and after each search, and of items found during the searches. The reports say nothing of significance was found.

Exhibit #29 - The hallway outside Dr. Ivins' office
(Photo taken by the FBI on July 12, 2008)

Exhibit #30 - Ivins' office & desk
(Desks used by Ivins' assistants' were located to the
left and right as you enter the door.)

A Crime Unlike Any Other

Exhibit #31 - Closeup of Dr. Ivins' Desk

At Ivins' home, however, they found a number of items of interest. They found the recently-purchased bulletproof vest he had mentioned during the therapy session. They found some homemade body armor. They found 236 rounds of ammunition, not including seventeen rounds of .40 caliber hollow-point bullets. And, they found a large canister of smokeless gunpowder.[3]

Meanwhile, at Sheppard-Pratt, an FBI agent had arrived at their security office at 10:30 a.m. to coordinate the transmission of a search warrant via a fax machine. Thirty minutes later, after all the formalities had been completed, Sheppard-Pratt security officers escorted the FBI agent to the second floor where Ivins was observed walking around in the common area with other patients.[4]

The FBI agent and a security officer escorted Ivins to his room. When the agent showed Ivins the search warrant, Ivins stated that he wouldn't talk to any FBI agent without his lawyer being present. It was then explained that the agent wasn't there to talk, he was there to execute a search warrant for his room and his personal effects. Ivins immediately emptied the contents of his pockets onto the bed and stripped down to his underwear. After he'd been given back his eyeglasses, Ivins began reading the search warrant.

Ivins Locked Up

When asked if he understood what they were looking for, Ivins replied something the effect of, "There is no list; I don't have a list here, at home or at work. My family does not have a list."

The search found no list. The only items in his wallet were the standard things such as money, his driver's license, credit cards, a phone card, and business cards. There was also a Post-it note containing a list of phone numbers. However, none of the items were listed in the search warrant, so they were all returned to Ivins.

Ivins sarcastically asked the FBI agent if he also wanted to search under the bed, but the bed was bolted to the floor and there was no way to put anything under it.

When they exited the room, the FBI agent noticed that Ivins had taken his phone card out of his wallet. As he walked away, the FBI agent asked the nearby staff members if Ivins had used the phone that day. The response was that he had indeed used the phone several times that morning.

Another Phone Call

Later it was learned that, at 11:17 a.m., while the FBI agent was waiting in the security office for the paperwork to be completed, Ivins had called Duley's number again. This time, he'd rambled on in his menacing monotone voice for several minutes. He began by saying, "Jean, this is Bruce Ivins. I'm calling from Shepp-Pratt. I just wanted to tell you how just disappointed and betrayed I feel about what happened with the EP [Emergency Petition] because the information not only went to the police, it went to the FBI, and now they're all over me on this."[5]

He then began going through the reasons on the Emergency Petition for its use. He said, "I was looking at the information on EP and what is called for. It says you must have a mental illness. That's true. You must need in-patient care treatment. That's true. You must present a danger to yourself or others. Okay. I agree with that. If there is no available less-restricted form of care treatment to meet your needs. That's true. Then it says, you must be unable or unwilling to be admitted voluntarily. I would never have said no. I've never said no to your suggestions. When you wanted me to go to Suburban, I said 'Sure.' When you wanted me to go to Massie, I said

'Sure.' If you had said on a scale of 1 to 10 you are an 11 and you need to go away today and you need to go away within an hour, I would have done it. But, in this EP, I got arrested by the police, I had the two guys with the guns, I got roughed up, and it was a terrible experience. They got me released to the FBI, and now they're all over my family and all over my case. I have to have a counsel that I can trust. And, I don't have that trust anymore. I'm sorry."

But, Ivins' counselor, Jean Duley, didn't go into her office on that Saturday, so she still hadn't heard the messages.

Monday, June 14, 2008

When Duley reported to work on Monday, July 14, she listened to the seemingly threatening messages Ivins had left on her answering machine over the weekend. After hearing the messages, she did some research into Ivins' past history, and a secretary turned over to Duley a folder of documents. "I think you should see this," she said, and for the first time Duley read about the plan Ivins had voiced to counselor Judith McLean in 2000 to poison Mara Linscott. And, the folder contained comments by Ivins' earlier psychiatrist, Dr. David Irwin, who considered Ivins the "scariest" patient he had ever treated.[6]

Duley called FBI agent Daniel G. Borsuk to tell him about what she had just learned. The Amerithrax task force immediately began writing up a request to get a judge to order the release of Ivins' mental health records maintained at CCA.

Based upon what he already had learned, Borsuk called Judith McLean. He told her he needed to discuss a former client she had once counseled, but before he provided the name, McLean said, "There's only one client in my twenty-five years of counseling who the FBI would ever contact me about. There's only been one client that I ever felt was that dangerous, that scary and that I had a sense of evil about." And, of course, that client was Bruce Edwards Ivins.

When Agent Lawrence Alexander heard about the conversation, he realized that McLean was the mental health counselor that Ivins had once written about in an email, stating that she had wanted to put him in jail.

Lots of pieces were beginning to fall together.

330

On that same Monday, Amanda Ivins had to travel to Washington to be interviewed by the Grand Jury. Before the session, she met for an hour with two FBI agents and AUSA Rachel Lieber. They questioned her about her father's mental condition, his ongoing relationship with former associates Mara Linscott and Patricia Fellows, whether she or her father had ever visited Princeton, New Jersey, and whether Amanda had ever heard her father talk about the Kappa Kappa Gamma sorority. He'd never mentioned KKG to her.

Also that same Monday, the FBI sent letters to AOL, Hotmail and Yahoo! telling each of them that a subpoena was coming to obtain all records related to the various email addresses used by the subject of an ongoing criminal investigation, Bruce Ivins, and they should take measures to preserve all such emails sent, received *and* deleted until the subpoena arrives. Furthermore, Ivins was not to be notified of the subpoena.[7]

Ivins the Menace

On Tuesday, July 15, the FBI obtained copies of the menacing voice mail messages Ivins had left on Jean Duley's answering machine so the calls could be used in the involuntary commitment hearing that was to be held the next day, Wednesday July 16.[8]

However, on the advice of his lawyers, Ivins managed to avoid being committed involuntarily. He accomplished this by committing himself voluntarily before the hearing was held, which meant that, since he was voluntarily committed, he could also leave whenever he wanted. He had once again outwitted the system.

Since there was nothing technically preventing Ivins from leaving Sheppard-Pratt any time he wanted, on Thursday, July 17, an FBI agent and a Postal Inspector asked the Army officials at Ft. Detrick to ban Ivins from the base due to the homicidal threats he'd made against people working on the base.

The Army official refused, stating that the request had been shown to the Judge Advocate General (JAG) and other base officials, and they denied the request because the police report was "third hand information."[9]

The law enforcement officials then asked what kind of information or document would cause the JAG to reconsider barring Ivins from Fort Detrick until he was of better mind. What the Army wanted was some first hand information, which was provided later that day - personal statements of finding multiple guns in Ivins home, a bullet proof vest, and statements from witnesses that Ivins had made the threats. The Army finally agreed to the request, and Ivins would no longer be allowed on the base until the situation was fully resolved and it was deemed safe to let him reenter.

On Monday, June 21, the DNA swabs were obtained from Ivins. His lawyer, Paul Kemp had driven to Sheppard-Pratt twice and advised Ivins not to submit, but Ivins had decided not to fight it. So, the judge's order was given to Ivins, and a Sheppard-Pratt security guard stood watch as the agent swabbed the inside of Ivins' cheeks three times.[10]

On the 23rd, Sheppard-Pratt doctors advised the FBI that they planned to release Ivins the next day. Rachel Lieber learned of it and contacted Sheppard-Pratt to urge them to reconsider. But they saw things differently and planned to proceed with the release on schedule.[11]

FBI agent Borsuk advised Jean Duley that Ivins was about to be released. Duley, too, called the staff psychiatrist at Sheppard-Pratt to urge that they continue to hold Ivins there, but her pleadings changed nothing. Borsuk then recommended that Duley obtain a Peace Warrant

On Thursday, July 24, Duley and her lawyer Mary McGuirk Drawbaugh appeared before Maryland District Judge W. Milnor Roberts to petition for a Peace Order (also known as a Restraining Order). As part of the process, Drawbaugh questioned Duley to provide the judge with the information he needed to make a decision. The questioning was recorded and the recording later appeared on the *New York Times*' web site.[12]

Duley considered the first message Ivin left on her answering machine to be just ramblings, but she considered the last of the three messages to be "rather scary."

"He very calmly thanked me for ruining his life and allowing the FBI to prosecute him for the murders," Duley said. "And that it was all my fault. And it's going to be my fault that they can now get him." She also explained that the tape wasn't available to be played in court because it was at that time being entered into evidence for the Grand Jury hearing.

Drawbaugh then asked, "At this time, Ms. Duley, are you fearful for your personal safety?"

Duley replied, "I am, and so is the FBI."

Drawbaugh then asked Duley to describe why she was fearful for her safety.

And Duley answered, "As far back as the year 2000, the respondent has actually attempted to murder several other people, either through poisoning ... He is a revenge killer. When he feels that he has been slighted -- or has had -- especially toward women, he plots and actually tries to carry out revenge killings. He had been forensically diagnosed by several top psychiatrists as a sociopathic, homicidal killer. And, I have that in evidence. And also, through my working with him I find that to be very true."

Drawbaugh then asked her about getting protection from the FBI, but how the FBI is unable to do that.

"They're going to be following him," Duley explained. "He's being released today. And my assigned FBI agent very much recommended that I get a protection order."

When asked if there was anything else the judge needed to know before signing the protection order, Duley responded, "I'm scared to death."

The judge then immediately signed the order and started to set Friday, August 1, 2008, as the date for the final hearing where both Duley and Ivins would be required to appear. But, on that date Duley was scheduled to appear before the Grand Jury, so the judge set the hearing date for July 31, 2008, at 9:45 a.m.

It was probably while Duley and her lawyer were sitting in court waiting for copies of the judge's order to be printed that, over fifty miles away, Diane Ivins picked her husband up at Sheppard-Pratt and proceeded to drive him home.

Chapter 44

The Death of Bruce Ivins

Bruce Ivins appears to have been determined to commit suicide as soon as he was out of the hospital and as soon as he could muster together the courage.

On the afternoon of the July 24th, the same day he had been released from Sheppard-Pratt, Ivins set about purchasing the drugs he would use to kill himself. It was just a two minute drive to the Giant Eagle supermarket on Seventh Street where he went to buy a few items of groceries and a bottle of seventy pills of Tylenol PM, a popular over-the-counter pain killer and sleep aid containing acetaminophen.[1]

Acetaminophen?

Acetaminophen is a very common pain killer and fever reducer that most people probably consider to be no more dangerous than aspirin. But, it can be very deadly.

Acetaminophen overdose is, by far, the leading cause of calls to the Poison Control Centers across the US. It is estimated that acetaminophen poisoning calls exceed 100,000 per year. Studies indicate that acetaminophen overdose results in over 56,000 injuries, 2,500 hospitalizations, and an estimated 450 deaths per year.

There's an antidote, N-acetylcysteine, but it has to be administered within 8 hours of the overdose.

After his adopted daughter had tried to commit suicide by taking Tylenol, Bruce Ivins almost certainly knew the dangers inherent with overdosing with acetaminophen, and that severe liver damage can be a terrible way to die. But, for reasons of his own he was preparing to commit suicide that way.

He checked out at the Giant Eagle at 12:31 p.m., drove home in about two minutes. Then, he returned to the same store a short while later, at 1:44 p.m., to pick up three filled prescriptions for Celexa, an antidepressant, Seroquel, an antipsychotic drug used in the treatment of schizophrenia and bipolar disorder, and Depakote, a drug for treating mania and migraine headaches.

Checking the Internet

The FBI had confiscated Ivins' home computer, and he couldn't go in to work to use a computer there. So, that evening Ivins drove to downtown Frederick and used computers at the Frederick Public Library. There were dozens on the second floor available to the public, with a limit of one hour per person per computer. While FBI agents observed from a distance, Ivins had to switch from one computer to another as he spent about an hour and a half accessing his various email accounts and checking the latest news on a web site dedicated to developments in the Amerithrax investigation: www.anthraxinvestigation.com.[2]

The latest news on the site was about a CNN interview with FBI Director Robert Mueller. The FBI had been created on July 26, 1908, and the topic of the interview was the Bureau's upcoming 100th anniversary. The site contained a video clip of the interview, and a transcript of what was said about the anthrax attacks of 2001:

Kelli Arena: Are you still confident?

FBI Director Mueller: I am still confident, and people who are not familiar with the investigation -- ah -- could criticize. I'm confident in the course of the investigation. I'm confident in the steps that have been taken in the course of the investigation. And I'm confident that it will be resolved.

Arena: Is there any –

Mueller: I tell you, we've made great progress in the investigation. It's in no way dormant. It's active.

Arena: Would you say ... describe it as there have been breakthroughs?

Mueller: In some sense there have been breakthroughs, yes. [3]

In the video clip, the FBI Director seemed very confident and upbeat.

The web site also contained newspaper articles and information from other sources about what else had happened in the case during the time Ivins had spent at Sheppard-Pratt.

Director Mueller had also given an interview to ABC News in which he mentioned unsolved mysteries the FBI continued to pursue:

The most obvious is the hunt for Osama Bin Laden, the Sept. 11 suspected mass murderer, who is at the top of the FBI's famed Ten Most Wanted list.

FBI historian John Fox said Bin Laden "is the first murderer on that scale" that's made the list.

But beyond Bin Laden, FBI Director Robert Mueller says there are many mysteries the FBI wants solved — such as the anthrax attacks. Five people were killed, 17 sickened and nearly seven years later no arrest appears imminent.

"I never give time frames, because you never know where you'll have sufficient evidence to go public with a prosecution," Mueller said. [4]

At Home

The news wasn't very hopeful for Ivins. Later that evening, he called his daughter Amanda to cancel a lunch they had planned for the next day. Ivins claimed to have a bad headache. They agreed to try to get together on Monday or Tuesday of the following week. [5]

"I love you, dad," Amanda said as the conversation came to an end.

"I loved you first," Ivins replied.

Amanda thought that to be a strange response, since her father had never expressed himself quite that way before.

On the evening of July 24, Diane Ivins wrote her husband a letter, evidently feeling there was no other way she could get him to listen to the things she had to say. While he was sleeping, she placed the letter on his nightstand:

> Bruce,
>
> I'm hurt, concerned, confused, and angry about your actions over the past few weeks. You tell me you love me but you have been rude and sarcastic and nasty many times when you talk to me. You tell me you aren't going to get any more guns then you fill out an on line application for a gun license. You pay Paul Kemp an enormous amount of money then ignore his advice by contacting Pat and Mara, going into work at odd hours, and walking in the neighborhood late at night. You are jumpy and agitated from the extreme amount of caffeine you drink each day. Peter [a financial advisor] asked us not to cash any more EE bonds because we pay so much tax on them and you cashed one in June. The FBI is convinced you're having an affair with Mara every time you email her they are more suspicious. Can you honestly say you are following the plan you developed at Massie Clinic for stress reduction and coping with this?[6]

The next day, Friday, July 25, Ivins called his lawyer and made an appointment for Monday. Paul Kemp had arranged for the government to pay his legal fees if Ivins was indicted on a capital murder charge. But, Kemp was still hoping that the charge wouldn't be anything more than lying to the FBI about the sample he'd provided in April 2002 that was supposed to be from flask RMR-1029, but the evidence said it clearly wasn't.[7]

Kemp and his associate Tom DeGonia were planning to meet with the Amerithrax detectives and the prosecutors on Tuesday, at which time Kemp expected them to lay out exactly what the charges would be, along with providing a detailed account of the evidence to support the charges.

Suicide Watch

It was probably on the evening of the 25th that Ivins turned over the letter Diane had written and wrote a response on the back: "I have a terrible headache. I'm going to take some Tylenol and sleep in tomorrow. Please let me sleep, please." Then, he crossed out the last sentence. He may have been contemplating suicide that evening. If so, he couldn't yet get himself to go through with it.

Ivins spent most of Saturday, July 26, in bed. His wife went up to check on him from time to time. In the evening, she went up to check at 7 p.m and again at 9 p.m. Then she lay down on a couch while reading a book, and she fell asleep there.

At 1 a.m. in the morning of Sunday, July 27, Diane Ivins went upstairs to check on her husband once more before going to bed. She found Ivins lying on the floor in the bathroom, in a pool of his own urine, wearing only his underwear. He was still breathing, but he wouldn't wake up when Diane called his name. She checked his pulse and pinched his arm to see if that would rouse him. It didn't. He seemed very cold to the touch.

Diane rushed to a phone and at 1:06 a.m. dialed 911.

An FBI agent and a postal inspector were watching the house. They'd taken over from the previous surveillance team at 10:30 p.m. Their logs showed:

10:30P   All vehicles present. No lights 1st floor. 2nd floor bathroom and hallway lights on. No activity noted.

12:25A   No lights 1st floor. 2nd floor bathroom and hallway lights on. No activity noted.

1:15A   Fire and rescue responds to the residence.[8]

At 1:16 a.m., officers of the Frederick Police Department were dispatched to assist in the 911 call to the Fire Department. Officer Robert Pierce was in charge. Pierce's report showed that he talked with Diane Ivins, and she showed him all the medications her husband was taking. They quickly but carefully counted the pills in each of the three prescription bottles he'd picked up at the Giant Eagle a few days earlier. All 28 Depakote pills were in their bottle. All 14 Citalopram (Celexa) pills were in their bottle. Only 1 of the 14 Seroquel pills seemed to be missing. Diane stated that she had no idea what else her husband could have taken, or if he indeed had taken anything that might have caused his condition. She explained that "he quit drinking, and he only takes celexa for depression." She also pointed to what appeared to be a partially empty soda bottle in the sink. Pierce opened the cap and smelled the contents. He believed it smelled like orange soda.

On the night stand beside Ivins' bed was another bottle of red liquid and a green glass containing some of the liquid.

At 1:30 a.m., the federal officers watching the house saw Ivins being carried to the ambulance in a stretcher. Mrs. Ivins also came out of the house and got into her blue Civic to follow the ambulance to the hospital. The FPD led the way for the ambulance. The agents followed Mrs. Ivins.

Diane Ivins claimed she believed that one of her neighbors was following her on the way to the hospital, so she made a turn to throw off her tail. The paramedics noticed her turn at Tollhouse Avenue and made a note of it.

As the FPD officers who had led the way for ambulance #18 watched Ivins being carried inside, they were approached by Federal agents in the parking lot. The agents stated that, even though Bruce Ivins was a suspect in a federal case, they didn't want to enter the hospital. But, they needed to be advised of what was happening.

The hospital recorded Ivins arrival at 1:47 a.m. on Sunday, July 27th. His blood pressure was extremely low, and his breathing was rapid. The Emergency Room doctor suspected a drug overdose or a stroke.

Outside of the hospital, watching from the hospital parking lot, the federal agents saw Diane Ivins turn a corner and approach the hospital. She entered the building a 1:50 a.m. carrying what appeared to be a paperback book. It appears that her diversion had been to stop at the CVS Pharmacy across the street to buy the book.

339

A Crime Unlike Any Other

At 2:15 a.m. the Frederick PD advised the federal agents that Bruce Ivins was going to be admitted. He was currently paralyzed and appeared to have suffered some kind of overdose.

At 2:30 a.m., the federal agents terminated their surveillance and left the parking lot.

Death Watch

As soon as he was admitted, the emergency room doctors began suspecting from his symptoms that Ivins was suffering from acetaminophen poisoning. They began intravenously administering the antidote N-acetylcysteine. A blood sample was taken, and the results showed 196.1 micrograms per milliliter positive for Acetaminophen. The normal range is between 10-30 micrograms per milliliter. From his blood test results, it also appeared that Ivins had ingested Valium with the Tylenol tablets. Although he'd purchased 70 Tylenol tablets just a few days earlier, no bottle and no tablets were observed in the bathroom where he'd been found.

By 6:45 a.m., the acetaminophen level in Ivins' blood was down to 129.1 micrograms per milliliter, but still many times higher than normal.

By 8 a.m., Ivins seemed to be improving somewhat. The intensive care nurse watching over him, Megan Shinabery, saw that he was able to open his eyes and could nod his head in response to yes and no questions. She asked, "Did you intentionally try to commit suicide?" And Ivins nodded in response.

Realizing that he was still alive and that he had apparently failed in his suicide attempt, Ivins began to try to pull out the tubes that were giving him intravenous medicines. He had to be strapped down.

The next day, his condition was worse. Doctor Myung Hee Nam had a lengthy discussion with Diane Ivins to see if they should transfer Ivins to an institution where a potential liver transplant could be contemplated. Diane Ivins responded that in her opinion her husband would not have wanted a liver transplant. So, Ivins would be kept at Frederick Memorial. Dr. Nam also asked about what should be done in the event of a cardiac arrest. Dr. Nam reported, "The wife is again fairly adamant that her husband would not want resuscitative efforts in the event of a cardiac arrest."

At the FBI, the word spread that Ivins had attempted suicide. When FBI Agent Edward Montooth heard the news early on the morning of July 27, he immediately realized that the conspiracy theorists would have a field day if the case against Ivins couldn't be presented in court. Speculation could overshadow the evidence. "They better save [him]," he snapped at a colleague as he hung up the phone.[9]

When AUSA Rachel Lieber heard about it, she called Ivins lawyer Paul Kemp to advise him. Kemp rushed to the hospital, but there wasn't anything he could do.

On Tuesday morning, July 29, 2008, Bruce Ivins body was turning a sickly yellow as a result of jaundice from liver failure. His wife and two children were at his bedside when, at 10:47 a.m., he died.

Chapter 45

A Never-Ending Story

At 1 p.m. on the day Bruce Ivins died, the scheduled meeting between Ivins' lawyers, the Amerithrax investigators and the DOJ prosecutors went ahead as scheduled.

In a session that lasted nearly two hours, Rachel Lieber laid out the case they had against Bruce Ivins, going into far greater detail and disclosing evidence that had never been shared with the defense lawyers before. AUSA Leiber had reportedly been planning to offer Ivins a deal to take the death penalty off the table and a punishment of life imprisonment in exchange for a plea of guilty. But, that plan was now moot. When the meeting was over and everyone was preparing to leave, Paul Kemp reportedly said to Rachel Lieber, "It would've been a fun case. Would've been a fun case to try. You would've cooked our goose." [1]

But when interviewed by reporter David Willman nearly three years later for his book *The Mirage Man*, Kemp characterized the statement as a "false compliment." [2]

It was Willman who, in the August 1 issue of the *Los Angeles Times*, broke the story that the anthrax killer had committed suicide. Facts for the article, *Anthrax suspect dies in apparent suicide* were sparse, and for days the media was printing incorrect information about how long Ivins had worked at Ft. Detrick and repeating an incorrect Frederick police department report which stated that Ivins had "overdosed on Tylenol with codeine," a prescription medicine.

A Never-Ending Story

Nearly every reporter mentioned that the FBI had pursued Steven Hatfill as being the anthrax mailer for years before admitting that he wasn't the anthrax mailer. Many questioned whether or not the FBI's investigation of Bruce Ivins was equally incorrect. The media organizations which played a major role in the crusade to get Hatfill investigated seemed the most aggressive in unleashing a storm of questions regarding the validity of the investigation of Bruce Ivins.

"Extraordinarily Complex"

According to the Department of Justice, the Amerithrax investigation had been "extraordinarily complex" and "one of the largest and most complex in the history of law enforcement." It was not a case that could be easily explained in 10-second sound bites or 20-second video clips.

The media was clamoring for more information about the evidence against Bruce Ivins, and the FBI and DOJ had to provide it. On August 8, 2008, the FBI and DOJ, along with key scientists who had been involved, held a "roundtable discussion" to address some of the scientific aspects of the Amerithrax investigation for reporters.[3]

The questioning from reporters seemed to be mainly directed toward finding holes in the science, but much of it could also have been a serious effort to understand the complex science used in the case. By the time the session was over, it was clear that not every reporter understood every word. But, that wouldn't stop them from printing their interpretations of what was said.

Ivins' Memorial Service

Ivins' memorial service was held at St. John the Evangelist Catholic Church in Frederick on Saturday, August 9, 2008. The church was surrounded by a dozen officers from the Frederick Police Department under instructions to keep the media from disrupting the private service.[4]

Nothing was mentioned about Ivins' crimes in the ceremony. It was all fond memories and descriptions of the "talented musician, funny and entertaining" person he had seemed to be to most of those who knew him. And, although the media was banned, there were plenty of quotes in the media about what was said of Ivins during and after the ceremony.

"If there had been problems with him getting along with people, I would have heard about it," Ivins co-worker Russell Byrne said. "I can't imagine he had anything to do with the anthrax letters. I never seriously considered it, just from what I knew about him and how the place worked."

"They haven't got a real case. It's all circumstantial," fellow Red Cross volunteer Kathleen O'Connor said after the service. "There's just no way he could do it. ... They just grabbed a convenient person."

But none of them knew of the numerous other crimes Ivins had admitted to the FBI. They didn't know of his harassment of Nancy Haigwood or his burglaries at KKG sorority houses. And, when told of those things, they still couldn't believe it.

And, there was the Hatfill case as proof. The FBI had tried to blame Steven Hatfill for the killings, and then, after they were sued, they were forced to admit they were wrong. Ivins just wasn't made of the same stern stuff as Hatfill. Ivins had crumbled under the pressure, and that's why he committed suicide.

Or the FBI killed him and made it look like suicide. A few months after Ivins' death, his lawyer Paul Kemp told David Willman, "I have received ten thousand e-mails from every lunatic in America, suggesting it wasn't suicide."[5]

Conspiracy Theorists & True Believers

Most who claimed Ivins to be innocent had their own theories about who had sent the anthrax letters. Many thought it was Saddam Hussein or al Qaeda who had sent the letters. Some thought it was the Jews. Others believed their odd next door neighbor did it. Still others believed it was former Vice-President Dick Cheney who did it to start the war with Iraq. There were those who thought that a former USAMRIID or Battelle employee was the real killer. If there were a thousand people with theories, that meant there were a thousand *different* theories, since, even if they agreed on who was responsible, virtually none of them would agreed on details of how it was done or exactly why it was done.

A Never-Ending Story

The only thing they agreed upon was that the FBI was wrong, since, if the FBI was right, that meant that everyone in the thousand was wrong. And that just didn't seem possible.

By any impartial measure, the Amerithrax investigation was a case for the text books. In many respects, the crime was a crime unlike any other. It was done by a respected scientist working in a secure government lab who committed criminal acts under the noses of his co-workers. The culprit had no intention of harming anyone, but he ended up killing 5 innocent people, injuring at least 17 others and causing billions of dollars in damage.

The case began as a global investigation that could have involved international terrorists living in caves in Afghanistan, and it ended as a very local investigation of a mentally ill scientist known to the investigators from almost the very beginning. It involved developing new scientific techniques that had never been used in any previous criminal case. It involved questioning hundreds of scientists in dozens of laboratories.

According to the case Summary Report, "In the seven years following the attack, the Amerithrax Task Force expended over 600,000 investigator work hours, involving in excess of 10,000 witness interviews conducted on six continents, the execution of 80 searches, and the recovery of over 6,000 items of potential evidence. The case involved the issuance of over 5,750 federal grand jury subpoenas and the collection of 5,730 environmental samples from 60 site locations."

However, like so many other criminal investigations, there was also a large amount of luck involved. It was pure luck that the culprit believed that the Ames strain of anthrax was common, widely distributed and virtually impossible to trace, while in reality it was a very rare strain that was almost immediately traced to its primary source. It could also be considered pure luck that Terry Abshire let some inoculated plates sit in the incubator longer than normal, but it was her alertness and experience that caused her to notice that unusual colonies had formed. Without the stroke of luck, the case might never have been solved. But, there's also a famous quote from movie mogul Samuel Goldwyn that is known and repeated by many types of investigators: "The harder I work, the luckier I get."

A Crime Unlike Any Other

Disbelievers

At a September 17, 2008 hearing of the Senate Judiciary Committee, Senator Patrick Leahy said this about Bruce Ivins: "If he is the one who sent the letter, I do not believe in any way, shape, or manner that he is the only person involved in this attack on Congress and the American people. I believe there are others who could be charged with murder."[6]

Senator Leahy wasn't the only politician to disbelieve the findings. On March 3, 2009, Representative Rush Holt of New Jersey began efforts to set up a commission to investigate the investigation. He did it apparently to satisfy his own personal belief that Muslim terrorists were responsible for the attacks, a belief that may have been shared by the majority of his constituents. In a crime of such magnitude, it just seems like it *should* be the work of some global terrorist organization instead of being a stupid act by some absent-minded professor-type nut case who didn't realize that what he was doing could result in the deaths of innocent people.

Clarifying the Science

In what may have been the FBI's biggest blunder in the case, the FBI announced in late July 2009 that they were going to pay the National Academy of Sciences (NAS) nearly $880,000 to review the science used in the Amerithrax investigation. Director Mueller seemingly failed to realize that, in the world of science, time and costs are irrelevant. After all, it was not totally *impossible* that a scientific analysis might show that the attack spores contained silicon because they were grown by space aliens working in underground lab on the far side of the moon. Hundreds of scientists could earn a good living working their entire lives to find the scientific answers.

On the other hand, although the NAS would take almost two years to complete their review, the process produced some valuable and interesting information fairly quickly when scientists who had worked with the evidence gave public presentations.

Photographs of the powders were made public via the NAS web site. They showed clumps of thousands of spores, and chunks of dried slime with embedded spores. Dr. Joseph Michael of Sandia

346

National Laboratories presented spectrograph images showing where the silicon was located inside the spore coat, including a color image of a spore from the *New York Post* letter that already had silicon in its coat even though it was still inside the mother germ, indisputable evidence that the silicon was incorporated during spore formation, *not* added after the spore was fully formed.

When Dr. Michael's findings were combined with published information from scientists who had detected silicon in the coats of anthrax and other *Bacillus* spores found under natural conditions[7], one could hypothesize that 25 to 35 percent of the spores in the attack powders had been grown at or near incubator temperatures, where the fast growing conditions didn't allow time for the absorption of silicon from the surroundings. And the remainder of the spores had grown in more natural-like, lower temperatures inside autoclave bags stored in a corner or in a basement, where the slow growing conditions allowed the time for the absorption of silicon into the spore coats.

Closing the Case

On February 19, 2010, the FBI and Department of Justice officially closed the Amerithrax investigation. They produced the 92 page *Amerithrax Investigative Summary* which made public for the first time many other details about the evidence against Bruce Ivins, most notably the evidence related to decoding the hidden message in the media letters. And, with the *Summary* report, the FBI also released 2,720 pages of FBI documents, search warrants and other supplementary information.

Not long afterward, the U.S. Army and USAMRIID began releasing hundreds of Bruce Ivins' emails sent while at work.

It was an enormous flood of information. But, it wasn't enough for Congressman Rush Holt, who again pressed for an investigation of the investigation. A *New York Times* editorial supported Holt's call for an investigation stating that the "report leaves too many loose ends to be taken as a definitive verdict." And they reasoned, "We need to head off conspiracy theories that are apt to be fostered if the only judgment available comes from an agency eager to clear its books."[8]

It was far too late to head off any conspiracy theories. They'd been vocalized and promoted since the letters were first discovered in October 2001.

The media had a field day reporting on all the people who disagreed with the findings. Ivins' lawyer, Paul Kemp declared in an interview, "There's not one shred of evidence to show he did it."[9] And, Henry Heine, a former friend and co-worker of Bruce Ivins had left USAMRIID and made himself available to newspaper reporters and radio talk show hosts to give his opinion about the case. *The New York Times* reported on his briefing of NAS panel members where Heine declared that "producing the quantity of spores in the letters would have taken at least a year of intensive work using the equipment at the army lab. Such an effort would not have escaped colleagues' notice, he added later, and lab technicians who worked closely with Dr. Ivins have told him they saw no such work." [10]

In the supplementary documents released along with the FBI/DOJ *Summary*, there were documents written by Bruce Ivins in which he stated that he routinely made a trillion spores *per week*.[11]

Legalese

One major problem with the statements and documents produced by the FBI and the Department of Justice in the Amerithax investigation was the fact that there were many different ways the anthrax spores could have been produced, and there was either no way or no definitive *affordable* way to determine *exactly* which way Ivins had used. But, in a federal court of law it isn't required that the prosecution identify the exact method used to commit a crime. It is only necessary to prove that the defendant had the *means*.

Ivins had multiple ways to grow the spores, he had multiple ways to dry the spores, and he had multiple ways to purify the spores. Many of those ways would produce exactly the same results.

So, in court, the prosecution would show that Ivins had the means to create the attack spores. They would *not* speculate on which method was *most likely* used. If they did that, the defense immediately would jump on it as "speculation" and not fact.

It was a fact that Ivins had the means.

The defense could not believably argue that he didn't have the means.

The same legalese argument was used on the matter of motive. Since only Bruce Ivins knew his exact motive -- and, given his mental condition, it's possible that even he wasn't certain exactly why he did what he did -- the DOJ lawyers could only list some of Ivins' apparent motives. In court, the defense would have to try to argue that Ivins had *no* motive.

Another unsatisfying subject was the handwriting. It seemed that no two handwriting experts could agree on how Ivins had written the letters. So, for courtroom purposes, the handwriting evidence was simply considered "inconclusive." If they figured out which child had written the letters, the 12 year old child may not even have remembered what he had written when he was 6. And, there wasn't a critical need to identify to world the child who had written the anthrax letters. The case was solid without it.

The NAS Report

The FBI evidently learned in late 2010 that the NAS report was not going to be to their liking, and they supplied the NAS with a large amount of additional information, which caused a two month delay in the release of the report.

The report was released on February 15, 2011 and, while it basically supported the findings, it cast doubt on how solid the FBI's scientific evidence was. Although flask RMR-1029 seemed to be the "murder weapon," it was *scientifically possible* that some unknown operative could have put together a flask of spores in exactly the same way and got the exact same morphological variants.

The FBI had asked labs to submit samples of every stock of the Ames strain they had, but there was no way to be *scientifically certain* that every lab supplied samples from every supply - specifically supplies which existed in 2001 but not in later years when the FBI asked for samples. And, even worse, there was no guarantee that some unidentified lab that couldn't have gotten a supply of Ames via some undocumented route. So, the FBI could not be *scientifically certain* that they had a sample from every stock of Ames in the world.

It was scientific certitude versus evidence proving a legal case beyond a reasonable doubt.

There was no attempt by the NAS to claim that the FBI didn't get the right man, but the emphasis on the lack of scientific certitude was more than enough to send the conspiracy theorists and anti-government, anti-FBI media reporters into a frenzy that continues to this day.

And along with the NAS report, 9,600 pages of additional information were released. The pages included countless details of the scientific work that had not been previously made public, including facts which showed the spores had been grown on agar plates at lower than incubator temperatures.

The EBAP Report

On March 23, 2011, an Expert Behavioral Analysis Panel (EBAP) released a 285 page report about Ivins mental problems that was a total surprise to most people following the case. It was done in such secrecy - due to the sensitivity of the subject matter and the problems associated with doctor-client confidentiality - that it seemed to come out of nowhere.

Unlike the committee behind the NAS report, the EBAP report showed that its members had no doubt that Bruce Ivins was the anthrax mailer. And the report provided "considerable additional circumstantial evidence" confirming Ivins' guilt that had never been released before. But, its main purpose was to provide a lesson for the future by showing how Ivins did what he did without people at USMARIID noticing, although they *should have* noticed since they had plenty of clues indicating that Ivins was mentally ill.

The Stevens vs. USA Lawsuit

The compelling evidence against Ivins prompted the lawyers for Maureen Stevens to revise their claims against the government to accept that Ivins was the person who had killed Bob Stevens. Then they apparently realized they had fallen into a legal trap, since it made Bruce Ivins responsible, *not* the government. It wasn't the government that had failed to keep track of deadly pathogens, allowing some to fall into the hands of some killer, it was an individual who had access to the pathogens but used them for his own purposes, purposes having nothing to do with any government project.

So, Stevens' lawyers then began a process of trying to show that Ivins was innocent. That involved having people who worked with Ivins talk about how they didn't believe he could have done it. But, that also meant that they could not have foreseen what Ivins did, therefore it helped the government's case in arguing that Ivins crime was not foreseeable.

But the government also made a mistake. In a document filed on July 15, 2011, a lawyer in the civil division of the Department of Justice misunderstood an important fact in the case and wrote this sentence as point #28 in a 10 page "Statement of Facts" while calling for a summary judgment in the case:

> 28. USAMRIID did not have the specialized equipment in a containment laboratory that would be required to prepare the dried spore preparations that were used in the letters.

The media, particularly the McClatchy newspapers chain, jumped all over this misstatement and declared it meant the government was changing its position on Ivins' guilt and declaring he could not have committed the crime because he didn't have the "required" equipment. It was "yellow journalism" in its most basic form, wild distortions of a single erroneous sentence in a legal document.

On July 27, the document was re-filed and the erroneous sentence was corrected to read:

> 28. Although USAMRIID had equipment that could be used to dry liquid anthrax in the same building where anthrax research was conducted, USAMRIID did not have a lyophilizer in the specific containment laboratory where RMR-1029 was housed to prepare the dried spore preparations that were used in the letters.

It wasn't until November 29, 2011 that the Stevens case was finally settled, with the government admitting no guilt but paying $2.5

million to Maureen Stevens and her family in order to avoid the costs and uncertainties of going to trial.

Scientists with Beliefs

In July 2011, Pulitzer Prize winning science writer Laurie Garrett self-published a book via Kindle titled *I Heard the Sirens Scream* in which she seemingly argued that al Qaeda sent the anthrax letters. In September 2011, scientist Jeanne Guillemin was basically neutral in her book *American Anthrax*, but in his review of her book in *Science* magazine, Dr. David Rehlman, who had been co-chair on the review of the Amerithrax case by the National Academy of Sciences, also argued that al Qaeda could have done it.

On June 11, 2011, Dr. Martin Hugh-Jones, Dr. Barbara Hatch Rosenberg and Dr. Stuart Jacobsen began distributing a paper they had written which was eventually printed in the October 2011 edition of the obscure scientific periodical *The Journal of Bioterrorism & Biodefense*. The paper titled *The 2001 Attack Anthrax: Key Questions, Potential Answers* presented their theories about the source of the silicon found in the attack spores, along with arguments about exactly where and how the attack spores were created and other questions the FBI had not answered to their satisfaction.

Bill Broad and Scott Shane wrote about it on the front page of the October 9, 2011 issue of *The New York Times* under the headline: *Scientists' Analysis Disputes F.B.I. Closing of Anthrax Case.*

The following year, when several FBI scientists published a scientific report titled *Trace Detection of Meglumine and Diatrizoate from Bacillus Spore Samples Using Liquid Chromatography/Mass Spectrometry* in the April 26, 2012 issue of *The Journal of Forensic Sciences* explaining one of the tests they performed which proved that the attack spores did not come *directly* from flask RMR-1029, it was major news to some uninformed scientists.

On May 25, 2012, Dr. Amesh A. Adalja wrote on *Clinicians' Biosecurity News*:

> The major implication of this study, as the authors note, is "that the evidentiary spore material was not diverted di-

rectly from RMR-1029." This fact means that if the anthrax spores used in the attack were taken from RMR-1029, their preparation would have required extra steps prior to mailing. That type of purification would have required specialized machinery and likely would have left traces of the material on machinery. No such material was found, though, and in a recently settled civil case in Florida, the U.S. Department of Justice acknowledged that the specialized machinery was not available at USAMRIID.

And, on May 29, 2012, a similar article was published on GlobalDefense.com titled *FBI Study Raises More Questions in Bruce Ivins Anthrax Cases.*

The July 20, 2012 issue of the *Journal of Bioterrorism & Biodefense* contained an article by Dr. Yurii V. Ezepchuk titled *The Bioterrorist Attacks on America* which declared that an Iranian-born scientist named Waly Samar was the anthrax mailer, and the FBI pointing the finger at Dr. Ivins was "obviously the consequence of complete incompetence of the investigators."

So, the story isn't over. It's just waiting for someone to find something - or make up something - to write about.

Notes & Resources

Abbreviations:

Summary pp 10 = "Amerithrax Investigation Summary" by the U.S. Department of Justice, February 19, 2010, page 10.

FBI #847357 pp 10 = FBI pdf file #847357, page 10. These are the 2,720 pages of supplementary documents released along with the Amerithrax Summary as they were originally identified.

NAS pp 10 = "Review of the Scientific Approaches Used During the FBI's Investigation of the Anthrax Attacks of 2001," The National Academy of Sciences, 2011, page 10

NAS CD B1M2 pp 10 = The CD of supplementary documents released by the National Academy of Sciences with their "Review" consisted of 9,600 pages of documents in "Batches" and "Modules" or "Documents" within the Batches. Each "module" or "document" was a pdf file. Therefore, B1M2 pp 10 means Batch 1, Module 2, page 10. And B3D2 pp 10 means Batch 3, Document 2, page 10.

EBAP pp 10 = "Report of the Expert Behavioral Analysis Panel," Research Strategies Network, 2011, page 10.

Willman pp 10 = David Willman's book "The Mirage Man" (Bantam Books, 2011), page 10.

Preston pp 10 = Richard Preston's book "The Demon In The Freezer" (Random House, 2002), page 10

USAMRIID Personnel File 004B pp 10 = USAMRIID personnel files on USAMRIID's web site, page 10.

UCLA, Case 10 = UCLA's Department of Epidemiology web site "American Anthrax Outbreak of 2001," Case 10. Site location: http://www.ph.ucla.edu/epi/bioter/detect/antdetect_intro.html

Chapter 1

1 - FBI #847547 pp 10
2 - EBAP pp 143
3 - EBAP pp 51
4 - EBAP pp 52
5 - Willman pp 21
6 - USAMRIID personnel files 004B pp 25
7 - EBAP pp 51
8 - EBAP pp 27
9 - EBAP - 164 - 165
10 - EBAP - 165
11 - EBAP - 47
12 - Willman pp 22
13 - Willman pp 22
14 - EBAP pp 56
15 - EBAP pp 59

Chapter 2

1 - Science magazine, 1994, Volume 266, pages 1202 - 1208
2 - USAMRIID personnel files 004B pp 4
3 - Willman pp 37
4 - Floor plan originally from a Materials License application filed by USAMRIID circa 1991.
5 - Floor plan for Suite B3 constructed from 2 different Building 1425 floor plans and using information gathered from a variety of USAMRIID and FBI reports.
6 - FBI #847547 pp 11
7 - The Oregonian, Aug. 8, 2008 - "Director of Oregon's primate lab says she was stalked by anthrax suspect"
8 - EBAP pp 59
9 - EBAP pp 63
10 - EBAP pp 275
11 - EBAP pp 63 - 64
12 - EBAP pp 57
13 - FBI #847545 pp 193 - 199
14 - Mother Jones magazine, May 1984, pp 55

15 - FBI #847447 pp 12 - 13

Chapter 3

1 - CDC image
http://phil.cdc.gov/PHIL_Images/10032002/00006/PHIL_2266 _lores.jpg
2 - Associated Press, Laura Meckler, Oct. 3, 2002, "Fewer Shots for New Anthrax Vaccine"
3 - Willman pp 57
4 - FBI #847443 pp 99, FBI #847423 pp 1 & 5
5 - August 18, 2008 FBI/media "Roundtable discussion"

Chapter 4

1 - Willman pp 52
2 - Summary pp 40
3 - Willman pp 48 - 49
4 - EBAP pp 63
5 - Summary pp 43 - 44
6 - Summary pp 43
7 - en.wikipedia.org/wiki/Ahmed_Ressam
8 - Willman pp 50
9 - Hypothesis: The decoding of the hidden message is described on pages 58 - 64 of the FBI/DOJ Summary report. It seems to be too complicated a code for Ivins to have constructed it in the few days he had between 9/11 and the sending of the media letters. Ivins' purchase of ammonium nitrate to build a bomb in January 2000 suggests that Ivins had developed a different plan for using the coded message at that time. And the timing of the LAX bomb plot makes it a likely connection. The fact that the date on the media letter seems to have been added by a different hand is also part of the hypothesis. So is the fact that the handwriting on the media letter appears to indicate it was written before 9/11 and weeks before the envelopes were addressed.

Chapter 5

1 - EBAP pp 28
2 - Willman pp 50
3 - Summary pp 42 & Washington Post, Aug. 7, 2008,
    "Acquaintances and Counselor Recall the Scientist's Dark Side"
4 - Summary pp 44
5 - Washington Post, Aug. 7, 2008, "Acquaintances and Counselor
    Recall the Scientist's Dark Side"
6 - Willman pp 64 - 66
7 - Washington Post, Aug. 7, 2008, "Acquaintances and Counselor
    Recall the Scientist's Dark Side" & Los Angeles Times, Aug. 7,
    2008, "Delving into the suspect's state of mind"
8 - Willman pp 67
9 - Summary pp 45 - 46

Chapter 6

1 - Summary pp 39 (footnote)
2 - Ivins email dated Sept. 10, 2001, subject "CpG progress update"
    & FBI #847406 pp 18
3 - FBI #847373 pp 3, FBI #847377 pp 77 & FBI #847406 pp 8 - 9
    and 19
4 - NAS pp 77 states that a minimum of 463 plates would have been
    needed to make all the spores in the anthrax letters.
5 - USA Today, Aug. 4, 2008, "Anthrax suspect was a prolific
    scientific author"

Chapter 7

1 - There are numerous additional facts which say a child wrote the
    anthrax letters and addressed the envelopes. Also, on Sept. 17,
    1993, Ivins had a letter to the editor published in the Frederick
    News-Post. The letter defended pedophilia and said it was just a
    matter of "sexual orientation." So, using a child to write the
    letters would be a far less terrible act than other acts with children
    he seemed to think about.

2 - The author has high resolution copies of the Brokaw letter and envelope, the New York Post letter and envelope, and the Leahy letter and envelope obtained via an FOIA request.
3 - The National Enquirer, Oct. 31, 2001, "The Nightmare That Came In The Mail"

Chapter 8

1 - FBI #847362 pp 101
2 - EBAP - pp 79
3 - EBAP pp 43
4 - EBAP pp 44
5 - In his 2012 book "How Sherlock Holmes Deduced 'Break the Case Clues' on the BTK Killer, the Son of Sam, Unabomber and Anthrax Cases," former NYC police Captain Tom Walker noted that the ZIP for Franklin Park, NJ (08823) subtracted from the ZIP for Monmouth Junction (08852) equals 29. If viewed as a number code, the 2nd letter in the alphabet is B and the 9th is I. And Bruce Ivins' initials are B.I. Thus, the ZIP codes *could be* another code to allow Ivins to prove he wrote the letters.
6 - Summary pp 46

Chapter 9

1 - Summary pp 31
2 - Summary pp 33
3 - USAMRIID emails by Ivins - Batch 35, pp 7
4 - EBAP pp 81
5 - EBAP pp 9
6 - EBAP pp 82
7 - USAMRIID emails from Ivins, "2001 activity," item #1
8 - EBAP pp 41
9 - Summary pp 31
10 - EBAP pp 83
11 - Atlanta Journal-Constitution, Oct. 14, 2001, "Florida doctor found first clue of anthrax." & USA Today, October 15, 2001, "On the trail of anthrax: A detective story"
12 - USAMRIID emails by Ivins, Batch 35, pp 19

Chapter 10

1 - The Arizona Republic, Dec. 16, 2007, "Finding link to anthrax, professor set NAU apart"
2 - New Scientist magazine, May 9, 2002, "Anthrax attack bug 'identical' to army strain"
3 - Time Magazine, Apr. 8, 2002, "Tracking the Anthrax Attacks"

Chapter 11

1 - CDC - Emerging Infectious Diseases, Volume 8, Number 10, October 2002, "First Cases of Bioterrorism-Related Inhalation Anthrax in the United States, Palm Beach County, Florida, 2001"
2 - The National Enquirer, Oct. 31, 2001, "The Nightmare That Came In The Mail"
3 - Washington Post, Oct. 14, 2001, "Problems in Bioterror Response"
4 - Florida Sun-Sentinel, Oct. 10, 2001, "Anthrax found in Boca appears to be manmade in Iowa Lab: CNN"
5 - Infection and Immunity, May 1986, Volume 52 Number 2, Pages 509 - 512, "Comparative Efficacy of Bacillus anthracis Live Spore Vaccine Protective Antigen Vaccine against Anthrax in the Guinea Pig"
6 - Salisbury Medical Bulletin, 1996 Special Supplement, Number 87, pages 125-126
7 - See exhibit #28
8 - The New York Times, Oct. 11, 2001, "A Nation Challenged: A Medical Mystery"
9 - San Francisco Chronicle, Oct. 11, 2001, "Iowa Strain of anthrax tied to Florida death"
10 - Center for Counterproliferation Research - Working Paper: Anthrax in America, pp 30
11 - Iowa State Daily, Feb. 1, 2002, Ames anthrax famous, but strain from another state"
12 - USAMRIID emails by Ivins, Batch 36, page 15
13 - USAMRIID emails by Ivins, Batch 36, page 15 - 16

Chapter 12

1 - UCLA, case 2
2 - Newsday, Oct. 13, 2001, "America's Ordeal"
3 - ABC News, Oct. 14, 2001, "Three More in NYC Exposed to Anthrax"
4 - Las Vegas Review-Journal, Oct. 14, 2001, "Anthrax bacteria in Reno letter"
5 - FBI #847418 pp 41
6 - Willman pp 105
7 - Book: "The Killer Strain" by Marilyn W. Thompson, pp 118

Chapter 13

1 - EBAP pp 83
2 - Book: "The Demon in the Freezer" by Richard Preston, pp 164. Most information about Peter Jahrling and Tom Giesbert in this chapter comes from Preston's book.
3 - Willman pp 109
4 - Preston pp 165
5 - Preston pp 166
6 - Willman pp 110
7 - FBI #847443 pp 29
8 - PBS NewsHour, Oct. 17, 2001 transcript: http://www.pbs.org/newshour/bb/health/july-dec01/anthraxgi_10-17.html
9 - FBI #847443 pp 29
10 - Willman pp 110 -111

Chapter 14

1 - UCLA, case 9
2 - UCLA, case 4
3 - UCLA, case 1
4 - The Wall Street Journal, Oct. 18, 2001, "The Iraq Connection"
5 - USAMRIID emails by Ivins, Batch 36, page 49
6 - Preston pp 175 - 176

7 - Email to author from Don Weiss of the NYC DoH, Nov. 30, 2007

8 - In a November 29, 2010 "seminar" held by conspiracy theorists at the University of California Washington Center in Washington, DC, a member of the audience, John Ezzell, said the New York Post powder was "multi-colored" and added, "The only way you can get those three different colors is to take this pellet - which is essentially as I described - and dry it as a pellet, and then chop it up. To me, that's the only way you could prepare material like that." Color photos of the New York Post powder are available on the Internet.

9 - FBI #847418 pp 44

Chapter 15

1 - The Guardian, Oct. 19, 2001, "Don't blame Saddam for this one"

2 - The Atlanta Journal-Constitution, Oct. 19, 2001, "Experts doubt anthrax a domestic plot"

3 - UCLA, case 15

4 - UCLA, case 16

5 - Preston pp 179 - 180

6 - ABC News, Oct. 17, 2001, "Dozens on Capital Hill Exposed to Anthrax"

7 - UCLA, case 14

8 - UCLA, case 13

9 - Center for Counterproliferation Research - Working Paper: Anthrax in America, pp 41

10 - USA Today, Oct. 21, 2001, "Experts seek clues in a bioterrorist's penmanship"

11 - Preston pp 180

12 - John Ezzell, Nov. 29, 2010 conspiracy theorist "seminar" held at the University of California Washington Center in Washington, DC.

13 - NAS CD, B1M2 page 20

14 - Preston pp 181

15 - Preston pp 183 - 186

16 - The Los Angeles Times, Sept. 18, 2008, "Scientist admits mistake on anthrax" by David Willman.

Chapter 16

1 - The Washington Post, Oct. 25, 2001, "Additive Made Spores Deadlier" by Rick Weiss and Dan Eggen
2 - Preston pp 192 - 193
3 - ABC News, Oct. 26, 2001, "Troubling Anthrax Additive Found"
4 - Willman pp 121 - 122
5 - Willman pp 118 - 121
6 - ABC News, Nov. 1, 2001, "Additive Search Requires More Study"
7 - Book: "Taking the Heat" by Ari Fleischer, page 201

Chapter 17

1 - UCLA, case 17
2 - UCLA, case 19
3 - UCLA, case 18
4 - UCLA, case 20
5 - UCLA, case 21
6 - UCLA, case 22
7 - When envelopes go through the sorting machines, a bar code is printed on each envelope to help with sorting and distributing mail further down the line and in the next postal facility. The bar code identifies the destination. When the bar code is printed, a computerized record is made of the time and the bar code. Thus, Postal Inspectors were able to locate the time the letters when through the sorting equipment and many of the letters that went through the same sorting equipment around the same time.
8 - Email discussions with a NYC DOH official
9 - My analysis.
10 - Book: "Scientific and Technical Means of Distinguishing Between Natural and Other Disasters" pp 81 (also elsewhere)
11 - UCLA, case 23 (There were only 22 victims. Case #10 was determined to be unconfirmed and deleted from the statistics.)

Chapter 18

1 - CNN, Nov. 18, 2001, "FBI tests Leahy letter" (plus other sources)

2 - USA Today, Nov. 19, 2001, "FBI: Leahy anthrax letter 'sent by same person'" (plus other sources)
3 - Los Angeles Times, Oct. 24, 2001, "Look-alike anthrax letters provide clues" (and other sources)
4 - USAMRIID emails by Ivins, Batch 40, page 3
5 - FBI #847443 pp 2 & Willman pp 132 - 133

Chapter 19

1 - www.shesource.org/experts/profile/barbara-rosenberg
2 - CNN, Nov. 1, 2001, "Bush urges improvements in biological weapons convention" and many other sources.
3 - Testimony of Barbara Hatch Rosenberg, PhD - Before the Subcommittee on National Security, Veterans Affairs and International Relations, House Committee on Government Reform Hearing on The Biological Weapons Convention Protocol: Status and Implications - June 5, 2001
4 - CNN, July 26, 2001, "U.S. rejects germ warfare accord"
5 - Steven Jay Hatfill's curriculum vitae (cv)
6 - The Washington Post, June 28, 2002, "Biological Warfare Experts Questioned in Anthrax Probe" & The New York Times, Dec. 3, 2001, "Terror Anthrax Linked to Type Made by U.S."
7 - The New York Times, July 2, 2002, "Anthrax? The F.B.I. Yawns" & Hatfill v New York Times lawsuit court documents
8 - The Washington Post, Jan. 4, 2002, "2nd letter to land in Daschle's office"
9 - The Washington Times, Aug. 3, 2002, "Scientist says FBI asked about setup"
10 - Science Magazine, Aug. 22, 2002, "Unconventional Detective Bears Down on a Killer"
11 - "Statement by Barbara Hatch Rosenberg, Federation of American Scientists, Before the Delegates to the Fifth Review Conference of the Biological Weapons Convention" - Geneva, 21 November 2001.

Chapter 20

1 - USAMRIID emails from Ivins, Batch 38, page 19

2 - Willman pp 207 - 208
3 - Willman pp 136 - 138 & other sources & images of the morphs
4 - The New York Times, May 7, 2002, "Anthrax Sent Through Mail
    Gained Potency by the Letter"
5 - The New Jersey Star-Ledger, Nov. 2, 2001, "Investigators focus
    on domestic culprit"
6 - The Los Angeles Times, Nov. 10, 2001, "Loner Likely Sent
    Anthrax, FBI Says"
7 - Feb. 14, 2003 email to email forum by microbiologist Richard
    Ebright & Newsday, Dec. 27, 2001, "Scientists at Loss in Anthrax
    Probe"
8 - Time Magazine, Nov. 19, 2001, "Profile Of A Killer'
9 - 1 mutation per billion divisions used as estimate for all living cells,
    per "Microbial Forensics" by Bruce Budowle et al, page 246.
    Other estimates range from 1 per 200,000 to 1 per 20,000,000,000
    (Geographical Distribution of Genotypic and Phenotypic Markers
    Among Bacillus anthracis Isolates and Related Species by
    Historical Movement and Horizontal Transfer," J.L, Kiel, et al,
    Folia Microbiology, Sept. 2008.)
10 - USAMRIID emails from Ivins, Batch 38, page 29
11 - FBI #847447 pp 125
12 - FBI #847443 pp 16 - 19 & USAMRIID "15-6 Investigation -
    Anthrax Contamination" report
13 - FBI #847376 pp 6 - 7

Chapter 21

1 - The Washington Post, Mar. 29, 2002, "Memo on Florida Case
    Roils Anthrax Probe"
2 - Hartford Courant, Jan. 20, 2002, "Anthrax Missing From Army
    Lab"
3 - Willman pp 136
4 - Summary pp 84
5 - NAS CD, Ancillary Documents, pp 135 - 138
6 - FBI #847443 pp 3 - 6
7 - Willman pp 245 - 246
8 - The Washington Post, January 29, 2002, "One Anthrax Answer:
    Ames Strain Not From Iowa"

9 - USAMRIID emails from Ivins, Batch 40, page 65
10 - USAMRIID emails from Ivins, Batch 40, page 67
11 - USAMRIID emails from Ivins, Batch 40, page 71
12 - The New York Times, January 30, 2002, "Geographic Gaffe Misguides Anthrax Inquiry"
13 - Summary pp 48

Chapter 22

1 - Scripps Howard News Service, Jan. 23, 2002, "Amateur sleuths offer clues to anthrax killer"
2 - The Trenton Times, Feb. 19, 2002, "Expert: Anthrax suspect ID'd"
3 - The Daily Princetonian, Feb. 19, 2002, "Investigators explore new anthrax suspect"
4 - The Guardian, Feb. 20, 2002, "'US scientist' is suspect in anthrax investigation"
5 - The Trenton Times, Feb. 20, 2002, "FBI says no prime anthrax suspect"

Chapter 23

1 - Willman pp 208 - 209
2 - *ibid*
3 - NAS CD, B3D10, page 2 & 6
4 - USAMRIID emails from Ivins, Batch 40, page 3
5 - The Wall Street Journal, Feb. 7, 2002, "FBI's New Approach in Its Search For Anthrax Mailer Focuses on Labs"
6 - EBAP pp 34
7 - My understandings based upon emails exchanged with Paul Keim in January 2009.
8 - ScienceNOW Daily News (Science magazine), Aug. 18, 2008, "The Anthrax Case: The Trail of the Spores "
9 - Dr. Joseph Michael's presentation to the National Academy of Sciences, Sept. 25, 2009
10 - Aerosol Science and Technology magazine, March 1, 2008, "Development of Aerosol System for Uniformly Deposting Bacillus Anthracis Spore Particles on Surfaces"

11 - Technical Guide 265 by the U.S. Army Center for Health Promotion and Preventive Medicine, Aug. 2003, page A-5 & discussions between the author and William Patrick III, Kenneth Alibek and others.

12 - Dr. Joseph Michael's presentation to the National Academy of Sciences, Sept. 25, 2009

13 - FBI/DOJ "Roundtable Discussion" with journalists on Aug. 18, 2008

14 - NAS CD, "Supplemental Documents," item #3: "Preparing and Shipping TSA Slants for *B. anthacis Ames*"

15 - FBI #847443 pp 54

Chapter 24

1 - The Hartford Courant, Mar. 4, 2002, "Anthrax Probe Remains Slow Go"

2 - FBI #847443 pp 31

3 - The Wall Street Journal, Mar. 26, 2002, "Anthrax Probe Was Complicated By Muddled Information, FBI Says"

4 - The New York Times, Sept. 26, 2003, "F.B.I. Names Top Scientists for Advisory Panel on Germs"

5 - The Wall Street Journal, Mar. 26, 2002, "Anthrax Probe Was Complicated By Muddled Information, FBI Says"

6 - Summary pp 78

7 - FBI #847551 (original version) pp 77

8 - Willman pp 262 - 263

9 - Summary pp 78

10 - USAMRIID "15-6 Investigation - Anthrax Contamination" report, page 80

11 - *ibid* pages 35 & 76

12 - *ibid* pages 89 - 90

13 - FBI #847443 pp 16 - 19

Chapter 25

1 - The New York Times, Feb. 26, 2002, "U.S. Says Short List of 'Suspects' is Being Checked in Anthrax Case"

2 - The New Yorker, Mar. 18, 2002, "The Anthrax Culprit"

3 - GlennBeck.com, Mar. 20, 2002, "British Suggest Anthrax Attacks Were CIA Backed"

4 - USA Today, Mar. 26, 2002, "Ask the FBI: The Anthrax Investigation"

5 - The Weekly Standard, Apr. 29, 2002, "Remember Anthrax? Despite the evidence, the FBI won't let go of its 'lone American' theory"

6 - The New York Times, May 24, 2002, "Connecting Deadly Dots"

7 - The Wall Street Journal, June 3, 2002, "FBI Reform: Connect the Anthax Dots: The 'lone wolf' theory is evidence of the Bureau's ineptitude"

8 - The Scotsman, June 16, 2002, "War on Terror: FBI 'guilty of cover-up' over anthrax suspect"

9 - Case 1:03-cv-01793-RBW Document 102 Filed 11/18/2005, page 11

10 - Salon.com, June 21, 2002, "I'm ready for my close-up, Sen. Daschle"

11 - The New York Times, June 26, 2002, "Search of Biologist Is Uneventful"

12 - The Hartford Courant, June 26, 2002, "FBI Searches Home In Anthrax Case"

13 - ABC News, June 17, 2002, "Blueprint for Anthrax Attack"

14 - The New York Times, July 2, 2002, "Anthrax? The F.B.I. Yawns"

Chapter 26

1 - The Advocate, Aug. 25, 2002, "Hatfill to reveal new data" & Newsweek, Aug. 12, 2002, "The Hunt for the Anthrax Killer"

2- The Weekly Standard, Sept. 16, 2002, "The Hunting of Steven J. Hatfill" & Newsweek, Aug. 12, 2002, "The Hunt for the Anthrax Killer"

3 - Book: Amerithrax: The Hunt for the Anthrax Killer" by Robert Graysmith, page 366

4 - ABC News, Oct. 23, 2002, "Bloodhounds Lead Investigators to Ex-Government Scientist in Anthrax Case"

5 - Washington Post, Aug. 15, 2002, "Evidence Lacking as Probe Intensifies"

6 - Baltimore Sun, Oct. 29, 2002, "FBI's use of bloodhounds in anthrax probe disputed" & author's telephone discussions with William Patrick III

7 - ABC News, Oct. 23, 2002, "Bloodhounds Lead Investigators to Ex-Government Scientist in Anthrax Case" & Newsweek, Aug. 12, 2002, "The Hunt for the Anthrax Killer"

8 - FBI #847418 pp 43

9 - Accuracy in Media, Sept. 27, 2002, "A Shaggy Dog Story"

10 - Lawsuit document, Hatfill v Alberto Gonzales et al, Deposition of Daniel S. Seikaly, Oct. 10, 2007

11 - The Baltimore Sun, Aug. 3, 2002, "Ex-Fort Detrick scientist is put on leave from new job at LSU"

12 - The Washington Times, Aug. 3, 2002, "Scientist says FBI asked about setup"

13 - The Washington Post, Aug. 11, 2002, "Ex-Army Scientist Denies Role in Anthrax Attacks"

14 - The Associated Press, Aug. 11, 2002, "Steven Hatfill's Statement"

15 - "Analysis of the Anthrax Attacks" by Barbara Hatch Rosenberg, part III "Statement by Barbara Hatch Rosenberg, 11 August 2002"

Chapter 27

1 - The Wall Street Journal, Aug. 12, 2002, "Anthrax Investigators Test Mailbox in Princeton Area" & The Trenton Times, Aug. 13, 2002, "Anthrax found in mailbox"

2 - The Trenton Times, Aug. 14, 2002, "Anthrax probe goes door to door" & North Jersey News, Aug. 14, 2002, "The Scientist and the mailbox"

3 - Lawsuit document, Hatfill v John Ashcroft, the FBI, the DOJ, Complaint dated Aug. 26, 2003

4 - The Washington Post, Dec. 13, 2002, "Justice Dept. Says It Intended To Shield Anthrax Probe Figure"

5 - The Associated Press, Aug. 14, 2002, "Hatfill Novel Depicts Terror Attack"

6 - The New York Times, Sept. 4, 2002, "Anthrax Figure Loses Job as Researcher"

7 - The Washington Post, Sept. 19, 2002, "Senator Questions Anthrax Investigation"

8 - The Baltimore Sun, Aug. 19, 2002, "FBI anthrax investigation smells funny" & The Baltimore Sun, Oct. 29, 2002, "FBI's use of bloodhounds in anthrax probe disputed" & Accuracy In Media, Oct. 23, 2002, "ABC News Repeats Shaggy Dog Story"

9 - EBAP pp 69

10 - EBAP pp 84

11 - NAS CD, B3D1, page 12, "AMERITHRAX Sample Status and Benefit Analysis for 6/27/02"

12 - NAS CD, B3D1, page 3

13 - NAS CD, B3D1, page 6

14 - NAS CD, B3D1, page 9

15 - NAS CD, B3D1, page 99 & Ancillary Documents page 48

16 - NAS CD, B3D1, page 69

17 - NAS CD, B3D1, page 9

18 - NAS CD, B3D1, page 14

19 - NAS CD, B3D1, page 14

20 - NAS CD, B3D1, page 91

21 - CDC, Oct. 2002, "First Case of Bioterrorism-Related Inhalation Anthrax in the United States, Palm Beach County, Florida, 2001" & book "American Anthrax" by Jeanne Guillemin, page 17

22 - NAS CD, B3D1, page 7

23 - NAS CD, B3D1, page 49

24 - NAS CD, B3D1, page 64

25 - The Washington Post, Nov. 5, 2002, "Anthrax Under The Microscope"

Chapter 28

1 - The Baltimore Sun, Dec. 3, 2002, "FBI investigators search Md. forest for anthrax"

2 - Associated Press, May 12, 2003

3 - EBAP pp 265 - 267 & The Washington Post, Aug. 2, 2008, "A science nerd with a dark side"
4 - FBI #847443 pp 22 - 27
5 - FBI #847443 pp 32 - 34
6 - FBI #847443 pp 35
7 - FBI #847443 pp 36 - 39
8 - FBI #847443 pp 40 - 42
9 - The Los Angeles Times, Aug. 2, 2008, "Suspect stood to gain from anthrax panic"

Chapter 29

1 - NAS CD, B3D1, page 99
2 - Summary pp 35
3 - Willman pp 385 - 386
4 - NAS CD, Supplemental Documents, "FBI WFO [Washington Field Office] Report on Samples from an Overseas Site Identified by Intelligence," June 2008.
5 - FBI #847443 pp 43 - 44 & 45
6 - FBI #847443 pp 43 plus Internet research about the MPL PA vaccine.
7 - The Washington Post, April 18, 2003, "Washington Chief To Retire From FBI"
8 - Willman pp 197, 199 & 203
9 - The Washington Post, Sept. 30, 2003, "D.C. FBI Chief Regrets Leaks and Labels in Anthrax Case"
10 - CNN, May 11, 2003, "Traces of disease found on object near Fort Detrick, Maryland" & retraction on May 12, 2003: "Anthrax Investigation" transcript
11 - ABC News, June 9, 2003, "Underwater Evidence?" & Associated Press, June 9, 2003, "FBI Drains Maryland Pond in Anthrax Probe"
12 - The Baltimore Sun, May 20, 2003, "FBI vehicle hits Hatfill, but he gets the $5 ticket"
13 - The Washington Post, June 29, 2003, "FBI Ends Anthrax Probe Of Pond Near Frederick"
14 - The New York Times, July 2, 2003, "Subject of Anthrax Inquiry Tied to Anti-Germ Training"

15 - The Washington Post, July 3, 2003, "Anthrax Suspect Trained U.S. Team on Bioweapons"
16 - The Baltimore Sun, July 3, 2003, "Hatfill's biowar classes may have led to scrutiny"
17 - Frederick News-Post, July 3, 2003, "Germ lab links Hatfill, anthrax"
18 - www.anthraxinvestigation.com, July 17, 2003, email from Ivan Oelrich to author
19 - Southeast Missourian, Aug. 16, 2003, "FBI's 'person of interest' loses traffic ticket appeal" & other reports
20 - Hatfill v John Ashcroft lawsuit documents
21 - Hatfill v The New York Times lawsuit documents & Hatfill v Foster lawsuit documents

Chapter 30

1 - FBI #847443 pp 51
2 - FBI #847443 pp 50
3 - FBI #847443 pp 52 & 56
4 - FBI #847443 pp 54 - 61
5 - FBI #847443 pp 70
6 - Presentation to the National Academy of Sciences by Dr. Joseph Michael on Sept. 25, 2009
7 - The Chicago Tribune, Mar. 2, 2004, "FBI hits wall in anthrax investigation"
8 - The Washington Post, Mar. 30, 2004, "Judge Postpones Hatfill's lawsuit" & The Associated Press, Apr. 18, 2004, "Judge grants six-month stay in anthrax civil suit"
9 - FBI #847443 pp 71 - 72
10 - FBI #847443 pp 73 - 79
11 - FBI #847443 pp 80 - 81

Chapter 31

1 - The Oxford (CT) Republican-American, Nov. 21, 2004, "Anthrax Revisited"
2 - FBI #847443 pp 83 - 87
3 - FBI #847443 pp 88 - 90

4 - FBI #847443 pp 91 - 92

5 - Fox News, July 20, 2004, "Anthrax Probe Takes Over Army Labs' & Baltimore Sun, July 21, 2004, "Closing of lab marks renewed intensity in anthrax probe" & Associated Press, July 26, 2004, "FBI Completes Search At Fort Detrick"

6 - FBI #847443 pp 93

7 - FBI #847443 pp 100

8 - FBI #847443 pp 94

9 - Wellsville Daily Reporter, Aug. 10, 2004, "Helms: FBI owes Berry big-time apology; Pastor calls Dr. Berry a 'national treasure'

10 - The New Jersey Star-Ledger, Aug. 6, 2004, "FBI searches houses tied to doctor from Jersey" and many other newspaper articles

11 - USA Today, Dec. 17, 1997, "Clinton sees little anthrax threat to civilians"

12 - The Hartford Courant, Aug. 6, 2004, "Residences Searched in Anthrax Probe"

13 - The New York Times, Oct. 3, 2004, "Interest in Bioterror Issue Puts Doctor Under Scrutiny and His LIfe in Turmoil"

14 - Pittsburgh Tribune-Review, Aug. 7, 2004, "FBI queried ex-neighbors of anthrax probe figure"

15 - Pittsburgh Tribune Review, Aug. 11, 2004, "Doctor aided Defense Dept."

16 - The Washington Post, Aug. 6, 2004, "N.Y. Home Searched In Anthrax Probe" & KDKA.com, Aug. 6, 2004, "Local Ties in Federal Anthrax Probe"

Chapter 32

1 - FBI #847443 pp 95

2 - The Los Angeles Times, Aug. 20, 2004, "Anthrax Leaks Blamed on Lax Safety Habits"

3 - FBI #847423 pp 3 -12

4 - FBI #847443 pp 96 - 97

5 - FBI #847443 pp 98

6 - FBI #847443 pp 99

7 - NBC News, Oct. 4, 2004, "Hatfill strikes back in anthrax case" & Hatfill v Donald Foster et al lawsuit documents

8 - The Washington Post. Nov. 30, 2004, "Judge Dismisses Hatfill Suit Against N.Y. Times" & other reports & court documents
9 - Willman pp 212 - 214
10 - Willman pp 218
11 - Willman pp 217
12 - FBI #847444 pp 1 -23 & 24 - 26
13 - FBI #847545 pp 93 -96
14 - FBI #847444 pp 27
15 - FBI #847551 (original) pp 76 & Willman pp 222
16 - FBI #847444 pp 27

Chapter 33

1 - FBI #847376 pp 41 - 53
2 - FBI #847447 pp 132 - 177
3 - Willman pp 222 -223.
4 - The Frederick News-Post, Aug. 7, 2008, "Ivins alone responsible for attacks, feds claim" & The New York Times, Sept. 13, 2008, "Another Twist in Case of Dead Anthrax Suspect"
5 - FBI #847376 pp 1 - 27
6 - FBI #847376 pp 38 - 40
7 - FBI #847376 pp 32
8 - FBI #847376 pp 99 - 102
9 - FBI #847376 pp 97

Chapter 34

1 - USAMRIID emails by Ivins, Batch 63, page 7
2 - Willman pp 225
3 - Summary pp 76 - 77 & EBAP pp 86
4 - Willman pp 226
5 - Slate magazine at slate.com, Aug. 7, 2008, "The Adventures of Jimmyflathead" - The Internet postings of Bruce Ivins
6 - Summary pp 55 - 60
7 - Roundtable Discussion, Aug. 18, 2008
8 - NAS CD, B3D10, page 1 - 8
9 - Willman pp 229 - 230

10 - Scripps-Howard News Service, Nov. 17, 2006, "Senate chairman critical of FBI's anthrax mail probe" & NBC News, Sept. 18, 2006, FBI official leading anthrax probe off the case"

11 - The Florida Sun Sentinel, Oct. 15, 2005, "Anthrax attacks remain unsolved" & The Washington Post, Oct. 15, 2006, "The Unsolved Case of Anthrax" & The Miami Herald, Oct. 5, 2006, "Solving case may take many years"

12 - Willman pp 231 - 243

13 - The Washington Post, Sept. 15, 2006, "FBI Is Casting A Wider Net in Anthrax Attacks"

14 - Willman pp 233

15 - Author's email from Paul Keim dated Dec. 17, 2011

Chapter 35

1 - Willman pp 238

2 - The New York Sun, Feb. 27, 2007, "Hatfill settles $10M Libel Lawsuit"

3- FBI #847443 page 1

4 -FBI #847444 page 37 -39

5 - FBI #847444 pp 48 - 54 & Willman pp 244 - 245

6 - The Frederick News-Post, Sept. 17, 2008, "Ivins put cash on cremation" & The Baltimore Sun, Sept. 14, 2008, "Ivins will compel scattering of his ashes" & Willman pp 246

7 - FBI #847444 pp 41

8 - FBI #847444 pp 43

9 - FBI #847444 pp 67

10 - Willman pp 250

11 - Willman pp 251

12 - FBI #847551 pp 33

13 - FBI #847551 pp 19

14 - FBI #847551 pp 28

15 - Summary pp 68

Chapter 36

1 - The Los Angeles Times, Jan. 12, 2008, "U.S. Attorney's Office Accused of Anthrax Case Leaks"

2 - Court Documents - Steven Hatfill v Alberto Gonzales &
   University of Minnesota Bulletin, Oct. 21, 2009, "Reporters
   Ordered to Testify and Reveal Government Sources in Hatfill
   Case"
3 - WFMD radio interview with Henry Heine, Feb. 25, 2010
4 - USAMRIID emails by Ivins, Batch 88, pages 124, 132 - 136
5 - Willman 253
6 - FBI #847444 pp 171 - 172
7 - FBI #847447 pp 50 - 52
8 - FBI #847447 pp 53 - 56
9 - FBI #847447 pp 61

Chapter 37

1 - FBI #847545 pp 153 - 158 & Willman pp 261
2 - FBI #847545 pp 200 - 227 & FBI #847447 pp 71 -76, 94 - 116 &
   FBI #847551 (original) pp 72 & Willman pp 263 - 269
3 - FBI #847447 pp 68 - 70

Chapter 38

1 - FBI #847447 pp 88 - 186
2 - Summary pp 64 & Willman pp 272 - 273
3 - Summary pp 58 - 59

Chapter 39

1 - Willman pp 271
2 - Willman pp 275
3 - FBI #847362 pp 84 - 87
4 - FBI #847362 pp 79 -80
5 - FBI #847362 pp 89 - 91
6 - FBI #847551 pp 44 - 47
7 - PBS Frontline interviews with Rachel Lieber and Edward
   Montooth, Oct. 10, 2011
8 - FBI #847545 pp 193 - 199

Chapter 40

1 - Willman pp 279
2 - FBI #847545 pp 176- 177
3 - FBI #847547 pp 18 - 23
4 - FBI #847547 pp 10 -17
5 - FBI #847547 pp 119
6 - FBI #847547 pp 136
7 - *Ibid* & Willman 287 - 289 & FBI #847547 pp 138

Chapter 41

1 - Willman pp 298
2 - *Ibid*
3 - FBI #847551 pp 8
4 - Willman pp 291 - 293
5 - FBI #847551 pp 68
6 - PBS interview with Nancy Haigwood, Oct. 10, 2011, "Nancy Haigwood: "I Had a Gut Feeling It Was Bruce"
7 - FBI Summary pp 70 - 71 & FBI #847551 pp 66 - 69 & Willman pp 294 - 295
8 - PBS interview with Rachel Lieber, Oct. 10, 2011, "Rachel Lieber: The Case Against Dr. Bruce Ivins"

Chapter 42

1 - FBI #847551 originally contained this "off the record" interview on pages 70 - 77, but it was later deleted. I saved a copy before it was altered. Also see Willman pp 297 - 302
2 - FBI #847572 pp 53 - 55
3 - FBI #847572 pp 56
4 - FBI #847551 pp 54
5 - Court documents & ABC News, June 27, 2008, "DOJ Settles Hatfill Suit for $5.8 Million"
6 - Summary pp 49 - 50, & http://www.truecrimereport.com/2008/08/bruce_ivins_trolled_youtube.php
7 - FBI #847551 (original) pp 133
8 - Summary pp 50

9 - *Ibid* & EBAP pp 96
10 - Willman 308 - 309
11 - Jean Duley interview by author
12 - Willman pp 309
13 - EBAP pp 97 - 98
14 - Willman pp 310
15 - FBI #847572 pp 25

Chapter 43

1- The New York Times, Aug. 2, 2008, "Anthax Suspect's Death Is Dark End for a Family Man" (on-line version includes audio of the testimony) & Frederick News-Post, Aug. 5, 2008, "'I'm scared to death' of Ivins, Duley testifies"
2 - FBI #847551 pp 136
3 - Summary pp 7 - 8
4 - FBI #847551 pp 136 - 137
5 - http://www.fredericknewspost.com/media/audio/duleyvoicemail/duleyvoicemail.html
6 - Willman pp 312
7 - FBI #847551 pp 81 - 87
8 - FBI #847551 pp 132
9 - FBI #847551 pp 160 - 161
10 - FBI #847551 pp 134
11 - PBS interview with Rachel Lieber, Oct. 10, 2011, "Rachel Lieber: The Case Against Dr. Bruce Ivins"
12 - http://www.nytimes.com/2008/08/02/us/02scientist.html?_r=1&hp

Chapter 44

1 - Willman pp 315 - 316
2 - I first learned that Ivins had visited my site via an Associated Press article dated Aug. 7, 2008, "Despite demons, Ivins stayed at high-security lab" and I checked my web site logs to confirm the visit by Ivins. Ivins did a Google search for "Ed Lake," indicating that he was familiar with the quickest way to find my site without too much typing.

3 - CNN video clip and my transcription of what was said

4 - ABC News, July 19, 2008, "At the FBI, Cold Cases Are Not a Thing of the Past"

5 - Willman pp 316

6 - Medical reports, the contents of the letter written by Diane Ivins, and various police reports are available for viewing (at the current time) at http://www.fredericknewspost.com/media/pdfs/ivins_investigation001.pdf

7 - Willman pp 317

8 - FBI #847572 pp 43

9 - The Los Angeles Times, Oct. 16, 2011, "Science in anthrax letter case comes under attack"

Chapter 45

1 - Willman pp 321

2 - Willman pp 419

3 - https://docs.google.com/View?docid=dc3wqmd7_33d2tjs5ct&pli=1

4 - Associated Press, Aug. 9, 2008, "Ivins remembered for intelligence, compassion"

5 - Willman pp 419

6 - The Associated Press, Sept. 17, 2008, "Leahy: Suspect had help in anthrax attacks"

7 - "The Silicon Layer Supports Acid Resistance of Bacillus cereus Spores," by Ryuichi Hirota et al, Journal of Bacteriology, Jan 2010

8 - New York Times editorial, Feb. 27, 2010, "The F.B.I.'s Anthrax Case"

9 - AOL News, May 10, 2010, "Lawyer Doubts Case Against Anthrax Suspect"

10 - The New York Times, Apr. 22, 2010, "Colleague Disputes Case Against Anthrax Suspect"

11 - FBI #847423 pp 5 & USAMRIID emails from Ivins, Batch 57, pages 14 - 15

Index

Index

Index

Index

Index

Index

Index

Index

Index

Index

Index

Valium, 159, 258, 290, 309, 340
Villanova University, 299
van der Waals forces, 231
Vanity Fair, 29, 31, 229, 246-247, 270-
    271
Vassar College, 167
Vickers, Michael L., 164
Victoria, British Columbia, 32
Virginia Military Institute, 247
Vollum anthrax strain, 24, 163

W

Walker, Tom, 358
Wallingford, CT, 130
Wall Street Journal, 106, 172, 182, 192
WalMart, 276, 319
Walter Reed Army Institute of
    Research, 215
Walton, Reggie, 236, 278
Washington, D.C., 1, 48, 72, 112, 123,
    127, 133, 151
Washington Times, 205
Washington Post, 42, 44, 122, 134, 136,
    147, 162, 204-205, 212-213, 227-
    229, 278
weaponized anthrax, 98-100, 102, 108-
    109, 119-126, 131, 168, 175-177,
    191, 231, 239, 266
Weekly Standard, The, 192
Wellsville, NY, 241
West Trenton Post Office, 111
"wet" anthrax, 26
White Sands Ocean Front Resort, 241
Whitford, Howard W., 164
White House, 115, 119, 122, 124-126,
    162, 169, 208
Wikipedia, 261, 307
Willman, David, 103, 121, 342, 344
Wilmington, DE, 66
Wood, Cindy, 321
Woodrow Wilson School of Public
    and International Affairs, 167
Woods Hole Oceanographic Institute,
    211
Woolsey, R. James, 106-107

World Health Organization (WHO),
    136
World News Tonight, 126
World Trade Center, 48, 59, 75
Worsham, Patricia, 52, 70-71, 156, 158,
    170-171, 173, 182, 184, 186-187-
    189, 232, 279, 281, 300, 309

Y
Yemen, 55

Z
Zaid, Mark S., 48
Zavareei, Hassan A., 271
Zimbabwe, 198, 229
Zyprexa, 258

389

About the Author

I first became interested in the anthrax attacks of 2001 around October 11 of that year, when Bill Maher on his now defunct TV talk show "Politically Incorrect" discussed the idea of atom bombing Afghanistan if it turned out that al Qaeda or the Taliban were behind the unexplained inhalation anthrax case in Florida.

The idea of atom bombing *anyone* in that crowded part of the world stunned me, and I tried to get discussions started about it on the alt.tv.pol-incorrrect Internet newsgroup. My background in business systems analysis and other investigative work drove me to try to separate solid facts from people's personal opinions and beliefs.

Within the next few weeks, newspaper articles began appearing saying that facts were showing that the attacks could be from "domestic" sources. The serious debates began with those articles, and on November 22, 2001, I began gathering information on a web site I had set up to show and explain all the available facts.

Because of that web site, in early January of 2002, Scott Shane of the *Baltimore Sun* called me for an interview. That caused me to obtain the domain name www.anthraxinvestigation.com and to be more professional about what I was writing. My site was soon the leading site reporting and commenting on the case. On October 28, 2002, *Time* magazine printed a full page story about me and my site. To clarify issues and learn more about anthrax, I was contacting scientists who had published articles about anthrax and the case - including at least one scientist with the FBI. If I made a mistake, they would help me understand what corrections I needed to make.

Meanwhile, all the "Anthrax Truthers" (conspiracy theorists *and* True Believers) who felt they knew the *real* truth, were attacking me, which I considered to be confirmation that I was on the right track. They would state their (usually) baseless beliefs, and I would research the facts to find out what was true and what was just someone's personal opinion.

390

A Crime Unlike Any Other

Over the years, my web site grew and grew. It's still growing, and the arguments with the "Anthrax Truthers" continue to this day.

It's a seemingly endless debate over an extremely complex subject that has kept me fascinated for over 11 years.

In 2005, I self-published a book of my thoughts about the known facts, the opinions of conspiracy theorists, and how there seemed to be no way to resolve the endless disputes. I hypothesized that the anthrax killer probably lived in New Jersey, but I also stated:

> All the pieces fit. But, I also know that I probably do not have all the relevant information. Some *solid* piece of evidence that I've failed to find or properly evaluate could easily change things. That's what a "working hypothesis" is all about: to present it for others to tear apart with *new* facts which the hypothesis cannot explain.

It turned out that there was a *mountain* of solid facts that neither I nor anyone else outside of the FBI knew anything about.

When it was announced on August 1, 2008 that Bruce Ivins was the anthrax mailer, it was a name I had never heard of before. But the facts proving Ivins' guilt seemed undeniable to me, even though every item of new evidence that was released generated more endless debates with the "Anthrax Truthers."

This book is an attempt to summarize everything I've learned and figured out about the Amerithrax case during the past 11 years.

Ed Lake
Racine, WI
November 10, 2012

38282225R00225

Made in the USA
Lexington, KY
31 December 2014